APPROACHES TO QUALITATIVE RESEARCH: THEORY & ITS PRACTICAL APPLICATION

A GUIDE FOR DISSERTATION STUDENTS

Edited by

John Hogan, Paddy Dolan & Paul Donnelly

Published by
OAK TREE PRESS
19 Rutland Street, Cork, Ireland
www.oaktreepress.com

A catalogue record of this book is
available from the British Library.

ISBN 978 1 904887 31 7

CONTENTS

Tables   v

Figures   vii

Contributors   ix

Acknowledgements   xiii

Chapter 1: Introduction   1
John Hogan, Paddy Dolan & Paul Donnelly

Chapter 2: Research Topic Selection & Development   19
Conor Horan

Chapter 3: Ethnography: Visions & Versions   37
Marian Crowley-Henry

Chapter 4: Postcolonial Redirections in International   65
Management Research & Fieldwork
Banu Özkazanç-Pan

Chapter 5: Researching the 'Doing' of Gender, Work-   99
Family & Entrepreneurship: Methodological
Considerations
Kristina A. Bourne

Chapter 6: Focusing on Process & History: Path   125
Dependence
Paul F. Donnelly

Chapter 7: Piercing the Armoured Policy: Ideas &   151
Macroeconomic Policy Change in Ireland & the UK
John Hogan & David Doyle

Chapter 8: Using Documents: A Figurational Approach   185
Paddy Dolan

Chapter 9: An Overview of Discourse Analytical   209
Approaches to Research
Brendan K. O'Rourke

Chapter 10: Analysing Focus Group Data   229
Olivia Freeman

Chapter 11: Qualitative Methodology Discussion   261
Discussants: *Marian Crowley-Henry, Paddy Dolan, Paul
Donnelly, Olivia Freeman, Conor Horan, Brendan K. O'Rourke*

Index

TABLES

Table 2.1: The Process from Topic Selection to Topic Development   20

Table 2.2: Finding a Broad Research Topic   22

Table 2.3: Refining the Broad Research Topic with the Research Idea   24

Table 2.4: Developing the Research Rationale   26

Table 2.5: Agents of Evaluation & The Problem of Value Judgements   27

Table 2.6: Directionally-focused Research   29

Table 2.7: Is there an Identifiable Group that can be Researched?   32

Table 2.8: The Research Idea – The Functional Focus of the Research Project   33

Table 4.1: Study Sites & Data Collection Venues   81

Table 4.2: Data Collected During Fieldwork   82

Table 4.3: Summary of Fieldwork Participants & Types of Data Gathered   84 / 85

Table 5.1: Sample Description & Demographics   110 / 111

Table 6.1: The Primary & Secondary Archival Sources   138

Table 7.1: The Identification of Macroeconomic Crisis   161

Table 7.2: The Identification of Ideational Change   168

Table 7.3: The Identification of Change in Government Economic Policy   173

FIGURES

Figure 2.1: Identifiable Groups & Concepts   31

Figure 6.1: Analytic Structure of Path-dependent   134
Explanation

Figure 6.2: Sample ETHNO Output, Showing Associations   142
between a Series of Events

Figure 7.1: Critical Juncture Approach   154

Figure 9.1: Discourses Studies, Organised by Type of   215
Discourse & Analysis Used

Figure 10.1: Focus Group Phases   235

CONTRIBUTORS

Kristina A. Bourne, BBA, BA, MBA, PhD. Kristina is Assistant Professor of Management at the University of Wisconsin – Eau Claire in the US. She received her PhD in Organisation Studies at the University of Massachusetts in Amherst, after completing an MBA and Women's Studies Graduate Certificate there. Kristina's research interests include gender, work and family, entrepreneurship, and feminist theories. She has published articles in the *Academy of Management Review* (2009), *Business Horizons* (2009), *Organization Management Journal* (2007), and *Organisational Dynamics* (2003).

Marian Crowley-Henry, BBS, MSc. Marian Crowley-Henry is an international business theorist, who has taught in University College Cork, Ceram Graduate School of Management (Sophia Antipolis, France), and the Dublin Institute of Technology. She currently lectures in International Business, HRM, and Organisational Behaviour. Marian has published extensively in some of the top journals in the world, including the *Journal of Organizational Change Management* (2007), and *International Studies of Management & Organization* (2007). She has presented her research work at international conferences, including the International Labour Process conference, Workshop on Expatriation, the International Conference on Labour Flexibility, and the Academy of Management. Marian's PhD research (Lancaster University, England) is an ethnographic study on international careers. Her research interests include international HRM, migration, career theory, identity and critical management.

Paddy Dolan, BSc, MSocSc, PhD. Paddy Dolan is a sociologist, who has taught at Dublin City University, Trinity College Dublin and currently lectures in the Dublin Institute of Technology. He has published in *Journal of Consumer Culture, Sport in Society* and *Journal of Macromarketing*, and has presented his research at various conferences, including the American Sociological Association and the European Social Science History Conference. Paddy completed his PhD in Sociology at Goldsmiths College (University of London) in 2005. His thesis (*The Development of Consumer*

Culture, Subjectivity and National Identity in Ireland, 1900–1980) was supervised by Don Slater, London School of Economics, and examined developing and contesting cultures of consumption using the theories of Norbert Elias. Paddy was awarded a Government of Ireland Senior Research Scholarship in 2004–5 by the Irish Research Council for the Humanities and Social Sciences (IRCHSS) to facilitate the completion of his PhD. He continues to examine consumer subjectivity from a figurational (Eliasian) perspective, and has recently extended this theoretical focus to the study of Gaelic games in Ireland (with Dr John Connolly of DCU). He is co-founder, with Olivia Freeman, of the consumption & leisure studies research group at DIT (www.dit.ie/cls). He currently supervises four MPhil / PhD students within the DIT Faculty of Business.

Paul Donnelly, BA (TCD), MBA (TCD), PhD (UMass), GradDipMM (DIT), DipPR (PRII), CDipAF (ACCA). Paul is an organisational theorist, who studied for his PhD in the areas of organisation studies and international business at the University of Massachusetts at Amherst, where he also taught in the areas of global business, behaviour in the global economy, organisational behaviour, management and human resources management. At the Dublin Institute of Technology, he teaches strategy at the undergraduate level, and business ethics, negotiation, organisation behaviour and theory, and global marketplace at the postgraduate level. His research interests cover organisational studies (particularly from a processual perspective, through such lenses as actor-network theory and path dependence theory), international business, globalisation, and management education, and he has presented his work at conferences in Ireland, Europe, North America and South America. Currently, he is supervising three PhD students engaged in work that entails qualitative approaches to research. He is a Fulbright Scholar, having been awarded the Smurfit Scholarship in Business Studies by the Irish Fulbright Commission in 1999. He is also a recipient of the Irish Management Institute's Charles Harvey Award (1997) and Trinity College Dublin's John Good Prize for Best MBA Student (1996). In addition to his teaching and research activities, he is Vice President of the Irish Fulbright Alumni Association (2009-11), having previously served as Membership Secretary (2004-09). Prior to studying for his PhD in the US, he worked in various roles (business analyst, executive assistant to the commercial director, head of internal communications and head of customer relations) with Telecom Éireann (now eircom).

David Doyle, BBS, MA, PhD. David is a political scientist, who currently teaches in the School of Law and Government at Dublin City University. His research is concerned with Latin American politics, political institutions, partisan politics, political economy and creating models to understand policy change. He has published in journals such as *Canadian Journal of Political Science, Irish Political Studies* and *Acta Politica.* His teaching broadly reflects his research interests. David has also presented his findings at numerous conferences in Ireland and Europe. Currently, David's research is focused upon the impact of partisanship on policy outcome in the current international political economy, and upon developing ideational models for understanding policy change.

Olivia Freeman, BA, MSc Marketing. Olivia lectures in consumer behaviour and communications in the Faculty of Business at DIT. Olivia's current PhD work involves examining preschoolers' talk-in-interaction around branded commodities through the lenses of conversation analysis (CA) and discourse analysis (DA). Major research interests include children's consumer culture and advertising and marketing to children. Other interests include gendered consumer culture, tribes of consumption and sponsorship and advertising in schools. Olivia is co-founder, with Brendan O'Rourke, of the discourse analysis group (DAG) (www.dit.ie /DAG) and, with Paddy Dolan, of the Consumption & Leisure Studies research group (www.dit.ie/cls), both at DIT.

John Hogan, BBS, MA, PhD. John is a political scientist, who has taught in the School of Law and Government, DCU, the Department of Political Science, Trinity College Dublin, and in the Dublin Institute of Technology. He teaches Irish Politics, American Politics, and Comparative International Political Economy. His research interests are developing frameworks for identifying policy change, and studying the regulation of the lobbying industry internationally. He has published in the *Canadian Journal of Political Science, Political Quarterly, Acta Politica, and Irish Political Studies,* in addition to a number of book chapters. John has presented conference papers in Ireland, North America, and Europe. John has also won two Government of Ireland Postgraduate Research Scholarships, one for his Master's research and a second for his PhD research. He is currently working on a book on international lobbying regulations for Manchester University Press, with Professor Gary Murphy of DCU and Dr. Raj Chari of TCD.

Conor Horan, BBLS, MBS (Marketing). Conor is a research methodologist, who has previously lectured and researched in the Smurfit School of Business (UCD), and at the Czech University of Life Sciences in Prague. Conor teaches marketing theory and research methodology courses at the DIT. His research interests include Inter-Organisational Knowledge Creation and Markets-as-Networks. He is published internationally in the *Journal of Business Research, Journal of Strategic Marketing*, and *Industrial Marketing Management*. Conor is currently completing his PhD at the University of Strathclyde, Glasgow.

Brendan K. O'Rourke, BA, MA, PhD. Brendan is an management researcher, working in the area of economic discourses at the Dublin Institute of Technology. There, Brendan has supervised a range of research in issues such as volunteering organisations, industrial buying and creativity. His academic publications includes articles on interview methodology, owner-managed firms and on the nature of economics expertise. Currently, he is particularly interested in discourses of strategy and enterprise. Brendan is also the co-founder (with Olivia Freeman) of the Discourse Analysis Group (DAG) within DIT. DAG is a specialist group of academics who have published extensively in the area of discourse analysis.

Banu Özkazanç-Pan, BA (Johns Hopkins University), MBA (Loyola College), PhD (University of Massachusetts, Amherst). Banu is an assistant professor of management and international business at the College of Management, University of Massachusetts, Boston, teaching both undergraduate and graduate business courses. Her prior positions include the University of Massachusetts in Amherst, Hofstra University on Long Island, NY, and New York University's Wagner School of Public Policy. She has extensive teaching experience in organisational behaviour, management, and international business. Her research interests include transnationalism, postcoloniality and entrepreneurship theory and research, international and cross-cultural management, and diversity. Banu was the inaugural recipient of the Stanley J. Young scholarship award at the University of Massachusetts, Amherst. Her work has appeared in the *Academy of Management Review* (2008).

ACKNOWLEDGEMENTS

First of all, we would like to thank Brian O'Kane of Oak Tree Press. We are particularly indebted to Brian for his support of, and belief in, this project. Oak Tree Press was a delight to work with, and we are grateful for the team's efficiency throughout this process.

We acknowledge the support of the Faculty of Business, Dublin Institute of Technology, and thank Paul O'Sullivan, Dean and Faculty Director, and Kate Uí Ghallachóir, Head of the School of Marketing, for their support and guidance. We also acknowledge the support of the universities of the other contributors to this book, including Dublin City University, the University of Massachusetts at Boston and University of Wisconsin at Eau Claire.

We are especially grateful to all those who agreed to be interviewed, surveyed, or took part in focus groups, as part of the research conducted herein. Their participation, and honest answers, and the views they expressed, have contributed immeasurably to the quality of research on display here.

As always, we thank our families and friends for their unwavering support.

The editors and contributors
Dublin
March, 2009.

CHAPTER 1
INTRODUCTION

John Hogan, Paddy Dolan & Paul Donnelly

Undertaking a dissertation can be a daunting prospect, irrespective of whether a student is an undergraduate or a postgraduate. The idea of having to start with a blank sheet of paper and finish with anything between 15,000 words for an undergraduate dissertation, and 100,000 words for a PhD dissertation, is an arresting thought. But, even these coarse figures fail to capture the true extent of the work involved, as a finished dissertation is usually only a distillation of volumes of work and words that far exceed the finished product ultimately presented. However, the process can be made significantly easier if the student is genuinely interested in her / his topic of research, and can achieve clarity of vision through formulating, early in the research process, exactly what it is she / he wants to find out. This can be achieved by having a clearly-defined research question and a research methodology that is carefully structured to investigate that exact research question. However, even this prescription risks simplifying a complex and dynamic task. Qualitative research, in particular, is rarely linear, with each phase seen as a discrete entity. Researchers tend to work in a circular way, devising and rephrasing their research questions as they engage critically with existing theories. The research question will grow and evolve, as it becomes more theoretically informed and precise. The central question is, in effect, the 'translation' by the researcher of the various theories purporting to explain the phenomenon of interest in a form of words that captures his or her interpretation and understanding of the explanations (theories). In longer-term research projects, such as MPhil and PhD dissertations, the researcher may get the opportunity to go through this circular process several times, with each iteration representing an advance in understanding and methodological practice. Often, initial analysis of emerging data will lead the researcher to refine the research question at the very least. Sometimes, it may be entirely rewritten, or new theories may be identified as potential explanatory resources for hitherto unseen phenomena that have become interesting to the researcher.

For such projects, accidents and serendipitous encounters with people and data should not be avoided for fear of diversion from the imagined linear path of research. In qualitative inquiry, paths are rarely linear. But, minor dissertations at both undergraduate and postgraduate levels may not offer the same scope for unexpected discovery. This is simply a matter of 'time constraints'! In such circumstances, we argue that it becomes even more important to develop a tentative research question early in the process. This will guide reading for the literature review and aid the refinement of a theoretically-informed research question. Of course, the precise constraints any student faces depend on many factors, the most important of which will be the guidelines of the examining institution or university.

In terms of writing a research dissertation, one of the most difficult issues facing a student is selecting her / his research methodology – should this be qualitative, quantitative, or some mixture of the two? Each of these approaches is better suited to answer certain kinds of research questions and it is critical that the researcher understands which approach addresses which type of research question best. Thus, choosing a research methodology is not always as easy as it seems. The fact that the issue of methodology selection arises after the research question has been selected, but prior to the carrying out of the actual research, means that the methodology will determine the kind of research that is conducted and whether the findings will fit with the research objectives of the dissertation. Generally speaking, research questions focused on *how* certain processes, events, or structures are inter-related tend to suit qualitative methods. This is because the researcher is interested in particular modes of development and needs to see precisely how these change, or how they are expressed and articulated. Of course, quantitative methods also examine the inter-relationships between 'factors' or 'variables' (this is the purpose of statistical regressions and correlations, for example), but here the analysis tends to show *that*, rather than *how*, such factors are related. The precise mechanisms and processes, intended or unintended, are usually obscured, rather than revealed, by purely statistical approaches. But, mixing qualitative and quantitative approaches can be very useful in providing more complete explanations of social phenomena. While such mixed methods are not addressed in this book, we believe that qualitative methods can by themselves produce compelling knowledge of how and why people behave as they do, whether in organisational, family, personal, or other social roles.

It is in order to address these complex issues that that we have produced this book on qualitative research. The various chapters present examples for dissertation students in terms of how they might go about conducting qualitative research. Additionally, the chapters' findings show how students might consider presenting their own findings. To this end, each of the chapters has been structured like a mini dissertation with introductions, brief literature reviews, methodology sections, and finally analysis. Thus, the book was written with the intention of assisting dissertation students as they grapple with the difficulties of selecting and implementing a research strategy. Somewhat unusually for a qualitative research textbook, we have not addressed philosophy of knowledge issues to any great extent and certainly not through separate chapters. We would suggest that trying to deal with philosophical problems is not really the purpose of most organisational, consumer and other social research. While philosophical debates between positivism and interpretivism have often been superimposed upon quantitative and qualitative debates, this was always an oversimplification. Some qualitative methods and principles have positivistic origins and deciding finally on your own position in these philosophical debates is likely to close off important options and opportunities in the research process. Where philosophical concerns were of interest and relevance to the research studies discussed in the book, the contributors have sought to integrate the discussion of philosophy into their research strategies. Happily, the former strict opposition between qualitative and quantitative researchers has significantly receded and, with that, perhaps the reliance on philosophy as a source of research direction has declined to some extent, too.

THE QUALITATIVE APPROACH TO RESEARCH

Qualitative research is a multifaceted approach that investigates culture, society and behaviour through an analysis and synthesis of people's words and actions. Unlike quantitative approaches, it does not try to transform verbal symbols into numerical ones; the data remains at the level of words, either the research participants' own words, the words written in documents or the words used by the researcher herself / himself to describe the activities, images and environment observed. It tries to get to the heart of what exactly led to decisions, or choices, that were made, and how these choices came to take the form that they ultimately did.

Generally speaking, qualitative research has 'traditionally' been conducted by means of direct observation of a sample, case studies, personal experiences, introspection, an examination of relevant texts, interviews, focus groups, life stories, and the researcher's own participation in the settings that she / he is researching. But, with the advent of various new types of information technology devices and media, the range of things to be directly observed in qualitative research has greatly increased. Thus, in addition to observation, interviews, and documentation, there are now emails, text messages, instant messages, Twitter, online chat, as well as various online forums and blogs that can be examined. As Marshall & Rossman (2006: 2) point out, 'qualitative research is pragmatic, interpretive, and grounded in the lived experiences of people'. As we can see from the above, the media through which people communicate have greatly expanded in recent years, giving qualitative researchers a much broader field to inquire into. Qualitative research is a 'broad approach to the study of social phenomena' (Marshall & Rossman, 2006: 3). This 'allows qualitative research to pay special attention to the "qualities" of experience, aspects of life that quantitative approaches typically gloss over' (Gubrium & Holstein, 1997: 11). Put crudely, qualitative research is all about researching specific meanings, emotions, and practices that emerge through the interactions and interdependencies between people. It is concerned with social and personal processes and relations. Rather than reduce or abstract from these relations various static properties of individuals or groups in isolation, it seeks to examine how various sub-units and sub-processes derive their functions due to parts played in broader, composite units. As such, the so-called 'micro' aspects of life are connected to the 'macro' level, which reflects the links between many people and organisations. The emphasis on process and fluid relations tends to make qualitative inquiry more suitable. Of course, not all research dissertations will prioritise these aspects, so each student must think, or be reflexive, about the specific combination of research methods that will answer her / his research questions.

Denzin & Lincoln (2005: 10) argue that the term 'qualitative' suggests qualities, processes and meanings that are not examined through experimentation, or measured in terms of quantity. Each qualitative research approach possesses a series of unique steps in the analysis of findings and uses a range of strategies of inquiry. We stress that qualitative research is not subjective research; it is not based on one person's point of view, or biased towards one particular outcome. The findings from this research must be rigorous and dependable. Qualitative research sometimes takes place in natural settings, where researchers can conduct their research in the presence of the people they are studying, or within the environment they are examining. Thus, 'qualitative research is uniquely suited to discerning humans' participation in what happens to them' (Fischer, 2005: 411). However, perhaps the most common qualitative methods – interviews and focus groups – do not occur in 'natural' situations as such. Here, the researcher has arranged a social situation specifically, and usually exclusively, for the generation of data. The research participants would not be in these situations but for the efforts of the researcher. These situations, however, can be treated as social encounters and accomplishments, as well as being an opportunity to encourage the participant to recall memories and experiences regarding prior or recurring events and activities.

Frankfort-Nachmias & Nachmias (1996: 281) argue that qualitative researchers 'attempt to understand behaviour and institutions by getting to know the persons involved and their values, rituals, symbols, beliefs and emotions'. This encapsulates the idea that qualitative research tries to make sense of phenomena in terms of the meaning people bring to them. This can prove very important in evaluating research, in that an understanding of how certain events came about can be as important as what the particular events actually were.

WHAT SETS QUALITATIVE RESEARCH APART FROM QUANTITATIVE RESEARCH?

The qualitative approach to research differs from the quantitative approach in a number of distinct and important respects. Qualitative research tends to focus upon small samples, rather than the larger samples associated with quantitative research. Sampling in qualitative research is generally purposive, that is, the subjects, or cases, selected for examination are chosen specifically, due to some characteristic of interest to the researcher and her / his research topic. Researchers also play a key role in the research process itself. They are not observing events from a remove, but tend to be intimately involved in the research process. They bring with them particular theoretical frameworks and concepts, which influence how they interpret what they uncover. The data is examined by the researcher in a manner that requires her / his own interpretation of the results, based on the interplay between theoretical foregrounding prior to data generation, experience, understanding, and certain coding techniques that she / he has developed to analyse and synthesise data. Thus, 'qualitative research is multimethod in focus, involving an interpretive, naturalistic approach to its subject matter' (Denzin & Lincoln, 1994: 2). This use of multiple methods is representative of an attempt to gain an in-depth understanding of a phenomenon, with the recognition that objective reality can never fully be captured. As Flick (1998: 7) argues, 'qualitative research is not based on a unified theoretical and methodological concept'. Instead, the approach's strength is derived from the diverse approaches to qualitative research used in the world today.

'Qualitative research is concerned with collecting and analysing information in many forms, chiefly non-numeric' (Blaxter *et al.*, 1999: 60). Qualitative research, when done properly, can involve the designing of an approach that does justice to the complexity of the object under study. In this regard, the object of study is not reduced to single variables, but is studied in all of its complexity (Flick, 1998: 5).

Exceptional situations, and persons, are often the focus of qualitative research. While the objective of this research can be to examine, support or refute exiting theories, the researcher can also develop new understandings, modify or extend prior theoretical frameworks, or even formulate new theories. Thus, the qualitative researcher seeks examples of both expected and unforeseen relationships within the data, which are compared and contrasted. However, 'qualitative methods cannot be regarded independently of the research process and the issue under study' (Flick, 1998: 1). Qualitative research recognises a researcher's interaction with the topic of study as part of the knowledge creation process. Researchers' reflections on their own research actions become an element of the project, constituting part of the data.

Perhaps a final word needs to be said on the popular representation of qualitative research in some textbooks, for example, marketing research. Often, qualitative data and methods are portrayed as 'exploratory', 'soft' or 'inconclusive'. This implies, of course, that the use of a particular method can guarantee the findings of research inquiries. This is plainly unrealistic. Throughout scientific history, researchers have relied purely on quantitative methods for the generation of theories, only for those theories to be rejected later. No method is 'conclusive', if by that we mean that the results are universal, eternal or definitive. Explanations can always be improved and research is an ongoing process, hopefully extending our knowledge of the social world we inhabit. Some phenomena, like an organisation's sales levels, or workforce, can be easily quantifiable, and others, like organisational culture and structure, less so. The ability to count things does not make them more real, more precise or more accurate. Counting is just one means by which we, as human beings, make sense of our world. Often, we need to understand action and strategy from the perspectives of the actors and thinkers. People act and think through language, the social symbols that are passed on and extended from one generation to the next, and so it is sometimes more appropriate, more realistic and precise, to explain social action in terms of verbal symbols.

However, in the end, neither a qualitative nor a quantitative research approach is better, and they are not mutually exclusive (Best & Kahn, 1989: 89). Like any other tool, a research methodology is neither good nor bad, its true value being determined by the skills and understanding of researchers using and moulding it in their pursuit of answers to the unique research questions they are asking. In that respect, an understanding of what qualitative research is, what it can achieve, what its limitations are, and what sets it apart from quantitative research, is very helpful.

THE AIMS OF THE BOOK

The primary objective of this book is to introduce students to the concepts underlying qualitative research and how this kind of research can be conducted in a practical manner. To this end, it discusses various approaches to qualitative research and provides examples of these approaches being carried out in practice. In doing so, the book shows how various disciplines all use qualitative research in order to discover answers to their own particular research questions. We also show how qualitative methods can never be completely divorced from the intellectual adherence of their practitioners. Researchers' worldviews inevitably influence the qualitative approach they adopt, the tools they use, develop and employ, and the interpretations they bring to the findings uncovered. This is why researchers need to reflect (to be reflexive) on their own social position in the research process, to examine their dispositions and inclinations that may close off certain research possibilities. In doing so, their results can become more dependable and theoretically generalisable. The intention of all this is to familiarise students with the underlying tenets of qualitative research, so that, instead of being intimidated by it, they feel that they can take ownership of the concept.

The book is primarily designed to be a qualitative research guidebook for undergraduate and postgraduate students undertaking dissertations as part of their course of study. As qualitative methodologies can be applied across a broad spectrum of disciplines, the book can be used by students working in any area of research from business studies to the social sciences. One of our intentions in writing this book is to disabuse students of the often-voiced misconception that there must surely be one qualitative methodological approach for researching in one discipline and another, completely different, methodological approach for researching in another discipline. In fact, across a range of disciplines, as divergent as business, politics, and sociology, authors may take the same qualitative approach, for example, a discourse analytical approach, to examine a series of in-depth interviews conducted with a small number of interviewees. By setting out various qualitative approaches, showing how these overlap, and how they are applied across a broad range of disciplines, our aim is to remove this misconception.

Although the book is highly theoretical, and methodologically rigorous, it is full of practical examples. These examples show how the theories and approaches discussed can be employed to acquire information that goes into constructing valid academic arguments that answer basic research questions. In most of the chapters, the authors set out a specific qualitative methodology to be employed in investigating a unique research question. This allows students to follow the process through from research question, to methodology formulation, to analysis, and finally to findings and conclusions. In this regard, we feel that the book shows how methodology can be applied in practice, making clear both the use and value of qualitative approaches in research. Thus, the chapters deal with a range of real world problems and not abstract conundrums often found in research theory texts. Ultimately, most of the dissertation students reading this book will be conducting dissertation research for the first time and that puts an onus on the authors to impart as much theoretical and practical knowledge as possible in as concise a manner as is feasible. By avoiding chapters that focus on general rules of thumb and certain 'central' principles of research that must be adhered to at all times, we did not engage in an overly prescriptive approach to the research process. What we provide is methodology, informed by research questions, and real world analysis informed by theory, so as to provide answers to those research questions.

Students should use this book as a handy reference guide, and sample exemplar, when conducting their own research and they should see the chapters as mini-templates of what they should be aiming to produce themselves. Our hope is that students will see from the chapters that it is the theoretically-informed research question that sets the tone for all that comes in its wake. This question determines the particular qualitative methodology adopted, which determines the nature of the findings produced, which in turn influences how these findings are interpreted. Thus, each stage in a research process must fit with what came before it and with what will come after it. All aspects of the research must align. However, the ultimate value of a piece of research is not judged for the kind of questions that it asks, but from the quality of the results produced. Mismatches between research questions and methodologies are a problem that has dogged many a potentially great dissertation, as the results produced have failed to properly address the questions asked.

THE STRUCTURE OF THE BOOK

This book provides a unique insight into various approaches to qualitative research, as practiced at the cutting edge of academia in both Ireland and further afield. It brings together a number of academics from various universities and disciplines, each of whom contributes a chapter utilising a qualitative methodology of their own particular design. Additionally, the final chapter of the book contains a discussion conducted amongst a number of the contributing authors on various issues surrounding qualitative research methodologies, in general, and the conduct of research, in particular.

Whereas other methodology books seek to separate the section discussing methodology and the theories behind it from the practical application of those methodologies, this book integrates the two in its various chapters. Most chapters begin with a research question followed by a brief examination of the literature, then a discussion on the qualitative methodology being used, before employing this methodology in researching the specific question. In this manner, the chapters show how a qualitative methodological approach is constructed, then employed in practice, and how the results are interpreted by the researcher. The reader can clearly see how each author carefully tailors the qualitative approach to suit her / his own research question's requirements. Each methodology section flows seamlessly into the case studies in which it is employed in searching for answers to the overarching research question initially set out. An essential element of all the chapters is that that they are grounded in the reality of their research questions. In this respect, the chapters, in many ways, resemble small dissertations in themselves. Thus, the student is presented with a book made up of chapters that, in many instances, constitute smaller versions of what they themselves will have to produce when required to complete a research dissertation. Roth (2006) argues that a book with a layout such as this can lead to advanced thinking by students on the issues surrounding research. This structure addresses one of the primary criticisms of qualitative methodology books, namely, authors failing to speak from experience and successfully imparting the learning they possess.

As the various contributors to this volume work in such diverse fields as economics, sociology, organisational theory, research methodology, international business, human resource management and politics, their range of research interests are very broad. Nevertheless, what the book clearly shows is that, irrespective of the topics studied, there are certain commonalities and consistencies in relation to qualitative approaches to research that bridge the broad range of disciplines and research interests. Thus, there is continuity between the chapters, as there is a certain crossover between a number of the contributions. From this, readers will see how methodological approaches can have similarities, to a certain extent.

Thus, qualitative approaches to economics can employ methodologies that are almost identical to those employed in studies of international business. Qualitative approaches to researching organisational structure and forming can be very similar to, even complimenting and overlapping with, approaches used to understand policy change in a political science context, as well as methods to illuminate developing consumer cultures. So, for example, the chapter focusing on processual and historically-informed organisational theorising uses a path dependence approach and is followed by a chapter focusing on identifying critical junctures in macroeconomic policy. Critical junctures are a concept used to explain periods of radical change in historical institutionalism, a concept akin to path dependence, and are used to explain continuity in political institutions and policies. This chapter is followed by one addressing the apparent discontinuities embedded within long-term continuities of structural change in consumer culture and society. Thus, overlaps exist within the methodological approaches to what, on the surface, appear to be very different research questions. It is this apparently unobtrusive similarity that allows the methodological approaches to overlap to such an extent. A similar situation arises in relation to the chapters on discourse analysis. One chapter outlines, in broad brushstrokes, an overview of discourse analytical approaches to research, while the following chapter examines consumer culture amongst preschoolers, using a conversation analysis form of discourse analysis. Thus, although the topics studied here using qualitative approaches can be different, the tools employed to find the answers to the questions asked can be similar.

It should be noted that, whether it is academics or students who are doing the research, the approach is generally the same. In many instances, the research skills that academics developed as students, when writing their own dissertations, are the same skills that they employ here. Ultimately, both academics and students are seeking answers to research questions and using methodology to help them work their way through that process. The only difference is that academics have more experience, and therefore more knowledge, of the process than students.

THE PRESENTATION OF THE BOOK

The qualitative research, as set out in this book, acknowledges biases and values, recognition of something that is integral to qualitative research today. As Mertens (2003) points out, this recognition of bias represents honesty, and openness, in research. It also acknowledges the reality of the situation. All contributors recognise that, as researchers, they have inherent biases, irrespective of their efforts to achieve the most impartial results possible. As Gubrium & Holstein (1997: 12) acknowledge, 'qualitative research is distinguished by a commitment to studying social life in process, as it unfolds'. As part of that social life, researchers, and all they bring to the research process, influence how they collect information, analyse this information and interpret the findings.

The chapters of the book show that there is no one best way to conduct qualitative research, or that there is one methodological 'silver bullet' to enable us to answer exactly the research question we pose. Here, we stress that formulating the right methodology to address a research question is a reflexive, iterative process, often involving trial and error until the proper approach is defined. While choice of methodology is reflexive, the results it achieves are not, and, thus, care is the watchword when it comes to the selection of methodology.

Turning to the content of the book itself, in **Chapter 2,** Conor Horan addresses the absence of work in business academic literature, textbooks, and practical teaching tools aimed at guiding students toward selecting and developing research topics for dissertations. The first part of the chapter, dealing with topic selection, provides guidelines and questions that student researchers should think about when embarking on a research process. These guidelines reflect the challenges faced during the research process. Their application will vary depending on the context and rationale underpinning the proposed research. The questions included here are intended to provoke some thought relating to the research process and are written with a generalised and somewhat standardised research process in mind. For this reason, these guidelines must be regarded as broad considerations and are not prescriptive in nature. It must be remembered that every student researcher's process will be highly personalised and it is the decisions made within this research process that are of interest in relation to how knowledge claims are arrived at. These decisions will be made in the context of the issues raised in this section. The second part of this chapter provides an outline for topic development, guiding students toward writing and continuous re-writing of the purpose statement, the broad research question and sub-research questions. A process of arriving at sub-research questions, in the context of the overall broad research question, is highlighted using the research topic and the research idea. Research students are required to tackle key questions underpinning the rigour of their research as they deal with each stage of the research process. The importance of this is discussed throughout the chapter.

In **Chapter 3**, Marian Crowley-Henry presents an aspect of the evolving research approach of ethnography and participant observation, delineating the complexities involved in classifying research as ethnographic, given underlying discrepancies in how the approach is applied and the respective philosophy behind its use. The chapter offers an overview of contemporary literature concerning ethnography in social research, from classic ethnography (such as Clifford, 1988; Mead, 2001[1928]) to the placement of all qualitative research as ethnographic (Mason, 2002). The author's own research (Crowley-Henry, 2007; Crowley-Henry & Weir, 2007, 2009) is considered in order to provide a concrete example of a contemporary ethnographic piece of research. Practical examples of real fieldnotes and extracts from interview transcripts are presented in the chapter. Key guidelines for conducting ethnographic research are shared, meriting the adoption of an ethnographic approach to research, even for undergraduate students who may not have the opportunity to conduct longitudinal studies for their dissertations.

In **Chapter 4**, Banu Özkazanç-Pan discusses an auto-ethnographic research project, which was carried out based upon the postcolonial frameworks of Homi Bhabha, Edward Said, and Gayatri Spivak. Guided by postcolonial concerns raised by each of these scholars, the chapter examines and critiques existing approaches to international management theory and research on representation and globalisation. To this end, the chapter discusses fieldwork carried out that addresses issues of power, gender and identity during the fieldwork encounter, as relevant to postcolonial research projects, by providing excerpts of observations and interviews. The chapter focuses on the international entrepreneur as a way to demonstrate how international fieldwork, with a focus on globalisation, might be carried out using a postcolonial framework and also discusses theoretical and methodological implications of postcolonial approaches to research.

In **Chapter 5**, Kristina A. Bourne, supported by socialist feminist theorising, which addresses the assumption of a public / private divide, considers how the 'social fact' of work and family as separate domains is produced and sustained. Based on ethnomethodology and symbolic interactionism, the chapter shows how the author shadowed ten women entrepreneurs as they went about doing 'work-family'. In this chapter, the author describes the theory that underpins her study's methodology and details how she identified the participants, and the strategies she used to collect, manage, and analyse the data. Lastly, she provides a snapshot of her ethnographic findings.

In **Chapter 6**, Paul Donnelly seeks to address calls for more processual and historically-informed organisational theorising. The chapter considers the notion of path dependency, an approach which holds that a historical path of choices has the character of a branching process with a self-reinforcing dynamic, such that preceding steps in a particular direction induce further movement in the same direction, thereby making the possibility of switching to some other previously credible alternative more difficult. Path dependence seeks to assess how process, sequence and temporality can best be incorporated into explanation, the focus of the researcher being on particular outcomes, temporal sequencing and the unfolding of processes over time. Thus, proceeding from a consideration of the position afforded history in the organisational literature, this chapter outlines the tenets of path dependence theory, before sketching out its application in the practice of doing research.

In **Chapter 7**, John Hogan and David Doyle show how hypotheses, and the observable implications derived for those hypotheses, can be tested in researching a real world phenomenon. They do this by developing a testable framework for examining critical junctures in macroeconomic policy in Ireland, the US, Britain and Sweden throughout the latter half of the 20th century. The chapter begins with a brief introduction, followed by a short review of the literature on the concept of critical junctures. Thereafter, the chapter sets out the reasons for case selection, followed by the methodology to be employed and the testing of that methodology against the countries selected for examination. The sequence of methodology development, and its testing, occurs in three discrete stages, each of which logically follows on from the one preceding it. From this, it is possible to see how a theoretical framework can be developed and tested, and the ensuing results examined. Based upon these results, we can determine whether the revised framework 'works', by which we mean that it accurately captures something of the reality of the world political economy, or does not work and is therefore in need of further revision.

In **Chapter 8**, Paddy Dolan focuses on the fact that consumer and organisational research has undergone a significant shift in favour of qualitative methods over the last 20 years, but interviewing, whether 'in-depth' or group, continues to dominate the literature. However, the use of documents offers considerable scope for the development of processual explanations. Such texts reflect, and in part constitute, the social realities pertaining to particular organisations and even societies. By tracing the changes in the meaning and emotional connotation of specific words, phrases and practices, the researcher is able to gain a purchase on social and cultural change over time. The chapter illustrates this method, which is adapted from the figurational approach of Norbert Elias, through an analysis of the development of consumer culture in Ireland. The process of analysis and synthesis involves the fluid coding of relevant extracts of parliamentary speeches. Individual parliamentary debates have been analysed separately based on the 'codes' developed for each debate. This ensures that the meaning of parliamentary speech is not decontextualised from the flow of the speech itself, but is rather understood holistically. From the interpretations of individual analyses, key themes across time were identified. The approach diverges from conventional qualitative data analysis, whereby codes are established to represent homogenous data extracts, which are internally uniform and externally heterogeneous in relation to other codes.

In **Chapter 9**, Brendan K. O'Rourke provides an overview of discourse analytical approaches to research. The field of discourse analysis (DA) is vast, varied and contested, with traditions ranging from the conversational analysis of Sacks (1995; origin. 1964-1972), to more Foucauldian-inspired approaches (e.g., Kendall & Wickham, 1999), to critical discourse approaches (Van Dijk, 2001; Fairclough, 2003) to the differing psychological perspective of Potter & Wetherell (1987) and Harré (2004). This diversity means that this overview is necessarily selective, but nonetheless aims to give an introduction from where the interested readers can further investigate those currents of DA that are of interest. In order to locate DA within the range of methodology discussed in this volume, and to argue for the unity of various DA approaches, a short history is provided. A survey of DA is then provided, organised by what various approaches mean by 'discourse' and by what theories they use for analysis. A guide to further reading is provided for those wishing to explore exemplars of empirical work in business in various DA traditions.

In **Chapter 10**, Olivia Freeman argues that consumer culture is viewed as a social resource, which children can draw on as they engage with one another through talk-in-interaction. The chapter addresses children's conversation around the artefacts of consumer culture, including toys, TV programmes and movies, to illustrate a conversation analysis (CA) informed discourse analytic (DA) approach to research. This research was motivated by questions around what children 'do' with brand knowledge in a social context. The CA-informed DA approach draws upon a number of influences, including Gilbert & Mulkay (1985), Edley & Wetherell (1999) and Goodwin (2006). CA focuses on people's own interpretation of interaction, as revealed in the turn-by-turn unfolding of conversation, while DA critiques the representational view of language, focusing instead on the performative dimensions of talk interaction (Woofitt, 2005). The CA-informed discourse analytic approach is intended to provide textured description and a rich interpretation of multi-party interactions. This chapter demonstrates the possibilities for direct engagement between consumer researchers and preschoolers.

Chapter 11 is a discussion on the nature of qualitative research. In this chapter, a number of contributors to the book contribute to a roundtable discussion on qualitative methodologies. Here, they express their thinking in relation to a range of questions on qualitative methodologies put to them by the moderator, one of the editors of the volume. The objective of the chapter is to provide readers with an insight into a free-flowing discussion amongst academics on the nature of qualitative research. This takes the readers outside of the carefully-structured arguments of the authors, as set out in their various chapters, and presents their thinking on the topic at an 'instinctual' level. This is also something that dissertation students are not often exposed to – an insight into the debates that occur between academics on the nature of research. Such an insight will show that, even amongst those using qualitative research as a tool, there are widely-differing opinions as to how to approach this topic. Hopefully, readers will also be able to take from this chapter the idea that stimulating discussions amongst peer groups is a great way of teasing out the intricacies of complex subject matters. They will see that failure to reach consensus on an issue is not a bad thing as, in research, as in many other areas of life, there are often no right or wrong answers, only results that require interpretation. Most of all, this chapter presents a myriad of ideas on the ways in which qualitative research can be used in the search for answers to questions.

CONCLUSION

Qualitative research employs complex reasoning that is multifaceted and iterative (Creswell, 2002) and the reality of qualitative research reflects the reality of human thinking in its iterative approach to questions. When researchers collect data, this is analysed and thereafter they have to decide whether this is answering the question that they are asking, or whether further research is necessary, or whether a reformulation of the question might be what is required. Thus, there is a process at work, with data collection followed by analysis, back to the reformulation of the problem again, and so on.

In essence, this approach to research is grounded in the 'real' world in which we live. Researchers, and the topics that they research, are constituent and interacting parts of that world. The approach is quite different from quantitative research. The primary tool used to gather the required information in qualitative research is the researcher himself or herself, as opposed to an inanimate instrument, such as a questionnaire or online survey, in quantitative research. The findings in qualitative research, as can be seen in the chapters that follow, are presented, usually, though not exclusively, in the form of thick description. The use and presentation of words and arguments, as opposed to 'facts and figures', is the essence of the findings in this approach. The focus is on the experiences of those within the case studies (Fraenkel & Wallen, 1990). The findings are usually case-specific and it must be noted that empirical generalisability will always be limited where qualitative research is involved, though findings can, and should be, related to prior or emergent theories. However, what all of the chapters in this book show is that well-constructed research, well-conducted research and well-written findings go a long way towards enabling the reader to understand how findings may be transferable into a wider context (Marshall & Rossman, 2006: 206). The ultimate object of the research, despite the researcher's integration into the entire process, is the production of dependable and credible findings.

A qualitative methodology takes the form of an investigation. Research questions can change based upon the investigation's early findings. The researcher can set out in search of specific information, only to discover quickly that such material no longer exists, if it ever did. This can be an issue, for example, in relation to such things as historical records in Europe, certain of these having been lost in the various conflagrations that have consumed the continent over the past centuries. In response to this situation, the researcher must either change the focus of the research question, or revise the research question itself. Thus, the iterative process in qualitative research can take hold very quickly.

In order to engage in qualitative research, it is necessary to consider it as a network of various approaches, or a combination of approaches. Qualitative research is not a value-free activity devoid of social, economic and environmental impacts. Findings have relevance and the nature of those findings is influenced by the choices made by the researchers and the academic community's appreciation of those findings.

Our aim in producing this book is to introduce students to the concepts fundamental to qualitative research and the conduct of such research in practice. Numerous qualitative research approaches are discussed and formulated, and examples of their application are then provided. This shows how answers to research questions can be uncovered by qualitative research. The chapters show how the qualitative approaches, in many respects, are linked to the intellectual background of the researchers, to their own interests and preferences. We want students to see qualitative methodology as a tool that can be used to maximise the potential of their research, rather than being intimidated by the notion of this methodology. Our ultimate hope is that students, from across a range of fields, will find this a useful volume in assisting them in conducting research of a qualitative nature.

BIBLIOGRAPHY

Best, J. & Kahn, J. (1989). *Research in Education,* 6th ed. Englewood Cliffs, NJ: Prentice Hall.

Blaxter, L., Hughes, C. & Tight, M. (1999). *How to Research*. Buckingham: Open University Press.

Clifford, J. (1988). *The Predicament of Culture*. Cambridge, MA: Harvard University Press.

Creswell, J.W. (2003). *Research Design: Qualitative, Quantitative and Mixed Method Approaches*. London: Sage.

Crowley-Henry, M. (2007). 'The Protean Career: Exemplified by First World Foreign Residents in Western Europe?', *International Studies of Management and Organization* 37(3): 44–64.

Crowley-Henry, M. & Weir, D. (2007). 'The International Protean Career: Four Women's Narratives', *Journal of Organizational Change Management* 20(2): 245-258.

Denzin, N.K. & Lincoln, Y.S. (1994). *Handbook of Qualitative Research*. London: Sage.

Edley, N. & Wetherell, M. (1999). 'Imagined Futures: Young Men's Talk About Fatherhood and Domestic Life', *British Journal of Social Psychology* 38(2): 181-94.

Fairclough, N. (2003). *Analysing Discourse: Textual Analysis for Social Research*. London: Routledge.

Fischer, C.T. (2005). *Qualitative Research Methods for Psychologists: Introduction through Empirical Studies*. Boston, MA: Academic Press.

Flick, U. (1998). *An Introduction to Qualitative Research*. London: Sage.

Fraenkel, J.R. & Wallen, N.E. (1990). *How to Design & Evaluate Research in Education*. New York, NY: McGraw-Hill.

Frankfort-Nachmias, C. & Nachmias, D. (1996). *Research Methods in the Social Sciences*, 5th ed. New York, NY: St. Martin's Press.

Gilbert, G.N. & Mulkay, M. (1984). *Opening Pandora's Box: A Sociological Analysis of Scientists' Discourse*. Cambridge: Cambridge University Press.

Goodwin, M.H. (2006). *The Hidden Life of Girls*. Malden: Blackwell Publishing.

Gubrium, J.F. & Holstein, J.A. (1997) *The New Language of Qualitative Method*. Oxford: Oxford University Press.

Harré, R. (2004). 'Staking Our Claim for Qualitative Psychology as Science', *Qualitative Research in Psychology* 1(1): 3-14.

Kendall, G. & Wickham, G. (1999). *Using Foucault's methods*. London: Sage.

Marshall, C. & Rossman, G.B. (1999). *Designing Qualitative Research*. Thousand Islands, CA: Sage Publications.

Mead, M. (2001[1928]). *Coming of Age in Samoa: A Psychological Study of Primitive Youth for Western Civilisation*. New York, NY: Harper Perennial Modern Classics.

Mertens, D.M. (2003). 'Mixed Methods and the Politics of Human Research: The Transformative-Emancipatory Perspective,' in Tashakkori, A. & Teddlie, C. (eds) *Handbook of Mixed Methods in Social and Behavioral Research*, pp. 135-164. Thousand Oaks, CA: Sage.

Potter, J. & Wetherell, M. (1987). *Discourse and Social Psychology: Beyond Attitudes and Behaviour*. London: Sage.

Roth, W-M. (2006). *Textbooks on Qualitative Research and Method / Methodology: Towards a Praxis of Method* [Online]. Available: http://www.qualitative-research.net/fqs-texte/1-06/06-1-11-e.htm (last accessed 14 March 2009).

Sacks, H. (1995 [1964-1972]). *Lectures on Conversation Volumes I & II*. Oxford: Basil Blackwell.

Van Dijk, T.A. (2001). 'Critical Discourse Analysis', in Schiffrin, D., Tannen, D. & Hamilton, H.E. (eds), *The Handbook of Discourse Analysis*, pp. 352-371. Oxford: Blackwell Publishers.

Woofitt, R. (2005). *Conversation Analysis and Discourse Analysis, A Comparative and Critical Introduction*. London: Sage.

CHAPTER 2
RESEARCH TOPIC SELECTION & DEVELOPMENT

Conor Horan

INTRODUCTION: AN OVERVIEW OF THE FIRST STAGE IN THE RESEARCH PROCESS

Easterby-Smith *et al.* (1991:18) comment that: 'It is very rare for students to have a clear focus from the outset of their research, and yet many find the lack of a clear focus is a major impediment to getting started'. Research methods textbooks allude to vague guidelines on topic selection by prescribing a course of action, i.e., stating that 'you must select a core topic' and / or 'you must write a purpose statement'. This approach rarely attempts to explain to student researchers 'how' to actually go about selecting and developing topics further and can often involve language with laden meaning. Indeed, the process of deriving hypotheses is very much based on exacting causal logic that is associated more with quantitative research. A discussion relating to this falls outside the focus of this book, although causal logic is used as a basis of some of the considerations in this chapter, e.g., the relationship between the research topic and research idea, and should not be ignored even within the context of qualitative research.

Very little research into this first stage of the research process has been conducted (L'Anson & Smith, 2004). This chapter aims to deal with this ambiguous gap, as highlighted by Easterby-Smith *et al.* (1991), by providing a framework (**Table 2.1**), albeit linear, toward overcoming some difficulties faced by the student researcher.

Topic Selection	Step 1: Finding a Broad Research Topic
	Step 2: The Research Idea
	Step 3: Developing the Research Rationale
	Step 4: Understanding Evaluation and Value Judgements
	Step 5: Directionally Focused Research
	Step 6: Is there an Identifiable Group that can be Researched?
	Step 7: The Functional Focus of the Dissertation
Topic Development	The Purpose Statement
	The Broad Research Question
	Sub-Research Questions

Table 2.1: The Process, from Topic Selection to Topic Development (Source: adapted and developed from Saunders *et al.* (2007) and Creswell (1994))

It should be noted that each stage of topic selection and topic development can be approached from multiple perspectives. There is no 'one way' of approaching research, but ensuring justified and informed choices are made and supported will ensure the research process is rigorous. Using the conceptual framework from Saunders *et al.* (2007) and Creswell (1994), this chapter intends to open a debate on some non-prescriptive issues around dissertation topic selection and development. By discussing this, the researcher should become aware of the possible relationships and configurations that underpin viable research topics. The aim here is to provide the student researcher with some items to consider, to assess the relative importance of these items and to provide food for thought as the researcher reflects on the research process.

TOPIC SELECTION: ISSUES RELATING TO THE RESEARCH TOPIC

Step 1: Finding a Broad Research Topic

The first step in the research process is to identify a *broad research topic* representing a broad area, discipline or function. One way to look at this is to consider the different subject areas in your course of study and / or functional areas or types of jobs you might wish to work in. This is invariably a good place to start, as it should reflect your academic interests. For example, a research project in finance is fundamentally different, in terms of associated academic literature, to one in organisational behaviour or consumer behaviour. By identifying a disciplinary / functional area, a distinct, coherent body of literature should be found. The references at the end of textbook chapters in your chosen topic area can indicate seminal articles associated with an appropriate research topic. This literature can then be used to represent the *boundary* of concerns guiding you forward. As you consider different topics, be conscious that your broad topic area will naturally shift as you become acquainted with the available literature. By focusing on the *boundary* between topic areas at this early stage, you can consciously manage the direction your research activities can take.

There is also a macro dimension influencing research topic selection. The field of *scientific choice* (Montgomery, 1967) discusses the allocation of scarce societal resources toward different research agendas. Currently, there is much debate about emphasising research relating to sustainability, climate change and recycling. In return for an allocation of resources, society expects a level of transparency in how these resources are used. Therefore, research projects mirroring the needs of society will receive greater emphasis from policy-makers (Gibbons *et al.*, 1992; Nowotny *et al.*, 2001). In other words, the results of research projects in these areas can be of interest to practitioners and academics alike. In considering the macro debate around 'scientific choice', the lessons to be learnt have a clear application to the choices to be made by the student researcher regarding the relevance of the research topic. Should a research project contribute only to theory, i.e., pure research, and not societal needs or practice, i.e., applied research, a question mark might be raised. The student researcher would do well to have a broad appreciation for the theory–practice debate and how it influences the research rationale and the writing of the research question and sub-questions. This scrutiny over research funding allocation reflects the macro discussion relating to transparency in research activity in society. Student researchers should inform themselves about the macro issues in their fields, as this can provide a great starting point in identifying a broad research topic for the dissertation.

Step 1: Finding a Broad Research Topic
Issues to be addressed by the Researcher: ♦ What is my broad research topic area? ♦ What disciplinary area or organisational function might this topic be related to?
The Recommendation: ♦ Identify key textbooks with chapter references that interest you. Follow up on these references. ♦ Use the identified literature as a *boundary* guiding your thinking as you move forward. ♦ Consult recent academic literature so as to gain an overview of research in your field. ♦ Consult recent trade literature so as to gain an overview of issues being discussed at an industry level. Also talk to practitioners (including managers, employees, consumers, etc.) to see what 'problems' they face– these problems may represent a broad research topic.
The Assessors will ask: ♦ Has the student identified a clear topic area with an identifiable body of literature indicating a clear research agenda?

Table 2.2: Finding a Broad Research Topic

Step 2: Refining the Broad Research Topic with the Research Idea

A more specific area of research then needs to be considered within the broad topic area. After identifying the discipline or functional area, a sub-topic or *research idea* can be identified (Saunders *et al.*, 2007). This can be done by looking at the different concepts considered in seminal sources or textbooks and asking what research is currently being pursued on this concept. The specifics of the research, most likely referenced at the end of the chapter, should represent what is called the *research front*, reflecting where the current research thinking is in relation to this concept.

The reason it is important to arrive at a *research idea* is a practical issue of resources and time. For example, studying the topic of 'marital relations' is of course a noble pursuit; however, from the perspective of a research project where we can assume limited resources and limited time, it would be impossible to cover every possible angle. This would arguably lead to a dilution of the dissertation, i.e., breadth without depth. Marital relations might well be considered from anthropological, sociological, legal or financial perspectives, to name but a few. It is important which perspective you have chosen in Step 1, as this will have a direct influence over the body of literature you will consider and the 'lens' with which you assess available literature. For example, Corporate Social Responsibility (CSR) is such a broad area that one has to ask from what perspective it will be studied. As mentioned, not every angle can be taken into account and we can assume that each angle will be a full study in itself (within the constraints of the resource-strapped student dissertation). An ethical approach to CSR, a consumer perspective on CSR, a corporate perspective on CSR strategy, or financial returns relating to CSR, etc., all represent different research projects, due to the nature of the research ideas linked to the broad research topic of CSR. The research idea will also have an impact on the methods used during data collection.

The key issue here is that academic research requires you to narrow your topic down by choosing one of these perspectives. It also requires the student researcher to become conscious of the consequences this decision will have on her / his own research process. By being aware of this connection at this early stage, you can progress the focus of the dissertation in a dramatic way. As awareness of the research idea develops, an alternative angle could be considered later within the scope of the research topic. Moving to this alternative angle would not cause too much trouble, as the literature relating to the research topic will still be considered.

In short, the *research idea* qualifies the *research topic*, in that the dissertation only considers the research topic from the perspective of the research idea. This is one clear way to break down broad research topics into manageable parts. While this is but one approach, for a further discussion, consult Saunders *et al.* (2007).

Step 2: Refining the Broad Research Topic with the Research Idea
Issues to be addressed by the Researcher: ♦ Within my identified topic area, what concepts interest me? ♦ Within the research topic area, what concepts are researchers focusing on? ♦ What problems do these researchers find to be of interest? ♦ Do these problems represent a 'research front' in the field? ♦ How are researchers currently studying these concepts? ♦ What specific concepts interest me? ♦ From what angle will I be approaching my research topic? What is my research idea? ♦ What 'level of analysis' interests me? The individual, the group, or the organisation?
The Recommendation: ♦ Identify one angle you would like to focus on. Be prepared for this to evolve and change as you progress through your study. ♦ Continue to try to narrow the research focus of your topic by actively looking for possible research ideas in the literature (within the boundary discussed above).
The Assessors will ask: ♦ How manageable is this research topic and idea within the time frame and resources available? ♦ Can the refined topic be completed sufficiently?

Table 2.3: Refining the Broad Research Topic with the Research Idea

Step 3: Developing the Research Rationale

At this early stage of the process, it can be helpful for the student to surmise who would benefit from potential results and who might be interested in reading the research. There must be a reason for conducting the research and that reason must have its basis in adding some value. A more focused way of considering this is by asking *'to what end?'* as a way of validating the research exercise. To start addressing this, consider what practitioners and academics might find interesting in your research. These will represent just two distinct communities or audiences for your research.

Research findings that are of particular interest to academics can relate to existing theories within a discipline and may even progress a discipline in some way, albeit in more advanced research projects. One way to progress a discipline might be the development of new data collection methods themselves and / or to refine the meaning of a particular concept used within a given discipline. This can be referred to as *pure research*. More often than not, research findings will have something to say about the discipline itself and how it is being researched, e.g., how we generate knowledge within a particular discipline. This is an important consideration for student researchers and is relative to the level of research being conducted.

Research findings that are of particular interest to practitioners, on the other hand, can aim to solve (or contribute towards a solution) managerial problems in a particular context. So if there is a problem with, for example, defecting customers, solutions could include research on the success of competitor offerings (often an uncontrollable external issue) or research into customer service issues (a controllable internal issue). Research conducted in the commercial setting with the above goals is often referred to as *applied research*. In some cases, this research can be conducted in the absence of referring to academic theories, i.e., commercial research. While recognising the characteristics of this type of research, most academic research requires student researchers to relate their research topic to available academic literature and theories. A discussion relating to the use of 'pure' and 'applied' research terms can be found in (**Chapter 11**) of this book.

In reality, very few student dissertations are so polarised that their results fall only into one category or the other; indeed the findings will likely be of interest to both academics and practitioners. Realising this will not only influence the way research questions will be written at the early stages of research process, but will have a significant impact on the structure and writing style in the findings chapter, where the relevance of the findings are discussed. It should be noted that the relevance to practitioners may influence the topic that is selected, but dissertations are primarily written for the evaluating academic audience. It is your academic audience that will grade the dissertation as discussed below.

Research that aims to add something new to the body of knowledge, and does not merely replicate what has gone before, is prized. Whereas different academic departments have different guidelines on this matter, the goal of writing in the context of existing theories is always an important one in terms of doing research and should be considered by all researchers. Requiring the researcher to address, for the reader, why her / his research is of interest focuses the researcher toward 'selling' the rationale of the research and why the reader should care. Without a clear rationale for a research topic, the context for the research questions becomes very loose and the overall impact of the research project can be diminished. In addition, the research will fail to achieve its potential, even if the methods are rigorous and the results meaningful.

Step 3: Developing the Research Rationale
Issues to be addressed by the Researcher:
♦ What contribution will this research bring? To what end?
♦ Who potentially is interested in the results from this research process?
♦ To what degree will academics and practitioners be interested in my results?
♦ How will these audiences influence the way I write my research questions?
The Recommendation:
♦ Identify the audience(s) for your research.
♦ Identify who would benefit from, or be interested in, your results.
♦ Write your draft research questions with the audience in mind.
The Assessors will ask:
♦ Has the student identified a clear audience, while noting that the academic audience will be the evaluators of the research?
♦ In what way will the results be of benefit?
♦ How has this been tackled in terms of justification for the research?
♦ How has the student rationalised this argument in the dissertation?

Table 2.4: Developing the Research Rationale

Step 4: Understanding Evaluation & Value Judgements

Following on from the last step, academic audiences will evaluate the rigour underpinning decisions made during the research process. Rigour in research relates to the justified and informed choices (Saunders *et al.*, 2007) made by the researcher during the process. Rigour ensures a broad consensus as to the quality of results within the particular chosen research tradition. This concept of rigour is underpinned by the transparent process called the 'peer review system'. The practicality behind this discussion is that the peer review system requires your research rationale to be as strong as possible – like a chain, where each link must support, and be supported by, the research questions in terms of contributing something to the body of knowledge, with the requirement for 'new' knowledge being found at the PhD level. In any case, an appreciation of the peer review system is important in understanding how value judgements will influence the development of your research rationale. While these judgements are criticised as being partial and biased, i.e., the problem of value judgements, Montgomery (1967) warns that any attempt to develop a science of authoritative value measurement would fail. Dunning (2007), in his podcast on peer-reviewed literature, mirrored this sentiment, stating that no one authority should, or could, have the power to make absolute value judgements and that the scientific community at large reviews published materials through a transparent process. It is this transparency itself that is both the strength and weakness in the system. For this reason, the 'methodology' chapter is so important, as it reveals, in a transparent fashion, the 'methods' and the decisions considered by the researcher, allowing for open comparison with alternative research choices made by other researchers.

Step 4: Agents of Evaluation & the Problem of Value Judgements
Issues to be addressed by the Researcher: ♦ What is the benefit to society and / or academe of my results?   ♦ How will the academic community evaluate the process and the results of my research?   ♦ Who are the agents of evaluation in the audience for your research?   ♦ How will the agents of evaluation, using the peer review system, evaluate my research?
The Recommendation: ♦ Be aware of the need for rigour and the purpose of the peer review system.
The Assessors will ask: ♦ Has this student addressed possible weaknesses in her / his rationale in the body of the research project?   ♦ Has the student attempted to apply rigour to her / his research decisions?

Table 2.5: Agents of Evaluation & the Problem of Value Judgements

At this point, it should be noted that developing the rationale for the research topic is an ongoing iterative process that, theoretically, should never be finalised during the writing process. More work can always be done! Student researchers need to inform themselves, during the research process, as to what constitutes rigour within their disciplinary area and what standards they are expected to meet in relation to the goal of producing something 'new'. Undergraduate dissertations do not require something new, but the goal in itself is still a valid one for improved research. This task is a difficult one and should not be underestimated. Faculty guidelines should be consulted in this regard.

Step 5: Directionally-focused Research

The approach taken here is a pedagogical one, where the focus is to provide guidelines that can be followed in the early stage of the research process, rather than a discussion about the structure of disciplines. So, as a general observation, much of the literature and research produced in the fields of business and management can be seen to handle concepts that have different biases or directional foci.

When we look at the structure in textbooks used in psychology or consumer behaviour (Solomon, 2006; Schiffman, 2008), for example, a distinction between studies of and within the individual (e.g., leadership, memory, learning, attitudes) and topics relating to the environment in which the individual operates (e.g., culture, social class, demographics, religion) can be seen. These reflect very different areas within the one discipline.

An example showing the practical distinction here can be illustrated when we study individual consumers and their behaviour (e.g., their ability to recall advertising, opinions of or attitudes toward a brand or their consumption habits) *versus* macro trends in a market (e.g., societal needs to focus on sustainable consumption). This might represent one way, but not the only way, of placing an arbitrary mental boundary on a topic refining the focus of your research.

This mental boundary can also be illustrated on a different level of analysis from the individual. If we move the level of analysis to the organisation level, we can find similar distinctions that can aid the development of a focused research topic and idea. In the field of economics, which is predominantly concerned with 'the firm', a topic studying resource allocation within 'the firm' reflects issues relating to organisational decision-making procedures. This is a different research process to a study on inter-organisational relationships or market dynamics. One way to illustrate why this difference is important is to identify the body of literature required to do either study. The former body of literature is fundamentally different to that which will be consulted for the latter, as the concepts being considered are completely different. This can be used to reflect on whether the sub-questions are all written in a consistent manner toward a common goal.

Research questions should be guided by theory and academic concepts and, in most cases, these theories derive from the social sciences. Sometimes, students undertaking research degrees at MPhil and PhD level can synthesise apparently separate literatures across several disciplines in the social sciences. Indeed, this is sometimes part of originality claims by PhD candidates. However, staying within a known boundary is useful, due to the time constraints imposed for minor dissertations.

Step 5: Directionally-focused Research
Issues to be addressed by the Researcher: ♦ How is my research focused? ♦ How will this focus influence the type of research objectives I will write? ♦ What broad body of literature am I considering? ♦ Does this body of literature broadly focus on more than one concept? ♦ Are the concepts being considered reflecting either an externally- or internally-focused research project?
The Recommendation: ♦ Particularly at undergraduate level, a project that attempts to encompass several disciplines may well divide the efforts of the student through the necessity to generate data pertaining to both consumers and organisations.
The Assessors will ask: ♦ Is there is a cohesive focus to the body of work? ♦ Is the literature review connected to a core concept (where possible)? ♦ Does the literature review deal adequately with the concepts being considered?

Table 2.6: Directionally-focused Research

The discussion here is not a discussion about structures of disciplines, but a discussion about developing mental schemas that are reflected in research questions. The embedded nature of concepts, and their laden meanings, in the social sciences makes this separation difficult for students to comprehend and this section is aimed at simply highlighting this consideration which is useful at the commencement of the research process.

Step 6: Is there an Identifiable Group that can be Researched?

A common requirement for a research project is that primary data is generated or used. The group can constitute a group of consumers, a group of employees and managers within an organisation, and even the group at a higher level of social integration such as the nation-state. In qualitative research, primary documents often provide evidence of the actions, beliefs, values and strategies of particular groups.

It is useful for the student researcher to consider 'identifiable groups' that business and management research projects focus on. A dissertation proposal that focuses on organisational processes, but then considers researching consumers, is bound to cause problems of coherency. There must be some alignment between the focus of the dissertation and the identifiable group being researched. This is a useful consideration and a useful way of reviewing and reflecting on the focus of your research as you move forward. Some questions the researcher should think about include:

♦ 'What group do I want / need to collect 'data' about?' When I have identified the group, 'how will this re-shape my research questions?'

♦ 'What are the types of questions I can ask about my identified group, either directly through interviews or indirectly through documentary sources?' Questions must be linked in some way for relevancy. For example, there is little use in asking consumers what they think of a managerial decision to choose TV advertising over internet advertising (internal managerial decision-making), unless those consumers have some identifiable connection with the issue. The logic behind this connection is usually discussed in the rationale section of the dissertation and is an important issue to think through.

♦ 'Do I intend to ask questions about more than one group?' Particularly at undergraduate level, by asking questions of more than one group the chances are that there will be some variability in your resultant research questions. One way of identifying this is to look to see whether there is more than one concept being researched. For example, a study looking at the creative decision in the execution of a particular advertising brief and the reaction of consumers to the final advert will result in two different studies with two different bodies of literature: the first being a study of decision-making in creative situations and the second focusing on consumer recall or perhaps consumer attitudes. A list of research questions written up to reflect both groups undoubtedly will reflect multiple concepts and potentially two bodies of literature. Therefore, dilution of research questions can occur as the number of identifiable groups increases (**Figure 2.1**). For this reason, these broad guidelines can provide some direction in editing down and refining a research topic and research idea.

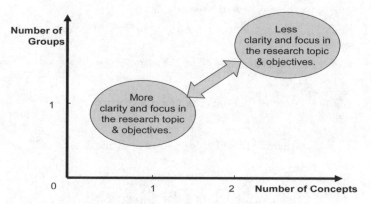

Figure 2.1: Identifiable Groups & Concepts

It is recommended to focus broadly on one identifiable group. This helps to focus the writing of the research questions around this group and highlight the bias within the research. This is purely a practical concern. It is not that multiple groups are incorrect, but, as a consequence of focusing on one group, the literature that the researcher considers will begin to take on a unified form. There are examples of research topics that cover more than one group, e.g., opinions of employees and managers about workplace conditions. This is a more demanding project, requiring access to two different perspectives. Where this happens, for methodological reasons, the researcher's skills will also be tested further.

Step 6: Is there an Identifiable Group that can be Researched?
Issues to be addressed by the Researcher: ♦ Will an identifiable group be approached for data collection? ♦ What group do I want / need to collect 'data' from? ♦ If no group is being researched, what sources of data are being considered? ♦ Are my research objectives written to reflect the perspective of this identifiable group? ♦ What connection does this identifiable group have to the concepts being researched? ♦ What are the types of questions I can ask this identifiable group?
The Recommendation: ♦ If it is clear a 'group' of people is to be approached, write this explicitly into your research objectives. ♦ Relate the group you are collecting data from to the concepts being studied. ♦ Ensure your research objectives are formulated in this context.
The Assessor: ♦ Will look to see that the identifiable group from which you have collected data has a valid connection to your research objectives.

Table 2.7: Is there an Identifiable Group that can be Researched?

Step 7: The Functional Focus of the Dissertation

A dissertation that is focused upon organisations, and with questions directed at managers or employees, will result in explanations of how or why organisations function as they do. Such explanations will need to be related to existing academic explanations (theories) in the discussion of the results. This can be distinguished from a piece of research about a market phenomenon. The difference might be seen in the emphasis and importance that will be placed on the literature used to complete the study.

By addressing managers, the issues that can be tackled in detail tend to be limited to strategic 'decision-making' or 'resource allocation'. This reflects principles in strategy texts (DeWit & Myer, 1998). In the same vein, as mentioned above, questions that are addressed to shareholders, by their very nature, tend to be of a financial or strategic nature, unless they have a vested interest that can be shown in other non-strategic topics. As mentioned in the Introduction to this chapter, many researchers fail to see the broad body of literature and thrust of a potential topic early on

(Easterby-Smith *et al.*, 1991). By becoming aware of the type of research process they are going to engage in at an early stage, students can avoid 'locking' themselves into a topic they are not interested in. At this stage of the process, it can be helpful to revisit this issue of the 'functional focus', so as to ensure it is aligned with the previous six steps in topic selection.

Step 7: The Research Idea – The Functional Focus of the Research Project
Issues to be addressed by the Researcher: ♦ What type of dissertation do I want to produce?   ♦ For example, am I interested in the decision-making processes of managers? How can this lead to the making of strategy? If so, what are the implications for my research questions?   ♦ For example, do I want to produce a piece of research that is looking at the behaviour and attitude of consumers? If so, what are the implications for my research questions?
The Recommendation: ♦ The recommendation here is to ensure that a research project fits within a discipline or organisational function. For research degrees, several functions or disciplines may be synthesized to provide fuller explanations.

Table 2.8: The Research Idea – The Functional Focus of the Research Project

TOPIC DEVELOPMENT: THE PURPOSE STATEMENT & FRAMING THE RESEARCH QUESTION

While the Topic Development Guide (Steps 1 to 7) is shown in linear fashion in practice, the path of research is anything but linear. There is a need to revise and develop a research topic continually, as you gain a better understanding of the body of knowledge relating to a research idea and the practical data collection and methods that can be employed. The need to revise and rewrite this core section of the dissertation continually is an important exercise and a skill that requires constant development over the course of your study. For this reason, the previous steps outlined here should be reviewed on an ongoing basis. Failing to rewrite and revise research questions from an early stage in the research process proves time and time again to be one of the key failings of the student researcher.

This following section intends to deal with three main issues: Development of the Purpose Statement; the Broad Research Question; and the Sub-Research Questions. It should be noted at this stage that many research projects will vary from this structure and language. For a further discussion on these three items, consult Creswell (1994). The issues raised below are intended to provoke thought into the intricacies of the concepts you are studying and to encourage you to engage with the decisions made by previous researchers in your field.

The Purpose Statement

The purpose statement is the core statement that indicates the direction and focus of the research being conducted in the dissertation. In many ways, it is related to the ideas that should come from thinking about the research topic and its relationship with the research idea, as discussed above. Creswell (1994: 59) provides an interesting script for the purpose statement, highlighting certain issues that should be considered. These include the purpose of the study; the central concept being studied; the level of analysis (i.e., the individual, the organisation or society); and, possibly, the method of inquiry. Of course, at this early stage in the research process, it is hard for the student researcher to have filled in all of these items knowledgeably. But, there is an important lesson here that illustrates that these issues have to be worked toward over the course of your research process. As the student progresses, these issues should be tackled and the pieces of the jigsaw completed before submission of the dissertation.

Framing the Research Question

Every dissertation must have one core overarching research question. It is a difficult task, especially when the student researcher becomes increasingly close to her / his topic, to write the core research question as one single question. Not only is this a writing challenge, but it is also a difficult intellectual challenge, and only comes about after engaging, reviewing and digesting the literature over the course of the research process. Students should refer to the following chapters in the remainder of the book for examples of research questions in the business and social science disciplines. It should be borne in mind throughout that, as this is a qualitative research guide, the research questions have been formulated accordingly.

What is the difference between the broad research question and the research sub-questions? For the purposes of this chapter, the sub-questions tend to be linked more to the 'research idea' mentioned in the first part of this chapter. In the CSR example above, it was mentioned that such a vast topic could be researched from many different disciplinary perspectives. Indeed, two researchers could have very similar research questions, but deal with these core questions in different ways, reflecting disciplinary or methodological perspectives. In that case, their written research objectives will be quite different.

One researcher looking at 'effectiveness in advertising' might look into brand recall as a way of understanding effectiveness. A second researcher alternatively might consider the execution of the creative content in the chosen medium as a way to assess effectiveness. In this context, the specific sub-questions (functionally, disciplinary and possibly methodologically) will differ, yet be subservient to the aspirational broad research question. All these research questions, when answered, will go some way toward meeting the overarching research question.

After writing sample objectives, the steps provided above should provide food for thought. What functional area is this topic related to and how might I consider getting the primary data?

CONCLUSION

This chapter is directed at the student researcher embarking on the research process for the first time. Broad attempts are often made to deal with the process of developing and refining a viable research topic; however, specific details on how to go about developing and refining viable topics requires further research. This chapter presents different considerations and guidelines that student researchers should consider when selecting and developing their research topic.

The second part of this chapter discussed, broadly, guidelines for developing the research question and sub-questions, considering how the development of the research topic is progressing, its functional focus and whether there is an identifiable group being approached for data collection. By thinking these considerations through, a student researcher can reduce significantly the time it takes to develop and refine a viable research topic. By reviewing these guidelines later in the research process to reflect on the direction and focus of the research, students can also ensure their research dissertation is coherent and purposeful.

REFERENCES

Creswell, J.W. (1994). *Research Design, Qualitative and Quantitative Approaches*. Thousand Oaks, CA: Sage.

DeWit, B. & Myer, R. (1998). *Strategy: Process, Content, Context*, 2nd ed. London: Thomson International Business Press.

Dunning, B. (2007). How to Identify a 'Good' Scientific Journal [Online]. Available: http://skeptoid.com/episodes/4050 (last accessed 14 March 2009).

Easterby-Smith, M., Thorpe, R. & Lowe, A. (1991). *Management Research: An Introduction*. London: Sage.

Gibbons, M., Limoges, C., Nowotny, H., Swatrzman, S., Scott, P. & Trow, M. (1994). *The New Production of Knowledge: The Dynamics of Science and Research in Contemporary Societies*. London: Sage.

Holbrook, M.B. (1987). 'What is Consumer Research?', *Journal of Consumer Research* 14(1): 128-32.

Horan, C. (2006). 'Toward Non-Prescriptive Issues: A Teaching Framework for Selecting Marketing Dissertation Topics', in Jorgensen, B. (ed), *Marketing Educators' Association 2006 Conference Proceedings*. San Francisco, CA: Marketing Educators Association.

L'Anson, R.A. & Smith, K.A. (2004). 'Undergraduate Research Projects and Dissertations: Issues of Topic Selection, Access and Data Collection Amongst Tourism Management Students', *Journal of Hospitality, Leisure, Sport & Tourism Education* 3(1): 19-32.

Nowotny, H., Scott, P. & Gibbons, M. (2001). *Re-thinking Science: Knowledge and the Public in an Age of Uncertainty*. Cambridge: Polity Press.

Montgomery, D.J. (1967). 'The Basis of Scientific Choice or On Criteria for Public Support of Science and Technology,' Internal Working Paper No 48, Social Sciences Group, Space Science Laboratory, University of California, Berkeley.

Porter, K.A. & Powell, W.W. (2006). 'Networks and Organizations', in Clegg, S.R., Hardy, C., Lawrence, T.B. & Nord, W.R. (eds), *The SAGE Handbook of Organization Studies*, 2nd ed, pp.776-99. London: Sage.

Saunders, M.N.K., Lewis, P. & Thornhill, A. (2007). *Research Methods for Business Students*, 3rd ed. London: Pitman Publishing.

Schiffman, L.G. (2008). *Consumer Behaviour: A European Outlook*. Harlow: Pearson Education.

Solomon, M.R. (2006). *Consumer Behaviour: A European Perspective*. Harlow: Financial Times / Prentice Hall.

CHAPTER 3
ETHNOGRAPHY: VISIONS & VERSIONS

Marian Crowley-Henry

INTRODUCTION

Ethnography, as with all research approaches, continues to evolve and develop, as new research agendas present themselves and as researchers – faced with limitations of time and access – come to terms with working with whatever tools may be available to them at any given point in time. This chapter presents an overview of traditional and contemporary literature concerning ethnography and participant observation in social research.

Ethnography is concerned with the study of a particular culture and relies, either partially or mainly, on participant observation (where the researcher immerses himself / herself in the customs and lives of the sample population under exploration and notes his / her observations in extensive fieldnotes). Given that all research approaches can be presented from different aspects, it should be noted from the outset that this chapter is written from the perspective of a hermeneutic researcher. Hermeneutics refers to an interpretive methodology, where the researcher commits to interpreting texts taking his / her previous experience and role in the research into consideration, as well as the data collected from observation, interviews, etc. Due to the integral part the hermeneutic researcher plays in his / her research undertaking, the chapter is purposely written in the first person.

Ethnography has evolved as a research approach since the classic ethnography period (as exemplified by ethnographers,[1] such as Margaret Mead's study about adolescents in Samoa (2001 [1928])) to the placement

---

[1]   Note that the terms 'ethnographer' and 'ethnographic researcher' are used interchangeably in this chapter.

of all qualitative research as ethnographic (Mason, 2002). The initial sections of this chapter map out some of the different major ethnographic approaches, as they have evolved over time. Next, the key elements in a research undertaking, which render a particular study 'ethnographic', are shared. The chapter includes concrete examples of an ethnographic study I undertook over a three-year period (2002-2005) in the South of France (Crowley-Henry, 2007; Crowley-Henry & Weir, 2007; 2009) to enable students to grasp the content and approach of a particular recent ethnographic research study in practice. Finally, recommendations for researchers interested in undertaking ethnographic research are shared. Given the variation in the underlying assumptions of the different ethnographic approaches considered in this chapter, it is stressed that ethnographic researchers should be clear as to where their ethnographic affiliations lie and lucidly include their ontological,[2] epistemological and methodological justification for embarking on their respective ethnographic journey.

Ethnography is a particular research *approach*, as opposed to being a particular method of research. Indeed, an ethnographic study can use several different methods, depending on the aim of the research and the methodological positioning of the researcher with regards to how the relevant research question(s) can be answered. Typical methods include interviews (structured or exploratory), observation (keeping diaries, writing fieldnotes), collecting narratives, undertaking document and / or historical research, participation in the context (and accumulating first-hand, contextual information about the culture or population sample in question). Given the variety of methods and data collection tools open to ethnographers, ethnography can be malleable to suit a particular research agenda, provided it is made clear how the researcher is using the approach in his / her particular research undertaking. The underlying elements of ethnography are the specificity of its study of a particular culture / sub-culture or population, and the use of observation in amassing field and contextual notes pertaining to (and used in the analysis and interpretation of) that culture / sub-culture or population.

Ethnography has its origins in anthropology, with the initial aim being to study exotic and unfamiliar cultures. Ethnographic research 'takes place in the natural setting of the everyday activities of the subjects under investigation' (Gill & Johnson, 1991: 124). 'Inquiry from the inside'

---

2   A description of the terms 'ontology', 'epistemology' and 'methodology', and their inter-linkages, is shared in the endnotes at the end of the chapter.

assumes 'that the researcher can best come to know the reality of an organization by *being there* – by becoming immersed in the stream of events and activities, by becoming part of the phenomena of study' (Evered & Louis, 1991: 11, italics in original). Fetterman (1998: 2) describes the ethnographer as:

> ... interested in understanding and describing a social and cultural scene from the emic, or insider's, perspective. The ethnographer is both storyteller and scientist; the closer the reader of an ethnography comes to understanding the native's point of view, the better the story and the better the science.

The ethnographic approach has evolved to 'encompass such a range of perspectives and activities that the idea of adhering to *an* ethnographical position, as though there were only one, is faintly ridiculous' (Mason, 2002: 55; italics in original). Ethnography, in practice, has evolved from the classic approach, where it was assumed the researcher could retain objectivity when exploring a new culture, to reflexive ethnography, where the role and background of the researcher is included as an integral element of the ethnographic undertaking. The following paragraphs give an overview of differing approaches in ethnography.

ETHNOGRAPHIC APPROACHES

Cultural & Social Anthropology

Ethnography has evolved from the field of anthropology (Junker, 1960). Sanjek (2000) distinguishes between cultural and social anthropology as a potential approach in studying people. He describes the approach and aim of *cultural* anthropology as being to focus on the meaning contained in people's heads, whereas *social* anthropology is characterised by its focus on the meanings constructed from social arrangements and speech in action (Sanjek, 2000: 280; see also Junker, 1960). Participant observation and 'naturally occurring speech in action' (Sanjek, 2000: 281) would fall more under the social anthropology heading than would interviews and instruments seeking to find meaning in people's heads, which would be placed under the cultural anthropology direction of study.

For instance, the ethnographic research I conducted between 2002 and 2005 would fall under cultural anthropology, as the objective of that particular piece of research was interpretive. That is, the focus of that particular study was to find meaning in the minds of the sample *vis-à-vis* their identity and career construction as 'foreigners' or non-nationals living permanently in the South of France. This was done through in-depth, qualitative, exploratory interviews, supplemented by contemporaneous contextual information gathered by maintaining fieldnotes, while I (the author / researcher), myself, was a member of that community (prior to, during and immediately following the interview process). The interviews and contextual notes were then interpreted by me (hermeneutically), in light of the more complete picture (from the interviewees' narratives and interview data, from the contextual fieldnotes, from my own experiences as a member of the sub-population under investigation), in order to present as comprehensive a text as possible pertaining to the sample in question.

Classic Ethnography

Mead (2001[1928]) and Clifford (1988) are exemplars of the 'classic realist ethnographic text' (Denzin, 1997: xiii). In classic ethnography, the researcher enters a completely foreign culture, far removed from his / her own; remains there for some time, observing the natives[3] and taking copious field-notes; then returns to the home country culture where he / she shares the knowledge and observations made during the period of time spent in the exotic location with readers from the same home culture where he / she originates (Van Maanen, 1988). This approach assumes an objectivity, whereby the ethnographer is able to put aside any

---

3   There is a continuum between participation and observation, depending on the extent of the researcher's involvement in the study. In observation, the researcher remains aloof, and notes traits and characteristics peculiar to a particular sub-culture. In participant observation, the researcher actively engages in the rituals of the culture under investigation. He / she lives in the particular culture for an extended period of time; he / she 'goes native'. The primary advantage of participant observation is in being able to collect a richness and depth of data as regards being part of the culture (as an insider) that would not be possible simply from observation as an outsider. The primary disadvantage is that the culture under investigation may resent the intrusion into their lives. Furthermore, depending on the methodological tendencies of the researcher, participant observation may be seen negatively as clouding objectivity, rendering a more subjective account of the experience in 'going native'. Alternatively, hermeneutic researchers would argue that only in participating and experiencing a culture first-hand is a researcher adequately skilled in meeting the task of reporting about a culture.

preconceived perceptions or unconscious prejudices, in order to relate the facts concerning the new culture in an unbiased way. The classic ethnographer remains an outsider in the study.

Sanjek's (2000) fieldwork dissertation, studying ethnic relations among residents of a city block in Accra, the capital of Ghana, West Africa, is a more contemporary example of ethnography engaged in describing an exotic culture. In his study, Sanjek (2000: 281) conducted detailed interviews with 40 informants, but also 'grounded this network study in neighborhood residence over a year and a half, participant observation in the locations people traveled to throughout the city, and the everyday conversations that found their way into my fieldnotes'.

Urban Ethnography

Notably, from the 1960s, 'urban ethnography' replaced classic ethnography as the trend in ethnographic research, with the Chicago School widely accredited for this evolution. Where classic ethnography was engaged in anthropological fieldwork, researching primitive, exotic, foreign cultures, urban ethnography was concerned with sociological fieldwork, studying sub-populations within a single country's national culture.

The Chicago School encouraged '[s]tudents ... to bring anthropology home by learning of the vigorous, dense, heterogeneous cultures located just beyond the university gates' (Van Maanen, 1988: 18). Whyte's (1993[1943]) *Street Corner Society* is exemplary of urban ethnography. In his study from 1937 to 1940, Whyte lived in a Boston inner city Italian slum, 'Cornerville', and mixed with young urban gang members, being a participant observer and taking fieldnotes of his observations. In urban ethnographic texts, 'deviant subculture' co-existing in the same country, state, or even city, is the unit of research.

The urban ethnographer engages with the sub-culture in much the same way as classic ethnographers. He / she conducts interviews, observes and engages in sub-cultural activities (such as Whyte getting involved in the bowling prize contest in the 'Cornerville' slum) and keeps fieldnotes. However, urban ethnographers consider their subjective involvement as an aid in understanding the objective elements and recordings of the study (objective observations and fieldnotes concerning elements, such as key players, key relationships and key characteristics). Whyte (1993: Appendix A: 279) explains that when:

... the researcher is living for an extended period in the community he is studying, his personal life is inextricably mixed with his research. A real explanation, then, of how the research was done necessarily involves a rather personal account of how the researcher lived during the period of study.

While relationships may build up with members of the sample under scrutiny during the course of the study, the researcher remains an 'outsider', and on leaving the study breaks the ties / links to the sample, reporting about her / his activities, rituals and ways of life in an objective manner.

My own ethnographic study can be categorised as urban ethnography, since it considered a sub-culture: the non-French, Western / First World foreign residents who had decided to live in the South of France on a potentially permanent basis and to follow their careers as French residents. For my study, I focused on a geographical case study, Sophia Antipolis, in the South of France, where I myself was a member of the community I was exploring (an active participant). All my observations and interviews took place in this location. Moving from classic to urban ethnography, the role of the researcher in the study becomes more integral. The next section considers the movement toward an even more subjective / reflexive role of the ethnographer in ethnography.

Critical & Reflexive Ethnography

In traditional classic ethnographic texts, it is assumed and accepted that the researcher is able to provide an unbiased 'indepth, holistic analysis of structure and processes of culture' (McQueen & Knussen, 2002: 22). Malinowski (1961[1922]) describes the ethnographer's job as to '[f]ind out the typical ways of thinking and feeling, corresponding to the institutions and culture of a given community and [to] formulate the results in the most convincing way' (1961[1922]: 3; also quoted in Van Maanen, 1995: 6; Denzin, 1997: xv-xvi). This thinking shows the realist nature of classic ethnography, where the background, experience and motivations of the ethnographer are ignored as irrelevant, or are considered not to influence or colour the resulting ethnographic reports and texts.

However, the supposed objectivity that is synonymous with classic ethnographic texts has come under fire. Denzin (1997: xiii) propounds that 'it is no longer possible to take for granted what is meant by ethnography. The classic realist ethnographic text is now under attack'. Classic ethnography's focus on the scientistic[4] approach, with the researcher's supposed impartiality or objectivity, has met with critique from social science researchers, who argue that the social world consists of multiple realities, rather than one single objective one. Thus, it is posited that a major limitation of traditional ethnography approaches was the failure to include detailed information regarding the researcher / ethnographer in question and his / her journey in understanding through the course of the study and participant observation. The extent any research can be impartial has been questioned, for the researcher makes personal decisions and choices on sampling, method of data collection and analysis, and core theories to highlight in any given research undertaking.

Ethnography is a study of culture and of people's lived experiences in that respective culture. The ethnographer normally comes from a culture other than that which he / she is researching. It is the ethnographer's oft unconscious, but, nevertheless, pre-conceived beliefs, based on his / her past experiences, that shape the direction of the research. Thus, the possibility of any ethnographer being able to give one 'true', objective picture of an exotic or under-examined sub-culture's lived reality is hotly contested among present day academics (Denzin, 1997; Sanjek, 2000).

Contemporary discussions on ethnography consider the researcher's role as an integral part of the research process and should be contemplated upon in depth as part of the research study. As Barth (1975: 226; quoted in Sanjek, 2000: 282) declares: 'My strong suspicion is that the bodies of native explanation that we find in anthropological literature are often created as an artefact of the anthropologist's activity'. Thus, in keeping with Whyte's (1993: 249) earlier quote, it is imperative that the researcher's role and background are included, in order to present a more complete picture of the research methodology and motivations of the study. The moving perspectives that the ethnographer encounters on his / her journey during the ethnographic study should be recorded and included as integral

---

4   To differentiate between scientistic and scientific: A scientistic approach
     prioritises method over discovery. The assumption is that only science can
     render absolute truth; that the only way to investigate the world is through the
     established methods and procedures of science (such as Mathematics or
     Physics), thereby ignoring more philosophically qualitative approaches. The
     scientific method, on the other hand, is but one method that can be used in
     (social) research. It does not claim to be the only true, valid method. Scientific
     methods are, however, based on rigor and relative detachment from the object
     under investigation.

components (along with fieldnotes and interview transcripts) in analysing and interpreting the ethnographic texts. The researcher's contemplations of his / her role and part in the study is considered and reflected upon, highlighting the reflexivity of the approach. This reflexive component of contemporary ethnography can be classified under critical or reflexive ethnography. In comparison with classic ethnography, in critical ethnography the role of the researcher in the process of inquiry and the other structural and contextual factors (such as the political and economic situation, temporal relativity, emphasising the specific period of time in which the study is conducted) are considered just as relevant as the actual ethnographic fieldwork and observation of the sample / culture (Hammersley & Atkinson, 1995; Denzin, 1997; Sanjek, 2000). The inclusion of reflexive reporting in ethnographic texts can allow a more transparent view of the culture under investigation to emerge because the role of the researcher as participant is addressed as an integral component of the study, and is, thereby, problematised and not ignored.

In reflexive ethnography, the ontological and epistemological[5] position of the ethnographer is integral to the research. It is necessary, therefore, to gain a deeper insight about the writer / ethnographer / researcher in order to be able to view and understand a more comprehensive picture of the ethnographic texts / study. The role of the researcher in qualitative research has been stressed by Lincoln & Denzin (1994). The self-contemplative and reflexive nature of qualitative research is both espoused and stressed in interpretive ethnography. This imbedded reflexivity in ethnographic research is aptly summarised by Emerson *et al.* (1995: 3):

> No field researcher can be a completely neutral, detached observer, outside and independent of the observed phenomena (Pollner & Emerson, 1988). Rather, as the ethnographer engages in the lives and concerns of those studied, his perspective 'is intertwined with the phenomenon which does not have objective characteristics independent of the observer's perspective and method' (Mishler 1979: 10). The ethnographer cannot take in everything; rather, he will, in conjunction with those in the setting, develop certain perspectives by engaging in some activities and relationships rather than others. ... the task of the ethnographer is not to determine the 'truth' but to reveal the multiple truths apparent in others' lives.

---

[5]   Refer to the endnotes at the end of the chapter for a glossary explaining terms such as 'ontology' and 'epistemology'.

Critical and reflexive ethnography suitably describe my ethnographic study. Given that I was a member of the population under investigation (that is, I was a non-national, from a Western / First World country, residing in the South of France on a potentially permanent basis and maintaining a professional career), my identification with the sample could not go unmentioned. While critics would argue such involvement detracts from the objectivity of a study, I counter-argue that it was my insider status that enabled my access to the respondents and their willingness to open up and share intimate life events with me. For instance, members of my sample recounted specific, difficult life circumstances, such as redundancies, miscarriages, deaths in the family, which affected their acculturation to France and their identity reconstruction as 'locally-residing foreigners'. My study includes a full chapter detailing my role in the research, outlining my position from the onset, during and after the interviewing and participant observation process, when I was more removed from the culture. I would contest that such depth of reflexive writing serves to provide a full, rich account of the sub-culture, from my perspective and the interviewees' perspectives, as well as from contemporaneous contextual fieldnotes pertinent to the time. For instance, during part of my fieldwork, there were national elections in France, where the results for the area in question showed a strong far-right-wing (nationalist) affinity to Jean-Marie Le Pen. The anti-foreigner feeling that my sample perceived from the results was tangible in their narratives. They told me how 'funny' they felt that their French neighbours or colleagues could be so anti-foreigner with regards to African or non-Western immigrants (many stemming from previous French colonies), while claiming to be in favour of Western immigrants, such as my sample. This classification of immigrants, based on their countries of origin, was discriminatory and left my sample ill-at-ease. Nonetheless, they were committed to remaining foreign residents, due to the lifestyle offered in the area (weather, environment (Alps for skiing, Mediterranean for beaches), French social policies concerning 35-hour week, childcare, etc.) and the fact that they had not directly experienced adverse discrimination.

Conclusions to Ethnographic Approaches

The ethnographic positions presented in the preceding paragraphs explain and promote the rise in critical ethnographic approaches in qualitative research. Critical ethnography is case- and researcher- specific. However, discussion persists on how different approaches to ethnography can forward social research, taking those elements from the varying ethnographic approaches in order to best suit the particular research sample and / or agenda. This flexibility is encouraging, but also confusing for students considering ethnography as a potential research approach; it necessitates a deep, considered reflexivity on behalf of the researcher / ethnographer in order to justify her / his own individual ethnographic approach and position.

Students do not need to undertake a longitudinal study if they want to adopt an ethnographic approach. An ethnographic approach can consist of shorter periods of participant observation in a particular sub-cultural context. For instance, if exploring the motivations of employees in a particular firm, the student (if he / she has been granted access to that firm) could visit that firm on a number of occasions, going to meetings and / or lunch with employees in order to build up observations concerning what it is like to be an employee in that firm. The important aspect is that the researcher engages with the sample under investigation and notes his / her observations as meetings with the sample progress. The next section gives some practical guidelines on what ethnographic research involves.

POSITIONING RESEARCH AS ETHNOGRAPHIC

This section describes the features common across ethnographic approaches. It is noteworthy that, in contemporary qualitative research, approaches may be widely described as ethnographic (Mason, 2002). However, I argue that, in order to position a research undertaking as ethnographic, the researcher needs to understand the alternative ethnographic approaches and the implications of following a particular direction over another.

Hammersley (1992) highlights the general features of the ethnographic research approach as follows:

♦ People's behaviour is studied in their normal environment, not under experimental conditions.

♦ Data is collected from different sources, with observation and relatively informal conversations the primary ones.

♦ The focus is generally a single setting or group.

♦ The analysis involves interpretation of meaning.

These features are echoed by Denzin & Lincoln (1998a: xvi), who note that ethnographic 'methods are characterized by the collection of relatively unstructured empirical materials, a small number of cases, and a writing and style of analysis that are primarily interpretive, involving descriptions of phenomena'. Ethnography is primarily about **describing** cultures. ·

In my own ethnographic study, I went further than simply describing the sample under investigation which I term 'bounded transnationals' (Crowley-Henry, 2008), and comparing them to other international assignee categories. I also used and interpreted the data collected to inductively build-up models and frameworks concerning the identification (evolving identity construction as members of a non-national community) of the sample. I went into the field wanting to research the particular group of self-initiated international assignees that remains in the host country environment for a potentially permanent duration (that is, the bounded transnational community). I did not have any pre-defined theories or concepts to test or prove on going into the field. I simply wanted to collect the experiences and stories from the interviewees regarding their lives in the area, and how they feel their lives (and careers) had progressed since they moved to the area. It was only after extensive examination of the narratives and uncovering patterns in the interviews that I began to pull together elements that built up, from my research, a framework of the bounded transnational's career influences. Then, when looking more at career literature and international human resource management literature, I was able to categorise some of the concepts that emerged from my findings with labels that other researchers had coined to explain similar phenomena. The inductive nature of my study, which was admittedly more longitudinal than many, specifically undergraduate, research dissertations are practically able to be, is specific to my particular research journey.

The aim of the ethnographer is paramount in determining the direction the ethnographic study is going to take – purely descriptive or also seeking to offer explanation for why a particular culture is how it is. It is important, and may be a requirement, for some dissertation students that they at least attempt to explain and / or develop the research question or phenomenon under exploration during the analysis and interpretation of the findings stage of their research.

In describing ethnography, Hammersley & Atkinson (1995: 1-2, emphasis added):

> ... see the term as referring primarily to a particular method or set of methods. In its most characteristic form it involves the ethnographer participating, overtly or covertly, in people's daily lives for an extended period of time, watching what happens, listening to what is said, asking questions – in fact, collecting whatever data are available to throw light on the issues that are the focus of the research. Equally though, ... there is a sense in which all social researchers are participant observers and, as a result, the boundaries around ethnography are necessarily unclear.

It is this blurring of boundaries between ethnography and qualitative research that presents confusion and requires researcher contemplation when classifying a particular piece of research as ethnographic. The following paragraphs consider key features apparent in ethnographic approaches in more detail.

Context

The relevance of context is paramount across ethnographic research positions (Denzin, 1997; Sanjek, 2000). Denzin (1997: xiii, emphasis added) notes the importance of the actual context from undertaking the fieldwork to the final ethnographic text produced:

> Ethnographic texts are the primary texts given for the interpretive, ethnographic project. These texts are always dialogical – the site at which the voices of the other, alongside the voices of the author, come alive and interact with one another. Thus, the voices that are seen and heard (if only imaginatively) in the text are themselves textural, performative accomplishments. *These accomplishments have a prior life in the context of where they were produced.* Texts... are easily reproduced; contexts are not.

Including the social context provides a more rounded description of the culture under scrutiny. Omitting this information reduces the relevance of the findings, as they must be considered in light of the temporal context in which they occurred.

In my ethnographic study, I collated contemporaneous contextual fieldnotes (concerning policies, economic and political circumstances at the point of time I was conducting the fieldwork). I included those fieldnotes in presenting a description of the sample in question, concerning their motivations to remain resident in the South of France, as well as their hesitation in moving to another location or returning to their home countries. The next paragraph is an example of a fieldnote I made during the study:

> The legal working hours in France were 35 hours a week for all companies. Any overtime in excess of these 35 hours must be compensated by time off in lieu (so called RTT days). In addition employees are entitled to a minimum 25 days annual leave. With the RTT days on top of annual vacation, total annual leave of over 50 days is not uncommon. This is a major incentive for the sample in their desire to remain in France, where they can avail of such policies.

By including fieldnotes, such as the above, the reader is made aware of the temporal and social context during which the study was conducted, which, for my specific research, impacts upon the desire of the sample to remain resident in the South of France. Were such fieldnotes not included, a comprehensive picture of the sample's motivations to remain in France would not have emerged.

A further fieldnote entry concerns the Sophia Professional Women's Network (SPWN):

> The Sophia Professional Women's Network is a branch of the International Professional Women's Network, a network promoting women professionals. [Catherine[6]] co-founded the group in Sophia Antipolis with [Mary]. She uses her own time to organise the events, and is not paid for the post. She attends international conferences on women's issues, again at her own expense. It is her hobby as such, as well as a means of integrating with other non-French professional women in the area.

The following paragraphs present some of my observational fieldnote entries. These fieldnotes are specific observations noted in parallel with the interview process, which, together with the narratives, enabled me to interpret the transcripts from different perspectives.

> Both [Shaun] and [Gordon] speak about how they feel like foreigners in the general day-to-day, going about your business, part of life – whether it be comments about their French accent or level, or just nuances regarding their foreign status – they perceive themselves as different and as being seen in some ways negatively by members of the French public.

> Similar to [Sarah], [Alice] did not want to get into the International Women's group. She did not feel comfortable there – drinking coffee, etc. She was a professional woman who had put her career on hold for

---

[6]　Catherine and Mary are pseudonyms for two members in my research sample. Note that all interviewee names used for example purposes are pseudonyms.

child-rearing and until she found a suitable position. She did not fit the profile of women in that particular group / club.

Tendency among all interviewees who had previously worked in London, that they described and did not appreciate the commuter-centric environment, where the objective, overtly-conspicuous career was the number 1 priority, with people judged by others according to the objective career (salary and status) that they have.

[Tracy] had au pairs, [Kate] has a local child-minder / cleaner – someone to trust with the children, to fill in the 'parental space', while they concentrate on their careers and giving all to their careers. The support systems that they organised themselves enabled their objective career focus.

Some observation notes from my meeting with [Tracy]:

She used to work for [Clare] and there were some issues when she wanted to be promoted to senior manager to run the European Business Centre in the organisation. But they appear to be on friendly terms again now. She [Tracy] had tears in her eyes on the occasions I brought up about her not feeling happy in her job or not feeling valued. I got a sense of isolation from her. Perhaps on recounting her personal story, from becoming a young widow with young children, to the lack of support from her in-laws, to moving from the USA to France with her children, it hit a nerve with regards to how she had to do it alone. She is very career-driven. I get the feeling that she puts her career first, children first, and maybe herself always down the line... She is happy with her life – lovely, happy children, great job / career, nice house, nice friends in a nice environment ... Just I feel that, maybe on deeper level, there is still some sadness. As I expect there always will be, having lost her husband so young and really having coped alone with the children, without close family support nearby.

As can be seen from the above exemplars, some observations can be short one-liners regarding commonalities perceived from different interviews. Others then, as the final extract, can be much longer and work together with the particular interviewee's narrative in building up a more accurate description of someone's experiences and choices, albeit as perceived and interpreted by the researcher.

Using the information gathered through participant observation and fieldnotes (such as exemplified above) when analysing and interpreting the sample's identification enabled me to develop a more comprehensive systems framework, which included a number of elements with regards to identity construction. Undertaking participant observation is only useful if the information garnered during the process is included in analysing the data and in interpreting the information in order to present the findings.

Fieldwork / Participant Observation

Fieldwork refers:

> ... to observation of people *in situ*; finding them where they are, staying with them in some role which, while acceptable to them, will allow both intimate observation of certain parts of their behavior, and reporting it in ways useful to social science but not harmful to those observed. (Hughes, 1960: iii).

Fieldwork is often interchanged with participant observation. Participant observation has been described as when the 'ethnographer participates in the daily routines of this setting, develops ongoing relations with the people in it, and observes all the while what is going on' (Emerson *et al.*, 1995: 1). McQueen & Knussen (2002: 23) refer to it as 'observation of a group or society of which the observer has become a part'. Participant observation is a key element of ethnographic research (Atkinson & Hammersley, 1998). With participant observation, the researcher is committed 'to intimate, repeated, and prolonged involvement in the life and community of the respondent' (McCracken, 1988: 7). The researcher is a participant in, and accepted as part of, the culture that is under observation (Trochim, 2000). Hughes (1960: ix) compares the ethnologist and the sociologist, where the 'ethnologist was always an exotic to the people he studied' and the 'sociologist observed and reported upon a segment of his own world'. The sociologist was 'reporting observations made, not as a complete stranger, but in some measure as a member of an in-group' (Hughes, 1960: ix). With participant observation:

> ... [t]he ethnographer discovers the multiple 'truths' that operate in the social world – the stories people tell one another about the things that matter to them ... These stories move people to action, and they rest on a distinction between fact and truth. Truth and facts are socially constructed, and people build stories around the meanings of truth. (Denzin, 1997: xv).

In practice, there are wide variations between the degree of participation and fieldwork with which contemporary ethnographers engage in a particular research undertaking. Turnbull (1999) calls her study of middle managers' responses to a change programme in a large engineering company ethnographic. She visited the organisation in question on a number of occasions, conducting interviews and observing meetings, but her involvement with the participants was never that of an insider. Nonetheless, her study fits the four criteria given by Hammersley (1992, noted above) in determining a research study as ethnographic. Turnbull's (1992) approach is one that students conducting even minor dissertations can adopt. On the other hand, I was an insider during the course of my data collection; I was a member of the international community I was investigating. As such, participant observation was an integral component of my study. It was, perhaps, leaving the area and no longer being a member of the international community that enabled my further reflection on the interviews that had been conducted and the fieldnotes that had been gathered, and that further served in my reflexivity concerning the study. Previous perceptions I had had when a member of the community could then be seen more from the standpoint of a more neutral observer. It is this depth and reflexivity that has added much value to my particular ethnographic study, serving to un-bias it as much as possible, in offering different perspectives to the reader of my ethnographic texts.

The next section considers immersion in ethnography in more detail. In general, anthropological studies (ethnography) tend to have a longer duration in the field (up to several years) than their sociological counterparts, which may last less than a couple of weeks. The variation in fieldwork and immersion (see next section) renders a detailed description of the study's duration as vital information for the readers of ethnographic texts, in order that those readers fully understand the degree of immersion and fieldwork that was involved.

Immersion

The degree of immersion in the study is a further element of fieldwork / participant observation. Goffman (1989: 125, as quoted in Emerson *et al.*, 1995: 2) describes ethnography as:

> ... subjecting yourself, your own body and your personality, and your own social situation to the set of contingencies that play upon a set of individuals, so that you can physically and ecologically penetrate their circle of response to their social situation, or their work situation, or their ethnic situation.

Such 'immersion' allows the ethnographer to experience, first-hand, the everyday tasks and routines of the sample or culture in question. In reality, however, the extent to which an ethnographic researcher can immerse himself / herself in the research setting and with the research sample varies (see section 1.3 (ii)). Access into the respective 'social', 'work' or 'ethnic' situation may be restricted, limiting the researcher's immersion in the context. However, the research may still present important findings and be termed ethnographic due to the depth of information uncovered in the process.

Insider – Outsider

In ethnography:

> ... [e]ven with intensive resocialization, the ethnographer never becomes a member in the same sense that those 'naturally' in the setting are members. The fieldworker plans on leaving the setting after a relatively brief stay, and his experience of local life is colored by this transience. ... In these ways, research and writing commitments qualify ethnographic immersion, making the fieldworker at least something of an outsider and, at an extreme, a cultural alien. (Emerson *et al.*, 1995: 4).

There is a fine line between the ethnographer as insider and as outsider. As an outsider, it would suggest that the ethnographer would not be privy to the same level of understanding as the true insider. However, in line with classic ethnography, the suggestion persists from some authors that the ethnographer maintains a different position to the sample of the population under examination. I argue that, in reflexive ethnography, the insider position of the ethnographer is paramount in finding out as much as possible about the sample in question. However, this is only valuable research as long as the researcher details in full his / her background, thoughts and role in the process.

MY ETHNOGRAPHIC STUDY: ACADEMIC DISCUSSION ON AN EMPIRICAL UNDERTAKING

The discussion, as presented in the preceding paragraphs, on the evolving nature of ethnographic approaches is ongoing. This chapter, so far, has shown how the approach has developed from cultural anthropology to social research, where the researcher has unquestionably become a vital piece of the jigsaw in building up a representative picture of a particular culture or sub-culture. It has also presented the common elements in ethnographic research. This section provides more information on the ethnographic study I conducted, in order to provide concrete examples of what can be found out by using an ethnographic approach.

My research took place in France. In line with urban ethnography, the population sub-sample under investigation was a distinct grouping of international assignees, who relocated to the country for a potentially permanent duration. The research in question was a qualitative undertaking, an attempt to learn about the identity and career construction of a sample of foreign assignees, something that has not been studied in the literature. They have moved to a 'foreign' country for different reasons, but have chosen to remain in that host country for lifestyle, rather than career or economic, reasons. They are not economic migrants, would not term themselves 'emigrants', nor are they expatriates in the widely-accepted description of expatriates (as individuals sent *by their organisation* on an international assignment of a *temporary* duration). In the study in question, they were termed 'bounded transnationals' (Crowley-Henry, 2008).

The empirical research took place over a three-year period. I lived in that international community prior to (since September 2000), during (mid-2002 to early 2005) and immediately after (to mid-2005) the collection of qualitative data, namely through conducting exploratory, semi-structured interviews with individuals within that sample. To that extent, I was already an 'insider' of the international community before conducting the interviews and actively taking fieldnotes. For the period of time from 2000 to mid-2002, I was a participant observer, but it was only on commencement of the research project that formal research observations and fieldnotes were made. While my closeness to the community could be perceived as a bias or limitation to the research, the reflexivity of the study, including the observations on my removal from the community, present an in-depth account of life as a bounded transnational. Being part of the community enabled access to the sample and allowed me to amass a wealth of contextual information concerning the political, social and cultural conditions prevalent at the particular point in time the research took place. This contextual information positions the research in a particular context, which is impossible to replicate exactly. Fetterman (1998: 2) praises the process of contextualisation as a means of reducing researcher bias.

In my research study, I adhered to Emerson *et al.*'s (1995) description of ethnography as 'immersion' in the research subject. I was an active member of the international community in question. However, the depth of involvement in the everyday lives of the members of the sample I interviewed was neither an aim of the research nor a practical undertaking. Thus, there are limits to the degree of 'immersion' in the study. The research undertaking's methods of data collection were in-depth interviews, insider participant observation and contextual data. While I joined the community in question in the year 2000, the formal study commenced in 2002 and lasted for three years (2005), when I left the area. On interviewing respondents (commencement in July 2002), I supplemented their transcripts with any other contextual or observational data pertinent to the time of the interview. In addition, I kept a private journal, documenting my own perceptions as the study progressed. I used the interview transcripts as the core data, while the contextual fieldnotes were used in order to support argument development and model building, given the specificity of the case. Being an insider was an advantage, not a limitation of the study. It facilitated placing the narrative texts in a particular social and temporal context, along with being able to analyse and interpret the material from particular perspectives.

For instance, my discussions with females in the sample showed how perceptions varied regarding gender discrimination in their respective organisations. One particular female respondent felt that the glass ceiling was most prevalent in French culture, despite working for a multinational organisation. She expressed her anguish at not having been promoted in recent years, despite receiving exceedingly good performance reviews. However, another woman (working for the same organisation) reported that she was promoted immediately on returning to work after maternity leave (several years previously). Knowing the employment context at the time (recessionary), I was able to interpret both narratives (both true) accordingly. I wrote up the female's perception of gender discrimination, but was able to include background to this (such as: her manager was French (or not); the nationality / culture of the female in question; the labour climate at the time), thus providing as holistic a picture of the situation as possible to allow the reader to make up his / her own mind regarding the issue.

The next paragraph gives an extract from an interview transcript collected during my study, whereby another female respondent shares her experiences with gender discrimination in a professional capacity in France:

Marian: Have you had any experience in France about trying to get in anywhere without having a Grande École[7] background, or have you come up against that at all?

Respondent A: No, No. I've come up against other people telling me that it's existent.

Marian: But you haven't seen it yourself?

Respondent A: No. I haven't seen it. It doesn't exist in ... It didn't exist in, you know, the two organisations I know most closely here are [Organisation 1[8]] and [Organisation 2], and it doesn't exist in either of those. It may a little bit in the Paris office, probably does, but internationally not, where if you come from somewhere else you're forgiven for not having it [a Grande École education]. But I have heard ... I know of a couple of people who left and I'll cite the name [Organisation 3] for example, because they came to the point when they realised that not having Grande École, the next level they just would not get to and they left and joined other organisations because of that. So, it's anecdotal, but I haven't personally ever experienced it. But I think that's partly the point of it [being] cultural and a question of [me] not willing to join a French organisation.

The transcript shared above shows how contextually relevant the issue of potential gender discrimination in the workplace is. While Respondent A has never personally experienced discrimination, she has heard about it from others and notes that some organisations may be less tolerant of it than others. She, interestingly, names the same firm as the respondent who had claimed she was suffering from gender discrimination in her firm. Using the information from the interview transcript (above) and from other interviews, together with participant observation and fieldnotes on the importance and relevance of social status in France (such as the Grande École education), enabled me to build up and develop areas, such as identity and discrimination, into more complex systems than just a personal response from one respondent. Being part of the community facilitated access, understanding and interpretation of the interviews.

Being an insider also meant depth of self-analysis and reflexivity were prerequisite components of the final research piece. By virtue of membership status, I was a participant observer. However, for the purpose

---

[7]   In France, many influential political and business people have come through the traditional educational system of Grandes Écoles, which are private third level institutions ranked according to their profile and prestige.

[8]   The names of the organisations she mentioned have been removed for anonymity and confidentiality reasons.

of the data collection for the research undertaking, I followed Whyte's (1993: 305) example, in that 'I tried to avoid influencing the group, because I wanted to study the situation as unaffected by my presence as possible'. This stance toward interviewing is common in qualitative research undertakings, where the researcher attempts to reduce the degree of interviewer bias as much as possible. Thus, the interviews collected were recorded and transcribed in full, without prejudice. In interpretation, the different perspectives (mine, interviewees', taking the contextual circumstances into account) work together in triangulating the findings so that a more comprehensive account is presented.

Fetterman (1998: 9) argues that '[i]n many applied settings, long-term continuous fieldwork is neither possible nor desirable'. He compares an ethnographic study he undertook himself, where:

> ... I visited sites for two-week periods every few months during a three-year study. This approach allowed me to conduct intensive fieldwork, pull back and make sense of what I had observed and recorded, and then return to the field to test my hypotheses. The effort was successful because I was able to see patterns of behavior over time. In many applied contexts, limited resources compel the researcher to apply ethnographic techniques in a contract deadline time-frame rather than to conduct a full-blown ethnography.

His study is similar to many management research undertakings, where researchers can access a company for intensive, albeit brief, periods of time, using the breaks between the fieldwork to consider, reflexively, what was learnt on each occasion. Such breaks allow the researcher the opportunity to reflect upon the study's progress and enable him / her to test consistency and validity of the outcomes and of her perspective in each subsequent period in the field. This emphasises that individual specificity of the case under exploration is essential in determining what methods and approaches best suit that particular case or research study. For student mini dissertations, a scaled-down ethnographic study could be most appropriate, whereby the student visits a particular site or community for short periods of time, takes fieldnotes of his / her observations while at that site or community and supplements them with interview and other contextual information in analysing and interpreting how that particular group works.

Given the perspectives outlined in this chapter, my study can be classified as a cultural anthropological study. It would fit into the sociological school of ethnography – urban ethnography (studying a sub-group within a national cultural setting), and reflexive ethnography (where the role of the researcher in the interpretation of the material collected is paramount). While I provide a detailed personal account concerning my involvement in the study as an integral component of the research methodology, the research is not auto-ethnographic (Reed-Danahay, 1997; Russell, 1999; Ellis & Bochner, 2000), as my own experiences are not related in the findings or analysis. Rather, the insider contextual knowledge serves to add context to the interview data, with an acknowledgement that my own experiences and background shaped the direction of the study.

To conclude this section, I would like to express why one should engage in ethnographic research: what can ethnography allow you to find out, as a researcher? As mentioned earlier in this chapter, the research approach undertaken depends on what the researcher wants to find out. From my own personal experience, taking an ethnographic approach facilitated my development of the bounded transnational population as a sub-category of international assignees that had not received academic attention in the past. In using the interview transcripts, fieldnotes and observations, I was able to build up a comprehensive picture of what / who is a bounded transnational, of the bounded transnational sub-culture. This is in line with the aim of classic through urban ethnography.

One of my primary findings was a categorisation of international assignees, including the bounded transnational, which academics and researchers can use to differentiate the previously heterogeneous label of 'international assignee'. A further finding is an empirically-developed career framework of the bounded transnational sample, which includes objective and subjective career elements, as well as contingency influences (temporal, structural, economical, familial, and serendipitous). From that framework, I was able to develop the protean career concept (Crowley-Henry, 2007; Crowley-Henry & Weir, 2007, 2009) to encompass identification (Bauman, 2001) and career construction influences in a globalisation context. The reflexive and holistic nature of ethnographic research enabled that theory development.

Discussing the Extremes of Ethnographic Research

With ethnographic studies embracing from an objective, classic to an interpretivist, reflexive approach, it would seem that adopting a standard ethnographic research position is difficult. In essence, the individuality of the ethnographic texts is what makes ethnography so interesting. In reading about other cultural groupings, one is compelled to consider the findings presented in the texts, the position of the researcher / ethnographer, and to reflect upon the study from one's own perspective. Whyte (1993: 289) stresses the uniqueness of the ethnographic approach:

> I am not suggesting that my approach to Street Corner Society should be followed by other researchers. To some extent my approach must be unique to myself, to the particular situation, and to the state of knowledge existing when I began research.

All ethnographic research uses participant observation (and fieldnotes) as a means of data collection. This can be supplemented with interview data and through document sources in order to build up a detailed picture of a particular culture or sub-culture in society (Atkinson *et al.*, 2001; Mason, 2002). This illustrates the multi-method possibilities that ethnography offers.

LIMITATIONS OF ETHNOGRAPHY

Critics of ethnography argue that, because it usually involves a relatively small sample size, the findings cannot be generalised to the wider population (Gill & Johnson, 1991). In response to such critics, this limitation is shared by all qualitative research, with qualitative researchers reasoning that the depth and richness of qualitative findings outweigh the constraints of trying to generalise across time and context, which, in any case, qualitative researchers would argue is not reliable, given the proposition that all research (quantitative or qualitative) is context-, researcher-, and temporally-specific.

Sanjek (2000) considers the challenges that face modern ethnographers working in urban sites, notably dealing with vast numbers of people, vast sites of participant observation. He recommends taking a holistic approach when exploring a particular sub-culture and including contextual and temporal details (political, economical, and historical), which make the particular piece of ethnographic research specific. However, Sanjek (2000) warns that, if ethnographers try to include too much information, (that is, do participant observation, get historical / political / social / cultural knowledge and comparative theories), it may be to the detriment of participant observation: 'This could lead to ethnographies that were more frame than picture – a result that might be characterized as "thin description", or "history without people"' (Sanjek, 2000: 282). A compromise is required in order to ensure adequate description and information frame the picture of the actual people being investigated.

Bias is a limitation of all research. Emerson *et al.* (1995: 3) do not believe that 'consequential presence' is a negative bias, but, rather, the 'very source of that learning and observation'. A further response to the bias limitation is reflexive ethnography, whereby the ethnographer presents as complete a picture from his / her angle as he / she does of the sub-population or culture under investigation. The section above that outlined my personal ethnographic study emphasised the necessity in documenting the researcher's perceptions during the course of the fieldwork in order to limit researcher bias.

CONCLUSIONS

This chapter presents my perspectives concerning the ethnographic approach in social science research undertakings. It does not claim to be the definitive perspective in this evolving area. The early sections of the chapter presented an overview of differing concepts in ethnography, from the classic to the reflexive approach. As a qualitative researcher, I admit a bias toward the reflexive ethnographic approach, which I show in my own research. The positioning of a research undertaking, which I undertook as ethnographic, is discussed in depth in the latter part of the chapter, along with suggestions for students who would like to undertake an ethnographic study. Taking the loose description of ethnography (for instance, Hammersley, 1992), there is no question that much qualitative research can be termed ethnographic. However, I would consider such grouping of research under the ethnographic heading as misleading. Researchers should carefully consider how their study fits into ethnographic approaches before committing their respective research to that domain. For the study outlined in this chapter, elements of urban and reflexive ethnography are identified, reified by my involvement with the context and sample over the period of the study.

ENDNOTES

♦ **Ontology**: In philosophy, ontology refers to how a researcher considers the nature of reality and truth. Some may believe that reality and truth are external and exist, regardless of human interaction, while others may believe that reality and truth are socially-constructed, leading to each individual having a different interpretation of reality and truth. Along this dichotomy, there is a continuum depending on the particular ontological framework of a particular researcher.

♦ **Epistemology**: In philosophy, epistemology refers to how a researcher considers knowledge, or how a researcher can know 'reality' or 'truth'. For some researchers, the only way to 'know' may be in following scientistic research approaches. For others, it may be through transactions, such as language and semiotics. As with ontology, there is an epistemological continuum along which researchers position themselves.

♦ **Methodology:** The connection between ontology, epistemology and methodology should be explained in a research undertaking. Based on the researcher's particular ontology and epistemology, he / she will be guided to follow a methodology that he / she believes best informs knowledge (epistemology) in order to make sense of reality (ontology). Some researchers may conduct scientific research, believing in the ability to objectify truth; others may conduct interpretive research, focusing on individual cases in order to explain phenomena.

♦ **Positivism:** This refers to a philosophy espousing that knowledge is objective, generalisable and quantifiable, and that such knowledge is best investigated through observation and measurement (as in scientific experiments).

♦ **Hermeneutics:** This refers to an interpretive methodology where the researcher commits to interpreting texts, taking his / her previous experience and role in the research into consideration, as well as the data collected from observation, interviews, etc.

♦ **Naturalism** refers to the belief that reality can be investigated through scientific methods.

REFERENCES

Atkinson, P. & Hammersley, M. (1998). 'Ethnography and Participant Observation', in Denzin, N.K. & Lincoln, Y.S. (eds), *Strategies of Qualitative Inquiry*, pp. 110-36. London: Sage.

Atkinson, P., Coffey, A., Delamont, S., Lofland, J. & Lofland, L. (2001). *Handbook of Ethnography*. London: Sage.

Barth, F. (1975). *Ritual and Knowledge among the Baktaman of New Guinea*. New Haven, CT: Yale University Press.

Bauman, Z. (2001). 'Identity in the Globalising World', *Social Anthropology* 9(2): 121-29.

Clifford, J. (1988). *The Predicament of Culture*. Cambridge, MA: Harvard University Press.

Crowley-Henry, M. (2007). 'The Protean Career: Exemplified by First World Foreign Residents in Western Europe?', *International Studies of Management & Organization* 37(3): 44–64.

Crowley-Henry, M. (2008). 'A Narratives' Exploration of Non-Traditional International Assignees Locally Resident and Employed in the South of France', paper presented at 4th Workshop on Expatriation, Las Palmas, Gran Canaria, 23-24 October 2008.

Crowley-Henry, M. & Weir, D. (2007). 'The International Protean Career: Four Women's Narratives', *Journal of Organizational Change Management* 20(2): 245-58.

Crowley-Henry, M. & Weir, D. (2009). (forthcoming) 'Control and the Protean Career: A Critical Perspective from the Multinational's International Assignees', in Voronov, M., Wolfram Cox, J., Le Trent-Jones, T. & Weir, D. (eds), *Critical Management Studies at Work: Multidisciplinary Approaches to Negotiating Tensions between Theory and Practice*. Cheltenham: Edgar Elgar Publishing Ltd.

Denzin, N.K. (1997). *Interpretive Ethnography: Ethnographic Practices for the 21st Century*. Thousand Oaks, CA: Sage.

Denzin, N.K. & Lincoln, Y.S. (1998a). *The Landscape of Qualitative Research. Theories and Issues*. Thousand Oaks, CA: Sage.

Denzin, N.K. & Lincoln, Y.S. (1998b). *Strategies of Qualitative Inquiry*. Thousand Oaks, CA: Sage.

Ellis, C.S. & Bochner, A.P. (2000). 'Autoethnography, Personal Narrative, Reflexivity: Researcher as Subject', in Denzin, N.K. & Lincoln, Y.S. (eds), *The Handbook of Qualitative Research*, 2nd ed, pp. 733-68. London: Sage.

Emerson, R.M., Fretz, R.I. & Shaw, L.L. (1995). *Writing Ethnographic Fieldnotes*. Chicago, IL: University of Chicago Press.

Evered, R. & Louis, M.R. (1991). 'Alternative Perspectives in the Organisational Sciences: "Inquiry from the Inside" and "Inquiry from the Outside"', in Smith, N.C. & Dainty, P. (eds), *The Management Research Handbook*, pp. 7-22. London: Routledge.

Fetterman, D. (1998). *Ethnography: Step by Step*. Thousand Oaks, CA: Sage.

Foote Whyte, W. (1993). *Street Corner Society: The Social Structure of an Italian Slum*, 4th ed. Chicago, IL: University of Chicago Press.

Gill, J. & Johnson, P. (1991). *Research Methods for Managers*. London: Chapman Publishing Ltd.

Goffman, E. (1989). 'On Fieldwork', *Journal of Contemporary Ethnography* 18:123-32.

Hammersley, M. (1992). *What's Wrong with Ethnography?* London: Routledge.

Hammersley, M. & Atkinson, P. (1995). *Ethnography: Principles in Practice*, 2nd ed. London: Routledge.

Hughes, E.C. (1960). 'Introduction: The Place of Field Work in Social Science', in Junker, B.H. (ed), *Field Work. An Introduction to the Social Sciences*, pp. iii-xiii. Chicago, IL: University of Chicago Press.

Junker, B.H. (1960). *Field Work. An Introduction to the Social Sciences*. Chicago, IL: University of Chicago Press.

Lincoln, Y.S. & Denzin, N.K. (1994). 'The Fifth Moment', in Denzin, N.K. & Lincoln, Y.S. (eds), *The Handbook of Qualitative Research*, pp. 575-86. Thousand Oaks, CA: Sage.

Malinowski, B. (1961). *Argonauts of the Western Pacific*. New York, NY: E.P. Dutton.

Mason, J. (2002). *Qualitative Researching*, 2nd ed. London: Sage.

McCracken, G. (1988). *The Long Interview: Qualitative Research Methods*. Beverly Hills, CA: Sage.

McQueen, R. & Knussen, C. (2002). *Research Methods for Social Science: An Introduction*. Harlow: Prentice Hall / Pearson Education Limited.

Mead, M. (2001[1928]). *Coming of Age in Samoa: A Psychological Study of Primitive Youth for Western Civilisation*. New York, NY: Harper Perennial Modern Classics.

Mishler, E. (1979). 'Meaning in Context: Is There Any Other Kind?', *Harvard Educational Review* 119(1): 1-19.

Pollner, M. & Emerson, R.M. (1988). 'The Dynamics of Inclusion and Distance in Fieldwork Relations', in Emerson, R.M. (ed), *Contemporary Field Research: A Collection of Readings*, pp. 235-52. Prospect Heights, IL: Waveland.

Reed-Danahav, D.E. (1997). *Auto-Ethnography: Rewriting the Self and the Social*. Oxford: Berg.

Russell, C. (1999). 'Autoethnography: Journeys of the Self', in Russell, C. (ed), *Experimental Ethnography: The Work of Film in the Age of Video*, pp. 275-314. Durham, NC: Duke University Press.

Sanjek, R. (2000). 'Keeping Ethnography Alive in an Urbanizing World', *Human Organisation* 59(3): 280-88.

Trochim, W.M. (2006). *The Research Methods Knowledge Base*, 2nd ed [Online]. Available: http://www.socialresearchmethods.net/kb/ (last accessed 14 March 2009).

Turnbull, S. (1999). 'Corporate Values Programmes - What Do Managers Really Learn?', in Gilson, C.H.J., Grugulis, I. & Wilmott, H. (eds), *Critical Management Conference Proceedings*. Manchester: Manchester School of Management.

Van Maanen, J. (1988). *Tales of the Field. On Writing Ethnography*. Chicago, IL: University of Chicago Press.

Van Maanen, J. (1995). 'An End to Innocence: The Ethnography of Ethnography', in Van Maanen, J. (ed), *Representation in Ethnography*, pp. 1-35. Thousand Oaks, CA: Sage.

CHAPTER 4
POSTCOLONIAL REDIRECTIONS IN INTERNATIONAL MANAGEMENT RESEARCH & FIELDWORK

Banu Özkazanç-Pan

INTRODUCTION

Globalisation is an important topic of discussion and research across the social sciences, as sociology, anthropology, political science, history and economics scholars examine the complex geopolitical, social, and cultural activities taking place across integrated national economies (Adler, 2002; Castells, 1996; Hardt & Negri, 2000, 2004; Massey *et al.*, 1999; Schiller, Basch & Blanc, 1995).

Within the business and management academic community, there has also been a growing interest in understanding globalisation. These interests expand from Adler & Graham's (1989: 515) earlier concerns that, 'as the proportion of foreign to domestic trade increases, so does the frequency of business negotiations between people from different countries and cultures' to recent arguments about business functions now taking place over geographical and temporal distances in a 'virtual' world as global production chains span the globe. Through the circulation of technologies, ideas, and people, global business activities are thus made possible.

Appadurai (1990) puts forth his notion of 'scapes' to view globalisation as flows of people, technology, finance, media, as well as political ideas. In this sense, doing business under globalisation relies on a set of interconnections and exchanges between people and places, where, as suggested by Pieterse (1994: 161) 'a process of hybridization ... gives rise to a global mélange'. Thus migration, immigration, and hybridisation become important and relevant ideas in thinking about globalisation, for as 'transnational connections' (Hannerz, 1996) and new relationships between people and places occur, new ideas about who they / us are in those relationships also emerge.

STATE OF THE IM FIELD: STUDYING PEOPLE & GLOBALISATION

The approach to the study of people and globalisation within United States (US)-based international business and management research seems to lack dynamic conceptualisations of globalisation and the people involved in these processes. Traditionally, the literature has emphasised cross-cultural and comparative approaches, as scholars try to differentiate business people and business practices around the world (see Tsui, Nifadkar & Ou, 2007, for an overview). At the level of theory, this has meant a static and compartmentalising approach to the study of culture. Yet, this theoretical approach has also had effects on the way such studies have been carried out in the field. Namely, methodologies aiming to study culture and 'cultural differences', inclusive of both quantitative and qualitative work, have extended the unquestioned assumptions of theories to fieldwork. Below, I expand upon the problems of existing international management (IM) theoretical approaches as well as accompanying methodologies.

To be specific, the cross-cultural research I mention above addresses micro-level similarities and differences in / among individuals and groups 'across cultures.' In such work, 'culture' is generally defined as collective mental programming (Hofstede, 1980, 1998; Hofstede & Bond, 1988) or underlying norms and values individuals share with members of their own nations, regions, and groups (Triandis, 1983; Triandis & Suh, 2002; Trompenaars, 1996). The majority of this research focuses on similarities and differences in managerial behaviours / practices (Hofstede *et al.*, 2002; Huo, Huang & Napier, 2002; Kovach, 1994; Lee, 1999; Lowe, Milliman, De Cieri & Dowling, 2002). Others have been concerned with personal traits (Black, 1999; Oliver & Cravens, 1999; Soedarsono, Murray & Omurtag, 1998; Yousef, 1998), and attitudes (Hofstede, 1998; Kuehn & Al-Busaidi, 2000; Ramamoorthy & Carroll, 1998).

The cross-cultural and comparative international management literature also includes a subset of work focusing on gender differences in management values and practices across different cultural contexts. Scholars in this area examine gender differences regarding individualism / collectivism (Kashima *et al.*, 1995), self-regulation (Kurman, 2001), organisational justice (Lee, Pillutla & Law, 2000), and leadership activities (Bartol, Martin & Kromkowski, 2003; Gibson, 1995; Zander & Romani, 2004) across cultures. These scholars are, in effect, attempting to delineate how gender *and* culture make a difference in work-related values and management practices in diverse people around the world.

Thus, in general, questions around values in different countries have been of great interest (d'Iribarne, 2002; Gamble & Gibson, 1999; Kirkman & Shapiro, 2001). Notable among these is, no doubt, the enormous amount of publications generated by and through Geert Hofstede's frameworks and, more recently, through the GLOBE project (*cf.* JIBS, 2006) in an attempt to delineate what difference culture makes for leadership, among many other constructs (e.g., House, Javidan & Dorman, 2001).

In the light of these various research efforts ongoing in the IM field, there have also been voices from within the field that have questioned existing theories and approaches used to study people in a dynamic, globalised world. For instance, as Boyacıgiller & Adler (1991: 263) note, 'Americans have developed theories without being sufficiently aware of non-US contexts, models, research, and values'. Unfortunately, while some scholars have recognised that a problem exists, most solutions have been focused on finding appropriate theories and methods that fit the 'culture' or people under study, rather than on underscoring the possibility that all people in the world may not conceptualise themselves in the same way (e.g., Geertz, 1983). In other words, questions over the constitution of self / identity in the management literature have not been addressed, while the study of the self continues in a culturally-relative, but essentialist fashion (e.g., Americans are individualistic, Asians are collectivistic, see Hofstede, 1980).

Meanwhile, globalisation has been studied through decontextualised and comparative cultural approaches that privilege management ideas and practices from the West, while silencing those associated with the non-West. For instance, in the IM field, globalisation has been studied as a movement of management theories and practices from 'industrialised nations' to the 'rest of the world' (i.e., best practices) or as a 'global / local' dichotomy. Often these ideas have been presented as 'convergence' and 'divergence' with US management ideas and practices (*cf.*, Blyton, 2001; Khanna & Palepu, 2004; Leung *et al.*, 2005; Shenkar, 2004). That is, business ideas and practices have often been thought of as moving from the 'West' to the 'Rest' or as having identifiable aspects, which can be called either distinctly 'global' or 'local.' The global often implies universal applicability, while the local is frequently considered as idiosyncratic or lesser practices or ideas. In this same vein, the global / universal is more likely to be thought of as coming from dominant 'industrialised nations,' while the local / idiosyncratic is more likely to be associated with specific 'cultural practices' functioning as referent of non-dominant societies.

In these arguments, *the complex and necessary interconnections between all people and nations,* which make 'doing business' under globalisation possible, have not been sufficiently recognized. Under the current approaches, the study of these business activities has been based on cultural comparisons between people (i.e., cultural differences) that assume a static, Western-centric world of peoples and cultures, without consideration for the historic and ongoing relations among nations.

To clarify, there is no dearth of concerns over these issues. Recently, one important focus of US-based and Western international management scholarship, cross-cultural and comparative IM in particular, has been to outline how to think about people *from* and *in* different parts of the world engaged in international business transactions. A pressing issue is how to conceptualise such 'international business people' within international management theory and research: How can cross-cultural and comparative international management scholars represent the people they want to study? What must they consider in order to conceptualise and understand different people in international management? (Boyacıgiller, *et al.*, 2004; Earley & Singh, 2000). However, these questions are not innocent, but, rather, are implicitly sustained by strong *a priori* assumptions about the subjects scholars intend to study.

Guided by these latter remarks, I suggest that meta-theoretical considerations are needed before international management theory and research can articulate alternative approaches to understanding business people and practices in the context of globalisation. I further argue that an appropriate focus of analysis to address these encounters is through the notion of *identity formation* in relationships between people in the world. Therefore, I consider a relevant research question to be: How do business people in the context of globalisation *form* their identities?

Specifically, since globalisation involves the movement of people and ideas, these flows result in encounters and exchanges all over the world and give way to a series of *relational processes* as people engage in economic, cultural, and political activities more generally. As people interact with each other through these activities, new *identities* are produced, which perhaps better represent 'international business people' in the world today. To study identity formation in ways that recognise the voices of the various participants in 'the encounter,' including the researcher, it is necessary to go beyond theoretical and research approaches currently available in the IM literature.

Even when they may appropriately identify the problem (i.e., need to examine multiple contexts and move beyond US-based management theories), as a group, international management scholars do not seem to be able to break loose from formulating nation-specific theories and methodology to solve their predicaments. This is seen in calls to 'determine which management theories *de facto* embrace the North American cultural context' (Doktor, Tung & Von Glinow, 1991a: 260) and 'develop management theories that are effective and functional when applied in culture settings' (Doktor, Tung & Von Glinow, 1991b: 363). This emphasis on culturally-specific theories and new methodologies does not allow for a reconsideration of the Western philosophical assumptions guiding a more general assumption: that it is altogether possible to do cross-cultural and comparative international management theories and research. Paradoxically, even the articulation of *international* is done *in relation* to the US, and North America more generally, as suggested recently by the editors of the *Academy of Management Journal*:

> This journal has made a successful transition from being primarily North American in focus to being a truly international journal—one with (1) many authors who are international scholars, (2) many samples collected outside North America (Kirkman & Law, 2005: 7)

Evidently, scholars do not reflect upon the fact that their problem is that assumptions embedded within these very 'international' management theories end up reflecting back their own creators. Representations put forth in the cross-cultural and comparative international management fields already create a research subject / identity based on assumptions regarding the 'self' from Western modernist philosophy, no matter how 'culturally sensitive' (another modernist assumption) the specification. While this has not gone unrecognised, such recognition does not change the modernist philosophical assumptions (i.e., based on Humanism and Enlightenment philosophies) that imagine 'culture' as pure, fixed, and identifiable. Thus, 'the problem' is articulated more as a matter of the quantity of 'variables' that must be accounted for rather than a matter of re-thinking meta-theoretical assumptions in conceptualising the situation. Consequently, the issue at hand when carrying out fieldwork is not necessarily the choice of methods, but rather how methodological choices should reflect the underlying meta-theoretical concerns of research projects. In this sense, the question is not whether quantitative or qualitative work is better, but a concern over the goals of the research and the ability to use methods appropriate for the research questions at hand.

POSTCOLONIAL FRAMEWORKS

Postcolonial scholars highlight the importance of historical experiences among nations and peoples in critiques and analyses of Western philosophy. By highlighting the relevance of the 'non-West' to any theoretical argument guided by Western philosophical assumptions, postcolonial studies can offer another way to conceptualise the formation of international business identities under conditions of globalisation based on historic colonial relations between nations (for examples of research studies using postcolonial frameworks, see Banerjee & Linstead, 2001; Calás, 1992; Chio, 2005; Frenkel & Shenhav, 2003, 2006; Jack & Westwood, 2006; Kwek, 2003; Mir, Mir & Upadhyaya, 2003; Moulettes, 2007; Prasad, 2003).

Both international management and postcolonial approaches consider 'the rest of the world', but differ significantly in their theoretical approaches to the topic. Postcolonial studies, as a field of inquiry, is made up of diverse theorists engaged in critiquing Eurocentric and Western representations of non-Western worlds. As a group, these theorists want to call attention to privileged canonical knowledge that makes claims about non-Western peoples and to articulate, instead, knowledge that has been marginalised by Western epistemological interventions. In order to accomplish these objectives, postcolonial scholars rely on several theoretical approaches having their roots within Marxist, postmodern and poststructuralist frameworks (for an overview of postcolonial frameworks and their relevance for IM, see Özkazanç-Pan, 2008). Postcolonial studies is concerned not only with relations between former coloniser and colonised, but also with cultural representations of the 'non-West' from the perspectives of the 'West'. However, in order not to essentialise and reify these nation positions, it is important to recognize that 'non-West' countries and powers may themselves have engaged in colonising practices during their histories.

Not all postcolonial scholars agree as to what time or which people constitute 'post-colonial.' In addition, there is debate within the field about textual *versus* material approaches to resistance and reflexivity in the light of colonial encounters. Finally, key terms such as 'West' and 'non-West' are not unproblematic concepts for a number of postcolonial scholars, whose works challenge pure notions of culture. Moreover, although the postcolonial studies field may seem united by shared concerns of Western epistemological hegemony and knowing differently, as well as their emphasis on the formation of 'others' identities as a relational practice between colonisers and colonised, the analytic strength of postcolonial studies lies in the distinct theoretical approaches of various scholars to these very concerns and debates. To illustrate the importance of these differences, I rely on three key theorists who have made significant contributions to the postcolonial field: Homi K. Bhabha (1990a,b, 1994), Edward W. Said (1985, 1988, 1991, 1993a,b,c, 2000), and Gayatri C. Spivak (1985a,b,c, 1987, 1988, 1990, 1996, 1999).

Bhabha, Said, and Spivak each make distinct theoretical contributions to postcolonial studies and these contributions have different implications for international management theory and research (Frenkel, 2008; Özkazanç-Pan, 2008). In brief, Bhabha's work explores the connections among writing, identities, and nation-building. His framework for analysis considers psychoanalytic dimensions and repercussions of colonial rule, while simultaneously focusing on textual / theoretical manoeuvres, such as binary oppositions and mimicry as attempts to legitimise differences between Western and non-Western people. Bhabha's work challenges the rules by which Western texts create essential characteristics for people and focuses instead on the indeterminacy of identities. More importantly, his framework highlights how people produce culturally-based meanings around various practices and thus problematises the notion that ideas can be imposed or transferred mimetically between cultures.

In contrast, Said's postcolonial framework helps uncover the connections between Orientalism, as a discourse based on modes of representation, vocabulary and imagery, and Western material structures. His analytics also highlight the ways in which Orientalist discourses emanating from Western academic knowledge rhetorically feminise the non-West (i.e., as weak, in need of help) and, based on this, influence macro decisions, such as foreign or business policies embarked upon by Western nations and institutions.

Finally, Spivak's theoretical work focuses on the textual production of the gendered postcolonial subject as she outlines how this subject exists at the margin of Western feminist and academic writing. Rather than focusing exclusively on Western narratives and their consequences for postcolonial subjects, Spivak is equally determined to address the material. Her framework links texts to the material world, as she examines the living and working conditions of female postcolonial subjects with respect to the international division of labour and the interventions that are made on their behalf. To these effects, however, rather than becoming the 'native informant' within a Western academic institution, Spivak questions her own privileged position in studying the 'Third World.' In her arguments she highlights the 'Third World' as existing only in relationship to a 'First World' of Western invention, produced by a Western imagination that also produces 'native' populations and 'knowledge' about them. Consequently, one of the main contributions of Spivak's framework is the reflexive position and questioning that she requires of researchers who want to study postcolonial subjects. In effect, Spivak's work speaks directly to the problematic of representation: giving voice is neither an academic methodological issue nor necessarily possible to do. It is a practice that attempts to address the gendered power relations among different people and nations embedded in the global economy.

In terms of identity formation, each scholar allows for a different examination of identity / representation and resistances to dominant Western forms of knowledge, based on their distinct frameworks. Despite these differences, postcolonial scholars share theoretical assumptions regarding representational strategies and historic power relations. Firstly, postcolonial theories pay close attention to the language of representation in texts / writing and, in particular, to the theories, concepts, and words used to represent non-Western people textually, including how 'the research subject' is formed through specific signifiers. This focus allows theorists to consider who may benefit from a particular representation of the non-West / non-Westerner in Western academic writing and to highlight connections among academic theory, epistemology / research, and education regarding the 'Third World.'

Secondly, postcolonial theories focus on particular historical, economic, and political relations among nations in order to provide a context for relational differences. In other words, 'cultural differences' can only be understood by acknowledging the relevance of encounters between peoples under colonial / postcolonial and imperialist conditions. How are such 'differences' formed? In relationship to what? Who articulates them? In which ways, and for what purposes? Postcolonial theories thus highlight power relations that are embedded in these relationships.

Altogether, I argue that postcolonial theory is immediately relevant to understanding 'international management'. That is, from these perspectives, international management discourse of 'cultural differences' is another Western linguistic practice, whereby certain conceptualisations of self / difference are considered management 'knowledge', while other ways of understanding relationships among people in the world are marginalised.

EXAMINING POSTCOLONIAL CONCERNS IN CONTEXT: THE 'NON-WEST' & 'NON-WESTERNER'

Taken together, postcolonial frameworks emphasise how power relations and historic political and economic relationships among nations are relevant to present-day representations of the 'non-West' and contribute to the study of contemporary encounters between West and non-West under globalisation. As a way to demonstrate my concerns about existing approaches to IM theory and fieldwork, I focus on studying the US and Turkey through postcolonial lenses as an examination of postcolonial meta-theoretical concerns around West / non-West relationships and an articulation of identity-formation narratives in the context of such encounters. While the US and Turkey do not have an historical colonial relationship *per se*, postcolonial frameworks nonetheless help to acknowledge historic power relations, i.e., neo-colonial relations, which include political, military and economic issues – as important and relevant to academic writing, research, and education about Turkey in US business representations (i.e., IM literature about the 'Other'). By studying this ongoing relationship, I can also highlight experiences of globalisation related to identity formation that take place within the context of history and the present. To accomplish this and illustrate the analytical value of postcolonial approaches, I focus on a subset of the IM literature addressing the international entrepreneur.

THE INTERNATIONAL ENTREPRENEUR: A CASE IN POINT

Within the context of globalisation, entrepreneurs often reflect the movement of people and the interconnection of places. Such international entrepreneurs characterise simultaneous lives / identities: they know the 'native' business practices of their societies while travelling globally. The flexibility of identity formation can be represented by this group of people, who are doing business on 'their own' and are less constrained to identify themselves by the structural limitations of multinational organisations. Thus, international entrepreneurs are a good way to examine globalisation processes related to identity formation.

In recent years, there has been a growing academic interest in international entrepreneurship, as evidenced by management journals producing special issues on this topic, including the *Academy of Management Journal* (2000) and *Entrepreneurship: Theory & Practice* (forthcoming 2010). More importantly, the growth of the field has been marked by scholars attempting to define international entrepreneurship conceptually as the field continues to emerge, mainly by borrowing concepts from strategy, entrepreneurship, and international management / business fields (McDougall & Oviatt, 2000; Zahra & George, 2002). Thus, one of the pressing concerns in the field is how to conceptualise and study international entrepreneurship in light of globalisation. Despite these concerns, most work within this nascent field does not focus specifically on the mobility of business people and ideas through migration and movement, but, rather, on the static aspects of entrepreneurs and entrepreneurship, even if they acknowledge the existence of ethnic or immigrant aspects of entrepreneurial activities. As I will discuss, this subset of the literature brings to visibility, at its most immediate, the problems created by fixing 'identity' and 'culture' in the extant IM literature when addressing globalisation.

To this end, each postcolonial scholar promotes a different theoretical lens to study how identity / representation is formed within the context of this relationship. Bhabha's framework offers the possibility of understanding people through hybridity, rather than pure cultural selves (i.e., Turkish *versus* American identities). Hybridity is not only a self-construct, but a strategy for resisting colonising representations that offer no voice or agency and questioning mimetically-imposed cultural ideas and practices that assume business ideas and practices that exist in one part of the world also exist in the same way and have the same meaning in other parts of the world. By studying international entrepreneurs in the US and Turkey, I can uncover (or recover) other ways of understanding self and business practices as they occur in the West / non-West encounter.

Said's theoretical focus on historic power relations highlights how globalisation is a set of dependencies and relationships, such that people, nations, and cultural differences need to be understood within this particular context. Furthermore, his articulation of the terms of knowledge production (i.e., science is not neutral) highlights how cultural differences, as they exist in the IM literature, may perpetuate Orientalism and silence non-Western voices, particularly as Western management ideas and practices circulate hegemonically in the global economy through media and business school knowledge. Based on Said's work, studying the international entrepreneur in the US and Turkey allows for consideration of how such individuals exist in relational aspects in the context of historic geopolitical and economic interdependencies among nations.

Spivak's lens adds another layer of complexity to understanding the self and the West / non-West encounter in the context of globalisation. Her theoretical focus on the gendered postcolonial subject and the subaltern (i.e., that group of people existing beyond capitalist labour processes) highlights how gendered discourses (i.e., epistemological violence) and material practices (i.e., division of global labour) enable particular identities and practices to become the norm by marginalising others. More importantly, Western representational strategies of the 'Third World' produce a subaltern subject who occupies a gendered place in the text and in the world. By examining how discourses of international entrepreneurs and entrepreneurship take place in the US and Turkey, Spivak's lens uncovers a self embedded within gender(ed) relations among people and nations. Moreover, she calls attention to the role of the researcher in producing such academic knowledge about the 'Third World' and thus highlights power relations between an institutionally-located and privileged researcher and a research subject located institutionally in the gendered division of global labour.

In summary, although each postcolonial scholar offers a distinct theoretical approach to the examination of identity, as a group they find some common ground in their epistemology of conceptualising relational aspects of identities. This stands in contrast to the conceptualisation of research subjects under international management research. To demonstrate the value of postcolonial analyses for international management theorising and research, this chapter attempts to answer the following questions: How do international entrepreneurs in the context of globalisation form their identities? How are these possible identities formed and represented? Through these questions I examine Turkish entrepreneurs as an exemplar of international business people in the context of globalisation, and contrast the representations of their identities made in the IM literature with other possibilities allowed by my research questions. In other words, my project has a dual purpose: to show the limits of existing IM approaches to theorising and researching globalisation and business people under globalisation *and* to uncover the ways in which global encounters allow for the production of new identities (i.e., processual, hybrid, gendered).

My research question, 'How do international entrepreneurs in the context of globalisation form their identities?', is guided by postcolonial theoretical frameworks, and methodologically answering this question must attend to constructivist critical epistemology. To this effect, I examine narratives of identity formation occurring under globalisation. How are people telling stories about themselves in the context of globalisation? What stories do they tell? To whom do they tell them? Where do they tell them? For what purposes? To attend to these concerns, however, is more than a matter of choosing methods that can address the research question, e.g., ethnography: for postcolonial frameworks also highlight that issues such as the seemingly simple act of retrieving information from research participants, i.e., 'informing', is also in question. For instance, how do researchers speak for others and how do they speak of particular places? (Appadurai, 1988). That is, postcolonial positions (Spivak specifically) problematise how 'the researcher', the actual writing of the research, and the audience for whom it is written, are implicated in the very research that is conducted and, therefore, are part of the process of identity formation (Khan, 2005; Lal, 1996). Below, I discuss how the study design I employed addresses the research question *and* these other concerns.

METHODOLOGY: STUDY DESIGN

The postcolonial frameworks I rely on share a common interest with poststructuralist frameworks in the primacy of texts and language and, thus, allow me to make the argument that language constructs reality and is implicated in representing 'knowledge'. Yet, each of these postcolonial theoretical positions engages with texts written by the West about the Rest through distinct analyses. These philosophical arguments translated into the material reality of data collection mean that I needed a study design allowing me to pay attention to language and text to examine how identity formation happens through hybridity / mimicry, gender and subalternity, and historic power relations. Further, this meant that to study identity formation, I had to pay attention not only to its textual construction in the participant's narratives, but also my very implication in these processes.

The design that enabled me to fulfil these aims was a combination of ethnography and auto-ethnography (see Henry-Crowley's chapter in this book for further discussion of ethnography). I use ethnography loosely as a borrowed methodological tool from anthropology to engage in in-depth fieldwork through participant observations, interviews, and collection of artefacts (i.e., physical objects from sites). Although postcolonial positions have a problematic relationship with ethnography, as it was often the handmaiden of colonial rule (see Prasad, 2003a) and assumed a universal notion of culture (see Sokefeld, 1999), I rely on methods available from more recent reflexive and critical ethnographic approaches, such as Clifford's (1992) in 'Traveling Cultures', to examine identity formation as it occurs among encounters of different mobile people.

Yet ethnographic approaches focusing on mobility, rather than fixed place, are not sufficient in this case, for I am very much an interested participant in the research project. In other words, I am an (assumed) 'native' of Turkey, who has 'culture' in 'common' with study members and who returns 'home' to carry out this research. Yet these assumptions are quite problematic assumptions, as voiced by postcolonial positions. Specifically, guided by Spivak's theoretical concerns around this very issue, I take a reflexive stance that complicates the information retrieval function of ethnography; no longer could I simply report identity formation as the other's voice (identity) even if in mobile places (cultures) for, as researcher, I occupy a subject position parallel to, and in interaction with, that of the other participants in this project. For this reason, I took further recourse through auto-ethnography, 'the study, representation, or knowledge of a culture by one or more of its members' (Buzard, 2003: 61), or ethnonarrative (Hansen, 2006). Both of these approaches refer to a reflexive practice of considering the researcher as part of the context, both materially and textually (i.e., representations and language). Auto-ethnography materializes as the intersections of researcher's voice, place, and privilege that need to be considered in contacts with participants (i.e., observations, interviews) and in the writing of the research (i.e., informing, reporting).

Based on this position, gaining access to the research sites and participants is part of the question of researcher involvement and needs to be addressed. It is the story of the researcher's identity formation, as well as an entrance into the story of possible selves under globalisation.

Gaining Access: Entering the Field

I limited my research to an examination of high-tech entrepreneurs in the United States and Turkey. Since the high-tech sector is associated with modernisation, innovation, and Western-ness, high-tech entrepreneurs were a good test case to examine relational identity formation from postcolonial perspectives. Given the expected role of high-tech entrepreneurs in 'developing and commercialising technologies worldwide' (Kropp & Zolin, 2005: 1), was there convergence towards US modelling of their international high-tech entrepreneurial business activities? In other words, was there mimicry?

To accomplish these various inquiries into identity formation, from 2005 to 2008, I attended annual high-tech business conferences in the Silicon Valley area and a similar conference in Antalya, Turkey. I learned about the conference that ultimately became the first data collection site for my research upon receiving an email from a Turkish community listserv in 2005 discussing an upcoming high-tech conference in Silicon Valley. The fieldwork for the research began in the following conference, 'Bridging Silicon Valley & Turkey,' that took place at the Stanford University Schwab Residential Center in Palo Alto, California on 21 May 2005. The conference was organized by the Turkish American Business Connection (TABC) Association in Santa Clara, CA, the Stanford Turkish Student Association, and the Stanford Graduate School of Business High Tech Club. I attended the conference as a participant, after contacting members of TABC about my research interests. They forwarded me the names and emails of three entrepreneurs who wanted to speak to me during the conference. The conference aimed to bring together high-tech Turkish entrepreneurs to network and discuss investment opportunities in Turkey. My initial contact was with Baris,[1] an entrepreneur with whom I had exchanged emails regarding his participation in my study prior to arriving in California. He told me to call him once I arrived in Palo Alto, CA on 20 May 2005. Upon doing so, he invited me to a pre-conference gathering held at the hotel I was staying at for the duration of the conference. I found out that this gathering was for TABC members, conference speakers and organisers only. He introduced me to members of TABC, including the president of the organisation. Once I told the president of TABC that I had emailed them in the previous months about my research project, he welcomed me to the gathering and started to introduce me to all the

---

[1]   To keep the anonymity of interviewees, I changed their names.

Turkish entrepreneurs, as well as other TABC members, who had come to this pre-conference social. The president of TABC at the time, Kemal, was also one of the three entrepreneurs who agreed to be interviewed. The third entrepreneur, Hakan, said he had a business meeting and would be out of town during the conference. However, he agreed to be interviewed later on, if I came back to the area to carry out the rest of my project.

The next day, I attended the conference from 8am to 9pm, including welcome speeches by the Los Angeles Consulate General of Turkey, the president of TABC, and the chairman of the board of Cisco Systems. The conference ran two parallel tracks of panel discussions, including 'Turkish technology sector and opportunities' and 'Entrepreneurship and high-tech ventures'. I attended all the discussions and presentations in the second track, 'Entrepreneurship and high-tech ventures'. I chose this track, based on my research focus on high-tech and the related discourse around modernisation and Western-ness. All the presentations and discussions were carried out in English, although there were some Turkish phrases / sayings that were used intermittently to make certain points. During the conference, there were several breaks, which gave me the opportunity to have conversations with other conference attendees and to expand my contacts.

During the cocktail hour and networking session at the end of the conference, I was invited to a post-conference barbeque to be held the next day (Sunday, 22 May 2005) at the house of one of the TABC members, Cem (also an entrepreneur). During this time, I met members of TABC that I did not have the opportunity to meet at the conference. In addition, I was able to schedule an interview with Cem upon my return to the area and to obtain the names of other Turkish high-tech entrepreneurs who would be in the area at that point. During and after the conference, I made additional contacts with several other members of this entrepreneurial community for possible participation in my fieldwork.

I came back to the Silicon Valley area from July to October 2005 to carry out further preliminary interviews and, through these, I gained access to still other Turkish high-tech entrepreneurs in the area. I also attended First Thursdays, which were free, informal meetings where individuals got together to discuss social and cultural events affecting the Turkish and Turkish-American community. The conferences, in contrast, were formal gatherings (i.e., had to pay to attend) with sponsors, high-profile Turkish entrepreneurs, and Turkish politicians. Further, I went to Turkey from November 2005 to January 2006, and established links with high-tech entrepreneurs there, based on contacts provided by my interviewees in Silicon Valley, as well as other links obtained through a faculty member contact at the School of Management at Sabanci University in Istanbul, Turkey.

This initial access, and consequent returns to conferences put together by the TABC in 2006 (Turkey's Role in the Global High Technology Market) and 2007 (Financing our High-Tech Future: Investments in Turkey), as well as email communications throughout the course of the research, allowed me to become part of the conference over the several years of data collection. I became a participant observer, for instance, as members asked my advice about what they should present for topics, rather than treating me as a guest, as I was initially seen in 2005. In addition to attending the conferences in the Silicon Valley area put together annually by TABC, I attended a Turkish high-tech sector conference in January 2008 in Antalya, Turkey put together by Sinerjiturk.[2] I learned about this conference through the TABC website.

DATA COLLECTION METHOD & SITES

During the fieldwork, I carried out participant observations, self-observations, and interviews and collected various material artefacts (i.e., books, pamphlets, videos, PowerPoint presentations) at various empirical sites in the United States and Turkey. Since each of the postcolonial frameworks values language and text, I focused on discourse (language in use and in texts) during the data collection in order to understand how identity formation takes place through different narratives. Specifically, in order to study identity formation at the level of hybridity and mimicry (culturally-based meanings), I focused on the empirical sites themselves as allowing particular narratives of identity formation to take place. Next, to study identity formation at the level of historic power relations between nations, I examined economic and political historic events / relations between the United States and Turkey. I observed participant behaviours and material practices during the interviews, conferences, and get-togethers, e.g., the First Thursdays (see **Table 4.1**).

---

[2]   Sinerjiturk was a recently-formed (2007) non-profit Turkish organisation with
     members from business, academia, government branches and NGOs that
     aimed to foster dialogue and action in Turkey's technology sectors. See
     www.sinerjiturk.org.tr.

Year	Conferences	One-on-one interviews	First Thursday meetings
2005	20-22 May, Palo Alto: 2nd TABC conference, pre / post conference events (Bridging Silicon Valley & Turkey)	July-October, Silicon Valley; November-December, Istanbul and Ankara	July-October, Silicon Valley
2006	27 May, Berkeley: 3rd TABC conference, pre / post conference events (Financing our High-technology Future: Investments in Turkey)	January, Istanbul and Ankara	
2007	26 April, San Jose: 4th TABC conference (Turkey's Role in the Global High-technology Market)	January, Istanbul and Ankara	
2008	18-19 January, Antalya: 1st Sinerjiturk conference (Turkey in the Global Communication Sector)		

Table 4.1: Study Sites & Data Collection Venues

DATA

As part of the fieldwork, I collected data in the following empirical sites, depending on which postcolonial lens I was using: interviews, conversations, participant observations, websites, and conference materials (artefacts), including presentations, handouts, and any other text materials. The interviews took place one-on-one, while conversations took place either one-on-one or with me participating in small group (three to four people) discussions. Participant observations took place at the pre and post conference social gatherings, during the conferences, and at First Thursdays. Text data was obtained during the conferences through field notes, presentations, handouts, and by examining the TABC, Sinerjiturk and entrepreneurs' own corporate websites (if available) (see **Table 4.2**).

♦ 400 pages of interview transcripts.

♦ 45 hours of video recording from conferences (only available for TABCON 2007 and Sinerjiturk 2008).

♦ 40 PowerPoint presentations from all conferences (2005 to 2008).

♦ 250 pages from the websites of the organisations involved in putting together the conferences (TABC and Sinerjiturk) and from the corporate websites of the high-tech entrepreneurs (if available).

♦ 180 pages of fieldnotes from all conferences in the US and Turkey, including pre and post conference events (such as cocktails and dinners), First Thursdays informal gatherings in Silicon Valley.

♦ Multiple conference handouts (such as pamphlets, reports, and advertisements from sponsors).

Table 4.2: Data Collected During Fieldwork

During the interviews I carried out, I chose to use open-ended questions, such as 'Can you tell me about yourself?', in order to focus on how entrepreneurs decided to go into the business they did and become entrepreneurs. Follow-up questions focused on how entrepreneurs came to identify themselves as entrepreneurs and as business people, how they thought of themselves as 'Turkish' entrepreneurs in the context of the US and Turkey. I chose to focus on such open-ended questions, followed by more specific ones based on each of the distinct postcolonial lenses and the different contribution each made to understanding identity formation in the context of the US and Turkey. By using different methods depending on the postcolonial position, the act of producing data becomes inextricably linked to the theoretical assumptions guiding my fieldwork. Thus, what I pay attention to and how I pay attention to it in terms of what becomes called data can be properly called the 'politics of evidence' (Denzin & Giardina, 2008). It is questions such as 'for whom do "we" produce knowledge?' and "what are the consequences of such claims of knowledge?' arriving out of postcolonial concerns that sets apart postcolonial fieldwork as a political project from being simply a qualitative approach to fieldwork.

RESEARCH PARTICIPANTS: INTERVIEWEES & CONFERENCE & MEETING ATTENDEES

Research participants in this study can be separated into two kinds: those who participated in one-on-one interviews and those whom I observed during ethnographic fieldwork at conferences and meetings. For the one-on-one interviews, I interviewed a total of 15 individuals I had contacted either directly during the conferences or through contacts I established at the conferences and meetings. All 15 participants interviewed during the study identified themselves as entrepreneurs in the high-tech sector and as Turkish or Turkish-American when I initially asked them (either in person or via email) whether they would participate in my study. During my fieldwork in the US from July 2005 to October 2005, I carried out interviews with eight male Turkish high-tech entrepreneurs. The one-on-one interviews allowed me to collect textual data and make ethnographic observations during moments of encounters while they were participants attending the conferences and meetings could be observed using ethnographic field methods. Such observations allowed me to examine encounters among different people as I became embedded in the research process (see Table 4.3).

DATA ANALYSIS

In order to address the shared textual concerns of the postcolonial positions and to pay attention to their distinct approaches framing my argument, I use narrative analysis (see Czarniawska, 2004), as this type of analysis allows me to speak to the theoretical arguments I raise in regards to subjectivity / identity formation. If identity formation is positioned as a discursive process, whereby identities are formed through language and the stories people tell about themselves, then narrative analysis would allow me to analyse this process. As such, narratives do not await discovery by researchers, but are co-created among participants and researchers out of oral renditions when people tell stories about their experiences (i.e., through interviews, conversations, speeches) and tell stories about events (see Riessman, 2007, for an overview of narrative approaches).

Location	One-on-one interviews: Text data and ethnographic observations	Conference and meeting attendees: Ethnographic observations
California	◆ Ismail, male, 55 years old, bachelors degree, US and Turkish citizenship ◆ Fatih, male, 50 years old, PhD, US and Turkish citizenship ◆ Baris, male, 34 years old, MBA, Turkish citizenship ◆ Cem, male, 45 years old, PhD, US and Turkish citizenship ◆ Kemal, male, 31 years old, bachelors, Turkish citizenship ◆ Hakan, male, 36 years old, PhD, US and Turkish citizenship ◆ Tamer, male, 42 years old, PhD, US and Turkish citizenship ◆ Selim, male, 54 years old, PhD, US and Turkish citizenship	◆ About 200 attendees at each of the TABC conferences from 2005 to 2007 ◆ About 20-25 individuals at First Thursday meetings in 2005

Location	One-on-one interviews: Text data and ethnographic observations	Conference and meeting attendees: Ethnographic observations
Istanbul and Ankara, Turkey	♦ Bora, male, 40 years old, bachelors degree, Turkish citizenship ♦ Murat, male, 48 years old, bachelors., US and Turkish citizenship ♦ Osman, male, 46 years old, PhD, Turkish citizenship ♦ Zeynep, female, 45 years old, bachelors, Turkish citizenship ♦ Turgut, male, 59 years old, PhD, Turkish and German citizenship ♦ Alp, male, 47 years old, MBA, Turkish citizenship ♦ Semra, female, 50 years old, PhD, US and Turkish citizenship	♦ About 150 attendees during the Sinerjiturk conference

Table 4.3: Summary of Fieldwork Participants and Types of Data Gathered

I took the following steps in order to uncover identity formation processes. First, all audio recordings were transcribed into text format in the original language of the interview. In addition, fieldnotes based on conversations and behaviours and practices that I observed during participant observation, as well as materials from websites and conference proceedings (such as PowerPoints and handouts), were all recorded on paper and thus turned into written texts that could be read and analysed.

One important issue here is whether selves, ideas, concepts, and practices articulated through one language can be translated or made sense of in another, as postcolonial frameworks foreground the limits and, at times, impossibility of cultural translations and epistemological impositions. Nonetheless, translations were still necessary when using direct quotes given that I am writing in English for an international management audience. Such translations, when I used them, were verified by my contact at Istanbul's Sabanci University, who is a native Turkish speaker. Thus, part of the methodological concern in this study is *how* to translate and whether such translations (i.e., conceptual equivalence) are possible, despite the researcher's claims to be able to translate. Based on postcolonial frameworks, translation is not merely a methodological issue, but also a concern over researcher reflexivity and subaltern agency. Whose interpretation is valid? Whose voices have a say when 'the native speaker' can no longer speak as a native?

UNDERSTANDING OF FINDINGS GAINED THROUGH THIS RESEARCH

Having carried out the fieldwork, what can be said about postcolonial lenses and their contributions to IM theory and research? What about my own experiences in this project? Along the way, what seemed self-evident in terms of who I was and what my role would be in the fieldwork (i.e., business scholar) was challenged in different ways, particularly as I came to understand better what postcolonial analyses could illuminate about my own experiences. The notion of the native-self returning to her home nation to collect data on people-like-her never existed – instead, what I experienced and wrote about was the emergence of a hybrid gendered self that denied such an innocent return. The place I came to understand as home was not a stagnant and static nation, but, rather, my 'return' was much more akin to a dislocated state of being.

These attempts to 'get out' or 'become someone / something else' bring me to a concern I had over whether I was a tourist, a native, a traveller, or someone else in the research process. I never figured this one out, but understood that who I became during the different encounters was not necessarily out of choice as I had imagined – at times, I did not have the choice about which position I occupied, about which voice I had to speak from, and about which place I represented. Reflexivity in practice was much more difficult than I had imagined – there was no gauge to tell me that I had been reflexive or a moment where I felt comfortable doing the research reflexively. Moving back and forth among nations is an exhaustive process, physically, emotionally and epistemologically. Attempting to study this process as it relates to identity formation and exemplifies complex and contradictory processes of globalisation through the lens of the international entrepreneur is a much more difficult task than leaving one location and showing up in another; it necessitates examining displacement and placement, which cannot be done with the existing approach in the international entrepreneurship literature. This being said, to actually drop my theoretical tools and pick up another set was perhaps the most difficult challenge I faced in this research project.

The theoretical positions of Bhabha, Spivak, and Said each allowed for a distinct view of how identity formation processes take place in the context of globalisation. To clarify, Bhabha's postcolonial concerns establish that different hybrid selves take form in different sites of encounters between the West and the Rest. Moreover, his lens depicts how hybridity allows for a particular kind of resistance against mimetic impositions of ideas that dictate how individuals should understand themselves and particular practices – in the case of Turkish high-technology entrepreneurs, different hybrids evolved that were inevitably called the same name: Turkish-American. Yet, becoming Turkish-American looked different in Silicon Valley than it did in Turkey, depending on the site of encounter (i.e., Silicon Valley, TABCON conference, Turkey, Sinerjiturk conference) and the relational role of the individual in that encounter. The hybrid self emerged as a way to refuse the gaze of the West that had immobilised Turkey and Turkish entrepreneurs in a position they did not want to occupy: not known for their innovation and technology production. Yet, being Turkish was a slippery slope as how individuals understood what being Turkish meant changed with the particular context they were negotiating. Equally important was the fact that what or who was considered the embodiment of that immobilising Western gaze changed. For example, the excerpt below from an interview highlights how identities shift in the context of global encounters:

> **Ismail:** There was so much that both countries have given you that at some point, maybe I would identify myself as Turkish-American with the emphasis on the Turkish side. But depends on where I am. Here in the US, I'm Turkish-American and overseas, everybody knows that I'm from Turkey. But they look at me as American, not as Turkish.
>
> **BOP:** How about in Turkey, would you say you're Amerikali Turk (the American Turk)? Or how would you?
>
> **Ismail:** Except when I'm with my mother. People also look at me, too, except few friends that I still have that they may still see me as I was rather than Amerikali Turk (the American Turk).

BOP: But not your mother?

Ismail: Yeah, she doesn't want to see it any other way.

BOP: Just the Turk?

Ismail: Yeah.

Another example of shifting selves or identities is the following:

BOP: how would you identify yourself?

Semra: Well, that's a tough question. If I wanted that – because I lived 25 years in the US – when I went to US, I was 24, 25 years old, and then I lived 25 years there, so my life is almost – well, now considering I'm two more years, maybe I'm more Turkish now. It's sort of my adulthood, raising my child, enjoying income, having a career, building a career. Everything happened there, so the real enjoyment of life and learning to be a citizen, voting, understanding politics, and everything else as an adult happened there, so the aspect of – and I'm an American citizen, that is very American, and that will stay as it is, but there's also the cultural aspect. Being born here, raised by a Turkish family, learning my first language in Turkish, the culture, the religion, all the aspects of my upbringing, that brings that Turkish in me, so I have both identities, and can identify with both of them. I go to the US, I am the perfect US citizen. I come here, and I'm almost the perfect Turkish citizen … the company I'm in actually is very different than the rest of Turkey. We're like a little America here. It's an adventure.

In contrast, Said's focus on historic power relations among nations allowed for consideration of how relational identities form differently in Silicon Valley and Turkey. In Silicon Valley, Turkish high-technology entrepreneurs attempted to get out of the Orientalised position they were put in through visa status and the ethnic immigrant label associated with them by Orientalising others. This was accomplished by differentiating themselves from other Turks, other ethnicities in Silicon Valley, and through a cultural / political identification of self as 'technologically capable' in the context of ongoing US / Turkish geopolitical and economic relations. For example, one of the Orientalising discourses that enabled the Turkish identity to form was accomplished in reference to a Mexican identity. Individuals described themselves as a Turk by saying that they were not undocumented, which in the context of California meant not Mexican. One example of this is Kemal, who was having difficulty obtaining a green card but had nonetheless formed his own start-up while working for a major technology corporation in Silicon Valley. When I asked what being a Turkish entrepreneur meant, he stated:

> What does it mean? Well it means, do you mean my visa status?
> [laughs] It annoys the hell out of me, 'coz I can't do much. I have a
> company which I can't work for in reality, I can own the company, I can
> be a stakeholder but I can't work for the company, I have to hire people
> ... Right now, I'm here with an H1-B, so it's sponsored so that means
> I'm a slave of some corporation. I find the green card process
> humiliating, I don't know, I resisted it, I don't know, I've been offered it
> two times.

This situation of being unable to get a green card when he wants to be
documented as a legal immigrant who could work for his own corporation
was complicated by the fact that he saw himself as different from the
Others, the 'undocumented' people in California. In effect, he was trying to
get out of an Orientalised position by Orientalising another group of
people: the Mexicans as 'undocumented' workers.

In Turkey, entrepreneurial identity formation occurred in relation to
the West as Turkish entrepreneurs tried to overcome hegemonic Western
high-technology business knowledge that Orientalised business practices
in Turkey. As such, through Said's lens, entrepreneurial identity formation
processes needed to be seen as cultural / political acts of agency, and at
times acts of resistance to Orientalism, that highlighted how and why it
was necessary to position oneself as Turkish or Turkish-American,
depending on the context of national relations between the US, Turkey,
and other nations (i.e., EU, Turkey-Greece-Armenia, US-Mexico). In this
sense, globalisation did not mark the separation of nations, as implied by
the 'cultural differences' approach to identity formation. Rather,
entrepreneurial identity formation processes highlighted that context is
relevant for understanding how and why different identities emerged in
Silicon Valley and in Turkey (e.g., Tsui, 2007). Further, it also highlighted
that 'context' is an ongoing process as well, in this case, as the
interdependence of nations.

In contrast, Spivak's concerns over gender, subalternity and the
postcolonial subject allowed for an examination of how gendering and
subalternity functioned differently in different sites of encounters. As a
site, Silicon Valley enabled the formation of a macho male culture (i.e.,
Young Turks), which became associated with high-technology
entrepreneurship. This took place by silencing the Other of young, male
high-technology entrepreneurs: women and older men. In contrast, the
issue of women and gender was immediately articulated in the Turkish
context, where the subaltern spoke back to the masculinity associated with

the high-technology sector. Moreover, gendered practices of high-technology work came to light in distinct ways in Silicon Valley and Turkey, but were both nonetheless inscribed, albeit differently, in a broader context of global competition, division of labour, and 24-hour production cycles for high-technology goods and services. For example, based on my interviews, men have to work long hours in order to become high-technology entrepreneurs. These long hours are only possible if the spouse is assumed to be responsible for the family. Yet, how these high-technology selves emerge is not only based on the gendered assumptions about how to or who can become an entrepreneur – high-technology entrepreneurship already assumes a particular global division of labour that places Silicon Valley as the centre of technology innovation and the rest of the world as potential places for low-cost outsourcing. This global division of labour allows for US firms to stay competitive, as high-technology workers outside the US complete the job. Thus, the global division of high-technology is based on those nations that produce the innovation versus those that manufacture it. These activities are documented in the following ways:

> **Hakan:** Most of the work is done outside the country, we have, we outsource to two, three different teams in Russia, in three different cities actually, three in India, two in Pakistan, about two in Ukraine and one is about to go to China, oh, one is in Romania, so this, but getting the work done there is the cheapest thing you can imagine … as a start-up you have to watch out for resources and the money, how you spend, so they do good work, they do much better work than people here, they work hard, those people, and they are, actually managing them is easier, they're scattered and they don't have actual offices here, they finish their work … so most of the work here is integration and testing, things related to customer side here, other than that, the work is distributed.

In effect, global flows of capital (FDI) and labour (outsourcing) enabled Silicon Valley to become *the* place of technology and innovation and for Turkey to be left out. Within this context, the gendered high-technology entrepreneurial self in Silicon Valley emerged by disavowing spouse and family, while simultaneously subalternising high-technology entrepreneurship in Turkey as 'behind.'

Thus, each of the lenses highlights a distinct way of understanding identity formation processes and globalisation as processes taking place through encounters of people and ideas. Yet using each of these postcolonial frameworks separately does not imply that these processes are taking place separately at one point or another, depending on which lens one uses. Rather, these lenses also highlight that globalisation is a contradictory process, such that there is no neat set of ideas one can use to study it. In effect, it is impossible to use each lens one after another as if they were nested—the assumptions about self, translation, and resistance under each of the lenses are at times at odds with one another. Thus, what can be learned from these lenses that could be useful for international management?

CONCLUSION

Among one of the important issues that arise when conducting qualitative work is how to carry out the fieldwork, including questions on which methods to use, how to make sure these methods of choice are appropriate for the theoretical framing of the research project, and how these methods will help you address the research questions posed. To this end, there is no postcolonial method. Rather, researchers are reminded that the choice of methods depends very much on the meta-theoretical assumptions, theoretical framing, and research questions guiding the research project. Carrying out fieldwork based on postcolonial concerns is about realizing the political and gendered complexities of entering the field and the repercussions of representing people and their practices through particular lenses.

Equally relevant is the fact that postcolonial contributions to international management emanate from the complexity and contradictions they highlight, rather than from providing neat, stacked lenses. That is, postcolonial frameworks not only challenge assumptions about international management theory and research, but the very notion of what kind of research can be produced. In this sense, research context is not about including more variables or more levels of analysis (see Oviatt & McDougall, 2005). Based on postcolonial concerns, it is not, as Rousseau & Fried (2001: 11) suggest, possible to contextualise international research based on three tiers, including rich description of the setting, followed by analysis of contextual effects, and finally, through comparative studies in order to highlight 'powerful institutional and cultural differences'. In other words, postcolonial frameworks make impossible the micro, macro, and meso approaches or the level of analysis argument, as these arguments, more generally, prevent understanding the full complexity of business phenomena, particularly in the context of globalisation (see Kyriakidou & Ozbilgin, 2006).

Postcolonial frameworks highlight that 'the production of theory is in fact a very important practice that is worlding the world in a certain way' (Spivak 1990: 7). They also make relevant that ethico-political considerations are part of producing theory, particularly in international management, as the imposition of Western management concepts and the circulation of Western business ideas can end up colonising, and thus silencing, those very ideas and practices non-West scholars claim to value. Postcolonial work, then, attempts to dismantle this 'desire for a reformed, recognizable Other, as a subject of a difference that is almost the same, but not quite' (Bhabha, 1994: 86). In this sense, postcolonial research projects are always political and attempt to 'make concurrent those views and experiences that are ideologically and culturally closed to each other and that attempt to distance / suppress other views and experiences' (Said, 1993: 33). Altogether, thus, this research was a political project that attempted to speak back and recover (however problematically) the right to speak about 'the self' by rearticulating it, such that it fully questions the terms under which representation and knowledge have taken shape in the international management field as we know it. How 'the other selves' would reclaim the field is another project waiting to be written.

REFERENCES

Academy of Management Journal. (2000). 'Special Research Forum: International Entrepreneurship: The Intersection of Two Research Paths', 43(5): 902-1003.

Adler, N.J. & Graham, J.L. (1989). 'Cross-Cultural Interaction: The International Comparison Fallacy?', *Journal of International Business Studies* 20(3): 515-37.

Adler, R.H. (2002). 'Patron-Client Ties, Ethnic Entrepreneurship & Transnational Migration: The Case of Yucatecans in Dallas, Texas', *Urban Anthropology & Studies of Cultural Systems & World Economic Development* 31(2): 129-61.

Appadurai, A. (1988). 'Introduction: Place and Voice in Anthropological Authority', *Cultural Anthropology* 3(1): 16-20.

Banerjee, S.B. & Linstead, S. (2001). 'Globalization, Multiculturalism and Other Fictions: Colonialism for the New Millennium?', *Organisation* 8(4): 683-722.

Bhabha, H.K. (1990a). 'Introduction', in Bhabha, H.K. (ed), *Nation and Narration*, pp. 1-7. New York, NY: Routledge.

Bhabha, H.K. (1990b). 'DissemiNation: Time, Narrative & the Margins of the Modern Nation', in Bhabha, H.K. (ed), *Nation and Narration*, pp. 291-322. New York, NY: Routledge.

Bhabha, H.K. (1994). *The Location of Culture*. New York, NY: Routledge.

Bartol, K.M., Martin, D.C. & Kromkowski, J.A. (2003). 'Leadership and the Glass Ceiling: Gender and Ethnic Group Influences on Leader Behaviors at Middle & Executive Managerial Levels', *Journal of Leadership & Organization Studies* 9(3): 8-19.

Black, B. (1999). 'National Culture and High Commitment Management', *Employee Relations* 21(4): 389-404.

Blyton, P. (2001). 'The General and the Particular in Cross-National Comparative Research', *Applied Psychology: An International Review* 50(4): 590-95.

Boyacıgiller, N.A. & Adler, N.J. (1991). 'The Parochial Dinosaur: Organisational Science in a Global Context', *Academy of Management Review* 16(2): 262-90.

Boyacıgiller, N.A., Kleinberg, J., Phillips, M.E. & Sackmann, S.A. (2004). 'Conceptualizing Culture: Elucidating the Streams of Research in International Cross-Cultural Management', in Punnett, B.J. & Shenkar, O. (eds), *Handbook for International Management Research*, 2nd ed, pp. 99-167. Ann Arbor, MI: University of Michigan Press.

Buzard, J. (2003). 'On Auto-Ethnographic Authority', *The Yale Journal of Criticism* 16(1): 61-91.

Calás, M.B. (1992). 'An / Other Silent Voice? Representing "Hispanic Woman" in Organisational Texts', in Mills, A.J. & Tancred, P. (eds), *Gendering Organisational Analysis*, pp. 201–21. Newbury Park, CA: Sage.

Castells, M. (1996). *The Rise of the Network Society*. Malden, MA: Blackwell.

Chio, V.C.M. (2005). *Malaysia and the Development Process: Globalization, Knowledge Transfers and Postcolonial Dilemmas*. London: Routledge.

Clifford, J. (1992). 'Traveling Cultures', in Grossberg, L., Nelson, C. & Treichler, P. (eds), *Cultural Studies*, pp. 96-116. New York, NY: Routledge.

Czarniawska, B. (2004). *Narratives in Social Science Research*. Thousand Oaks, CA: Sage.

Denzin, N.K. & Giardina, M.D. (2008). *Qualitative Inquiry & the Politics of Evidence*. Walnut Creek, CA: Left Coast Press.

d'Iribarne, P. (2002). 'Motivating Workers in Emerging Countries: Universal Tools and Local Adaptations', *Journal of Organisational Behavior* 23(3): 243-56.

Doktor, R., Tung, R.L. & Von Glinow, M.A. (1991a). 'Incorporating International Dimensions in Management Theory Building', *Academy of Management Review* 16(2): 259-61.

Doktor, R., Tung, R.L. & Von Glinow, M.A. (1991b). 'Future Directions for Management Theory Development', *Academy of Management Review* 16(2): 362-65.

Earley, P.C. & Singh, H. (eds) (2000). *Innovations in International & Cross-Cultural Management*. Thousand Oaks, CA: Sage.

Entrepreneurship Theory & Practice. (forthcoming 2010). 'International Entrepreneurship: Do Institutions Matter?' (special issue).

Frenkel, M. (2008). 'The Multinational Corporation as a Third Space: Rethinking International Management Discourse on Knowledge Transfer Through Homi Bhabha', *Academy of Management Review* 33(4): 924-42.

Frenkel, M. & Shenhav, Y. (2003). 'From Americanization to Colonization: The Diffusion of Productivity Models Revisited', *Organisation Studies* 24(9): 1537-61.

Frenkel, M. & Shenhav, Y. (2006). 'From Binarism Back to Hybridity: A Postcolonial Reading of Management and Organisation Studies', *Organisation Studies* 27(6): 855-76.

Gamble, P.R. & Gibson, D.A. (1999). 'Executive Values and Decision-making: The Relationship of Culture & Information Flows', *Journal of Management Studies* 36(2): 217-40.

Geertz, C. (1983). *Local Knowledge: Further Essays in Interpretive Anthropology*. New York, NY: Basic Books.

Gibson, C.B. (1995). 'An Investigation of Gender Differences in Leadership Across Four Countries', *Journal of International Business* 26(2): 255-79.

Hannerz, U. (1996). *Transnational Connections: Culture, People, Places*. New York, NY: Routledge.

Hansen, H. (2006). 'The Ethnonarrative Approach', *Human Relations* 59: 1049-75.

Hardt, M. & Negri, A. (2000). *Empire*. Cambridge, MA: Harvard University Press.

Hardt, M. & Negri, A. (2004). *Multitude: War & Democracy in the Age of Empire*. New York, NY: Penguin Press.

Hofstede, G. (1980). *Culture's Consequences: International Differences in Work-Related Values*. Thousand Oaks, CA: Sage.

Hofstede, G. (1998). 'Attitudes, Values & Organisational Culture: Disentangling the Concepts', *Organisation Studies* 19(3): 477-92.

Hofstede, G. & Bond, M.H. (1988). 'The Confucius Connection: From Cultural Roots to Economic Growth', *Organisational Dynamics* 16(4): 5-21.

Hofstede, G., Van Deusen, C.A., Mueller, C.B., Charles, T.A. & The Business Goals Network (2002). 'What Goals do Business Leaders Pursue? A Study in 15 Countries', *Journal of International Business Studies* 33(4): 785-803.

House, R., Javidan, M. & Dorman, P. (2001). 'Project GLOBE: An Introduction', *Applied Psychology: An International Review* 50(4): 489-505.

Huo, Y.P., Huang, H.J. & Napier, N.K. (2002). 'Divergence or Convergence: A Cross-National Comparison of Personnel Selection Practices', *Human Resource Management* 41(1): 31-44.

Jack, G. & Westwood, R. (2006). 'Postcolonialism and the Politics of Qualitative Research in International Business', *Management International Review* 46(4): 481-501.

JIBS (2006). 'An Exchange Between Hofstede and GLOBE', *Journal of International Business Studies* 37(6): 881-931.

Kashima, Y., Yamaguchi, S., Kim, U., Choi, S., Gelfand, M.J. & Masaki. Y. (1995). 'Culture, Gender and Self: A Perspective from Individualism-Collectivism Research', *Journal of Personality and Social Psychology* 69(5): 925-37.

Khan, S. (2005). 'Reconfiguring the Native Informant: Positionality in the Global Age', *Signs: Journal of Women in Culture & Society* 30(4): 2017-35.

Khanna, T. & Palepu, K.G. (2004). 'Globalization and Convergence in Corporate Governance: Evidence from Infosys and the Indian Software Industry', *Journal of International Business Studies* 35: 484-507.

Kirkman, B.L. & Law, K. (2005). 'From the Editors: International Management Research in the AMJ: Our Past, Present and Future', *Academy of Management Journal* 48(3): 377-86.

Kirkman, B.L. & Shapiro, D.L. (2001). 'The Impact of Cultural Values on Job Satisfaction and Organisational Commitment in Self-Managing Work Teams: The Mediating Role of Employee Resistance', *Academy of Management Journal* 44(3): 557-69.

Kovach Jr., R.C. (1994). 'Matching Assumptions to Environment in the Transfer of Management Practices', *International Studies of Management & Organisation* 24(4): 83-99.

Kropp, F. & Zolin, R. (2005). 'Technological Entrepreneurship and Small Business Innovation Research Programs', *Academy of Marketing Science Review* 7: 1-14.

Kuehn, K.W. & Al-Busaidi, Y. (2000). 'A Difference of Perspective: An Exploratory Study of Omani and Expatriate Values and Attitudes', *International Journal of Commerce & Management* 10(1): 74-90.

Kurman, J. (2001). 'Self-Regulation Strategies in Achievement Strategies: Culture and Gender Differences', *Journal of Cross-Cultural Psychology* 32(4): 491-503.

Kwek, D. (2003). 'Decolonizing and *Re*-presenting Culture's Consequences: A Postcolonial Critique of Cross-Cultural Studies in Management', in Prasad, A. (ed), *Postcolonial Theory and Organisational Analysis*, pp. 121-46. New York, NY: Palgrave Macmillan.

Kyriakidou, O. & Ozbilgin, M.F. (eds) (2006). *Relational Perspectives in Organisation Studies.* Northampton, MA: Edward Elgar.

Lal, J. (1996). 'Situating Locations: The Politics of Self, Identity and "Other" in Living and Writing the Text', in Wolf, D.L. (ed), *Feminist Dilemmas in Fieldwork*, pp. 185-214. Boulder, CO: Westview Press.

Lee, C., Pillutla, M. & Law, K .S. (2000). 'Power-Distance, Gender and Organisational Justice', *Journal of Management* 26(4): 685-704.

Lee, H. (1999). 'Transformation of Employment Practices in Korean Business', *International Studies of Management & Organisation* 28(4): 26-39.

Leung, K., Bhagat, R.S., Buchan, N.R., Erez, M. & Gibson, C.B. (2005). 'Culture & International Business: Recent Advances and Their Implications for Future Research', *Journal of International Business Studies* 36: 357-78.

Lowe, K.B., Milliman, J., De Cieri, H. & Dowling, P.D. (2002). 'International Compensation Practices: A 10-Country Comparative Analysis', *Human Resource Management* 41(1): 45-66.

Massey, D.S., Arango, J., Hugo, G., Kouaouci, A., Pellegrino, A. & Taylor, J.E. (1999) *Worlds in Motion: Understanding International Migration at the End of the Millennium*. Oxford: Clarendon Press.

McDougall, P.P. & Oviatt, B.M. (2000). 'International Entrepreneurship: The Intersection of Two Research Paths', *Academy of Management Journal* 43(5): 902-6.

Mir, R., Mir, A. & Upadhyaya, P. (2003). 'Toward a Postcolonial Reading of Organisational Control', in Prasad, A. (ed), *Postcolonial Theory & Organisational Analysis: A Critical Engagement*, pp. 47-74. New York, NY: Palgrave.

Moulettes, A. (2007). 'The Absence of Women's Voices in Hofstede's "Cultural Consequences": A Postcolonial Reading', *Women in Management Review* 22(6): 443-55.

Oliver, E.G. & Cravens, K.S. (1999). 'Cultural Influences on Managerial Choice: An Empirical Study of Employee Benefit Plans in the United States', *Journal of International Business Studies* 30(4): 745-62.

Oviatt, B.M. & McDougall, P.P. (2005). 'Defining International Entrepreneurship and Modeling the Speed of Internalization', *Entrepreneurship Theory & Practice* 29: 537-53.

Özkazanç-Pan, B. (2008). 'International Management Meets "the Rest of the World"', *Academy of Management Review* 33(4): 964-74.

Pieterse, J.N. (1994). 'Globalisation as Hybridisation', *International Sociology* 9(2): 161-84.

Prasad, A. (ed) (2003). *Postcolonial Theory and Organisational Analysis*. New York, NY: Palgrave Macmillan.

Prasad, P. (2003a). 'The Return of the Native: Organisational Discourse and the Legacy of the Ethnographic Imagination', in Prasad, A. (ed), *Postcolonial Theory & Organisational Analysis*, pp. 149-70. New York, NY: Palgrave Macmillan.

Ramamoorthy, N. & Carroll, S.J. (1998). 'Individualist / Collectivism Orientations and Reactions Towards Alternative Human Resource Management Practices', *Human Relations* 51(5): 571-88.

Riessman, C.K. (2007). *Narrative Methods for the Human Sciences*. Thousand Oaks, CA: Sage.

Rousseau, D.M. & Fried, Y. (2001). 'Location, Location, Location: Contextualizing Organisational Research', *Journal of Organisational Behavior* 22(1): 1-13.

Said, E.W. (1978). *Orientalism*. New York, NY: Random House.

Said, E.W. (1985). 'Orientalism Reconsidered', *Race & Class* 27(2), Institute of Race Relations. Reprint in 2000, *Reflections on Exile and Other Essays*, pp. 198-215. Cambridge, MA: Harvard University Press.

Said, E.W. (1988). 'Representing the Colonized: Anthropology's Interlocutors', *Critical Inquiry* 15. Reprint in 2000, *Reflections on Exile & Other Essays*, pp. 293-316. Cambridge, MA: Harvard University Press.

Said, E.W. (1991). 'The Politics of Knowledge', *Raritan: A Quarterly Review*, 2(1). Reprint in 2000, *Reflections on Exile and Other Essays*, pp. 372-85. Cambridge, MA: Harvard University Press.

Said, E.W. (1993a). 'Nationalism, Human Rights and Interpretation', in Polhemus, R.M. & Henkle, R.B. (eds), *Critical Reconstructions: The Relationship of Fiction and Life*. Stanford, CA: Stanford University Press. Reprint in 2000, *Reflections on Exile and Other Essays*, pp. 411-35. Cambridge, MA: Harvard University Press.

Said, E.W. (1993b). 'Wild Orchids and Trotsky: Messages from American Universities', interview with Mark Edmundson in Viswanathan, G. (ed) (2001), *Power, Politics & Culture. Interviews with Edward W. Said*, pp. 164-82. New York, NY: Pantheon Books.

Said, E.W. (1993c). *Culture and Imperialism*. New York, NY: Routledge.

Said, E.W. (2000). 'The Clash of Definitions: On Samuel Huntington', in *Reflections on Exile & Other Essays*, pp. 569-90. Cambridge, MA: Harvard University Press

Schiller, N.G., Basch, L. & Blanc, C.S. (1995). 'From Immigrant to Transmigrant: Theorizing Transnational Migration', *Anthropological Quarterly* 68(1): 48-63.

Shenkar, O. (2004). 'One More Time: International Business in a Global Economy', *Journal of International Business Studies* 35: 161-71.

Soedarsono, A.A., Murray, S.L. & Omurtag, Y. (1998). 'Productivity Improvement at a High-Technology State-Owned Industry – An Indonesian Case Study of Employee Motivation', *IEEE Transactions on Engineering Management* 45(4): 388-95.

Sokefeld, M. (1999). 'Debating Self, Identity and Culture in Anthropology', *Current Anthropology* 40(4): 417-31.

Spivak, G.C. (1985a). 'Feminism and Critical Theory', in Treichler, P.A., Kramarae, C. & Stafford, B. (eds), *For Alma Mater: Theory and Practice in Feminist Scholarship*, pp. 119-152. Urbana, IL: University of Illinois Press. Reprint 1987 in *In Other Worlds*, pp. 77-92. New York, NY: Routledge.

Spivak, G.C. (1985b). 'Scattered Speculations on the Question of Value', *Diacritics* 15(4): 73-93. Reprint 1987 in *In Other Worlds*, pp.154-175. New York, NY: Routledge.

Spivak, G.C. (1985c). 'Subaltern Studies: Deconstructing Historiography', in Guha, R. (ed), *Subaltern Studies IV*, pp. 330-363. New Delhi: Oxford University Press. Reprint 1987 in *In Other Worlds*, pp. 197-221. New York, NY: Routledge.

Spivak, G.C. (1987). *In Other Worlds: Essays in Cultural Politics*. New York, NY: Routledge.

Spivak, G.C. (1988). 'Can the Subaltern Speak?', in Nelson, C. & Grossberg, L. (eds), *Marxism & the Interpretation of Culture*, pp. 271-313. Urbana, IL: University of Illinois Press.

Spivak, G.C. (1990). Interview in Harasym, S. (ed), *The Post-Colonial Critic: Interviews, Strategies, Dialogues with Gayatri Chakravorty Spivak*. New York, NY: Routledge.

Spivak, G.C. (1996). Interview in Landry, D. & MacLean, G. (eds), *The Spivak Reader*. New York, NY: Routledge.

Spivak, G.C. (1999). *A Critique of Postcolonial Reason: Toward a History of the Vanishing Present*. Cambridge, MA: Harvard University Press.

Triandis, H.C. (1983). 'Dimensions of Cultural Variation as Parameters of Organisational Theories', *International Studies of Management & Organisation* 12(4): 139-69.

Triandis, H.C. & Suh, E.M. (2002). 'Cultural Influences on Personality', *Annual Review of Psychology* 53: 133-60.

Trompenaars, F. (1996). 'Resolving International Conflict: Culture and Business Strategy', *Business Strategy Review* 7(3): 51-68.

Tsui, A.S. (2007). 'From Homogenization to Pluralism: International Management Research in the Academy and Beyond', *Academy of Management Journal* 50(6): 1353-64.

Tsui, A.S., Nifadkar, S.S. & Ou, A.Y. (2007). 'Cross-National, Cross-Organisational Behavior Research: Advances, Gaps and Recommendations', *Journal of Management* 33(3): 426-78.

Yousef, D.A. (1998). 'Predictors of Decision-Making Styles in a Non-Western Country', *Leadership & Organization Development Journal* 19(7): 366-73.

Zahra, S.A. & George, G. (2002). 'International Entrepreneurship: The Current Status of the Field and Future Research Agenda', in Hitt, M.A., Ireland, R.D., Camp, S.M. & Sexton, D.L. (eds), *Strategic Entrepreneurship: Creating a New Mindset*, pp. 255-82. Malden, MA: Blackwell.

Zander, L. & Romani, L. (2004). 'When Nationality Matters: A Study of Departmental, Hierarchical, Gender and Age-Based Employee Groupings' Leadership Preferences Across 15 Countries', *International Journal of Cross-Cultural Management* 4(3): 291-315.

CHAPTER 5
RESEARCHING THE 'DOING' OF GENDER, WORK-FAMILY & ENTREPRENEURSHIP: METHODOLOGICAL CONSIDERATIONS

Kristina A. Bourne

INTRODUCTION

There is an extensive body of qualitative inquiry literature (e.g., Denzin & Lincoln, 2000; Merriam, 2002; Patton, 1990; Rossman & Rallis, 1998; Silverman, 2000; Wolcott, 1994). Denzin & Lincoln (2000) point out that the design of any 'qualitative' study will be shaped by the philosophical underpinnings of the chosen theoretical orientation. Interpretive researchers begin with the notion that reality is socially-constructed and they aim to map out this process. They focus on words, artefacts, behaviours, and symbols, trying to explain the process of everyday life.

In Bourne (2006), I bring two interpretive schools of thought, symbolic interactionism and ethnomethodology, together with socialist feminist theory to examine the construction and re-construction of 'work' and 'family' as separate and attend to the gendering of entrepreneurship in the everyday life of women who work as entrepreneurs. This context is interesting because entrepreneurship has been positioned as a way for women to bridge the assumed fissure between work and family. Their lives are where work and family are 'allowed' to overlap as the best-case scenario of 'work-family balance', because it is assumed they have the freedom to organize their business policies, practices, and everyday life as they choose.

My empirical questions are: How do women business owners 'do' work-family? How do women who own small businesses negotiate the contradictions and ambiguities of what is 'business' and what is 'family' in their everyday life? How do they, and the people with whom they interact, sustain particular definitions of situations as business / not business, family / not family, work / not home, and home / not work? How is the 'social fact' of work and family as separate produced? What are the tensions that arise in trying to sustain this separation? Furthermore, how are their reality-constituting practices embedded in gendered processes that shape their everyday activity?

In this chapter, I describe the theoretical framework that underpins my study's (Bourne, 2006) methodological approach and provide a lens through which to view and interpret the phenomena of gender, entrepreneurship, and work-family. After that, I explain how I located, selected, and gained access to the lives of the 10 women business owners. Next, I discuss the strategies I used to gather and document the data. Then, I review my data management and analysis techniques. Finally, in the conclusion, I talk briefly about my findings.

TOWARDS A GENDERED STUDY OF WORK-FAMILY IN ENTREPRENEURSHIP

My point of departure is in the 'doing of gender.' In this perspective, women and men 'do' gender, not as a passive response to genetics or socialization, but, actively in social interactions. Gender is something individuals perform (Butler, 1990) and accomplish on a daily basis (West & Zimmerman, 1987). Specifically, I draw from the gendering of organisational analysis literature and feminist epistemology to outline my theoretical framework (e.g., Acker, 1990, 1992, 1998, 2006; Calás & Smircich, 1992a, 1992b, 1996, 2006; Gherardi, 1995; Martin, 2001, 2003; Smith, 1987).

I begin from the standpoint that gender is a basic organising principle of society (Acker, 1992). Gender is a relational system based on the logic of difference: female and male are distinct categories with asymmetrical positions of power. Separating femaleness from maleness is an everyday aspect of our lives. Like most binaries, the male / female dichotomy has an underlying hierarchy based on power relations. Woman, female, femaleness, and femininity are often considered inferior to man, male, maleness and masculinity, regardless of the individual women and men under consideration (Rantalaiho *et al.*, 1997).

The macro social structure of the gender system of difference and asymmetrical power relations is interrelated with micro-processes and practices of human action. Smith (1987: 126), inspired by ethnomethodology, developed the socialist feminist analytical approach that begins from the assumption that social reality is not permanent; rather it is 'always in the making' and the way to understand this social construction of reality is to examine the on-going activities of actual people. She studies how everyday activities or 'practices' produce and reproduce social structures and relations.

Acker (1990, 1992) focuses on the gendering processes and practices in organisations. She outlines interacting processes that reproduce gendered social structures, based on the perceived differences between women and men. For example, the production of divisions along gender lines, like divisions of labour, where women and men work in different industries, different organisational levels, and different jobs, the construction of symbols and images that reinforce those gendered divisions, the interactions between individuals that enact dominance and submission, and the expression of individual identity through the presentation of self as a gendered member of an organisation (e.g., choice of appropriate dress).

Other organisational scholars have also attended the processes that constitute work as gendered. Gherardi (1995) examines gender as a symbolic process in the workplace. Martin (2001) explores the social consequences of men 'mobilizing masculinity' in organisations. She proposes that men use masculinity(ies) in work situations and 'conflate' these processes with work processes. For example, in work meetings, when men assert their knowledge and skill by vying with each other for attention and a chance to talk, they conflate this 'one-upping' as 'normal' work behaviour.

Acker (1992: 255) argues that these gendering processes produce and reproduce a gendered substructure of organisations. In her words:

> The gendered substructure lies in the spatial and temporal arrangements of work, in the rules prescribing workplace behavior, and in the relations linking workplaces to living places. These practices and relations, encoded in arrangements and rules, are supported by assumptions that work is separate from the rest of life and that it has first claim on the worker. Many people, particularly women, have difficulty making their daily lives fit these expectations and assumptions. As a consequence, today, there are two types of workers, those, mostly men, who, it is assumed, can adhere to organizational

rules, arrangements, and assumptions, and those, mostly women, who, it is assumed, cannot, because of other obligations to family and reproduction.

Thus, a socialist feminist perspective pays attention to how 'working' is often associated with waged labour and 'familying' is assumed to be outside of it. It shows that waged work is fundamentally thought of as 'men's' work and how domestic work is treated as 'women's' work, rendering it invisible. This two-sphere ideology often restricts women's involvement in economic activity and men's involvement in family. Further, a socialist feminist analysis shows how the social construction of masculinity and femininity is reinforced through the sexual division between production / work and procreation / family as well as within them. Finally, socialist feminist theorising questions the taken-for-granted assumption that these are factual separate / separable domains.

In order to study these processes and practices of 'doing gender' and 'doing work-family' in the entrepreneurial activities of women business owners, I turn to an interpretive approach, which requires the researcher to start from the concrete of the everyday.

AN INTERPRETIVE APPROACH

Much of the feminist work cited above (e.g., Gherardi, 1995; Smith, 1987; West & Zimmerman, 1987) has roots in the interpretive paradigm, especially symbolic interactionism and ethnomethodology. A central ontological and epistemological underpinning of this perspective is that social worlds are on-going processes created and re-created by the people in them (Berger & Luckmann, 1966). From this standpoint, social reality is understood as 'a network of assumptions and intersubjectively shared meanings' (Burrell & Morgan, 1979: 30). Thus, researchers drawing from this perspective are concerned with *how* social reality is constructed in everyday situations. Various schools of thought make up the interpretive paradigm (for review, see Burrell & Morgan, 1979), two of which, symbolic interactionism and ethnomethodology, support the approach taken in my research.

Symbolic Interactionism

According to Silverman (2000: 47), 'interactionism is concerned with the creation and change of symbolic orders via social interaction'. Specifically,

I draw on Goffman's (1961) concepts of 'definition of the situation' and 'frame.' To understand what is going on in a situation, individuals construct a reality, based on symbolic social interpretations. In other words, an individual constructs the meaning of an experience through interacting with other people. Thus, meaning is formed through, and arises out of, social interaction. Goffman (1961: 19) suggests 'instead of beginning by asking what happens when this definition of the situation breaks down, we can begin by asking what perspectives this definition of the situation excludes when it is being satisfactorily sustained'. In this sense, we 'frame' situations to sustain one definition of a situation, and not another, as it unfolds. By doing so, we construct our 'unshaking' sense of reality (Goffman, 1961: 30).

Ethnomethodology

Once we frame / define the situation, we then use methods to sustain the 'unshaking' sense of reality we have created. Thus, I turn to ethnomethodology, the detailed study of everyday life, which details the actual processes and methods through which social reality of the everyday is constructed and sustained (Gubrium & Holstein, 2000: 488). Within this perspective, everyday life is 'accorded the status of a miraculous achievement' (Burrell & Morgan, 1979: 31).

Garfinkel developed this approach when he broke away from several theoretical assumptions of his teacher, Talcott Parsons. According to Gubrium & Holstein (2000: 490), Garfinkel criticised Parsons' belief that social order was achieved through 'socially-integrating systems of norms and values', on the grounds that it treats people as 'cultural dopes who automatically respond to external social forces and internalized moral imperatives'. Garfinkel argued that people are not merely following external rules or internal moral directives, but are 'actively using them, thus working to give their world a sense of orderliness' (Gubrium & Holstein, 2000: 490). The main interest of ethnomethodology then becomes people's 'methods' for accomplishing and sustaining this sense of an orderly reality. Said differently, an ethnomethodological approach focuses on the 'ordinary constitutive work that produces the locally unchallenged appearance of stable realities' (Gubrium & Holstein, 2000: 490).

Underpinning this focus is the assumption that the social construction of reality does not occur effortlessly or flawlessly. Contradictions and tensions abound. It takes a tremendous amount of work to maintain a sense of orderliness. Emerson (1970) aptly points out that the reality of many situations is precarious because there are competing definitions present. For example, she investigates the contradictory definitions of reality in a gynaecological examination: one medical, one sexual. She argues that a situation where the definition of reality is fragile allows the details of maintaining that reality to be more obvious. In her study, it is easy to see how patients, nurses, and doctors work hard to keep the dominant definition, i.e., medical, sustained through routines, conventions, talk, humour, and décor.

Scholarship in the area of symbolic interactionism and ethnomethodology has theoretically and empirically examined gender as a performance. For example, Garfinkel's (1967) ethnomethodological case study of Agnes, a young man who has a sex change and wants to be accepted as a woman. The study documents how Agnes works to become a 'normal, natural female' in her day-to-day interactions and behaviour, accomplishing 'normal' sexuality. Likewise, West & Zimmerman (1987) theorise gender as an accomplishment. They base their work on Goffman's (1979) understanding of gender as a 'display.' He argues that individuals learn to 'display' gender in situations with 'appropriate' appearances and behaviours.

The specific framework for my study of gender, entrepreneurship and work-family, is premised, precisely, on these socialist feminist and social constructionist arguments. Below, I detail my methodological approach to the construction and re-construction of 'work' and 'family' as separate and attend to the gendered implications of such processes.

METHODOLOGY: STUDYING THE GENDERED 'WORK' OF WORK–FAMILY

Using the above conceptual insights as a starting point, my research brings us into the lives of 10 women who own and manage small businesses. Thus, the everyday lives of women are a window into the ways in which 'work' and 'family' get done. To reiterate, my broader research questions are: How do women who own small businesses negotiate the contradictions and ambiguities of what is 'business' and what is 'family' in their everyday life? How do they, and the people with whom they interact, sustain particular definitions of situations as business / not business and family / not family? How is the 'social fact' of work and family as separate produced? What are the tensions that arise in trying to sustain this separation? Furthermore, how are their reality-constituting practices embedded in gendered processes that shape their everyday activity?

Procedurally, to answer these *how* questions, I ask another set of questions: What really goes on in these women's lives? What do they actually do on a daily basis? What activities and interactions make up their day? How do they organize their days? Where are they when they do what they do? With whom do they interact? What are these interactions about? What is said? In what manner? With what gestures? And finally, how do they account for their actions and interactions? How do they describe their lives, what they are doing and why?

Traditional work-family research tends to separate experience from its social location. Attempting to go beyond this shortcoming, I tried to capture the doing of work-family and gender in the moment. Thus, in order to document the everyday life experiences of the participants, I chose the method of shadowing, allowing me to be present as their day unfolded.

The observation method of shadowing as a research technique in the entrepreneurship field has already been employed (e.g., Bruni *et al.*, 2004). Bruni *et al.* (2004: 411) assert that shadowing in this setting is appropriate because 'entrepreneurial action is one of those activities that is constantly constructed through daily routines. It does not have rigidly pre-established boundaries (spatial and temporal) and tends to eliminate the dichotomy between public and private'. Thus, learning from Emerson (1970), I see the lives of women entrepreneurs as a window into the precariousness of maintaining a distinct divide between work and family.

Another advantage of this technique is that it allowed me to observe the minute details of each woman's day, especially her interactions. The vast majority of entrepreneur research focuses entirely on the owner and rarely includes employees. In contrast, because I was interested in understanding processes that are produced through social relations and interactions, I paid attention to the various people with whom the owner interacts (e.g., employees, business partners, children, life partners, bankers, spouses, parents, friends, suppliers). Thus, shadowing gave a rich picture and a detailed account of what people do in their ordinary daily routines.

I shadowed each woman over a one-week period. I negotiated access to their daily lives, without asking them *a priori* to separate it into work and family. This means I 'tagged along' to all activities and experiences that made up most of the waking hours of their day.

APPROACH TO SAMPLING &
GAINING ACCESS

In this section, I describe how I located, selected, and gained access to the lives of these 10 women business owners. The purpose of my research was not to examine an exhaustive set of women business owners, but to gain considerable insight into the way some lived their lives. Thus, I chose a sample size of 10. Lewis (2003: 107) claims '[t]he sample does not need to be large enough to support statements of prevalence or incidence, since they are not the concern of qualitative research'. In fact, the sampling technique used in qualitative studies is a result of the topic under examination and the methodology selected, not by the desire to produce empirically-generalisable findings (Higginbottom, 2004). Ten participants allowed me to view a diversity of everyday life situations, to which I will turn next.

The sampling approach used in this study is purposive sampling (also known as criterion-based). According to Patton (1990: 169), the objective of purposive sampling is to choose 'information-rich cases' from which the researcher can learn in-depth about the phenomenon under study. It requires the conscious selection of certain subjects to include in the research. In other words, participants are selected with a 'purpose' to represent a phenomenon in relation to specific characteristics, often socio-demographic, particular knowledge or experiences of interest to the research phenomena (Lewis, 2003).

To explore the complexities of 'doing' life, I set out to secure a sample with diverse life situations. I paid close attention to ensure that the final sample represented 'work' and 'family' in many different forms. I began by thinking about the factors that might influence how women 'do' work-family, such as family composition, household arrangement, life stage, age, career trajectory, type of business and industry, and location of business.

My approach to defining the sample derived directly from my interpretive perspective in which the researcher does not predefine the meaning of the phenomena of interest. For example, it is common in work-family literature to focus on women (and sometimes men) who have young children. In contrast, I allowed 'family' to be defined by those who participated. Furthermore, the entrepreneurship literature tends to focus on businesses in high-growth industries, excluding women in businesses that are in predominately female-dominated industries. Because my interest was in examining how women 'balance' owning a business with their everyday lives, I focused on those who were at least 51 per cent owner of their business and were involved in its daily operation. The reasoning was that with this arrangement they were most likely to have the freedom to organise their business practices and everyday life as they chose. Moreover, I was interested in both owners who employ others and those who work alone. As my aim was to explore social relations, I recognized that even those who work alone live in relation to other people, whether family members, friends, suppliers, customers, etc. I also wanted to have a balance of those who ran their business from their homes and those who have offices at another location. Lastly, I wanted to have a variety of ages and life stages.

In this way, I was open to women of all ages and in various living situations, as well as business types. The combination of these different life situations provided a unique opportunity for observing and comparing the different ways of 'doing' work and family. What is more, the different life situations allowed me to study how the local contexts affected the ways women did work, family, and gender, while at the same time allowing for broader patterns from the socio-political environment to emerge. In short, in trying to re-theorise how we think about work and family, a diversity of life situations may offer a glimpse of another way of understanding.

In order to locate my sample, I compiled a list of women business owners from several sources: the state small business development centre, colleagues, friends, women business owner organisations and directories, newspaper articles and advertisements, community members, and participants. After initial contact via phone, email, or in person, I sent a follow-up letter to each potential participant describing my project and made a subsequent phone call to answer any questions. In all, I contacted 24 women.

Ultimately, I used the following variety of means to locate the final 10 women who participated. First, I contacted the director of the Small Business Development Center, a governmental agency promoting entrepreneurship through business-consulting services. Due to confidentiality, the director contacted clients first to query their interest and forwarded me the names of those who expressed interest in my project. From these leads, I secured three participants. Second, I announced my project both at the local annual women business owners' conference and a local women business owner organisation's breakfast meeting. From these venues, I confirmed three participants. Third, I secured three participants through cold calls, after 1) reading a newspaper article about women with kids starting businesses; 2) seeing an advertisement in a women's business directory; and 3) frequenting a shop and meeting the owner. Finally, one participant came as a referral from another participant.

Of the 14 who said "No" or declined to participate, four women did not return my call or email or left a message declining without any explanation. The others gave a variety of reasons. One woman thought I could 'get someone better' because she did not have a set schedule. Four said "No" due to business reasons. For example, a woman who worked as a personal coach felt it would be a problem with clients. Two explained that it was not good timing because of a major project launch and an office move. The fourth had just sold her business when I contacted her.

The rest suggested more personal reasons. One woman who owned a clothing shop had just bought a house that needed many repairs and she did not feel she would have the energy for my project. In discussions with one woman, she agreed until I talked about attending her home activities, too, and then she said it probably was not going to work out. Three revealed that their lives were already so packed that my request was just too much. For example, one woman did not feel she had the 'space' for me among her responsibilities with her business and three children. Another woman left the following message on my voicemail.

> Hi, Kristina. This is Mary McGowan. I'm finally responding to your request. Right now for me, this is probably not a very good idea. I'm in the middle of … I just started my business in July, I'm in the middle of a divorce, and I've got two young kids, so I just … thought it might be a lot to look at, but it's really not going to be a very good thing.

In the same spirit, I received the following email from another woman.

> Hi, Kristina. I received your call and letter regarding your project. It sounds great but unfortunately I am not able to participate. Lots of reasons – I am too new to the business, it is tax season coming up, I have two children – and having someone that involved with my day-to-day just doesn't work with my personality! (Honestly!) If you ever conduct interviews or the like, I may be open to that. Good luck!

In the letter that I sent, I wrote that participants had the right to withdraw from the study at any time. I reiterated this sentiment again in the initial interview. However, all who eventually committed to the study did not withdraw once data collection started.

SAMPLE DESCRIPTION & DEMOGRAPHICS

All of the 10 women who participated in this study live and work in an area of the Northeast in the US, in different towns, ranging from a small town to the inner city of a metropolitan area. While the general area is renowned for its political engagement and cultural expression, mostly due to the concentration of academic institutions, there are many pockets of rural life as well. Thus, a diversity of living situations exists. For example, one participant lives and works from her home in a small, rural village of just under 4,000 residents. The room from which she works on her business overlooks woods and gardens. Likewise, another participant's house serves as the central location for her business. In contrast, however, her residential neighbourhood is in the heart of a city with a population of over 150,000. If the shades on her windows were open – which they rarely are – the view would be of cars speeding down the street and people passing on the sidewalk.

Seven of the 10 women live with male partners; six of these are married. One woman lives with a female partner and two had no partners at the time. Six of the women have children, four of them with children still living at home. Children, however, are not their only care-giving responsibility. Three have had to care for an elderly parent, one with Alzheimer's. Several of them care for pets, two of which feel their dogs are like their children. Nine of the women are Caucasian and one is African American. In **Table 5.1**, I describe the 10 participants and their various business and household situations.

Name	Age	Education	Business Type	Age	Business Location	# Employees	Current Household / Care-giving Situation
Susie	25	4-year degree	Children's Entertainment	4	Home	0	Lives with husband and their two children and part-time with a step-child
Amy	33	4-year degree	Daycare and Educational Products Direct Sales	3 &2	Home	0	Lives with husband and their two children
Lisa	38	High School	Sandwich Shop	2	Restaurant	10	Lives with husband and their three children
Molly	39	2-year degree	Personal Organizer	3	Home	0	Lives with husband and their dog
Anne	42	4-year degree	Sporting Goods Retail Store	9	Retail Shop	22	Lives with female partner
Barbara	45	High School	Youth Transportation	3	Home	10	Lives with her two children and has two older children living nearby
Fay	54	Master's Degree	Management Consultant	17	Home	0	Lives with male partner and a cat and has an older child who lives in another state

Name	Age	Education	Business Type	Age	Business Location	# Employees	Current Household / Care-giving Situation
Lynn	55	4-year degree	Gift Basket Designer	7	Retail Shop	0	Lives with husband and two dogs
Alice	55	4-year degree	Construction Representative	3	Home	0	Lives alone
Joyce	61	2-year degree	Promotional Products and Business Gifts	16	Office Building	18	Lives with husband and has two older children, one living nearby.

Table 5.1: Sample Description & Demographics

Now, I will complicate the information in **Table 5.1**. I presented the pieces of their lives as clean categories, but life is not so easily defined and sorted. For example, somebody might ask, 'How many women in your sample have employees?' I could answer that in several ways. Four have 'official' employees, meaning they report them to the Internal Revenue Service. However, the others rely on many people to keep their businesses running. For example, the woman who runs the children's entertainment company pays various family members to go to parties in costume; she just makes sure not to pay them over the legal amount by compensating them in other ways, such as, groceries. Thus, officially, she has no employees, but a half dozen people do 'work' for her company. Similarly, the management consultant is, as she calls it, a 'solepreneur', meaning she works for and with herself. However, she collaborates with a circle of other management consultants when need be for a project. Likewise, the woman who runs the multi-level educational toy business is a 'regional manager' of other business owners. Thus, while she does not have to report payroll, she spends much of her time 'managing' these people. Even the basket designer hires help during the Christmas holiday, but does not have to carry workers' compensation because the work is 'seasonal'.

Furthermore, the label 'employee' doesn't describe the complex relationship the women have with these various people. Some of their employees are their best friends; some are their family members, including their siblings, husbands, and children. In some cases, their children were paid employees, on the books, and in other cases the children were asked to do business-related tasks, but were not 'official' employees. In all of the married couple cases, the husband 'worked' for the woman's business. Despite the fact that they were not on the official payroll, husbands took days off from work to cover the day-care, came in over their lunch-hour to help make sandwiches for the noon rush, looked over presentation notes, reviewed employee applications, and did the accounting. Furthermore, they often acted as business advisors, suggesting ideas for marketing and employee relations.

Even trying to answer how many owners work from their home and how many have away-from-home offices is difficult. Four have a location away from their home where the majority of their business takes place, mostly because they own a retail shop. While the other six work from their homes, it does not necessarily mean they are home all day. The construction representative is often at building sites, the professional organiser spends much of her time in other peoples' homes, the management consultant is often at meetings, the toy-seller spends many evenings giving presentations, and the woman who owns the youth transportation company spends much of her time warming, gassing, and fixing buses, that is when she is not driving kids to school, to after-school care, and to home. In essence, they might do most of the administrative work from their homes, but much of their other activities are out of the home, interacting with various people.

DATA COLLECTION

In this section, I discuss the strategies I used to gather and document the data and describe my data management and analysis techniques. The women in this study allowed me to 'shadow' them from dawn until beyond dusk. I was present early in the morning, as their day began, to late in the evening, as their day ended. I followed the movements of their lives for one week each, mostly during the 'normal' workweek and, occasionally, on weekends. Each day would start when we agreed, so that, some days, I had to be at a specific location at 7 a.m. (whether it was their house, their business, or some other locale) and then I moved throughout their day with them. When to leave became one of the most difficult parts of this kind of research, because I wanted to 'see' as much as possible, but my departure depended on many factors, such as their schedules, their families' schedules and their activities, as well as my own.

In total, I completed 465 hours of observation over 56 contact days spread out over seven months from October 2004 to April 2005. The longest I spent with one woman was 57 hours and the shortest was 28 hours. I usually spent between eight to 12 hours a day with the women, and, in some cases, as long as 14 hours. When I arrived and left changed each day, depending on their schedule and desires, as well as my own, sometimes starting as early as 6 a.m. and sometimes ending as late as 10 p.m.

For this purpose, data was collected predominantly by using the standard ethnographic techniques of fieldwork, whereby activities were observed and documented by note-taking and audiotape-recording. Thus, observations, semi-structured interviews, informal interviews, and on-the-spot conversations formed the bulk of my data. Being there to observe their routines revealed opportunities to probe in greater depth.

I spent much time talking with the women throughout the day, both formally and informally. Interviewing took three forms in this project. The first type of interview used a more conventional approach, occurring prior to the shadowing period. After talking with each woman on the phone and obtaining their agreement, I set up an initial interview before the shadow week. These were tape-recorded, semi-structured interviews, in that I asked participants about their upbringing, education, career trajectory, business endeavour, and current living situation. I also asked what their 'typical' day looked liked. This initial interview was an important time in the fieldwork process, because it 'set the stage' for the shadowing portion in at least two ways. First, it allowed me to get a sense of their background and current situation. Second, it allowed each of them to get a sense of me before I entered their everyday life. These interviews lasted from one hour to as long as three hours.

The second form of interview is understood as 'talking with people' (DeVault & McCoy, 2002: 756). It took place during the field observation when I was observing the participant. I might ask for details on what she was doing or ask her to explain what she just did. In the field, I found that the participant herself often offered such details without prompting. It was more of an informal and on-the-spot conversation, than a formal or semi-formal interview, taking place mostly spontaneously in the situational everyday of the participants.

The third interview form also took place during the shadowing period, but was a bit more formal. I asked that we set aside several hours for intensive, open-ended interviews. During this time, I was able to ask for clarification of specific observations and other experiences. I encouraged the women to talk about what was on their minds, meaning I did not use an interview guide, leaving my questions open-ended and often circular. I responded and probed as the conversation developed around their understanding of their experiences. This type of interview added to the talk that occurred during observation, because it gave me an opportunity to follow-up on specific observations when it was not possible during the actual field activity. For example, in many of the cases, while we were driving between activities, I used that time to ask questions, turning on the tape-recorder.

Except in one case, the women were very open to me tape-recording their words. In fact, as one woman was getting a perm, I sat in the hairdresser chair next to her, tape-recorder in hand as we talked. Under the noisy hairdrier, she asked me to write down questions on my notepad so she could respond. In another case, we were halfway down the driveway to walk the dog when the woman stopped and asked, 'Where's the tape-recorder?'. I ran back in the house, retrieved it, and held it between us as we walked around her neighbourhood. In only one case, the tape-recorder seemed to make a participant nervous. She was guarded and said less when it was on. To make it more comfortable for her and to allow her to say what she felt, I did not tape often.

During the field observation, I kept a small notebook with me to jot down observations and experiences. I was often able to take notes on the spot right as things were occurring, but not always. In those cases, I might inconspicuously (often while in the bathroom) jot a keyword or phrase down and then later, when I got home, I would either type up notes directly on the computer or talk into the tape-recorder with more details to transcribe later. As I was with the participants for long hours, I was quite tired when I returned home (to my other life responsibilities), so, on my drive home, I often tape-recorded my thoughts about the day's events. The following day, I would reread my notes before leaving home and listen to the tape on the drive to the field site, refreshing my memory of the previous day's experiences.

Shadowing allowed me to 'participate' in their lives because I did most everything they did. I flowed with them through their day and each woman quickly included me in her routines and activities. I went to many different meetings: a Kiwanis lunch, a women's business support group, business networking meetings, and a board meeting for a women's business organisation. I also went to parks, grocery stores, a museum, and a home improvement store for wallpaper. I went to the bank with a woman to ask for a loan, with another woman to report fraudulent activity on her account, and another to deposit money.

I watched TV with them, watched as they gave presentations to potential clients, watched as they gave their children baths, and watched as they networked at Chamber of Commerce events. I listened in on phone conversations they had with clients and others – sometimes my presence was announced, sometimes not. I was present when they interacted with employees, significant others, kids, clients, friends, brothers, colleagues, and suppliers – some of whom counted in more than one category. I talked with these same people. I spent hours watching them work at their desks, write emails, type up reports and speeches, look over documents, enter information into their computers.

I shared many meals with them, their families, friends and clients, both in their homes and at restaurants. I attended a charity dinner event, a child's dance class, an awards presentation, a writing group, and an afternoon tea at the library. I also attended an interview for doggie daycare, several chiropractic sessions, a mammogram, and a trip to urgent care for a child's stomach-ache.

I sat at their dining room tables and kitchen islands, in their offices and living rooms, and once I found myself lying down on the spare bed in one woman's house while she napped before her evening event. I looked through wedding albums, business operating manuals, advertising campaigns, children's scrapbooks, trade magazines, office memos, and newspaper clippings. I witnessed tears brought on by taxes, emotional highs from a sale, arguments with husbands, problems with employees, and kids' meltdowns. As summed up by one participant, 'We laughed. We cried'.

In some instances, as participant-observer, I even actively participated in their lives. At times, it was inevitable that I helped and almost impossible not to. I acted as the audience in a dry-run of a presentation, painted a wall, filed business cards, helped cook, entered names and addresses in a computer database, made flip-charts, stapled packets together, taxied people in my car, organised shoes for a display, read off numbers to be entered in the computer, washed restaurant dishes, rang up sales, and watched kids for a short period of time. Yet, there were times in which I struggled with whether to help or not, because my aim was to observe how they negotiated certain situations. For example, one woman was in the kitchen on the phone with a client when her toddler, who was supposed to be napping, began crying, 'I want Mommy', from the hallway. When the woman stepped out onto the deck and shut the door to finish her phone conversation, I was not sure what to do. Should I tell him that his mom is outside? Or should I do nothing and see how the situation unfolds? I decided to wait for a short period of time and when his crying escalated, I gently told him that his mom would be right back.

My intention for this study was to observe life as it unfolded. As Emerson, Fretz & Shaw (1995: 3) note:

> The ethnographer cannot take in everything; rather, [s]he will, in conjunction with those in the setting, develop certain perspectives by engaging in some activities and relationships rather than others. Moreover, it will often be the case that relationships with those under study follow political fault lines in the setting, exposing the ethnographer selectively to varying priorities and points of view.

Indeed, I was sometimes limited in the extent to which I was allowed to 'see' their lives. One woman's partner was away when I shadowed, so the way she scheduled her days that week were not typical. Also, I came to learn that one woman was guarded with divulging information when her husband said, 'What? Quit poking me. I think she should hear this'. I consciously tried to be aware of how my presence changed what they did and said.

In a few occasions, I was asked not to participate in an activity. For example, one afternoon when the management consultant took a walk with her neighbour, who also runs a business from her home, her colleague asked that I not accompany them. She felt that, by having me there, it would change the dynamics. For the hour that they walked, I sat on the couch and looked through a few of the books from her shelf.

I was also excluded from several meetings because other people did not feel comfortable with me being present. One participant held a part-time job doing administrative work at another business and requested that I not shadow her that particular day. One event I chose not to attend. During one shadow week, a business colleague's father passed away suddenly and there was a wake. After talking with the woman, and sensing her hesitation, I chose not to attend so that she need not have to explain my presence.

While in the field, the categories of observation I paid most attention to were what kinds of activities they engaged in, the substance of their talk, and who they interacted with and the type of interaction. I noted situations where the tensions of 'balancing' work and family arose. I also looked for instances where the conceptualisation of work and family as separate spheres was lived and experienced. Lastly, I paid close attention to the underlying gendered processes in the women's everyday lives.

DATA MANAGEMENT & ANALYSIS

After the first few shadows, I fashioned this schedule: one week in the field, one week transcribing tapes and notes. Immediately transcribing the data helped me to remember the details, because each woman's life was so different. I manually transcribed every tape and typed up all field notes to develop an overall sense of each woman's everyday life at the moment in which I entered it. I created separate documents for each shadowee. The fieldwork resulted in 396 single-spaced pages of interview transcripts and 165 single-spaced pages of field notes, totalling 561 single-spaced pages of data.

As I was compiling these documents, I began to develop ideas about what was going on in my data. I created memos to document these hunches. After bringing together all handwritten notes, transcribed thoughts, and interview transcripts on the computer, I read through all of my data, immersing myself in each week's experience and the women's words and actions.

I then followed Esterberg's (2001) advice on how to get 'intimate' with my data, using a two-step coding process. According to Hesse-Biber & Leavy (2004: 411), 'coding is the analytic strategy many qualitative scholars employ in order to locate key themes, patterns, ideas, and concepts within their data'. It is a way to extract meaning from the textual material. It consists of labelling chunks or clusters of data that describe a theme or idea. The first step in the coding process is called open coding. Esterberg (2001: 158) points out that '… you don't want to limit potential insights by rigidly applying pre-established codes to your data. Instead, you want to use the process of coding to begin to reveal potential meanings'. Thus, I read through each document, line-by-line, identifying broad categories that seemed of interest.

How did I know how to 'read' the data? From an ethnomethodological perspective, the analytic focus is on the detailed processes and methods through which individuals construct and sustain perceivably stable features of their daily lives. I turned to Emerson *et al.* (1995: 146), who posed the following questions that I kept in mind as I worked intensively with coding:

♦ What are people doing? What are they trying to accomplish?
♦ How, exactly, do they do this? What specific means and / or strategies do they use?
♦ How do members talk about, characterise, and understand what is going on?
♦ What assumptions are they making?
♦ What do I see going on here? What did I learn from these notes?
♦ Why did I include them?

While open coding, I began to see themes emerge. I noted these themes in analytic memos. The next step in the analysis process is referred to as 'focused coding'. In this step, I returned to the data, continued to work line-by-line, but this time focused on the key themes I identified in open coding. The technique I used was to print out all the quotes for each one of my open codes. I then read through each cluster of quotes, highlighting passages and also taking more detailed notes on the theme.

To assist in the laborious task of data management, I used a computer software package. Specifically, I employed Atlasti to store, code, and retrieve my data. I did not, however, use it for data analysis purposes, like building conceptual networks, recognising patterns, or producing textual mappings. Instead, I hand-coded all the data and did not rely on the software to automatically code any of it, thus avoiding some of the pitfalls of using qualitative software (e.g., see Hesse-Biber, 1995). Like Coffey & Atkinson (1996: 165), I viewed using computer software in qualitative research as an 'analytic support' tool. I was able to locate useful quotes quickly by retrieving passages of the text that I had labelled with a given code name.

A SNAPSHOT OF FINDINGS

Below, I present the story of Susie to show how one woman negotiates the contradictions and tensions produced by an assumption of life as separable. Susie left full-time employment as a teacher after her children were born and subsequently started her own business, making her an ideal case of a woman 'balancing' work and family through entrepreneurship.

Susie: 'My Family Comes First'

It is 9:30 a.m. on a Wednesday morning when Susie, a 25-year-old woman who runs a characters (e.g., Sponge Bob, Snow White) entertainment business, is in the kitchen on the phone explaining the different entertainment packages and Ben, a two-and-a-half year old, is running around yelling, 'Mommy look! Mommy look!'. She hangs up the phone and tells me, 'It is abnormal for me to get a call in the morning like this', as she lifts Ben back into a chair at the dining-room table, which is covered in haphazard piles of papers. Before the phone rang, Ben and his older brother Scottie, who is three-and-a-half years old, were practicing writing the letter 'm' as part of their 'two hours of education' from 9.00 to 11.00, Monday through Thursday.

Susie feels that one of the major advantages of owning her own business is that she has control of her schedule. She describes:

> You get to make the rules. You get to adjust your schedule. If I don't
> want to work on a weekend, I block it off. My family comes first and I

don't want to be told to work on Christmas. I don't want to work on days when my family needs me. It's convenient working for myself. If I have to, I can always work around so that my kids come first. There are days that I am so busy that they seem like they come last, but … during the workweek, they really do come first, like during everybody else's workweek. My weekend is my biggest workweek. I barely get any business on the school days. I get about 10 educational programs a year and they are on school days but, other than that, all of my business is on the weekend.

Susie's 'workweek' is on Saturday and Sunday, because most of her business comes from children's birthday parties, which are most often held on weekends. For example, one Saturday morning, Susie is downstairs checking messages on her business phone that hangs on the wall of the basement hallway. A last-minute call for a Sponge Bob appearance came in, bringing the total appearances for that afternoon to three. As she returns the call, Ben comes down the steps, loudly voicing his frustration that he can't get a toy to work. 'Ben,' Susie says with exasperation and steps away to a quieter spot in the hallway to leave a message. She then carries a large Sponge Bob body out to the garage, saying, 'Ben, go back in. I can't watch you', as she stuffs it into the back of the minivan. He had followed her out to the garage, repeatedly asking, 'Mom, where are you going?'. Without answering him, Susie goes back into the house and finds that she just missed the phone. 'I'm always being interrupted with the kids. But I'm happy with that. They are good interruptions', she declares, as she returns the call and books another birthday party.

On Living the Separation: 'It's All About Priorities'

Throughout my time with Susie, I heard such phrases as, 'my priority is my family', 'I can always work around so that my kids come first', 'my family comes first and I don't want to be told to work on Christmas', 'my priority first was to spend time with them and school and then take them to the park and nothing was going to get in the way of that' and 'so my primary job is a mom and, if anything interferes with that, I would drop these two jobs in a heartbeat for them, anytime, because they do come first'. These 'priority' phrases are always said in relation to work, implying a clear conceptual understanding of work and family as separate spheres. In fact, she says, 'I try to keep as much as I can business and family separate, as much as I can'. She notes that she tries to do business work only when her children are eating or napping.

She not only sees work and family as separate components of her life but also sees them in a static, hierarchical relationship: family should always come first. Living the assumption of separation and hierarchy, however, is difficult; she feels tension when her beliefs and actions are in conflict. This is evident when the following sentence trails off: she says, 'I can always work around so that my kids come first. There are days that I am so busy that they seem like they come last, but …'. By believing that they should be separate, she has to expend a tremendous amount of mental work to keep up with the expectation that family is first. Another example is the morning she fields a business call during the morning education hours and notes, 'It is abnormal for me to get a call in the morning like this', indicating that she believes it is wrong for her take a few minutes away from her children. Likewise, during the chaotic Saturday morning when she is trying to get ready to go on a character run, she says, 'I'm always being interrupted with the kids. But I'm happy with that. They are good interruptions', suggesting that she feels like she shouldn't put work first. We can read in her comments the tension she feels when she is unable to maintain the separation. In these instances, she feels like she is not succeeding at her 'primary job' as a 'mom'.

My focus is not on her individual success or failure to 'balance,' but rather how she lives the belief that work and family are separate spheres, resulting in complex negotiations of where to be, what to do, and how to think inherent in the struggle for separation. The public-private dichotomy clearly organises Susie's day-to-day life, whether it is in her talk (e.g., 'family comes first') or in her actions (e.g., scheduling 'family time' and 'work time'). What we see in her story is the anxiety that arises from trying to live life as though it were made up of two mutually-exclusive domains.

CONCLUSION

In this chapter, I described the theoretical framework that underpins my methodological approach. To recap, symbolic interactionism examines the ways in which individuals attach symbolic meaning to everyday interactions and ethnomethodology explores how individuals sustain social interactions as orderly. Likewise, socialist feminism is concerned with how the gendered structure of the larger socio-economic environment impacts everyday lives of individuals. In particular, I focused on the critique of the public / private divide. As Jagger (1983: 146) explains, according to a socialist feminist perspective, 'the distinction between the so-called public and private spheres obscures their interpenetration and essential unity ... it is misleading to think of there being two distinct spheres at all'.

Thus, my methodological approach allowed me to capture the 'doing' of work and family by empirically locating it in the real-life experiences of women. In particular, I focused on the context of women-owned businesses, a context in which it is assumed these women have more freedom in organizing their everyday practices and routines, and thus more flexibility to 'integrate' work and family than if they are employed by somebody else. In my research, however, I found that they continue to live a daily life based on the assumption of separation. The method of shadowing allowed me to explore in detail what they did, what they said, and how they explained their behaviours. Specifically, I was able to document the concrete activities through which work and family are constructed as *if* separate, and demonstrated, in this chapter through the ethnographic case of Susie, the effort it takes to sustain a given definition of reality.

The broader implications of my research for the study of work and family in organisation studies is that the notion of 'work-family' as a theoretical construct to understand individual's lived experiences, especially those of women, is indeed misleading. Due to my methodological approach, I am able to show how work and family are negotiated accomplishments, rather than separate domains that need to be 'balanced'. 'Balance' conjures an image of a seesaw with work and family on opposite ends, separate realms that, once poised at the apex, can be maintained – a rather static view of the complexities of life. Thus, as I showed empirically, it takes a considerable amount of effort to sustain the idea of separation so that activities can be defined purely as 'work' and other activities can be defined purely as 'family.'

A more dynamic view conceptualises work and family as co-constituting each other in daily activities; both are in constant movement together on a day-to-day basis. Scholars studying work and family may do well to question the assumptions underpinning their theoretical concepts to open a space for reconsidering these notions as part of the complex field of socio-cultural power relations where gender (and class and race and sexuality) intersect.

REFERENCES

Acker, J. (1990). 'Hierarchies, Jobs, Bodies: A Theory of Gendered Organizations', *Gender and Society* 4: 139-58.

Acker, J. (1992). 'Gendering Organizational Theory', in Mills, A.J. & Tancred, P. (eds), *Gendering Organizational Analysis*, pp. 248-60. London: Sage.

Acker, J. (1998). 'The Future of "Gender and Organizations": Connections and Boundaries', *Gender, Work and Organization* 5: 195-206.

Acker, J. (2006). *Class Questions: Feminist Answers*. New York, NY: Rowman & Littlefield Publishers, Inc.

Berger, P.L. & Luckmann, T. (1966). *The Social Construction of Reality*. New York, NY: Doubleday.

Bourne, K.A. (2006). *In and Out of Balance: Women Entrepreneurs and the Gendered 'Work' of Work-Family*. PhD dissertation, ISBN: 978-0-542-65649-1. Amherst, MA: University of Massachusetts.

Bruni, A., Gherardi, S. & Possio, B. (2004). 'Doing Gender, Doing Entrepreneurship: An Ethnographic Account of Intertwined Practices', *Gender, Work and Organization* 11(4): 406-29.

Burrell, G. & Morgan, G. (1979). *Sociological Paradigms and Organizational Analysis*. Burlington, VT: Ashgate.

Butler, J. (1990). *Gender Trouble: Feminism and the Subversion of Identity*. New York, NY: Routledge.

Calás, M. & Smircich, L. (1992a). 'Re-writing Gender into Organizational Theorizing: Directions from Feminist Perspectives', in Reed, M. & Hughes, M. (eds), *Rethinking Organization: New Directions in Organization Theory and Analysis*, pp. 227-53. London: Sage.

Calás, M. & Smircich, L. (1992b). 'Using the "F" Word: Feminist Theories and the Social Consequences of Organizational Research', in Mills, A.J. & Tancred, P. (eds), *Gendering Organizational Analysis*, pp. 222-34. London: Sage.

Calás, M. & Smircich, L. (1996). 'From "the Woman's Point of View": Feminist Approaches to Organization Studies', in Clegg, S., Hardy, C. & Nord, W. (eds), *Handbook of Organization Studies*, pp. 218-57. London: Sage.

Calás, M. & Smircich, L. (2006). 'From "the Woman's Point of View" Ten Years Later: Towards a Feminist Organization Studies', in Clegg, S., Hardy, C., Nord, W. & Lawrence, T.B. (eds), *Handbook of Organization Studies*, 2nd ed, pp. 284-346. London: Sage.

Coffey, A. & Atkinson, P. (1996). *Making Sense of Qualitative Data*. Thousand Oaks, CA: Sage.

Denzin, N.A. & Lincoln, Y.S. (2000). *Handbook of Qualitative Research*, 2nd ed. Thousand Oaks, CA: Sage.

DeVault, M.L. & McCoy, L. (2002). 'Institutional Ethnography: Using Interviews to Investigate Ruling Relations', in Gubrium, J.F. & Holstein, J.A. (eds), *Handbook of Interview Research*, pp. 751-75. Thousand Oaks, CA: Sage.

Emerson, J. (1970). 'Behavior in Private Places: Sustaining Definitions of Reality in Gynecological Examinations', *Recent Sociology* 2: 74-97.

Emerson, R.M., Fretz, R.I. & Shaw, L.L. (1995). *Writing Ethnographic Fieldnotes.* Chicago, IL: The University of Chicago Press.

Esterberg, K.G. (2001). *Qualitative Methods in Social Research.* New York: McGraw Hill.

Garfinkel, H. (1967). *Studies in Ethnomethodology.* Englewood Cliffs, NJ: Prentice-Hall.

Gherardi, S. (1995). *Gender, Symbolism and Organisational Cultures.* London: Sage.

Glucksmann, M.A. (1995). 'Why "Work"? Gender and the "Total Social Organization of Labour"', *Gender, Work and Organisation* 2(2): 63-75.

Goffman, E. (1961). *Encounters: Two Studies in the Sociology of Interaction.* Indianapolis, IN: The Bobbs-Merrill Company, Inc.

Goffman, E. (1979). *Gender Advertisements.* Cambridge, MA: Harvard University Press.

Gubrium, J.F. & Holstein, J.A. (2000). 'Analyzing Interpretive Practice', in Denzin, N.A. & Lincoln, Y.S. (eds), *Handbook of Qualitative Research,* pp.487-508. Thousand Oaks, CA: Sage.

Hesse-Biber, S. (1995). 'Unleashing Frankenstein's Monster: The Use of Computers in Qualitative Research', in Burgess, R.G. (ed), *Studies in Qualitative Methodology,* Vol. 5: 25-41. Westport, CT: JAI Press.

Hesse-Biber, S. & Leavy, P. (2004). *Approaches to Qualitative Research: A Reader on Theory & Practice.* New York, NY: Oxford University Press.

Higginbottom, G. (2004). 'Sampling Issues in Qualitative Research', *Nurse Researcher* 12(1): 7-19.

Lewis, J. (2003). 'Design Issues', in Ritchie, J. & Lewis, J. (eds), *Qualitative Research Practice,* pp. 47-76. Thousand Oaks, CA: Sage.

Martin, P.Y. (2001). '"Mobilizing Masculinities": Women's Experience of Men at Work', *Organization* 8(4): 587-618.

Martin, P.Y. (2003). '"Said and Done" *versus* "Saying and Doing": Gendering Practices, Practicing Gender at Work', *Gender & Society* 17(3): 342-66.

Merriam, S.B. (2002). *Qualitative Research in Practice: Examples for Discussion & Analysis.* San Francisco, CA: Jossey-Bass.

Patton, M.Q. (1990). *Qualitative Evaluation Methods,* 2nd ed. Newbury Park, CA: Sage.

Rantalaiho, L., Heiskanen, T., Korvajärvi, P. & Vehviläinen, M. (1997). 'Studying Gendered Practices', in Rantalaiho, L. & Heiskanen, T. (eds), *Gendered Practices in Working Life,* pp. 3-15. London: MacMillan Press Ltd.

Rossman, G.B. & Rallis, S.F. (1998). *Learning in the Field: An Introduction to Qualitative Research.* Thousand Oaks, CA.: Sage.

Silverman, D. (2000). *Doing Qualitative Research: A Practical Handbook.* Thousand Oaks, CA: Sage.

Smith, D. (1987). *The Everyday World as Problematic.* Boston, MA: Northeastern University Press.

Wolcott, H.F. (1994). *Transforming Qualitative Data: Description, Analysis and Interpretation.* Thousand Oaks, CA: Sage.

West, C. & Zimmerman, D.H. (1987). 'Doing Gender', *Gender & Society* 1(2): 125-51.

CHAPTER 6
FOCUSING ON PROCESS & HISTORY: PATH DEPENDENCE

Paul F. Donnelly

INTRODUCTION

In taking issue with the largely ahistorical and aprocessual character of
much organisational theorising, this chapter seeks to depart from knowing
the organisational by way of classification and to move towards knowing
the organisational as an ongoing process. For example, extant theoretical
perspectives (such as structural contingency theory, transaction cost theory,
institutional theory, population ecology), which operate at the macro
organisational level, treat organisational form as an essence, as a durable,
tangible and relatively undeniable structure, which exists as an empirical
entity. Taken as a given 'out there', each approach equates form with, and
classifies form as, a set of essential and identifiable characteristics that
constitutes the organisational, the particular mix of characteristics serving to
distinguish one form from another. Central to each approach, therefore, is
the development of classification schemes and the construction and
maintenance of boundaries, not just to render forms distinct and identifiable,
but also to distinguish each theoretical view from the others.

Recognising calls for more processual and historically-informed
organisational theorising, path dependence theory offers a way of
articulating the organisational as an ongoing dynamic over more
dominant ways of thinking and knowing that are more static. With an
interest in how process, sequence and temporality can be best incorporated
into explanation, path dependence attempts to 'strike a better balance
between historically-insensitive causal generalization and idiographic
historicism' (Haydu, 1998: 367).

Re-inserting process and history into studying the organisational,
through the lens of path dependence, offers an approach to move out of
some of the organisational literature's current limitations. In the sections

that follow, I reflect on the position afforded history in the study of the organisational, which brings me on to path dependence theory itself. Having outlined the tenets of the theory, I then move on to sketch out its application in the practice of doing research.

REINSERTING HISTORY INTO 'THE ORGANISATIONAL'

While there have been calls to develop more historically-informed organisational theory, in turn facilitating a more process-oriented and more contingent / less deterministic approach, this does not mean breaking with modernity, for mainstream modernist history is no less foundational, rational, essentialist, logocentric or concerned with the notion of progress. With faith in reason, the modernist historian's unquestioned task has been to dig into the past, to investigate it, to discover a past reality and reconstruct it scientifically, to find the 'one line running through history' (Ankersmit, 1989: 153). Claiming authority for historical knowledge (White, 1995), the goal has been 'uniformization of the past' through integration, synthesis and totality (Ankersmit, 1989: 153). Critiques of history in this fashion, nonetheless, increasingly have appeared (e.g., Lukacs, 2002), including those such as Üsdiken & Kieser (2004), who argue that use of history in organisation studies are not all the same and can be demarcated according to three positions – supplementarist, integrationist and reorientationist, albeit with variations within each – consistent with how history is treated in relation to the social scientistic perspective that has come to dominate the field.

The Supplementarist Position

Theorising within the supplementarist position ranges from the timeless to limiting the value of history to add context for developing or testing generalisable theories (Kieser, 1994; Üsdiken & Kieser, 2004; Zald, 1990, 1993). As a useful check for ideas (Goldman, 1994), therefore, history becomes, substantively, an object of theoretical frames seeking to analyse and explain past events (Lawrence, 1984) and / or methodologically, an object of theory development and hypothesis generation (Goodman & Kruger, 1988). Claiming, for example, that organisational ecology and institutional theory already incorporate history into their analyses, Goldman (1994: 623) goes on to assert that assimilating history into organisation theory is only possible if it is acknowledged that 'insofar as theory refers to principles of organization that transcend time and space, historical and comparative (that is international and / or multicultural) data can test the generalisability and utility of a theory'.

With the exception of contingency theories, and their largely cross-sectional (in contrast to longitudinal) research focus, other organisational theories – transaction cost, institutional and ecological theories – each accommodate a historical take that could be considered supplementarist. However, such an accommodation is limited for, as Baum (1996: 107) notes, 'no theory can be general, precise, and realistic at the same time'. Hence, with realism (and precision) as the trade-off for generality, history becomes subordinated to contributing to the theory-driven scientistic enterprise substantively, i.e., through its potential for confirming and refining general theories, and / or methodologically, i.e., as an aid in selecting variables and in generating hypotheses within a theoretical context.

For instance, Clark & Rowlinson (2004) contend that transaction cost economics abides by the functional logic of efficiency, favouring theoretical explanations over historical narrative, with the latter only of value for purposes of illustration. With history subordinated to universally applicable economic models based 'on a combination of *a priori* theorizing and related natural selection arguments' (Williamson, 1985: 324), economic explanations for the existence of organisations or organisational forms need have no recourse to empirical historical research into their origins.

For Clark & Rowlinson (2004), the questionable use to which the transaction cost approach puts historical evidence in explaining the organisational, as noted by such critics as Jones (1982, 1997), is a sign of the approach's penchant for hypothetical (Swedberg & Granovetter, 1992) or stylised settings (McCloskey, 1994) over a perspective informed by history. Bolstering this reading is the view expressed by Fligstein (1990: 300) who, finding it problematical how what happened historically can be accounted for by economic arguments, contends that 'the plausibility of economic efficiency stories rests more on their abstract character and ability to round off the edges and provide a pleasing and simple version of what occurred'.

Both organisational ecology and institutional theory display a greater interest in history than structural contingency theory and research informed by both perspectives favours longitudinal over cross-sectional studies of organisational fields and populations. However, in their treatment of time, the temporal frame they adopt is generally that of a time-line which, in assuming a simple account of history and in smoothing time to achieve generalisability in exchange for realism and precision (Baum, 1996: 107), ignores that historical time is messy, uneven and infused with events that fracture the more or less enduring patterns of social life (Clark & Rowlinson, 2004).

Further, heavily influenced by biological analyses, organisational ecologists such as Hannan & Freeman (1989: 40) have been keen to distance themselves from being seen as deterministic and, in arguing that their analyses are subject to probabilistic modelling, they assert that '[i]n no sense do we think that the history of organizational populations is preordained to unfold in fixed ways'. However, as Clark & Rowlinson (2004) note, Hannan & Freeman (1989: 40) are very explicit in dismissing narrative history in asserting that 'the motivations and preferences of particular actors probably do not matter very much'. Thus, with no room for human actors in explaining organisational variability, organisational ecologists paradoxically leave little room for these very same human actors in using the insights of their approach to make organisational interventions (Astley & Van de Ven, 1983; Clark & Rowlinson, 2004; Perrow, 1986).

The Integrationist Position

In a criticism that can also be applied to mainstream organisational theory in general, Kieser (1994: 612) notes that sociologists, in favouring grand theories that bother little with historical details that disconfirm their theories, would be seen by many historians 'as people who state the obvious in an abstract jargon, lack any sense of differences in culture or time, squeeze phenomena into rigid categories and, to top it all, declare these activities as "scientific"'. Given the inferior position they accord history, Kieser (1994) calls for the abandonment of models that are conceptualised separately from that which is to be explained, in favour of analyses that are more interpretive and inductive, i.e., integrationist. For those of an integrationist position, the concern is with activating the potential of history to enrich organisation studies through both employing and challenging its social scientistic counterpart: 'Ultimately, the issue is how do we *combine* a positivistic programme of theoretical and empirical cumulation with the enriching possibilities of the humanities' (Zald, 1993: 516, emphasis in original). In similar vein, Kieser (1994: 619) proffers that '[h]istorical analyses do not replace existing organization theory; they enrich our understanding of present-day organizations by reconstructing the human acts which created them in the course of history.'

Thus, an integrationist position recognises that the organisational has been shaped by past events and that its course of development has been influenced by the broader context. More specifically, an integrationist position entails interest in 'processes of organizational change, development of organizational forms and variations across societal settings, path dependencies and continuities in organizational ideas and practices' (Üsdiken & Kieser, 2004: 323).

PATH DEPENDENCE AS AN INTEGRATIONIST POSITION

In recognition of the calls for more historically-informed organisational theory, therefore, I now turn to the notion of path dependency. Viewed as an idea through which 'history' is commonly made visible, path dependence emerged as an alternative perspective to 'conventional economics' in the 1980s through the work of David (e.g., 1985, 1987, 1994, 1997, 1999, 2001) and Arthur (e.g., 1988, 1989, 1990, 1994). Path dependence refers to dynamic processes involving irreversibilities, which generate multiple possible outcomes depending on the particular sequence in which events unfold. The path dependence approach holds that a historical path of choices has the character of a branching process, with a self-reinforcing dynamic in which positive feedback increases, while at the same time the costs of reversing previous decisions increase, and the scope for reversing them narrows sequentially, as the development proceeds. As already noted by David (2001: 23), 'the core content of the concept of path dependence as a dynamic property refers to the idea of history as an irreversible branching process'. Similarly, Hacker (2002: 54, emphasis in original) argues that 'path dependence refers to *developmental trajectories that are inherently difficult to reverse'*. Thus, preceding steps in a particular direction induce further movement in the same direction, thereby making the possibility of switching to some other previously credible alternative more difficult. 'In an increasing returns process, the probability of further steps along the same path increases with each move down that path. This is because the *relative* benefits of the current activity compared with other possible options increase over time' (Pierson, 2000a: 252, emphasis in original).

Those unfamiliar with the path dependence approach think that it is no more than recognition that 'history matters'. However, the approach not only recognises the impact of history, but also shows that a decision-making process can exhibit self-reinforcing dynamics, such that an evolution over time to the most efficient alternative does not necessarily occur. In general, path dependence refers to situations in which decision-making processes (partly) depend on prior choices and events. It recognises that a decision is not made in some historical and institutional void just by looking at the characteristics and expected effects of the alternatives, but also by taking into account how much each alternative deviates from current institutional arrangements that have developed in time. An outcome thus depends on the contingent starting point and specific course of a historical decision-making process.

Antonelli (1997: 661) attributes the emergence of path dependence to the failure of existing economic models to handle the dynamism and complexity of path-dependent processes, with Arthur (1990: 99) distinguishing between 'conventional economics', which largely avoids path dependence, and the 'new positive feedback economics', which embraces it. From an initial interest in the emergence of new technologies (e.g., David, 1985, 1987, 1997, 1999, 2001; Arthur, 1989, 1994; Cowan, 1990; Cusumano, Mylonadis & Rosenbloom, 1992; Puffert, 1991), path dependence arguments have since become prevalent in such areas as the spatial location of production (e.g., Arthur, 1994; Garnsey, 1998; Kenney & von Burg, 1999, 2000; Krugman, 1991), regional studies (e.g., Ackrill & Kay, 2006; Beugelsdijk, van Schaik & Arts, 2006; Hassink, 2005; Jakobsen, Rusten & Fløysand, 2005; Karlsen, 2005; Zukowski, 2004), the development of international trade (e.g., Krugman 1996), institutional sociology (e.g., David, 1994; Hacker, 2002; Krücken, 2003; Mahoney, 1999, 2000, 2001; Morgan & Kubo, 2005; North, 1990; Thelen, 2000), political science (e.g., Greener, 2005; Pierson, 2000a, 2000b, 2004; Pierson & Skocpol, 2002), policy studies (e.g., Béland & Hacker, 2004; Hogan, 2005; Howlett & Ramesh, 2002; Kay, 2003, 2005; Pierson, 1993; van der Klein, 2003), and entered into such areas as strategy (e.g., Booth, 2003; Brousseau & Chaves, 2005; Maielli, 2005; Mueller, 1997; Nerkar & Paruchuri, 2005; Rao, Vemuri & Galvin, 2004; Stack & Gartland, 2003, 2005; Teece, Pisano & Shuen, 1997) and organisation studies (e.g., Araujo & Rezende, 2003; Bruggeman, 2002; Greener, 2002; Heffernan, 2003; Noda & Collis, 2001; Schmidt & Spindler, 2002; Sonnenwald, 2003; Sydow, Schreyögg & Koch, 2005). Booth (2003) notes that path dependence has only recently entered organisation studies, due to the analytical problems encountered by existing approaches in accommodating the complexity and dynamism of path-dependent processes.

Path Dependence in Economics

Arguments about technology have provided the most fertile ground for exploring the conditions conducive to increasing returns. As David (1985, 1987, 1997, 1999, 2001) and Arthur (1988, 1989, 1990, 1994) have stressed, under conditions often present in complex, knowledge-intensive sectors, a particular technology may achieve a decisive advantage over competitors, although it is not necessarily the most efficient alternative in the long run. Once an initial advantage is gained, positive feedback effects may lock in this technology, excluding competing alternatives. With increasing returns, actors have strong incentives to focus on a single alternative and to continue down a specific path once initial steps are taken in that direction.

As Arthur, David and others contend, the key characteristic of a historical process that engenders path dependence is positive feedback, or self-reinforcement. Given this feature, every move down a particular path makes it harder to reverse course. In the presence of positive feedback, the probability of further moves in the same direction increases with each step along the way because the relative advantages of the current activity weighed against once-possible choices grow over time. Said differently, the costs of switching to a once plausible option would rise.

Couching his consideration of path dependence in terms of 'lock-in by historical events', Arthur (1989, 1994) focuses attention on a single condition: increasing returns to adoption that are realised not at a single point of time but rather dynamically, such that each step along a particular path produces consequences that increase the relative attractiveness of that path for the next round. As effects begin to accumulate, they generate a powerful cycle of self-reinforcing activity, which may result in path inefficiency and an equilibrium that may be inefficient. From an economic perspective, therefore, a process of allocation is called path-dependent when the sequence of allocations depends not only on fundamental, *a priori* determinants – typically listed as technology, factor endowments, preferences, and institutions – but also on particular contingent events. Instead of converging to a determinate, predictable, unique equilibrium, such processes have multiple potential equilibria, and which one is selected depends on the specific history of the process. Positive feedback among agents' choices lends persistence and, indeed, increasing impact to particular early choices and other events.

Institutional Path Dependence

From its roots in economics, path dependence has branched out to become a key concept in studying institutional evolution over the past decade (Crouch & Farrell, 2002). North (1990) proposed transforming the approach in such a way that it could be applied in an institutional context, noting that all the features identified in investigations of increasing returns in technology can equally apply to institutions, although with somewhat different characteristics, and that institutions are subject to considerable increasing returns. In situations of complex social interdependence, new institutions commonly require high fixed or start-up costs, and they entail significant learning effects, coordination effects, and adaptive expectations. By and large, established institutions engender powerful incentives that buttress their own stability (David, 1994).

North (1990) stresses that positive feedback applies not just to single institutions, but that institutional arrangements also produce corresponding organisational forms, which in turn may induce the development of new complementary institutions. Path-dependent processes will frequently be most marked not at the level of discrete organisations or institutions, but at a more macro level that comprises arrangements of corresponding organisations and institutions (Pierson & Skocpol, 2002).

For social scientists interested in paths of development, the key issue is often what North (1990: 95) calls 'the interdependent web of an institutional matrix', a matrix that 'produces massive increasing returns'. As North (1990: 3) sees it, institutions, broadly defined as 'the rules of the game in a society or, more formally, ... the humanly devised constraints that shape human interaction', account for the anomaly of enduring difference in economic performance. Once in place, institutions are difficult to alter, and they have an enormous impact on the potential for producing sustained economic growth. Individuals and organisations become accustomed to existing institutions and, when institutions do not encourage economic productivity, growth, if any, is unlikely.

For institutional and organisational scholars, North's insights are important for two reasons. First, he draws attention to the similarities between features of technology and certain features of social interactions. In this context, it is important to note that Arthur's points concerning technology are not really about the technology itself but about the features of a technology in interaction with particular qualities of related social activity. Second, he points out that institutional development is subject to positive feedback. Indeed, it is in elucidating patterns of institutional emergence, persistence, and change that path dependence may prove of considerable use to organisational scholars.

Social scientists, therefore, generally invoke the notion of path dependence to support a few key claims (Pierson, 2004): specific patterns of timing and sequence matter; from initially similar conditions, a wide array of social outcomes are often possible; large consequences may result from relatively small or contingent events; particular courses of action, once introduced, are almost impossible to reverse; and consequently, development is often punctuated by critical moments or junctures that shape the basic contours of social life. All of these features contrast sharply with more familiar modes of argument and explanation, which attribute large outcomes to large causes and emphasise the prevalence of unique, predictable outcomes, the irrelevance of timing and sequence, and the capacity of rational actors to design and implement optimal solutions (given their resources and constraints) to the problems that confront them.

Incorporating History & Process

Through the concept of path dependence, there is now the possibility to move beyond ahistorical organisational theorising. In the opinion of Hirsch & Gillespie (2001: 87), 'Path dependence deserves credit for bringing history back into analysis […] stimulating economists and other social scientists to address the limitations of their largely ahistorical models'. It seeks to assess how process, sequence and temporality can be best incorporated into explanation, the focus of the researcher being on particular outcomes, temporal sequencing and the unfolding of processes over time.

DOING PATH DEPENDENCE

Accounts of how and why events develop as they do necessitate a mode of causal logic that is grounded in time and in characteristically temporal processes (Abrams, 1982; Aminzade, 1992). As indicated before, path dependence seeks to assess how process, sequence and temporality can be best incorporated into explanation, the focus of the researcher being on particular outcomes, temporal sequencing and the unfolding of processes over time.

As Mahoney (2000: 511) notes, path-dependent analyses have at least three defining characteristics:

♦ They entail the study of causal processes that are very sensitive to events that occur early on in an overall historical sequence.

♦ Given the contingent character of these early historical events, they cannot be explained by reason of preceding events or initial conditions.

♦ When contingent historical events occur, path-dependent sequences are reflected in essentially deterministic causal patterns.

Mahoney (2001:112) elaborates these characteristics into an analytic structure, based on his view that path dependence refers 'to a specific type of explanation that unfolds through a series of sequential stages', as shown in **Figure 6.1**.

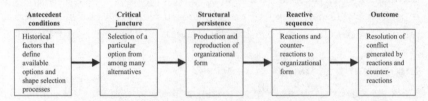

Antecedent conditions	Critical juncture	Structural persistence	Reactive sequence	Outcome
Historical factors that define available options and shape selection processes	Selection of a particular option from among many alternatives	Production and reproduction of organizational form	Reactions and counter-reactions to organizational form	Resolution of conflict generated by reactions and counter-reactions

Figure 6.1: Analytic Structure of Path-dependent Explanation
(Source: Adapted from Mahoney, 2001: 113).

Antecedent Conditions & Critical Junctures

In terms of deciding the critical juncture, Mahoney (2000) suggests that the period immediately prior to a critical juncture makes for a practical moment for specifying the start of the sequence. In the course of this pre-critical juncture, at least two alternatives are open for selection, e.g., policies or ways of organising, and potential processes influencing the choice made at the critical juncture become active. The choice is consequential because it leads to the creation of a pattern that endures over time. In practice, Mahoney (2000) notes that an event is considered contingent when it cannot be accounted for by existing scientific theory or when it contradicts the predictive capacity of a theory explicitly designed to explain a given result. In the case of the former, both small events too specific to be covered by existing theory and large events entailing apparently random processes are treated as contingent. In the case of the latter, no matter that a result may be consistent with the expectations of unexamined theories, events are treated as contingent where the result contradicts the theoretical framework of interest. Assessing critical junctures is achieved through counterfactual thought experiments, whereby the researcher posits another selection had been made and attempts to rerun history accordingly. Such analysis serves to demonstrate the importance of a critical juncture, by showing that the selection of this other option would have led to a final outcome that was significantly different.

Structural Persistence

Path dependence emphasises the contingency of historical turning points, with choices at critical junctures nudging history down tracks that then, through the stubborn persistence of subsequent continuities, become increasingly difficult to reverse. Thus it is that, once a specific selection has been made, it becomes increasingly difficult with the passing of time to return to the initial critical juncture when at least two options were still available.

Couching his consideration of path dependence in terms of 'lock-in by historical events', Arthur (1989, 1994) focused attention on a single condition: increasing returns to adoption that are realised not at a single point of time but rather dynamically, such that each step along a particular path produces consequences that increase the relative attractiveness of that path for the next round. As effects begin to accumulate, they generate a powerful cycle of self-reinforcing activity, contributing to structural persistence. Arthur (1994: 112) argues that four features of a technology and its social context generate increasing returns or positive feedback from the macro state of the system to the choices of individual agents, possibly resulting in *de facto* standardisation on a single technology:

♦ *Large set-up or fixed costs:* These create a high pay-off for further investments in a given technology. With large production runs, fixed costs can be spread over more output, which will lead to lower unit costs. When set-up or fixed costs are high, individuals and organisations have a strong incentive to identify and stick with a single option.

♦ *Learning effects:* Knowledge gained in the operation of complex systems also leads to higher returns from continuing use. With repetition, individuals learn how to use products more effectively, and their experiences are likely to spur further innovations in the product or in related activities.

♦ *Co-ordination effects:* These occur when the benefits an individual receives from a particular activity increase as others adopt the same option. If technologies embody positive *network externalities,* a given technology will become more attractive as more people use it. Co-ordination effects are especially significant when a technology has to be compatible with a linked infrastructure (e.g., software with hardware, automobiles with an infrastructure of roads, repair facilities and fuelling stations). Increased use of a technology encourages investments in the linked infrastructure, which in turn makes the technology more attractive.

♦ *Adaptive expectations:* If options that fail to win broad acceptance will
have drawbacks later on, individuals may feel a need to 'pick the right
horse'. Although the dynamic here is related to co-ordination effects, it
derives from the self-fulfilling character of *expectations*. Projections about
future aggregate use patterns lead individuals to adapt their actions in
ways that help to make those expectations come true.

From an institutional and organisational perspective, Arthur's discussion
of technology is important primarily because, as North (1990: 95) lays out,
all four self-reinforcing mechanisms apply, albeit with somewhat different
characteristics, and it clarifies a set of relationships typical of many social
interactions. Creating a new organisation usually entails significant start-
up costs; organisations learn by doing; the benefits of organisational
activities are often enhanced if they are co-ordinated or 'fit' with the
activities of other individuals, organisations or institutions; and it is
frequently important to 'pick the right horse', so organisations adapt their
actions in light of their expectations about the actions of others.

To the above self-reinforcing mechanisms can be added those of veto
points, or rules that make pre-existing arrangements hard to reverse, and
asset specificity (Pierson, 2004), the latter providing additional force to the
mechanisms of co-ordination effects and adaptive expectations. The concept
of asset specificity highlights variation in the degree to which the value of
assets is restricted to a particular setting or use, rather than being easily
reassigned to some other activity (Alt, Frieden, Gilligan, Rodrik & Rogowski,
1996; Lake, 1999). To the degree that assets are specific, there is likely to be
more constraint in how they are applied, so reinforcing path dependence.

Thus, in sequences with self-reinforcing properties, initial steps in a given
direction produce further movement along the same path, such that over
time it becomes difficult, if not impossible, to reverse direction. Increasing
returns processes are considered to apply to the persistence of a wide array
of institutions, with 'almost all institutional perspectives understand[ing]
"institutions" as enduring entities that cannot be changed instantaneously or
easily. This quality of persistence makes institutions a particularly useful
object of inquiry for analysts concerned with self-reinforcing sequences'
(Mahoney, 2000: 512). Once the selection is made, institutions endure
without recourse to that which brought about their creation.

Reactive Sequences & Outcomes

Mahoney (2001) notes that, in many path-dependent cases, the continued
existence of an institution over time activates a sequence of causally-linked

events that, when activated, materialise separately from the institutional factors that originally produced it. While ultimately connected to a critical juncture period, this chain of events can end in an outcome that is far removed from the initial critical juncture. He refers to these sequences of reactions and counter-reactions as 'reactive sequences' (Mahoney, 2000). In reactive sequences, comprising chains of events that are both temporally ordered and causally connected, the final event in the sequence is the outcome of interest. With each event within the chain a reaction to temporally antecedent events, and thus dependent on prior events, the overall chain of events can be viewed as a path culminating in the outcome. A reactive sequence is often set in motion by an initial challenge to the existing institution, with counter-reactions to this opposition then driving ensuing events in the sequence. Baring an 'inherent logic of events' (Abbott, 1992: 445), whereby reaction-counterreaction dynamics predictably see one event generate another, reactive sequences are normally marked by properties of reaction and counter-response as institutional patterns put in place during critical juncture periods are resisted or supported. Although such resistance may not lead to the transformation of these institutions, it can trigger an independent process that includes events leading to a result of interest. The tensions of a reactive sequence usually yield more stable final outcomes, which involve the development of new institutional patterns. While such outcomes suggest fairly stable equilibrium points, they will inevitably become displaced by new periods of discontinuity signalling the end of a particular critical juncture and possibly the start of a new one.

Methodologically, path dependence entails 'tracing a given outcome back to a particular set of historical events, and showing how these events are themselves contingent occurrences that cannot be explained on the basis of prior historical conditions' (Mahoney, 2000: 507-508). With path dependence characterising 'specifically those historical sequences in which contingent events set into motion institutional patterns or event chains that have deterministic properties' (Mahoney, 2000: 507), narrative analysis is considered most useful 'when temporal sequencing, particular events, and path dependence must be taken into account' (Mahoney, 1999: 1164). With causal narrative, which has been formalised through the procedure of event structure analysis (Corsaro & Heise, 1990; Griffin, 1993; Heise, 1988, 1989, 1991; Isaac, Street & Knapp, 1994), thick description of the sequence of events of a single case is used to identify the causal mechanisms at work in the sequence.

For the purposes of preparing for the path dependence analysis, for example, my first task when studying the forming of the Industrial Development Authority (IDA) was to source the raw material necessary to construct a running chronology of the events that constitute the organisational forming sequence for the IDA (Donnelly, 2007, forthcoming). The starting point for the chronology was the period immediately prior to the general election of 1932, to provide context for the creation of the IDA as an administrative body in 1949, when the alternative was to continue with the *status quo* option of the Department of Industry & Commerce, and the end-point marks the restructuring of the IDA into three separate agencies – Forfás, Forbairt (subsequently, Enterprise Ireland in 1998) and Industrial Development Agency Ireland– in 1994.

In terms of the data that I used to build the chronology and write the narrative, I had recourse to both archival and interview material. The primary and secondary archival sources to which I had access were those available in the public domain (see **Table 6.1**). In addition to archival material, I also conducted semi-structured interviews with three key decision-makers with intimate knowledge of the IDA and much of the period under study, namely the past and then current chief executives.

◆ Oireachtas (Parliament) archives, which cover debates and questions from the foundation of the State (1922) to the present.	◆ National Archives, which cover civil service department records from the foundation of the State (1922) up to 1976.
◆ Media archives.	◆ Legislation.
◆ Government-sponsored reports / reviews.	◆ IDA Annual Reports, 1969/70 to 1994.
◆ Government policies and economic programs.	◆ Published work (e.g., articles, books, reports, monographs) relating to the period under study.

Table 6.1: The Primary & Secondary Archival Sources

I was mindful that my work entailed historiography (Thies, 2002: 351) and, even though '*there is no such thing as a definitive account of any historical episode*' (Gaddis, 2001: 308, emphasis in original), I pursued a number of strategies to minimise the potential adverse effects of investigator bias and unwarranted selectivity in the use of materials from the historical record. Principally, I sought to cross-reference and triangulate with various sources of evidence, so as to maximise coverage and bring to light inaccuracies or biases in the individual sources, in the process constructing a more accurate account (McCullagh, 2000; Thies 2002). For example, to avoid the problems associated with interview data, e.g., analysing or describing the past from the viewpoint of the present (Butterfield, 1931; Thies, 2002) or interpreting interviewee accounts in favour of the way they saw events, I sought to triangulate with other sources of evidence – e.g., archives, newspaper and other contemporaneous accounts – so as to minimise inconsistencies, inaccuracies or biases in these individual sources and ultimately to provide a more accurate account. Equally, concerning secondary sources, I followed Thies' (2002) recommendation to start with the most recent contributions and then work backwards, the aim being to note the 'facts' that have stood the test of time.

In the knowledge that the record was incomplete, I am inclined towards viewing the 'results [of my research] as the uncertain product of an incomplete evidentiary record' (Elman & Elman, 2001: 29). Compounding this problem, the primary and secondary sources available to me were still too large to consider on my own, thus necessitating yet more selectivity in the sources I used. As such, I was upfront in acknowledging the potential impact of this selectivity on the judgments or inferences I made.

Data Analyses

In order to interpret sequential events as chapters of a coherent story, particularly where the narrative spans time periods with events located in different temporal contexts, it was necessary to isolate the mechanisms / steps through which a preceding event influenced a succeeding event. Approaching path dependency through the narrative method of event-structure analysis offered the rigorous means through which to sort events into temporally-explanatory sequences, by isolating conditions or choices that eliminated options and pointed history in a particular direction, for subsequent analysis and explanation.

Event structure analysis (ESA), and its associated computer program ETHNO (available as freeware from http://www.indiana.edu/~socpsy/ESA/home.html), permits the development of causal, interpretive-based explanations of narrative. Originally developed to study cultural routines (Corsaro & Heise, 1990; Heise, 1989), ESA has since been applied by many researchers to the study of historical narratives (e.g., Griffin, 1993; Isaac, Street & Knapp, 1994), including those of organisational change (Stevenson & Greenberg, 1998, 2000), industrial and interracial unionism (Brown, 2000; Brown & Brueggemann, 1997; Brueggemann & Boswell, 1998; Brueggemann & Brown, 2003), and organisational decline / life histories (Hager, 1998; Hager & Galaskiewicz, 2002; Pajunen, 2003). According to Griffin (1993: 1107), ESA can 'be used to illustrate or test virtually any processual theory.'

Narrative & Event Structure Analysis

As noted by Czarniawska-Joerges (1995: 15), narrative can be seen as 'a sequential account of events, usually chronologically, whereby sequentiality indicates some kind of causality, and action – accounted for in terms of intentions, deeds and consequences – is commonly given a central place'. Narratives have an explicit start-point, a sequence of intervening events, and an end-point that is reached through the many paths and the interrelationships between the intervening events (Griffin, 1992). A narrative explanation depends on these unfurling interconnections to explore the process leading to the outcome under investigation. As the story develops, there are contingencies, conjunctions and paths to be considered that might change the general flow of the narrative. As such, narrative explanation has to absorb the order of events and the position of an event in the story (Gotham & Staples, 1996).

With a coherent story line, it becomes possible to explain events at one point in time with reference to previous developments in the plot. Thus it is that the researcher-as-storyteller comes to identify the inherent logic that causes one event to follow from another (Abbott, 1992; Griffin, 1993; Isaac, 1997). Approaching explanation through storytelling provides what is considered a good way to represent how causal relations are rooted in particular contexts and performed over time (Haydu, 1998).

However, narrative alone does not provide causal explanations of path-dependent processes for, as Griffin (1993) notes, chronological order does not automatically yield causal significance. Further, on its own, narrative description can obscure explanation through its inability to recognise that an event may not have impact until much later in a sequence of events (Griffin, 1993). In order to shift from simple description towards understanding how causal processes are embedded in temporal streams, how some sequences have no tangible effect on the outcomes of events and how parallel sequences of events can emerge from an event and possibly converge on a significant turning-point, rigorous systematic methods for analysing narratives are essential (Griffin, 1993). Because it is based on a formal mathematical logic, ESA makes possible the development of a dynamic, causal interpretation of the primary narrative that can be replicated and generalised.

For example, having constructed the running chronology of events that constitute the organisational forming sequence for the IDA, I then used the ETHNO program to help me develop my interpretation of the causal relationships, the path dependencies, and the critical points in the organisational forming process. I entered each event into the ETHNO program in chronological order and, as each new event was entered, ETHNO posed a series of yes / no questions that asked for clarification about whether an event entered earlier was necessary for the occurrence of this new event. Through this process of interrogation, I was able to break down the running chronology of the narrative and reconstruct it with causal connections based on my 'expert judgments' (Griffin, 1993).

ETHNO, it has to be said, does not determine causality. Rather, I structured and interpreted the narrative events, based on information and knowledge I had to hand (Griffin, 1993, Isaac, Street & Knapp, 1994). Through the use of 'yes / no' queries, ETHNO obliged me to be clear-cut and thorough in my assessments about the association between particular events and to evaluate these events causally, not chronologically (Griffin, 1993). The heuristic of event structure analysis, and its associated ETHNO tool, allowed me to hone my understanding of the causal relationships between the different events. In so doing, I was in a position to verify which events had no effect and how certain events had consequences for the future, even though they did not trigger anything in the present. With the help of ETHNO, I decomposed organisational forming into a series of events such that path dependencies were identified and made clear. **Figure 6.2** below presents a sample ETHNO output showing associations between a series of events.

Path Dependence Interpretation & Explanation

The resulting event structure then facilitated causal interpretation and explanation of the process of organisational forming in respect of the IDA from a path dependence perspective. The resulting path dependence narrative covers the initial critical juncture, when events triggered creation of the IDA, and the period of reproduction, in which positive feedback mechanisms (e.g., large set-up or fixed costs, learning effects, co-ordination effects, adaptive expectations) reinforced the IDA. Thus, the path dependence narrative commenced with a historical fork in the road (contingency), pinpointed the turn taken and called attention to how ensuing developments rendered the choice irreversible.

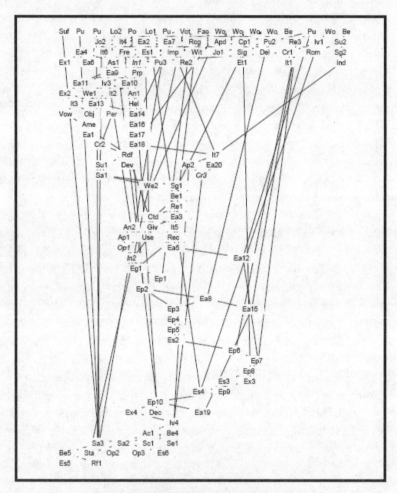

**Figure 6.2: Sample ETHNO Output, Showing Associations
between a Series of Events**

In the case of the IDA (Donnelly, 2007, forthcoming), we see its emergence at a critical juncture in 1949 and subsequent institutionalisation within the Irish industrial development landscape. Telling the story of the IDA from a path dependence perspective entailed charting the sequence of events at the centre of its emergence and evolution over time. At a key choice point or critical juncture, when antecedent historical conditions defined a range of available options, the industrial / economic development agency was selected and subsequently evolved, through self-reinforcing and positive feedback mechanisms, and was challenged, during periods of possible discontinuity, over time.

In the final analysis, from relatively contingent and unpredictable beginnings has evolved 'the IDA' as organisational form. Both the forces for structural persistence and those of reactive sequences have contributed to producing and reproducing an increasingly fine-tuned, specific asset, an organisational form that, *ex ante*, could not have been predicted when it was first established.

CONCLUSION

This chapter draws together the theoretical arguments underpinning the analysis of path dependent processes, organised around Mahoney's (2001) analytic structure (**Figure 6.1**). In the course of pre-critical junctures, when antecedent conditions are at play, at least two alternatives are open for selection and potential processes influencing the choice made at the critical juncture become active. The choice is consequential because it leads to the creation of a pattern that endures over time, nudging history down tracks that then, through the stubborn persistence of subsequent continuities, become increasingly difficult to reverse. It is here that positive feedback processes become active, with fixed costs, learning effects, co-ordination effects and adaptive expectations coming into play and contributing to structural persistence. Thus it is that, once a specific selection has been made, it becomes increasingly difficult with the passing of time to return to the initial critical juncture when at least two options were still available. In sequences with self-reinforcing properties, initial steps in a given direction produce further movement along the same path, such that over time it becomes difficult, if not impossible, to reverse direction.

The continued existence of the organisational over time activates a sequence of causally-linked events that, when activated, materialises separately from the institutional factors that originally produced it. In such reactive sequences, which comprise chains of events that are both temporally ordered and causally connected, the final event in the sequence is the outcome of interest. With each event within the chain a reaction to temporally antecedent events, and thus dependent on prior events, the overall chain of events can be viewed as a path culminating in the outcome. A reactive sequence is often set in motion by an initial challenge to the existing institution, with counter-reactions to this opposition then driving ensuing events in the sequence. Reactive sequences are normally marked by properties of reaction and counter-response as institutional patterns put in place during critical juncture periods are resisted or supported. Although such resistance may not lead to the transformation of these institutions, it can trigger an independent process that includes events leading to a result of interest. The tensions of a reactive sequence usually yield more stable final outcomes, which involve the development of new institutional patterns. While such outcomes suggest fairly stable equilibrium points, they will inevitably become displaced by new periods of discontinuity signalling the end of a particular critical juncture and possibly the start of a new one.

REFERENCES

Abbott, A. (1992). 'From Causes to Events: Notes on Narrative Positivism', *Sociological Methods and Research* 20(4): 428-55.

Abrams, P. (1982). *Historical Sociology.* Ithaca, NY: Cornell University Press.

Ackrill, R. & Kay, A. (2006). 'Historical-Institutionalist Perspectives on the Development of the EU Budget System', *Journal of European Public Policy* 13(1): 113-33.

Alt, J.E., Frieden, J., Gilligan, M.J., Rodrik, D. & Rogowski, R. (1996). 'The Political Economy of International Trade: Enduring Puzzles and an Agenda for Enquiry', *Comparative Political Studies* 29(6): 689-717.

Aminzade, R. (1992). 'Historical Sociology and Time', *Sociological Methods and Research* 20(4): 456-80.

Ankersmit, F.R. (1989). 'Historiography and Postmodernism', *History and Theory* 28(2): 137-53.

Antonelli, C. (1997). 'The Economics of Path Dependence in Industrial Organisation', *International Journal of Industrial Organization* 15(6): 643-75.

Arthur, W.B. (1988). 'Competing Technologies: An Overview', in Dosi, G., Freeman, C., Nelson, R., Silverberg, G. & Soete, L. (eds), *Technological Change and Economic Theory*, pp. 560-607. London: Frances Pinter.

Arthur, W.B. (1989). 'Competing Technologies and Lock-in by Historical Small Events', *The Economic Journal* 99(394): 116-31.

Arthur, W.B. (1990). 'Positive Feedbacks in the Economy', *Scientific American* 262(2): 92-99.

Arthur, W.B. (1994). *Increasing Returns and Path Dependence in the Economy.* Ann Arbor, MI: University of Michigan Press.

Araujo, L. & Rezende, S. (2003). 'Path Dependence, MNCs and the
    Internationalisation Process: A Relational Approach', *International Business
    Review* 12(6): 719-37.

Astley, W.G. & Van de Ven, A.H. (1983). 'Central Perspectives and Debates in
    Organizational Theory', *Administrative Science Quarterly* 28(2): 245-73.

Baum, J.A.C. (1996). 'Organizational Ecology', in Clegg, S.R., Hardy, C. & Nord,
    W.R. (eds), *Handbook of Organization Studies*, pp. 77-114. London: Sage.

Béland, D. & Hacker, J.S. (2004). 'Ideas, Private Institutions and American Welfare
    State 'Exceptionalism': The Case of Health and Old-age Insurance, 1915–1965',
    International Journal of Social Welfare 13(1): 42-54.

Beugelsdijk, S., van Schaik, T. & Arts, W. (2006). 'Toward a Unified Europe?
    Explaining Regional Differences in Value Patterns by Economic Development,
    Cultural Heritage and Historical Shocks', *Regional Studies* 40(3): 317-27.

Booth, C. (2003). 'Does History Matter? The Possibilities and Problems of
    Counterfactual Analysis', *Management Decision* 41(1): 96-104.

Brousseau, E. & Chaves, B. (2005). 'Contrasted Paths of Adoption: Is E-business
    Really Converging Toward a Common Organizational Model?', *Electronic
    Markets* 15(3): 181-98.

Brown, C. (2000). 'The Role of Employers in Split Labor Markets: An Event
    Structure Analysis of Racial Conflict and AFL Organizing, 1917-1919', *Social
    Forces* 79(2): 653-81.

Brown, C. & Brueggemann, J. (1997) 'Mobilizing Interracial Solidarity: A
    Comparison of the 1919 and 1937 Steel Industry Labor Organizing Drives',
    Mobilization 2(1): 47-70.

Brueggemann, J. & Boswell, T. (1998). 'Realizing Solidarity: Sources of Interracial
    Unionism during the Great Depression', *Work & Occupations* 25(4): 436-82.

Brueggemann, J. & Brown, C. (2003). 'The Decline of Industrial Unionism in the
    Meatpacking Industry: Event Structure Analyses of Labor Unrest, 1946-1987',
    Work & Occupations 30(3): 327-60.

Bruggeman, D. (2002). 'NASA: A Path Dependent Organization', *Technology in
    Society* 24(4): 415-31.

Butterfield, H. (1931). *The Whig Interpretation of History*. London: G. Bell & Sons.

Clark, P. & Rowlinson, M. (2004). 'The Treatment of History in Organization
    Studies: Towards an "Historic Turn"?', *Business History* 46(3): 331-52.

Corsaro, W.A. & Heise, D.R. (1990). 'Event Structure Models from Ethnographic
    Data', *Sociological Methodology* 20: 1-57.

Cowan, R. (1990). 'Nuclear Power Reactors: A Study in Technological Lock-in',
    Journal of Economic History 50(3): 541-67.

Crouch, C. & Farrell, H. (2004). 'Breaking the Path of Institutional Development:
    Alternatives to the New Determinism in Political Economy', *Rationality and
    Society* 16(1): 5-43.

Cusumano, M.A., Mylonadis, Y. & Rosenbloom, R.S. (1992). 'Strategic Maneuvering and Mass-Market Dynamics: The Triumph of VHS over Beta', *Business History Review* 66(1): 51-94.

Czarniawska-Joerges, B. (1995). 'Narration or Science? Collapsing the Division in Organization Studies', *Organization* 2(1): 11-33.

David, P. (1985). 'Clio and the Economics of QWERTY', *American Economic Review* 75(2): 332-37.

David, P. (1987). 'Some New Standards for the Economics of Standardization in the Information Age', in Dasgupta, P. & Stoneman, P. (eds), *Economic Policy & Technological Performance*, pp. 206-39. Cambridge: Cambridge University Press.

David, P. (1994). 'Why are Institutions the "Carriers of History"? Path Dependence and the Evolution of Conventions, Organizations & Institutions', *Structural Change and Economic Dynamics* 5(2): 205-20.

David, P. (1997). 'Path Dependence and the Quest for Historical Economics: One More Chorus of the Ballad of QWERTY', Discussion Paper in Economics and Social History, No. 20. Oxford: University of Oxford.

David, P. (1999). *At Last, a Remedy for Chronic QWERTY-Skepticism!* [Online]. Available: http://www.utdallas.edu/~liebowit/emba/david%20cure.pdf (last accessed 14 March 2009).

David, P. (2001). 'Path Dependence, Its Critics and the Quest for "Historical Economics"', in Garrouste, P. & Ioannides, S. (eds), *Evolution and Path Dependence in Economic Ideas: Past & Present*, pp. 15-40. Cheltenham, U.K.: Edward Elgar.

Donnelly, P. (2007). 'Organizational Forming in Amodern Times: Path Dependence, Actor-Network Theory and Ireland's Industrial Development Authority', unpublished PhD, University of Massachusetts at Amherst.

Donnelly, P. (forthcoming). 'Forming Ireland's Industrial Development Authority', in Hogan, J., Donnelly, P. & O'Rourke, B. (eds), *Irish Business and Society at the Start of the 21st Century.* Cork: Oak Tree Press.

Elman, C. & Elman, M.F. (2001). 'Introduction: Negotiating International History and Politics', in Elman, C. & Elman, M.F. (eds), *Bridges and Boundaries: Historians, Political Scientists and the Study of International Relations*, pp. 1-36. Cambridge, MA: MIT Press.

ETHNO [Online]. Available: http://www.indiana.edu/~socpsy/ESA/home.html (last accessed 14 March 2009).

Fligstein, N. (1990). *The Transformation of Corporate Control.* Cambridge, MA: Harvard University Press.

Gaddis, J.L. (2001). 'In Defense of Particular Generalization: Rewriting Cold War History, Rethinking International Relations Theory', in Elman, C. & Elman, M.F. (eds), *Bridges and Boundaries: Historians, Political Scientists and the Study of International Relations*, pp. 301-26. Cambridge, MA: MIT Press.

Garnsey, E. (1998). 'The Genesis of the High Technology Milieu: A Study in Complexity', *International Journal of Urban and Regional Research* 22(3): 361-77.

Goldman, P. (1994). 'Searching for History in Organizational Theory: Comment on Kieser', *Organization Science* 5(4): 621-23.

Goodman, R.S. & Kruger, E.J. (1988). 'Data Dredging or Legitimate Research Method: Historiography and its Potential for Management Research', *Academy of Management Review* 13(2): 315-25.

Gotham, K.F. & Staples, W.G. (1996). 'Narrative Analysis and the New Historical Sociology', *Sociological Quarterly* 37(3): 481-501.

Greener, I. (2002). 'Theorising Path-Dependency: How Does History Come to Matter in Organizations?', *Management Decision* 40(5/6): 614-19.

Greener, I. (2005). 'The Potential of Path Dependence in Political Studies', *Politics* 25(1): 62-72.

Griffin, L.J. (1992). 'Temporality, Events and Explanation in Historical Sociology: An Introduction', *Sociological Methods and Research* 20(4): 403-27.

Griffin, L.J. (1993). 'Narrative, Event Structure Analysis and Causal Interpretation in Historical Sociology', *American Journal of Sociology* 98(5): 1094-1133.

Hacker, J.S. (2002). *The Divided Welfare State: The Battle over Public and Private Social Benefits in the United States.* Cambridge: Cambridge University Press.

Hager, M.A. (1998). *Event Structure Analysis as a Tool for Understanding Organizational Life Histories* [Online]. Available: http://www.nonprofitresearch.org/ usr_doc/17310.pdf (last accessed 14 March 2009).

Hager, M.A. & Galaskiewicz, J. (2002). *Studying Closure Among Nonprofit Organizations Using Event-Structure Analysis and Network Methods* [Online]. Available: http://hcoc4.berkeley.edu/Galaskiewicz-abs.pdf (last accessed 14 March 2009).

Hannan, M.T. & Freeman, J. (1989). *Organizational Ecology.* Cambridge, MA: Ballinger.

Hassink, R. (2005). 'How to Unlock Regional Economies from Path Dependency? From Learning Region to Learning Cluster', *European Planning Studies* 13(4): 521-35.

Haydu, J. (1998). 'Making Use of the Past: Time Periods as Cases to Compare and as Sequences of Problem Solving', *American Journal of Sociology* 104(2): 339-71.

Heffernan, G.M. (2003). 'Path Dependence, Behavioral Rules and the Role of Entrepreneurship in Economic Change: The Case of the Automobile Industry', *The Review of Austrian Economics* 16(1): 45-62.

Heise, D. (1988). 'Computer Analysis of Cultural Structures', *Social Science Computer Review* 6(2): 183-96.

Heise, D. (1989). 'Modeling Event Structures', *Journal of Mathematical Sociology* 14(2): 139-69.

Heise, D. (1991). 'Event Structure Analysis: A Qualitative Model of Quantitative Research', in Fielding, N. & Lee, R. (eds), *Using Computers in Qualitative Research*, pp. 136-63. Newbury Park, CA: Sage.

Hirsch, P.M. & Gillespie, J.J. (2001). 'Unpacking Path Dependence: Differential Valuations History across Disciplines', in Garud, R. & Karnøe, P. (eds), *Path Dependence and Creation*, pp. 69-90. London: Lawrence Erlbaum & Associates.

Hogan, J. (2005). 'Testing for a Critical Juncture: Change in the ICTU's Influence over Public Policy in 1959', *Irish Political Studies* 20(3): 271-95.

Howlett, M. & Ramesh, M. (2002). 'The Policy Effects of Internationalization: A Subsystem Adjustment Analysis of Policy Change', *Journal of Comparative Policy Analysis* 4(1): 31-50.

Isaac, L.W. (1997). 'Transforming Localities: Reflections on Time, Causality and Narrative in Contemporary Historical Sociology', *Historical Methods* 30(1): 4-12.

Isaac, L.W., Street, D.A. & Knapp, S.J. (1994). 'Analyzing Historical Contingency with Formal Methods', *Sociological Methods & Research* 23(1): 114-41.

Jakobsen, S-E., Rusten, G. & Fløysand, A. (2005). 'How Green is the Valley? Foreign Direct Investment in Two Norwegian Industrial Towns', *The Canadian Geographer* 49(3): 244-59.

Jones, S.R.H. (1982). 'The Organization of Work: A Historical Dimension', *Journal of Economic Behavior & Organization* 3: 117-37.

Jones, S.R.H. (1997). 'Transaction Costs & the Theory of the Firm: The Scope and Limitations of the New Institutional Approach', *Business History* 39(4): 9–25.

Karlsen, A. (2005). 'The Dynamics of Regional Specialization and Cluster Formation: Dividing Trajectories of Maritime Industries in Two Norwegian Regions', *Entrepreneurship & Regional Development* 17(5): 313-38.

Kay, A. (2003). 'Path Dependency and the CAP', *Journal of European Public Policy* 10(3): 405-20.

Kay, A. (2005). 'A Critique of the Use of Path Dependency in Policy Studies', *Public Administration* 83(3): 553-71.

Kenney, M. & von Burg, U. (1999). 'Technology, Entrepreneurship and Path Dependence: Industrial Clustering in Silicon Valley and Route 128', *Industrial & Corporate Change* 8(1): 67-103.

Kenney, M. & von Burg, U. (2000). 'Paths and Regions: The Creation and Growth of Silicon Valley', in Garud, R. & Karnøe, P. (eds), *Path Creation and Path Dependence*, pp. 127-48. New York: Lawrence Erlbaum & Associates.

Kieser, A. (1994). 'Why Organization Theory Needs Historical Analyses – and How This Should be Performed', *Organization Science* 5(4): 608-20.

Krücken, G. (2003). 'Learning the "New, New Thing": On the Role of Path Dependency in University Structures', *Higher Education* 46(3): 315-39.

Krugman, P. (1991). 'History and Industry Location: The Case of the Manufacturing Belt', *American Economic Review* 81(2): 80-83.

Krugman, P. (1996). *Pop Internationalism*. Cambridge, MA: MIT Press.

Lake, D.A. (1999). *Entangling Relations: American Foreign Policy in its Century*. Princeton, NJ: Princeton University Press.

Lawrence, B.S. (1984). 'Historical Perspective: Using the Past to Study the Present', *Academy of Management Review* 9(2): 307-12.

Lukacs, J. (2002). *At the End of an Age*. New Haven: Yale University Press.

Mahoney, J. (1999). 'Nominal, Ordinal and Narrative Appraisal in Macrocausal Analysis', *American Journal of Sociology* 104(4): 1154-96.

Mahoney, J. (2000). 'Path Dependence in Historical Sociology', *Theory and Society* 29(4): 507-48.

Mahoney, J. (2001). 'Path-Dependent Explanations of Regime Change: Central America in Comparative Perspective', *Studies in Comparative International Development* 36(1): 111–41.

McCloskey, D.N. (1994). *Knowledge and Persuasion in Economics.* Cambridge: Cambridge University Press.

McCullagh, C.B. (2000). 'Bias in Historical Description, Interpretation and Explanation', *History and Theory* 39(1): 39-66.

Maielli, G. (2005). 'The Machine that Never Changed: Intangible Specialisation and Output-Mix Optimisation at Fiat, 1960s–1990s', *Competition and Change* 9(3): 249-76.

Morgan, G. & Kubo, I. (2005). 'Beyond Path Dependency? Constructing New Models for Institutional Change: The Case of Capital Markets in Japan', *Socio-Economic Review* 3(1): 55-82.

Mueller, D.C. (1997). 'First-Mover Advantages and Path Dependence', *International Journal of Industrial Organization,* 15(6): 827-50.

Nerkar, A. & Paruchuri, S. (2005). 'Evolution of R&D Capabilities: The Role of Knowledge Networks within a Firm', *Management Science* 51(5): 771-85.

Noda, T. & Collis, D.J. (2001). 'The Evolution of Intraindustry Firm Heterogeneity: Insights from a Process Study', *Academy of Management Journal* 44(4): 897-25.

North, D.C. (1990). *Institutions, Institutional Change and Economic Performance.* Cambridge: Cambridge University Press.

Pajunen, K. (2005). 'Comparative Causal Analysis in Processual Strategy Research: A Study of Causal Mechanisms in Organizational Decline & Turnarounds', in Szulanski, G., Porac, J. & Doz, Y. (eds), *Advances in Strategic Management* 22: 415-56. Amsterdam: Elseiver Publishing.

Perrow, C. (1986). *Complex Organizations: A Critical Essay,* 3rd ed. New York, NY: Random House.

Pierson, P. (1993). 'When Effect Becomes Cause: Policy Feedback and Political Change', *World Politics* 45(4): 595-28.

Pierson, P. (2000a). 'Increasing Returns, Path Dependence and the Study of Politics,' *American Political Science Review* 94(2): 251-67.

Pierson, P. (2000b). 'Not Just What, but *When*: Timing and Sequence in Political Processes', *Studies in American Political Development* 14(1): 72-92.

Pierson, P. (2004). *Politics in Time: History, Institutions and Social Analysis.* Princeton, NJ: Princeton University Press.

Pierson, P. & Skocpol, T. (2002). 'Historical Institutionalism in Contemporary Political Science', in Katznelson, I. & Milner, H.V. (eds), *Political Science: The State of the Discipline,* pp. 693-21. New York, NY: W.W. Norton.

Puffert, D.J. (1991). *The Economics of Spatial Network Externalities and the Dynamics of Railway Gauge Standardization.* Ph.D. dissertation, Stanford University.

Rao, P.M., Vemuri, V.K. & Galvin, P. (2004). 'The Changing Technological Profile of the Leading ICT Firms: Evidence from US Patent Data, 1981-2000', *Industry and Innovation* 11(4): 353-72.

Schmidt, R.H. & Spindler, G. (2002). 'Path Dependence, Corporate Governance and Complementarity', *International Finance* 5(3): 311-33.

Sonnenwald, D.H. (2003). 'The Conceptual Organization: An Emergent Organizational Form for Collaborative R&D', *Science and Public Policy* 30(4): 261-72.

Stack, M. & Gartland, M.P. (2003). 'Path Creation, Path Dependency and Alternative Theories of the Firm', *Journal of Economic Issues* 37(2): 487-94.

Stack, M. & Gartland, M.P. (2005). 'The Repeal of Prohibition and the Resurgence of the National Breweries: Productive Efficiency or Path Creation?', *Management Decision* 43(3): 420-32.

Stevenson, W.B. & Greenberg, D.N. (1998). 'The Formal Analysis of Narratives of Organizational Change', *Journal of Management* 24(6): 741-62.

Stevenson, W.B. & Greenberg, D.N. (2000). 'Agency and Social Networks: Strategies of Action in a Social Structure of Position, Opposition and Opportunity', *Administrative Science Quarterly* 45(4): 651-78.

Swedberg, R. & Granovetter, M. (eds) (1992). 'Introduction', in Granovetter, M. & Swedberg, R. (eds), *The Sociology of Economic Life*, pp. 1-28. Boulder, CO: Westview Press.

Sydow, J., Schreyögg, G. & Koch, J. (2005). 'Organizational Paths: Path Dependency and Beyond', paper presented at the 21st EGOS Colloquium, Berlin, Germany.

Teece, D.J., Pisano, G. & Shuen, A. (1997). 'Dynamic Capabilities and Strategic Management', *Strategic Management Journal* 18(7): 509-34.

Thelen, K. (2000). 'Timing and Temporality in the Analysis of Institutional Evolution & Change', *Studies in American Political Development* 14: 101-08.

Thies, C.G. (2002). 'A Pragmatic Guide to Qualitative Historical Analysis in the Study of International Relations', *International Studies Perspectives* 3(4): 351-72.

Üsdiken, B. & Kieser, A. (2004). 'Introduction: History in Organization Studies', *Business History* 46(3): 321-30.

van der Klein, M. (2003). 'The Widows of the Gasworks: Gendered Path Dependency and the Early Dutch Welfare State', *Social Politics* 10(1): 1-22.

White, H. (1995). 'Response to Arthur Marwick', *Journal of Contemporary History* 30(2): 233-46.

Williamson, O.E. (1985). *The Economic Institutions of Capitalism*. New York, NY: Free Press.

Zald, M.N. (1990). 'History, Sociology and Theories of Organization', in Jackson, J.E. (ed), *Institutions in American Society: Essays in Market, Political and Social Organizations*, pp. 81-108. Ann Arbor, MI: University of Michigan Press.

Zald, M.N. (1993). 'Organization Studies as a Scientific & Humanistic Enterprise: Toward a Reconceptualization of the Foundation of the Field', *Organization Science* 4(4): 513-28.

Zukowski, R. (2004). 'Historical Path Dependence, Institutional Persistence and Transition to Market Economy: The Case of Poland', *International Journal of Social Economics* 31(10): 955-73.

CHAPTER 7
PIERCING THE ARMOURED POLICY: IDEAS & MACROECONOMIC POLICY CHANGE IN IRELAND & THE UK

John Hogan & David Doyle

INTRODUCTION

Historical institutionalism is a method employed in the social sciences that focuses upon institutions, and their past. By the term 'institution', historical institutionalism can be referring to a bureaucratic institution, an association such as a trade union, an ideology, or even a law. It is very broad in its definition of institution. Historical institutionalism is generally employed in a comparative capacity in studies. As such, historical institutional studies tend to use a minimum of two case studies in order to achieve comparative findings, although many studies employ three, or more, case studies.

For historical institutionalism, the focus is on choices made early in the history of a polity, institution, law etc. These choices will have a persistent influence from that point onwards, making a reversal of course ever more difficult as time passes (Peters, 1999: 210). When, for instance, a government initiative starts down a particular path, there is a tendency for choices to persist. Put simply, choices made at time T influence choices at time T+1 (Berman, 1998: 380). Policies, for example, tend to be path dependent and, once initiated, continue until a sufficiently strong force deflects them (Krasner 1984: 240). Consequently, institutions are not easily altered when conditions change (Schickler 2001; Stark & Bruszt 1998). Thus, one of the concepts that historical institutionalists use in their research is that of path dependence.

Historical institutionalists focus on the conditions that led to the choice of a particular trajectory, while also considering the other trajectories that might have been selected at that time. As a result, the importance of the path followed is counterbalanced by considerations of the importance of those paths not chosen. Historical institutionalism is effective at explaining what happens, and in weaving a narrative that captures a good deal of the broad 'reality' of history. However, these characterisations of history come close to being functionalist. 'Historical institutionalism is not a fertile source of explanations for change in organisations and institutions' (Peters, 1999: 70). The problem is that there are cases in which institutions change in unexpected ways, and historical institutionalism appears at a loss to explain them. Rothstein (1996: 153) argues that this situation marks 'the weakest and most difficult point in [historical] institutionalist analysis.' Historical institutionalism is very good at explaining continuity, but not change.

Institutionalists (Steinmo, 1989; Thelen & Steinmo, 1992; Christensen, 1997; Mahoney, 2000; Pierson, 2000; Gorges, 2001) argue that crises result in abrupt institutional change. Often, crises are pointed to as the starting-points in a sequence of change, as in path dependence. Critical junctures have been regarded as initiating historical paths, as the catalysts that bring about the institutional / policy choices that are made at the time T. Consequently, scholars' interpretations of institutional change have resulted in the past being divided into periods of normalcy, and critical junctures.

Critical junctures are thus seen as pointing to the importance of the past in explaining the present. They 'suggest the importance of focusing on the formative moments for institutions and organisations' (Pierson, 1993: 602). As Collier & Collier (1991: 35) state, 'the distinctive contribution of the critical junctures framework is its approach to explanation'. It focuses on the historical causes. But, if focusing on the formative moments of institutions and organisations is critical, only being able to do so long after the fact constitutes a significant weakness for the concept, something this chapter seeks to remedy.

Pierson (2004: 5-6) states that critical junctures, 'a key concept needed in underpinning the analyses of temporal processes, have received only limited discussion'. Thelen (1999: 388) argues that good tools for understanding continuity have not been matched by equally sophisticated tools for understanding change. These arguments tie with the idea that historical institutionalism has tended to concentrate on the institutional side of the approach, rather than the historical. Historical institutionalism's inability to account for change has been compounded by the fact that the concept of a critical juncture has been left largely underdeveloped.

Lately, historical institutionalists have sought new means of demonstrating how institutions are remade (Thelen, 1999, 2000; Clemens & Cook, 1999; Pierson 2004). Consequently, the critical junctures concept, an only half-developed approach as it is entirely postdictive (as opposed to predictive), is being consigned to the rubbish bin. Simultaneously, some scholars are declaring particular events critical junctures, or watersheds, without the provision of the least evidence. This has rendered the concept of critical junctures largely meaningless, denigrating even what value it possesses as a postdictive approach.

In the past, critical junctures were examined by means of broad, sometimes unwieldy, frameworks (Collier & Collier 1991), or counterfactual analysis (Fearon, 1991; 1996). Of late, Hogan (2005; 2006) sought to endow the framework with greater rigour. But this involved the development of narrow, in many instances, case-specific criteria, as well as what amounted to arbitrary standards in certain cases. Consequently, scholars have yet to develop a framework for examining critical junctures that is both rigorous and widely applicable. Until now, all approaches used to examine critical junctures have been postdictive. Here we seek to develop a rigorous, widely applicable framework for examining critical junctures that incorporates a potentially predictive element.

We hypothesise that a critical juncture (a watershed or radical change) in macroeconomic policy consists of three discrete events or stages:

♦ Macroeconomic crisis.

♦ Ideational change.

♦ Radical change in economic policy.

Note, that this framework does not, as many have done in the past, conflate crisis and critical juncture. Instead, a crisis constitutes a part of a critical juncture, but does not constitute a critical juncture of and by itself. Until now, ideational change was not considered of importance in the analysis of critical junctures. However, we believe that the presence of ideational change links a crisis with the resultant policy change – that ideational change is an intermediating variable. As we are dealing with the idea of a radical change in macroeconomic policy, we assume this must be rapid in order to be synonymous with the concept of a critical juncture. Otherwise, the kind of change examined would constitute some other form or order of change, such as incremental change.

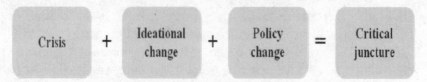

Figure 7.1: Critical Juncture Approach

Through examining four case studies of potential macroeconomic crises, one each from a different country, we aim to develop a set of criteria for examining potential critical junctures. The reason for so many cases is, as Hall (1993: 277) encourages, broad concepts deserve exploration in many contexts, and no single case can resolve all issues. The chapter seeks to show that, although there were four potential macroeconomic crises, not all were actual crises, and not all actual crises resulted in critical junctures in economic policies, and that the presence or absence of ideational change was the determining factor in this.

The chapter seeks to explain that what differentiates macroeconomic crises that result in radical economic policy changes, from those that do not, is ideational change. This differentiating factor is an essential element within the framework. If confirmed, it will be possible to look at countries experiencing economic difficulties, test to see whether the difficulties constitute a crisis, then test for the differentiating factor's presence, and thereafter interpret whether there is likely to be a radical change in economic policy. This development would remove the longstanding element of contingency associated with critical junctures by path dependence scholars (Mahoney, 2000: 513), and eliminate the necessity of having to wait decades to be able to conclude whether an event was a critical juncture.

The first section of the chapter discusses the critical junctures literature, focusing upon the frameworks developed, the range of issues the concept has been employed in, and its postdictive nature. The second section sets out the countries that make up the case studies. The third section, and its various subsections, discusses the criteria for examining macroeconomic crisis, ideational change, and macroeconomic policy change, and then tests these criteria in a series of case studies of the countries selected for examination. The conclusion will discuss how this framework can be used for examining potential critical junctures in future.

THE CHARACTERISTICS & USES OF THE CRITICAL JUNCTURES APPROACH

To be able to recognise what is a critical juncture, we equally must be able to recognise what is not a critical juncture. Not all events, even seemingly significant events, can be critical junctures. A critical juncture must be an event that puts our chosen unit, or units, of analysis onto particular development paths. Prior to the critical juncture, a range of possibilities must exist for those units, afterwards these possibilities will have mostly vanished, replaced by a particular and enduring legacy. It is here at the narrowing point, where possibilities close off, that we must seek to define critical junctures.

Thus, critical junctures are regarded as branching points that set processes of institutional, and / or policy change, in motion. The literature sees critical junctures as a point at which there was the adoption of a particular institutional arrangement from amongst a range of alternatives (Mahoney, 2000: 512). Thereafter, the pathway established funnels units in a particular direction, with the consequence of increasing returns, and the resultant irreversibilities (Mahoney, 2003: 53; Pierson & Skocpol, 2002: 9). The critical juncture is the point at which a radical change in the institution and / or policy takes place.

However, Pierson (2004) argues that institutional stability can result from non-path dependent causes too, implying that critical junctures should not be defined in part by the assumption that they initiate path dependent processes. Thus, it is conceivable that a critical juncture could lead to the existence of an institution whose persistence is not due to path dependence, but other sources of stability.

For some scholars, the duration of a critical juncture may involve a relatively brief period, while for others it can constitute an extended period of reorientation (Mahoney 2001). The analysis of critical junctures has been very influential in comparative politics, as well as in the wider social sciences. Collier & Collier (1991) developed a framework to determine whether certain periods constituted critical junctures in national development in Latin America. Their definition does not imply that institutional innovation occurs in short episodes (Thelen, 2004: 215). For Mahoney (2001), analysing the 19th century liberalisation of Central America, critical junctures took decades to come about, while their after-effects were of shorter duration. Hogan (2005; 2006) questioned whether these periods could rightly be called critical junctures at all, or were in fact instances of incremental change; more appropriately labelled as 'periods of conversion' by Streeck & Thelen (2005). Thus, even amongst those using the concept, there are differences of opinion as to what exactly qualifies as a critical juncture. This comes back to the fact that, up until now, there has been a failure to develop an unambiguous definition of what exactly constitutes a critical juncture – something this chapter is attempting to address.

However, critical junctures have also been employed in research into short-term change. Garrett & Lange (1995: 628) showed that electoral landslides create critical junctures by producing mandates for policy change. Casper & Taylor (1996) employed critical junctures in analysing periods when authoritarian regimes were vulnerable to liberalisation. Examining the *Reciprocal Trade Agreements Act* of 1934, Haggard (1988: 91) argued that economic depression brought into question existing institutions, and resulted in dramatic change. Karl (1997) used the concept in her analysis of how the 'petro-states' became locked into problematic development paths. Gal & Bargal (2002) used it to analyse the emergence of occupational welfare in Israel, while Vargas (2004) used the concept to examine the conflict in Chiapas. Hogan (2005; 2006) remoulded the framework to examine change in trade union influence over public policy.

THE COUNTRIES SELECTED FOR EXAMINATION

By studying politics comparatively, we can discover trends and achieve an understanding of broader characteristics (Blondel, 1995: 3). The value of comparison is the perspective it offers, and its goal of building a body of increasingly complete explanatory theory (Mayer, Burnett & Ogden, 1993; Mahler, 1995). But, as Lieberman (2001: 5) also recommends, in addition to cross-country cases, comparative historical analyses covering longer time spans are also beneficial. Thus, in order to provide a range of different, but comparable cases, we draw our case selection from four countries spread across four decades.

Cases from Ireland, USA, Britain and Sweden are selected for examination, this based upon 'most similar' and 'most different' selection criteria. The requirements for 'most similar' were long-standing democracy, and advanced capitalist state. The specific criteria were stable democracy since the first half of the 20th century, and founding membership of the Organisation for Economic Co-operation & Development (OECD). These conditions tied together the principles of representative democracy and free market economy. We used Lijphart's (1999) categories of majoritarian and consensual democracy as the 'most different' basis for selection, allowing us to control for varying institutional arrangements.

All of these countries' economies are very different, while their performances during the latter half of the 20th century, along with the policies governing them during that time, have varied dramatically. Nevertheless, their similarities ensure 'the contexts of analysis are analytically equivalent, to a significant degree,' while their differences place the 'parallel processes of change in sharp relief' (Collier, 1997: 40). Ireland is an interesting country to examine in this context, as it is often ignored in comparative studies of policy change. Comparing an Irish case to international cases of macroeconomic policy change may shed light on the country's economic development.

Identification of Macroeconomic Crisis

'An important part of the literature on critical junctures views them from the perspective of crises, placing a particular emphasis on the tensions leading up to the critical juncture' (Collier & Collier, 1991: 32). 'Traditionally, students of institutional change focused on the importance of crisis, situations of large-scale public dissatisfaction or even fear stemming from an unusual degree of social unrest and / or threats to national security' (Cortell & Peterson, 1999: 184). 'Exogenous shock, such as an international economic crisis, is often cited as an explanation for policy change' (Golob, 2003: 373). In this study, the crises being searched for are macroeconomic crises. 'Most scholars agree that severe recessions make significant structural changes possible because they render politics highly fluid' (Garrett, 1993: 522). Governments, and political parties, and their economic policies, are openly exposed to the impact of economic fluctuations, being readily affected by them. Such an event as a macroeconomic crisis can call into question existing institutions, policies, or even state projects (Tilly, 1975).

Drawing upon Frankle & Rose (1996: 351), we define a 'macroeconomic crisis' as a stagnant economy, in which inflation, interest rates, unemployment, economic openness, industrial disputes and the debt / GNP ratio are all at decade-long lows, while various actors in the economy perceive it to be in crisis. However, Pei & Adesnik (2000: 139) argue that defining any macro-economic downturn as a crisis requires subjective and objective deliberations. From this, we develop a range of observable implications to identify such a macro-economic crisis. These implications accept that a macro-economic crisis constitutes a severe economic low point. Apart from the first observable implication that is made up of quantifiable independent variables, the identification of the empirical-theoretical fit for the remainder of the observables and their independent variables, which are all qualitative, relies upon the researchers' interpretation of results. Defining an event as a crisis has as much to do with objective data, as subjective material involving emotions and perceptions surrounding the event. This is because there is a self-fulfilling prophecy element to many events that have been considered crises, particularly economic crises. As Blyth (2002: 9) argues, agents must diagnose a crisis, and impose on others their perception of this, before collective action to resolve uncertainty can take meaningful form. No one has developed a definitive set of criteria for identifying macroeconomic crisis, thus we are in uncharted territory.

O1.   If the main economic indicators were stagnant, then the economy may have been in crisis.

O2.   If opinion polls find the public regarded the economic in crisis, then the economy may have been in crisis.

O3.   If the national media regarded the economy in crisis, then the economy may have been in crisis.

O4.   If economic and political commentators regarded the economy in crisis, then the economy may have been in crisis.

O5.   If the central bank regarded the economy in crisis, then the economy may have been in crisis.

O6.   If both domestic and international organisations monitoring economic performance regarded the economy in crisis, then the economy may have been in crisis.

O7.   If elected representatives regarded the economy in crisis, then the economy may have been in crisis.

O8.   If government pronouncements on the economy were consistent with a crisis management approach, then the economy may have been in crisis.

While identifying one of these observables in isolation would be of little value, identifying many together would point to the possibility of a macroeconomic crisis. However, the question then becomes – how many observables must be identified in order for us to declare a situation to be a macroeconomic crisis? As there are no definitive criteria for identifying a macroeconomic crisis, we are also in uncharted territory on this issue. Borrowing a rule of thumb for statistics, which is that at least half the observables tested for need to be found, in order to have confidence that you have uncovered what you are searching for, we argue that at least two-thirds of all observables, for which there are findings, should point to economic crisis. This sets a higher standard for us to reach, but is not unreasonable in light of the opaqueness surround the issue of what exactly constitutes a macroeconomic crisis.

As space permits only a brief review of the vast amount of material examined, we concentrate on examining the most likely candidates of macroeconomic crises identified.

Ireland – 1959

In 1956, a stagnant, closed economy was finally opened to foreign investment. This was an admission of the failure of the economic philosophy underlying protectionism. However, this single act did not right the economy. By 1959, international organisations, the media, the Central Bank, and national commentators regarded the economy as in crisis. All economic indicators for Ireland had been at low ebb throughout the decade of the 1950s (**Appendix A**). The OECD (1962a: 6) stated that *per capita* GNP grew at 2.4 per cent per year throughout the 1950s, only because 'net migration averaged 41,000 a year'. However, this growth rate was among the lowest in the OECD (OECD, 1962a: 6). Ó Gráda & O'Rourke (1995: 214) argue that 'in the 1950s, Ireland's relative [economic] performance was disastrous'. Taoiseach Lemass stated that 1959 constituted a crucial year for consolidating the economic foundations of political independence.[1] The leader of the opposition remarked that the magnitude of the economic crisis could only be righted by a tremendous effort from all sections of the community.[2] The general consensus pointed to crisis in the economy.

USA – 1960

According to the OECD, by the late 1950s, the US was suffering from a large deficit (1962b: 5). *Time International* stated that the economy was in recession (1959: 14). The rate of unemployment stood at 5.5 per cent, or 3.7

---

[1]   *The Irish Times*, 25 June 1959.
[2]   *Dáil Eireann*, Vol. 171, 2 December 1958.

million. For the Labor Department, anything above three million indicated economic weakness (**Appendix A**). Inflation was at 1.5 per cent in 1959 and 1.3 per cent in 1960, while GDP growth fell from 7.2 per cent to 2.4 per cent in 1960 (Mitchell, 1998). 'By 1960 economists argued that the economy was slumping dangerously' (Heath, 1975: 63). The Secretary of the Treasury admitted as much to the IMF (*The Economist*, 1960: 42). Democratic presidential candidate Kennedy observed that, in 1959, the US experienced the lowest growth of any major industrialised country. 'You don't see a burgeoning economy', agreed his Republican rival, Nixon (*Time International*, 1960: 13). However, on thorough examination, this combination of factors was not sufficient to constitute an economic crisis based upon our criteria (**Table 7.1**).

Britain – 1979

During the first three months of 1979, Britain suffered severe industrial disputes. *The Times* commented that the economic heritage of 1979 would be dreadful.[3] During the 1979 election, Thatcher warned that returning Labour to office would be 'to accept our national decline as inevitable'.[4] Accelerating labour costs, and the appreciation of sterling, degraded competitiveness. Import penetration contributed to a £661 million balance of payments deficit (Bank of England, 1979: 116). The Bank of England (1979: 109) warned that failure to arrest the decline would result in decreasing living standards. For the public, the cost of living and unemployment were the main issues (Wybrow, 2001: 267). Thatcher, when elected, inherited 1 million unemployed (Kessler & Bayliss, 1995: 38), inflation running at 13 per cent, nonexistent growth,[5] and 29 million days lost through industrial disputes (**Appendix A**) (OECD, 1995). This period constituted Britain's worst post-war recession (Kessler & Bayliss, 1995: 39).

Sweden – 1982

The recession that began in the mid-1970s proved persistent. The OECD (1982a: 49) described the economy in 1982 as in difficulty. Government's expenditures had grown, while revenues stagnated. The budget deficits were financed by international borrowing (Siven, 1984: 17) and, as a consequence, the debt to GNP ratio increased by over 250 per cent in six years. In 1981, inflation reached 12.1 per cent, while GDP growth fell to -0.6

---

3   *The Times,* 25 April 1979, p. 7.
4   *The Guardian,* 17 April 1979, p. 3.
5   *ibid.,* 28 April – 4 May 1979, p. 13.

per cent (**Appendix A**).[6] Unemployment reached 3.1 per cent in 1982, its highest level since 1945, a political scandal in a country accustomed to full employment.[7] However, economists believed unemployment would have been closer to 16 per cent if it included the jobless in training programmes, workers forced into early retirement, and those who had given up looking for work.[8] *The New York Times* argued that the Swedish economy had been hobbled by foreign debt, low investment, and an adverse balance of payments.[9] The economy was in crisis.

The Observable Implications	Ireland	USA	Britain	Sweden
	1959	1960	1979	1982
O1. Were the main economic indicators stagnant?				X
O2. Did opinion polls find the public regarded the economic in crisis.			X	X
O3. Did the media regard the economy in crisis?	X	X	X	X
O4. Did economic and political commentators regard the economy in crisis?	X		X	X
O5. Did the central bank regard the economy as in crisis?	X		X	X
O6. Did domestic/ international organisations regard the economy as in crisis?	X		X	X
O7. Did elected representatives regard the economy as in crisis?	X			X
O8. Were government pronouncements on the economy consistent with a crisis management approach?	X		X	X
Economic Crisis	**Y**	**N**	**Y**	**Y**

Table 7.1: The Identification of Macroeconomic Crisis

---

6   *The Economist*, 28 August 1982, p. 41.
7   *The New York Times*, 20 September, p. 3.
8   *Time International*, 20 September 1982, Vol. 120, No. 38, p. 32.
9   *The New York Times*, 20 September p. 3.

Of the four potential macroeconomic crises examined, three satisfied most of the observable implications – constituting crises. As can be seen in **Table 7.1**, the USA in 1960 satisfied only one observable implication, and consequently could not constitute an economic crisis. The next section will examine the three identified macroeconomic crises to see whether ideational change occurred at these times and, central to our hypothesis, whether policy change followed ideational change.

Identification of Ideational Change

A crisis can discredit previous policies due to their implication in, or inability to right, the situation. Economic crises can shape a range of alternatives, but will not determine policy choices. This remains 'centred in domestic political and ideational processes' (Golob, 2003: 375). Thus, when an economic model is in flux, windows of opportunity will appear in which agents will contest the viability of the prevailing paradigm (Kingdon, 1995).

This is similar to Blyth's 'discursive phase', where 'agents interested in reforming existing distributional arrangements contest the definition, meaning and solution to the problems identified by opposing economic ideologies' (1997: 234). Agents will critique the old economic model, as economic shocks 'discredit earlier policy models that did not predict the crisis' (Golob, 2003: 374). These agents will introduce new ideas they believe can solve the problem, and will eventually coalesce around a set of ideas that will act as an alternative paradigm to the current model. 'Economic ideas facilitate the reduction of ... barriers by acting as coalition-building resources among agents who, in periods of crisis, attempt to resolve the crisis' (Blyth, 2002: 37). This reflects Blyth's 'instrumentalist phase', when ideas are co-opted and deployed by agents in an attempt to redefine existing institutional arrangements (1997: 234). Thus, ideas are the casual mechanisms of change in any critical juncture (Golob, 2003).

Once agents coalesce around a set ideas purporting to offer a solution to current economic woes, and an alternative to the current paradigm, *they* will attempt to 'inject' these ideas into the policy domain. We contend that this occurs through the actions of three broad groupings of *change agents*.

Newly-elected political parties constitute the first grouping. When elections occur during economic crisis, opposition parties run on platforms opposed to the current economic model. They propose new economic ideas as an alternative paradigm. The second grouping constitutes Kingdon's (1995: 179-183) 'policy entrepreneurs'. These are agents who promulgate specific economic ideas to replace the current paradigm. They may be civil servants, technocrats, academics, economists, or interest groups, who have access to decision-makers. This grouping roughly amalgamates Hall's economist-centred approach and coalition-centred approach in explaining economic change (Hall, 1989: 8-12). The final grouping consists of outside influences. Here, the media, and international organisations, such as the OECD, IMF, or World Bank, critique an existing economic paradigm, advocating a new paradigm instead.

Therefore, we hypothesise that an economic crisis will result in debate regarding economic policy, and its underlying ideas, and will see the generation of a new set of ideas about the economy. Consequently, we develop another set of observable implications, which suggest that, as agents debate the viability of the old economic model, they generate solutions to its ills in the form of new ideas.

O1.   The media questions the efficacy of the current economic model and / or specific policy areas.

O2.   Opposition political parties critique the current model and propose alternative economic ideas – at election time their platform will be built around these alternative ideas.

O3.   Civil society organisations, e.g., labour unions, employer organisations, consumer groups, critique the current model, reflecting Hall's coalition-centred approach (1989: 12).

O4.   Widespread public dissatisfaction with the current paradigm, observable through opinion polls, protests, etc.

O5.   External or international organisations critique the current model **and / or** actively disseminate alternative economic ideas to replace this model.

O6.   A clear set of alternative economic ideas is evident.

O7.   A clear agent of change to inject these new ideas into the policy arena is evident.

According to Legro's (2000: 419) two-stage conceptualisation of ideational change, if, despite its institutionalisation, agents agree that the prevailing paradigm is inadequate and should be replaced, then the first stage – ideational collapse – has occurred. These agents will propose solutions consisting of a hierarchy of contending ideas, *with one main challenger to the dominant creed*. But, 'even when ideational collapse occurs, failure to reach consensus on a replacement could still produce continuity, as society reflexively re-embraces the old orthodoxy' (Legro, 2000: 424). Thus, the critical issue becomes reaching consensus on a new set of ideas. If consensus is achieved, it constitutes the second stage of Legro's model – consolidation – agents co-ordinating a replacement set of ideas to the reigning consensus.

Once agents attempt to use the new ideas for change, it remains to be seen whether existing policies will change significantly. That is, following ideational collapse, can agents generate sufficient consensus around new ideas to reach consolidation, replacing the old ideas, and thereafter piercing 'armoured policies'. Referring to previous policies as 'armoured' builds upon the work of Hall, Blyth, and historical institutionalists in general. It is similar to Golob's notion of 'policy frontiers' (2003: 363). Armoured policies represent policy continuity, whereby once a policy has become institutionally embedded, 'policy-making becomes possible only in terms of these ideas' (Blyth, 2001: 4).

Ireland – 1959

Irish economic stagnation during the 1950s led to 'vigorous debate on the economy' (O'Day, 2000: 27). This debate, conducted at national levels, among civil society groups, and within the media, aggressively questioned the efficacy of protectionism. In turn, it was heavily influenced by the propagation of Keynesian ideas, or planned capitalism, that was gaining salience in the US, and much of Europe. The ideas associated with the outward-looking strategy that Ireland eventually adopted were first used by the coalition government of 1954-57. These saw tentative employment in the 1956 decision to allow the IDA distribute grants to export-orientated industries, and the creation of the Export Profits Relief Tax (Suarez, 2001). The Irish economy abandoned its traditional policy of protectionism and opened up to foreign investment for the first time (Tansey, 1998: 12).

These innovations, although doing little to alleviate the economic woes, were supported by employer groups and the trade unions (Suarez, 2001). As such, these moves, though only tentative, and the resultant media debate critiquing the old model of protectionism, ensured that '1957 is conventionally thought of as the end of an era, as marking the final exhaustion of the ideas of the first generation of political leaders' (Garvin, 1982: 37). In an environment of unfulfilled collective economic expectations, contestation of the existing economic orthodoxy by agents agreed on both its inadequacy, and need for replacement, resulted in its collapse.

Once a wide range of agents coalesced around a set of alternative ideas to replace the existing model of protectionism, the 1957 election was fought by Fianna Fáil on a platform attacking the old economic model, and the economic stagnation that had prevailed. As Hall (1993: 289) argues, 'politicians compete for office precisely by propounding new solutions to collective problems which appeal to the electorate'. Fianna Fáil won the election, and Seán Lemass became Minister for Industry & Commerce. Lemass was heavily influenced by the ideas of T.K. Whitaker, as set out in *Economic Development*. Whitaker constitutes a policy entrepreneur in this instance, as his ideas formed the backbone of the 1958 White Paper, *First Programme for Economic Expansion* (Horgan, 1997). This document laid out a coherent set of new economic ideas, based on an outward-looking strategy and / or planned capitalism.

With the retirement of de Valera in 1959, Lemass became Taoiseach. The state of the economy, and the new ideas propagated by Lemass and Whitaker, caused opposition parties to coalesce around these ideas such that, during the Dáil debate on Lemass' election as Taoiseach, Daniel Desmond of the Labour Party argued it was time for the political establishment to realise that solving the problems with the economy superseded their own struggles for power.[10] A range of agents had reached consensus on a replacement set of economic ideas, consolidating a new dominant ideational orthodoxy. Lemass now had the mandate and opportunity to inject these new ideas into the policy arena.

Britain – 1979

By the end of the 1970s, Britain was in an economic crisis. This was largely due to inflation, which in 1975 peaked at 25 per cent (Hall, 1992: 94). Seeking a solution, Labour Prime Minister Callaghan adopted monetary targets. This deviation from Keynesianism was regarded as being done without fully renouncing the approach (Hall, 1992: 93).

The crisis generated a range of critiques of Labour's economic policy. *The Times* warned that things would get worse before they got better for manufacturing industries,[11] while *The Financial Times* claimed there could be no quick fixes for the economy.[12] Margaret Thatcher, leader of the Conservative opposition, argued that there had been no economic

---

[10]   *The Irish Independent*, 24 June 1959.
[11]   *The Times*, 24 April 1979, 14.
[12]   *The Financial Times*, 28 April 1979, p. 26.

progress under Labour.[13] These criticisms began to generate consensus around alternative ideas, especially monetarism. For monetarists, inflation was the ultimate evil, and this resounded with the British public. Thatcher frequently reminded the public of Labour's legacy of inflation, while the media trumpeted monetarism. *The Economist* argued that the level of interference by the Labour government in the private sector had to end. If Britain was to go into the 21st century as a pluralist democracy, continued *The Economist*, there had to be a switch of emphasis to private wealth creation and choice.[14] As Hall (1993: 108) comments, 'four newspapers dominated the national market in Britain during the 1970s, and three gave an extraordinary amount of coverage to monetarist ideas'. Confidence in the extant economic orthodoxy had collapsed.

Under the influence of Sir Keith Joseph, Thatcher was introduced to the ideas of Enoch Powell, Friedrich Hayek, and Milton Friedman, who believed that high inflation was the critical problem for an economy. Joseph also argued for reducing trade union power, as this was impeding growth. The Conservatives' 1979 election manifesto set as its primary objectives controlling inflation and the unions.[15] It also pledged substantial cuts in all areas, apart from the health services and defence. These monetarist ideas enabled Thatcher to create an electoral coalition of capital, middle-class voters, and large segments of the working class (Hall, 1993: 106). Labour's inability to reduce inflation, public bitterness over the 'winter of discontent', and Thatcher's new economic ideas won the election for the Conservatives. As Booth (2001: 180) notes, 'the Conservatives came to power with a mandate to embark upon a new direction in economic policy'. Thus, a range of agents coalescing around the idea of monetarism consolidated it as the new economic orthodoxy.

Sweden – 1982

The recession of the 1970s saw the budget deficits supporting the social welfare system deepen. By 1981, the non-socialist coalition government held only 102 of the 350 seats in the *Riksdag*.[16] In autumn 1981, the krona was devalued by 10 per cent and, the following spring, the government introduced far-reaching austerity measures. However, the opposition parties gained ground (Hadenius, 1997: 129-130). The government hoped

---

13 *The Guardian*, 17 April 1979, p. 3.
14 *ibid.*, 28 April – 4 May 1979, p. 16.
15 *The Economist*, 14 – 20 April 1979, p. 17.
16 http://www.const.sns.se/swedishpolitics/.

its attempts to combat the economy's problems would generate respect for non-socialist policies; instead they generated widespread critiques, and initiated a debate on the economy. The *Financial Times* pointed out that the Swedes were nervous about the future, but reluctant to see the welfare state's benefits reduced.[17] 'The welfare state is in a crisis of legitimacy', observed Hans Vetterberg, Sweden's leading public opinion analyst. 'We can no longer afford to keep expanding it'.[18] Not surprisingly, the Swedish Employers' Federation (SAF) was unhappy with the government. However, the non-socialist government wanted neither to raise taxes, nor to dismantle the welfare state.[19] This situation, rife with unfulfilled economic expectations, and agents dissatisfied with the prevailing paradigm, constituted ideational collapse.

The 1982 election was deemed crucial, as it would determine whether public support had shifted, as in Norway and Denmark, away from the Social Democrats. The election campaign was dominated by talk of economic crisis – a $10 billion debt to foreign banks, inflation, declining exports, and increasing unemployment.[20] During the campaign, the Social Democrats (Socialdemokratiska Arbetarepartiet (SAP)) attacked the viability of another non-socialist government, and their economic policies. The SAP presented a program on how Sweden could save and work its way out of crisis. Ultimately, the election, and the debates surrounding it, failed to generate either a coherent set of alternative economic ideas to replace the existing ones, or a significant agent of change. The non-socialist parties failed to create a coalition around ideas alternative to the welfare state. Nearly all economic ideas presented were variations on existing themes. Despite the dominant orthodoxy's failure, agents re-embraced it. The ideas underpinning the policies of the welfare state endured. The SAP won the election, not on the back of a new economic paradigm that could cure the country's woes, but on a series of proposals to correct existing economic arrangements.

---

17 *The Financial Times*, 18 September 1982, p. 15.
18 *The Washington Post*, 21 September 1982, p. A15.
19 *Time International*, 20 September 1982, Vol. 120, No. 38, p. 32.
20 *The Washington Post*, 21 September 1982, p. A15.

The Observable Implications	Ireland 1959	Britain 1979	Sweden 1982
O1. Media questioning efficacy of current economic model and / or specific policy areas.	X	X	X
O2. Opposition parties critique current model and propose alternative economic ideas – at elections, their platform are built around these alternative ideas.	X	X	
O3. Civil society organisations will critique current model, reflecting Hall's coalition-centred approach.	X	X	
O4. Widespread public dissatisfaction with current paradigm, observable through opinion polls, protests, etc.		X	X
O5. External or international organisations which critique current model or actively disseminate alternative economic ideas to replace model.	X	X	X
O6. A clear set of observable alternative ideas are evident.	X	X	
O7. A clear agent of change to inject these new ideas into policy arena is evident.	X	X	
Adoption of New Economic Idea	Y	Y	N

Table 7.2: The Identification of Ideational Change

As can be seen from **Table 7.2**, each macroeconomic crisis was accompanied by ideational change. Each instance of ideational collapse was followed by agents reaching consensus upon, and consolidating around, a new economic ideational structure. The next section will examine these periods of macroeconomic crisis to determine whether they were accompanied by radical changes in economic policy.

THE IDENTIFICATION OF CHANGE IN GOVERNMENT ECONOMIC POLICY

The final issue this paper seeks to uncover is whether there were radical changes in the governments' economic policies. We identified macroeconomic crises in three of the four initial cases examined, along with ideational change in two of these three cases. The examination of change in economic policies is the final hurdle in determining which of these cases constituted critical junctures, and whether ideational change is central to the process. Golob (2003: 374) points out that, 'with demands for new solutions intensifying, the crisis-driven window for reform may actually broaden the scope of what constitutes an acceptable policy'. We base our final set of observable implications upon the concepts of first, second, and third order changes in policy, as developed by Hall (1993). Hall (1993: 291) argued that policy failures and exogenous shocks can set off processes that lead to great ideational change, to the extent of resulting in a re-examination of the very belief systems through which policy has been generated – a paradigmatic (third order) change. These observables will enable us identify, and differentiate, both the normal and fundamental shifts in a country's macroeconomic policies. However, the observables set out here also incorporate the ideas of both swift and enduring change developed by Hogan (2005). As we are searching for a paradigm shift in economic policy, this must encompass all three of the observables below:

O1.   If economic policy instrument settings changed (swiftly and for longer than one government's term of office), there may have been a radical change in government economic policy.

O2.   If the instruments of economic policy changed (swiftly and for longer than one government's term of office), there may have been a radical change in government economic policy.

O3.   If the hierarchy of goals behind economic policy changed (swiftly and for longer than one government's term of office), then there may have been a radical change in government economic policy.

Ireland – 1959

The late 1950s witnessed a dramatic shift in Irish economic policy, beginning with the opening of the economy to foreign investment. This decision, made amidst an economic crisis, was a clear admission of the failure of the policy of protectionism, the bedrock of Irish economic philosophy since the 1930s.

'On his return to office as Minister for Industry & Commerce in 1957, [Lemass] began the gradual process of opening the state to foreign investment' (Girvin, 1994: 125). This was despite fears over protected Irish industry.[21] Poor economic performance prompted a fundamental reappraisal of the policy package pursued since the 1930s. This reappraisal was embodied in the White Paper, *First Programme for Economic Expansion,* drawn up by the Department of Finance.

When Lemass became Taoiseach in 1959, he displayed a vigorous entrepreneurial leadership (McCarthy, 1973: 22). An outward-orientated economic strategy was adopted in a climate of severe balance of payments difficulty, recession, and emigration (O'Donnell, 1998: 4). Lemass remarked on the need for change in industrial development policy.[22] Tax breaks and grants were to be provided to foreign firms wishing to set up in Ireland. Adjusting industries to competition-led public policy into the realms of industrial relations, and pay bargaining. Lemass understood that government had to play a more active role in the Irish economy, but realised that the success of this strategy assumed a new partnership with different interest groups, which would become players in the policy game (Murphy, 1997: 58). The trade unions and employer organisations were brought into the policy-making environment, through the Employer-Labour Conference (ELC). Thus, 'the dialogue between state and major socio-economic groups quickly acquired a regular and institutional character' (Peillon, 1995: 370). For the OECD (1961: 12), the Fianna Fáil government's 1958 and 1959 budgets reflected a distinct change in fiscal policy. By 1961, the reshaping of public capital expenditure to give increased emphasis to directly-productive investment had stimulated economic growth. The OECD (1961: 10) found that the policy of grants and tax exemptions attracted a notable volume of foreign capital to Ireland.

In a short space of time, the setting, instruments, and hierarchy of goals behind Irish economic policy changed. Thus, economic crisis led to the collapse of the old economic orthodoxy, the consolidation of a new economic ideational structure, and a third order change in economic policy.

---

[21] *Budget,* 1958, p. 8.
[22] *Dáil Eireann,* Vol. 175, 3 June 1959.

Britain – 1979

Britain endured its 'winter of discontent' in 1978-79, as strikes ravaged the country. *Newsweek* observed that Thatcher's victory in May 1979 reflected disenchantment with Callaghan's failure to avert the winter's strikes.[23] The new government prioritised monetary stability and low inflation. Thatcher's government 'rejected reliance on active fiscal policy in favour of efforts to secure balanced budgets' (Hall, 1992: 91).

The Conservative government was determined to pursue different policies to the corporatism of earlier administrations. It argued that markets, left to themselves, perform better than markets subject to control. 'It was convinced that economic decline, unemployment, and inflation were all to be explained by the excessive role of successive post-war governments' (Coates, 1989: 113). 'They were committed to "roll back" the state, implement tougher policies on trade unions, reduce welfare benefits and aid to uncompetitive industry, and lower taxes' (Booth, 2001: 180).

The Conservatives' election marked the rejection of incomes policies and intervention, with the adoption of a *laissez-faire* approach to economic policy, relying upon monetarist measures to control inflation. The main instrument of the new approach was monetary policy (OECD, 1980: 26). Economic policy focused on control of the money supply, and the freeing of market forces (OECD, 1980: 29). The June budget saw the previous government's expenditure plans for 1979/80 cut to reduce the Public Sector Borrowing Requirement (OECD, 1980: 36). Personal income tax was reduced, VAT was increased, while financial assistance to industry and regional development programmes were reduced. The government also started selling off public sector holdings. There was a major revision of industrial, employment, and regional policies following mid-1979 (OECD, 1981: 7). In line with its market-orientated philosophy, the government, in a change of long-standing policy, abolished exchange controls (OECD, 1982b: 16). It sought to put the economy on a rapid non-inflationary growth path by diminishing the role of the state and giving greater economic responsibility to the individual (OECD, 1980: 29). To create a stable environment for the private sector, the government eschewed frequent changes of policy (OECD, 1981: 19).

If a government's radicalism is measured by the extent to which it breaks with the dominant assumptions of its predecessors, then the Conservative Government of 1979 must count amongst the most radical of

---

[23] *Newsweek*, 14 May 1979, p. 10.

the 20th century (Coates, 1989: 113). The Thatcher administration changed the setting, instruments, and hierarchy of goals behind economic policy. Economic crisis saw collapse of the dominant economic paradigm, and consensus develop around a new set of ideas leading to the consolidation of a new set of policies on how to run the economy.

Sweden – 1982

By the 1980s, the Swedish economy, once the envy of Europe, had been hobbled by crisis.[24] However, Swedes were reluctant to see their welfare state cut back.[25] But, economists argued that the state could not afford to keep expanding its range of benefits.[26]

The 1982 election saw economic problems deprive the non-socialist government of credibility (Mjoset, 1992, 346). However, the government argued that, under it, the welfare system had not been dismantled. The SAP, presenting a strategy on how Sweden could save and work its way out of the crisis, won the election (Lewin, 1985).

The result was an altered approach to economic management, with minor changes in economic policies. The SAP, admitting there were no ready solutions to the economy's problems,[27] implemented a recovery programme – *The Third Road*. This approach argued that renewed growth required redistribution of income from labour to capital. It constituted a shift in SAP economic planning, behind which course lay the influence of its research unit, as opposed to those of the unions. This marked an attempt to maintain a level of social democracy, which other countries were rolling back (Martin, 2000: 234). *The Third Road* sought to devise a wide-ranging stabilisation programme that included demand management measures, as well as initiatives to promote structural change and ensure the fair distribution of the burden of adjustment (OECD, 1984: 21). The SAP was also determined to pour funds into job-creating industries.[28]

The centrepiece of finance minister Feldt's strategy to boost corporate profits was devaluation of the krona. This measure was implemented in combination with a price freeze, and increases in sales and corporate taxes, in a sweeping 'crisis plan'[29] aimed at reviving the economy.[30] The main

---

[24] *The New York Times*, 20 September, p. 3.
[25] *The Financial Times*, 18 September 1982, p. 15.
[26] *The Washington Post*, 21 September 1982, p. A15.
[27] *The New York Times*, 20 September 1982, p. 3.
[28] *ibid.*, 21 September 1982, p. 3.
[29] *The Financial Times*, 12 October 1982, p. 1.

objective was to achieve export-led, and investment-fed, recovery (OECD, 1984: 21). The LO (*Landsorganisationen i Sverige*) accommodated devaluation by demanding average wage increases of 2.5 per cent in the ensuing wage-bargaining round. The devaluation and international economic recovery resulted in high earnings and excellent scope for export expansion (Ahlén, 1989: 333). The government also restored welfare entitlements cut by the non-socialists (OECD, 1984: 23).

To maintain the welfare state, by whatever means necessary, the government prioritised private sector growth, profits, and market forces. In this case, the economic policy instrument settings changed, but the instruments of economic policy, and the goals behind economic policy, remained much the same – the maintenance of the welfare state. This was a first order policy change.

The economic crisis in Sweden generated significant debate, and ideational collapse occurred. However, change agents did not consolidate around a replacement economic orthodoxy. As a result, the existing economic paradigm endured, providing the existing economic policies with sufficient armoured protection to remain largely intact. There was no critical juncture in economic policy.

The Observable Implications	Ireland	Britain	Sweden
	1959	1979	1982
O1. If economic policy instrument settings changed, there may have been a radical change in economic policy.	X	X	X
O2. If the instruments of economic policy changed, there may have been radical change in government economic policy.	X	X	
O3. If the hierarchy of goals behind economic policy changed, there may have been a radical change in government economic policy.	X	X	
Critical Juncture in Macroeconomic Policy	Y	Y	N

Table 7.3: The Identification of Change in Government Economic Policy

---

30 *The Washington Post*, 8 October 1982, p. A16.

Two of the cases examined (Ireland 1959; Britain 1979) witnessed third order changes (paradigm shifts) in macroeconomic policy. These third order policy shifts occurred following macroeconomic crises, collapse of the dominant economic orthodoxies, the introduction of new ideas into the policy arenas, and the consolidation of change agents around these ideas. They constituted critical junctures in macro-economic policy. However, neither of the other two cases witnessed critical junctures. In the US, in 1960, there was no macroeconomic crisis, while in Sweden, in 1982, although there was a macroeconomic crisis, there was no ideational change. In Sweden, ideational collapse followed an economic crisis, but change agents failed to consolidate around a replacement orthodoxy. The old orthodoxy endured, and, as a result, the hierarchy of goals behind Swedish macro-economic policy did not change.

These findings validate our hypothesis. A critical juncture in macro-economic policy consists of three stages: macro-economic crisis, ideational change, and radical policy change. Thus, a macro-economic crisis in itself is a necessary, but insufficient, condition for a paradigm shift in macro-economic policy. A macro-economic crisis not followed by ideational change will only lead to a first (Sweden 1982), or second order macro-economic policy change. Whereas a macro-economic crisis followed by ideational change (collapse and consolidation) will lead to a third order change in the dependent variable – macro-economic policy (Ireland 1959; Britain 1979) – which, combined, constitutes a critical juncture.

Ideational change is crucial in determining whether third order macro-economic policy change will occur after a macro-economic crisis. Existing ideational orthodoxy protects existing policy, ensuring continuity. However, in the wake of an economic crisis, if ideational collapse should occur, existing macro-economic policy is no longer armoured. If change agents, led by a political entrepreneur, consolidate around a new set of economic ideas, they will attempt to inject these into the policy domain. The result of this ideational change will be a third order change in macro-economic policy. However, if change agents fail to consolidate around a new economic orthodoxy, existing ideas will endure, and there will only be a first, or second, order policy change. Therefore, ideational change is the 'differentiating factor' between an economic crisis that leads to a third order change in macroeconomic policy, thereby constituting a critical juncture, and one that does not. This links with Pemberton's (2000: 771) argument that different network configurations are associated with different orders of policy change.

CONCLUSION

Here, we sought to develop an improved framework for examining critical junctures, a framework incorporating ideational change as a 'differentiating factor'. The case studies used in testing this framework initially were four potential macroeconomic crises, one each from Ireland, the US, Britain, and Sweden. We hypothesised that a critical juncture in macroeconomic policy consisted of three stages: macroeconomic crisis, ideational change, and radical change in economic policy. Of the four potential macroeconomic crises, three constituted actual economic crises. In each of the three macroeconomic crises, the paradigms underpinning economic policy came under intense scrutiny due to policy failures. The extant paradigms were attacked by various groupings of change agents advocating alternative paradigms. We uncovered paradigmatic (third order) changes in economic policy in the wake of the two macroeconomic crises in which ideational change occurred. Thus, of the four case studies examined, there were two in which there were critical junctures in their macroeconomic policies.

The framework, as set out and tested above, draws together some of the main theories on ideational and institutional change, to forge a rigorous and broadly applicable framework, that breaks new ground by incorporating ideational change into the concept of critical junctures. It shows us that, once a crisis occurs, existing policies come under attack. If the ideational orthodoxy underpinning these policies collapses, and new ideas purporting to provide a viable alternative are consolidated, then it is likely that a third order change in policy will occur. However, should existing ideas collapse, but change agents fail to consolidate around viable alternatives, extant policies will deflect whatever attack the crisis generates. As a result, only first or second order policy changes will occur. Thus, economic policy instrument settings (Sweden 1982) and the instruments themselves may change, but, without ideational change, the hierarchy of goals underpinning macro-economic policy will remain unaltered. Ideational change constitutes the differentiating factor between those macro-economic crises that are followed by a third-order change (paradigm shift) in macro-economic policy and those that are not.

In future, researchers, having identified a crisis (of whatever kind), and ideational change, should be able to predict that either a third order change in policy is coming, or if it has taken place, that it constitutes a critical juncture, and will endure for a long time to come. Researchers will no longer have to wait for years to pass after an event they feel to be a critical juncture to be able to declare it as such. The inclusion of ideational change broadens the applicability of the concept, deepens its incisiveness, while eliminating its exclusively postdictive nature.

REFERENCES

Ahlén, K. (1989). 'Swedish Collective Bargaining Under Pressure: Inter-union Rivalry and Incomes Policies', *British Journal of Industrial Relations* 23(3): 330-46.

Bank of England (1979). *Bank of England Quarterly Bulletin* 19(4).

Berman, S. (1998). 'Path Dependency and Political Action: Reexamining Responses to the Depression', *Comparative Politics* 30(4): 379-400.

Blondel, J. (1995). *Comparative Government: An Introduction*, 2nd ed. New York, NY: Harvester Wheatsheaf.

Blyth, M. (1997). 'Moving the Political Middle: Redefining the Boundaries of State Action', *The Political Quarterly* 68(3): 231-40.

Blyth, M. (2001). 'The Transformation of the Swedish Model: Economic Ideas, Distributional Conflict and Institutional Change', *World Politics* 54(1): 1–26.

Blyth, M. (2002). *Great Transformations: Economic Ideas and Institutional Change in the Twentieth Century*. Cambridge: Cambridge University Press.

Booth, A. (2001). *The British Economy in the Twentieth Century*. Basingstoke: Palgrave.

Casper, G. & Taylor, M.M. (1996). *Negotiating Democracy: Transitions from Authoritarian Rule*. Pittsburgh, PA: University of Pittsburgh Press.

Christensen, T. (1997). 'Utviklingen av direktoratene - aktører, tenkning og organisasjons-former', in Christensen, T. & Egeberg, M. (eds), *Forvaltningskunnskap*, pp. 53-77. Oslo: Tano.

Clemens, E.S., & Cook, J.M. (1990). 'Politics and Institutionalism: Explaining Durability and Change', *Annual Review of Sociology* 25: 441-66.

Coates, D. (1989). *The Crisis of Labour: Industrial Relations and the State in Contemporary Britain*. Oxford: Philip Allan.

Collier, R.B. & Collier, D. (1991). *Shaping the Political Arena: Critical Junctures, the Labor Movement and Regime Dynamics in Latin America*. Princeton, NJ: Princeton University Press.

Collier, D. (1997). 'Comparative Method in the 1990s', *APSA-CP: Newsletter of the APSA Organised Section in Comparative Politics* 9(1): 1-5.

Cortell, A.P. & Peterson, S. (1999). 'Altered States: Explaining Domestic Institutional Change', *British Journal of Political Science* 29(2): 177-203.

European Commission (1997). *Eurostat Yearbook*. Luxembourg: Office for Official Publications of the European Communities.

European Commission (2003). *Statistical Annex of European Economy*. Luxembourg: Office for Official Publications of the European Communities.

Fearon, J. D. (1991). 'Counterfactuals and Hypothesis Testing in Political Science', *World Politics* 43(2): 169-95.

Fearon. J.D. (1996). 'Causes and Counterfactuals in Social Science: Exploring an Analogy between Cellular Automata and Historical Processes', in Tetlock, P.E. & Belkin, A. (eds). *Counterfactual Thought Experiments in World Politics*, pp. 39-68. Princeton, NJ: Princeton University Press.

Gal, J. & Bargal, D. (2002). 'Critical Junctures, Labour Movements and the Development of Occupational Welfare in Israel', *Social Problems* 49(3): 432-54.

Garrett, G. (1993). 'The Politics of Structural Change: Swedish Social Democracy and Thatcherism in Comparative Perspective', *Comparative Political Studies* 25(4): 521-47.

Garrett, G. & Lange, P. (1995). 'Internationalization, Institutions and Political Change', *International Organization* 49(4): 627-55.

Garvin, T. (1982). *The Evolution of Irish Nationalist Politics*. Dublin: Gill & Macmillan.

Girvin, B. (1994). 'Trade Unions & Economic Development,' in Nevin, D. (ed), *Trade Union Century*, pp. 117-32. Cork: Mercier Press.

Golob, S. (2003). 'Beyond the Policy Frontier: Canada, Mexico and the Ideological Origins of NAFTA', *World Politics* 55(3): 361-98.

Gorges, M.J. (2001). 'The New Institutionalism and the Study of the European Union: The Case of the Social Dialogue', *West European Politics* 24(4): 152-68.

Hadenius, S. (1997). *Swedish Politics During the 20th Century – Conflict & Consensus*. Stockholm: Svenska Institute.

Haggard, S. (1988). 'The Institutional Foundations of Hegemony: Explaining the Reciprocal Trade Agreements Act of 1934', *International Organization* (42)1: 91-119.

Hall, P.A. (ed) (1989). *The Political Power of Economic Ideas: Keynesianism across Nations*. Princeton, NJ: Princeton University Press.

Hall, P.A. (1992). 'The Movement from Keynesianism to Monetarism: Institutional Analysis and British Economic Policy in the 1970s', in Steinmo, S., Thelen, K. & Longstreth, F. (eds), *Structuring Politics: Historical Institutionalism in Comparative Analysis*, pp. 90-113. Cambridge: Cambridge University Press.

Hall, P.A. (1993). 'Policy Paradigms, Social Learning and the State: The Case of Economic Policy-making in Britain', *Comparative Politics* 25(3): 275-96.

Heath, J.F. (1975). *Decade of Disillusionment: The Kennedy-Johnson Years*. Bloomington, IN: Indiana University Press.

Heston, A., Summers, R. & Aten, B. (2002). *Penn World Table Version 6.1*. Philadelphia, PA: Center for International Comparisons at the University of Pennsylvania (CICUP).

Hogan, J.W. (2005). 'Testing for a Critical Juncture: Change in the ICTU's Influence over Public Policy in 1959', *Irish Political Studies* 20(3): 23-43.

Hogan, J.W. (2006). 'Remoulding the Critical Junctures Approach', *Canadian Journal of Political Science* 39(3): 657-79.

Horgan, J. (1997). *Seán Lemass: The Enigmatic Patriot*. Dublin: Gill & Macmillan.

Karl, T.L. (1997). *The Politics of Plenty: Oil Booms and Petro-States*. Berkeley, CA: University of California Press.

Kessler, S. & Bayliss, F. (1995). *Contemporary British Industrial Relations*. London: Macmillan Press Ltd.

Kingdon, J. (1995). *Agendas, Alternatives and Public Policy*, 2nd ed. New York, NY: Harper.

Krasner, S.D. (1984). 'Approaches to the State: Alternative Conceptions and Historical Dynamics', *Comparative Politics* 16(2): 223-46.

Leddin, A.J. & Walsh, B.M. (1998). *The Macroeconomy of Ireland*, 4th ed. Dublin: Gill & Macmillan.

Legro, J.W. (2000). 'The Transformation of Policy Ideas', *American Journal of Political Science* 44(3): 419-32.

Lewin, L. (1985). *Ideologi och strategi*. Stockholm: Norstedts.

Lieberman, E.S. (2001). 'Causal Inference in Historical Institutional Analysis: A Specification of Periodization Strategies', *Comparative Political Studies* 34(9): 1011–35.

Lijphart, A. (1999). *Patterns of Democracy: Government Forms and Performance in Thirty-six Countries*. New Haven, CT: Yale University Press.

Mahler, G.S. (1992). *Comparative Politics: An Institutional and Cross-national Approach*. Englewood Cliffs, NJ: Prentice Hall.

Mahoney, J. (2000). 'Path Dependence in Historical Sociology', *Theory and Society* 29(4): 507-48.

Mahoney, J. (2001). 'Path Dependent Explanations of Regime Change: Central America in Comparative Perspective', *Studies in Comparative International Development* 36(1): 111-41.

Mahoney, J. (2003). 'Long-Run Development and the Legacy of Colonialism in Spanish America', *American Journal of Sociology* 109(1): 50-106.

Martin, A. (2000). 'The Politics of Macroeconomic Policy and Wage Negotiations in Sweden', in Iversen, T., Pontussson, J. & Soskice, D. (eds), *Unions, Employers & Central Banks*, pp. 232-66. New York, NY: Cambridge University Press.

Mayer, L.C., Burnett, J.H. & Suzanne O. (1993). *Comparative Politics: Nations and Theories in a Changing World*. Englewood Cliffs, N.J: Prentice Hall.

McCarthy, C. (1973). *The Decade of Upheaval: Irish Trade Unions in the 1960s*. Dublin: Institute of Public Administration.

Mitchell, B.R. (1993). *International Historical Statistics: Europe 1750-1988*, 3rd ed. Hong Kong: Stockton Press.

Mitchell, B.R. (1998). *International Historical Statistics: The Americas 1750-1993*, 4th ed. Basingstoke: Macmillan.

Mjoset, L. (1992). *The Irish Economy in a Comparative Institutional Perspective*. Dublin: National Economic and Social Council.

Murphy, G. (1997). 'Government, Interest Groups and the Irish Move to Europe', *Irish Studies in International Affairs* 8: 57-68.

O'Day, A. (2000). 'Nationalism and the Economic Question in Twentieth Century Ireland', in Teichova, A., Matis, H. & Pátek, J. (eds), *Economic Change and the National Question in Twentieth Century Europe*, pp. 9-32. Cambridge: Cambridge University Press.

O'Donnell, R. (1998). 'Ireland's Economic Transformation: Industrial Policy, European Integration and Social Partnership', Working Paper No. 20, Center for West European Studies, University of Pittsburgh.

Ó Gráda, C. & O'Rourke, K. (1995). 'Economic Growth: Performance and Explanations,' in O'Hagan, J.W. (ed), *The Economy of Ireland: Policy & Performance of a Small European Country*, pp. 198-227. Dublin: Gill & Macmillan.

Organisation for Economic Co-operation and Development (1962a). *Ireland 1962*. Paris: OECD.

Organisation for Economic Co-operation and Development (1962b). *The United Kingdom 1962*. Paris: OECD.

Organisation for Economic Co-operation and Development (1980). *The United Kingdom 1980*. Paris: OECD.

Organisation for Economic Co-operation and Development (1981). *The United Kingdom 1981*. Paris: OECD.

Organisation for Economic Co-operation and Development (1982a). *Sweden 1982*. Paris: OECD.

Organisation for Economic Co-operation and Development (1982b). *The United Kingdom 1982*. Paris: OECD.

Organisation for Economic Co-operation and Development (1984). *Sweden 1984*. Paris: OECD.

Organisation for Economic Co-operation and Development (1995). *Labour Force Statistics*. Paris: OECD.

Organisation for European Economic Co-operation (1961). *Ireland 1961*. Paris: OEEC.

Peillon, M. (1995). 'Interest Groups and the State in the Republic of Ireland', in Clancy, P. (ed), *Irish Society: Sociological Perspectives*, pp. 360-378. Dublin: Institute of Public Administration.

Pemberton, H. (2000). 'Policy Networks and Policy Learning: UK Economic Policy in the 1960s and 1970s', *Public Administration* 78 (4): 771–92.

Peters, B.G. (1999). *Institutional Theory in Political Science: The New Institutionalism*. London: Pinter.

Pierson, P. (1993). 'When Effects Become Cause: Policy Feedback and Political Change', *World Politics*, 45(4): 595-628

Pierson, P. (2000). 'Increasing Returns, Path Dependency and the Study of Politics', *American Political Science Review* 94(2): 251-67.

Pierson, P. (2004). *Politics in Time: History, Institutions and Social Analysis*. Princeton, NJ: Princeton University Press.

Pierson, P. & Skocpol, T. (2002). *Historical Institutionalism in Contemporary Political Science* [Online]. Available: http://www.polisci.berkeley.edu/Faculty/bio/permanent/Pierson,P/Discipline.pdf (last accessed 14 March 2009).

Rothstein, B. (1996). 'Political Institutions: An Overview', in Goodin, R.E. & Klingmann, H-D. (eds), *A New Handbook of Political Science*, pp. 133-66. Oxford: Oxford University Press.

Schickler, E. (2001). *Disjointed Pluralism: Institutional Innovation and the Development of the US Congress*. Princeton, NJ: Princeton University Press.

Siven, C. (1984). 'The Political Economy of Sweden in the 1970s', Research Papers in Economics, No.1, Department of Economics, University of Stockholm,

Stark, D. & Bruszt, L. (1998). *Postsocialist Pathways: Transforming Politics and Property in Eastern Europe*. Cambridge: Cambridge University Press.

Steinmo, S. (1989). 'Political Institutions and Tax Policy in the United States, Sweden, and Britain', *World Politics* 41(4): 500-35.

Streeck, W. & Thelen, K. (2005). 'Introduction: Institutional Change in Advanced Political Economies,' in Thelen, K. & Steeck, W. (eds), *Beyond Continuity: Institutional Change in Advanced Political Economies*, pp. 1-39. Oxford: Oxford University Press.

Suárez, S. (2001). 'Political and Economic Motivations for Labor Control: A Comparison of Ireland, Puerto Rico & Singapore', *Studies in Comparative International Development* 36(2): 54-81.

Tansey, P. (1998). *Ireland at Work: Economic Growth and the Labour Market, 1987-1997*. Dublin: Oak Tree Press.

Thelen, K. & Steinmo, S. (1992). 'Historical Institutionalism in Comparative Politics', in Steinmo, S., Thelen, K. & Longstreth, F. (eds), *Structuring Politics: Historical Institutionalism in Comparative Analysis*, pp. 1-32. Cambridge: Cambridge University Press.

Thelen, K. (1999). 'Historical Institutionalism in Comparative Politics', *Annual Review of Political Science* 2: 369-404.

Thelen, K. (2000). 'Timing and Temporality in the Analysis of Institutional Evolution and Change', *Studies in American Political Development* 14(1): 102-09.

Thelen, K. (2004). *How Institutions Evolve: The Political Economy of Skills in Germany, Britain, the United States and Japan*. Cambridge: Cambridge University Press.

Tilly, C. (1975). *The Formation of Nation States in Western Europe*. Princeton, NJ: Princeton University Press.

Vargas, V. (2004). 'The Political Dynamic of the Conflict in Chiapas: A History of its Critical Junctures', Centre of Latin American Studies Research Day, University of Cambridge.

Wybrow, R.J. (2001). *British Political Opinion 1937 – 2000: The Gallup Polls*. London: Politico's Publishing.

APPENDIX A

Ireland 1959

Year	Unemployment %	Inflation %	Government Debt to GNP ratio	Growth Rates in Real Gross Domestic Product	Industrial Disputes days lost (000)	Economic Openness
1949	9.0	1.2	N/A	4.1	273	
1950	7.5	0.0	N/A	1.9	217	70.93345
1951	7.3	11.25	49.9	1.9	545	82.55222
1952	9.1	10.1	N/A	2.26	529	69.63176
1953	9.6	2.04	N/A	2.5	82	66.85665
1954	8.1	2.0	N/A	0.9	67	65.45109
1955	6.8	1.9	N/A	1.9	236	67.17816
1956	7.7	4.4	N/A	-1.45	48	60.98576
1957	9.2	2.57	N/A	0.98	92	62.7357
1958	8.6	2.6	N/A	-2.2	126	62.86433
1959	8.0	-0.85	55.5	4.1	124	62.73207

USA 1960

Year	Unemployment %	Inflation %	Government Debt to GNP ratio	Growth Rates in Real Gross Domestic Product	Industrial Disputes days lost (000)	Economic Openness
1950	5.3	5.8	93.9	8.7	38,800	8.181615
1951	3.3	5.9	79.5	7.6	22,900	9.423225
1952	3.0	-.9	74.3	3.9	59,100	8.89649
1953	2.9	-59	71.2	4.5	28,300	8.374369
1954	5.5	-0.3	71.6	-0.67	22,600	8.466593
1955	4.4	0.3	69.4	7.09	28,200	8.66339
1956	4.1	2.8	63.8	1.9	33,100	9.409499
1957	4.3	3.0	60.4	1.9	16,500	9.792786
1958	6.8	1.7	60.7	-0.9	23,900	8.843573
1959	5.5	1.5	58.4	7.2	69,000	8.735885
1960	5.5	1.3	56.0	2.4	19,100	9.445088

Britain 1979

Year	Unemployment %	Inflation %	Government Debt to GNP ratio	Growth Rates in Real Gross Domestic Product	Industrial Disputes days lost (000)	Economic Openness
1969	2.3	5.32	74	1.5	6,846	42.50344
1970	2.5	7.06	67	2.2	10,980	43.82084
1971	3.4	8.94	60	2.7	13,551	43.5476
1972	3.7	7.84	58	2.2	23,909	42.3862
1973	2.2	6.84	52	7.5	7,197	48.48464
1974	2.1	13.89	50	-1.0	14,750	59.62696
1975	3.2	24.06	46	-0.7	6,012	52.59175
1976	4.8	14.13	47	3.6	3,284	57.26631
1977	5.2	13.03	48	1.3	10,142	58.77758
1978	5.1	10.75	49	3.7	9,405	55.20993
1979	4.6	13.44	46	1.6	29,474	55.21527

Sweden 1982

Year	Unemployment %	Inflation %	Government Debt to GNP ratio	Growth Rates in Real Gross Domestic Product	Industrial Disputes days lost (000)	Economic Openness
1972	2.0	6.0	22.2	2.2	11	45.83361
1973	2.5	6.7	22.6	3.9	12	50.90327
1974	2.0	9.9	24.2	4.3	58	63.73183
1975	1.6	9.8	24.4	2.2	366	55.24588
1976	1.6	10.3	23.6	1.2	25	55.70874
1977	1.8	11.4	26.5	-2.0	87	55.18196
1978	2.2	10.0	31.8	1.3	37	54.19376
1979	2.1	7.2	37.9	4.3	29	60.43795
1980	2.0	13.7	43.2	1.9	4,478	60.14818
1981	2.5	12.1	50.8	-0.6	209	59.64625
1982	3.1	8.6	59.3	1.1	2	64.93382

Data Sources: European Commission, 1997, 2003; Heston, Summers & Aten, 2002; Leddin & Walsh, 1998; Mitchell, 1993, 1998; OECD, 1995.

CHAPTER 8
USING DOCUMENTS:
A FIGURATIONAL APPROACH

Paddy Dolan

INTRODUCTION

Notwithstanding significant changes in the research cultures of many social science disciplines, there remains a certain orthodoxy in the selection of qualitative methods for consumer research in particular. In this field, focus groups and depth (or qualitative) interviews reign supreme, while the use of documentary evidence is sparse. The obvious exception is the growing number of studies written by historians of consumer culture (see for example, Cohen, 2003; De Grazia, 2005; Donohue, 2006). Historians traditionally have used documents as evidence of particular events, values, ideas and practices at specific times and places. These events can then be organised into a sequence over time, thereby constituting a narrative of change. Historians, though, are *less* likely to try to build an explanatory model of change based on broader social scientific theories (there are of course exceptions, and this is a matter of degree rather than an absolute difference).

In this chapter, I discuss the analysis of documents following the concepts and theories of the sociologist Norbert Elias (for an excellent introduction, see Mennell, 1998). Elias distinguished between history and sociology, insofar as the latter discipline should seek to find the structures (or order) of social change beneath the apparent discontinuities from one historical period to the next. For example, in his study of French court society, Elias (1983: 2) notes that, while history 'throws light on particular individuals, in this case individual kings', the sociological perspective 'illuminates social positions, in this case the development of the royal position'. Elias's approach became known as figurational or process sociology, as it stresses the development of social and personality structures over time, and therefore the need to generate data in terms of historical flows. Such changes are neither linear nor teleological, but careful analysis often reveals an unplanned order to the sequences. The emphasis on 'process' reflects the theoretical position that such apparent 'facts' as organisational structures or consumer attitudes actually have developed over time, and therefore in order to understand them, they need to be researched as flows. They cannot be isolated or frozen in time and explained outside of their temporal context. The word 'figuration' refers to 'a structure of mutually orientated and dependent people … the network of interdependencies formed by individuals' (Elias, 2000: 482). Importantly, this network of people must also be understood as dynamic, or 'in process'. Before elaborating on this specific approach, I will briefly outline the advantages of documents as data sources in general.

THE USE OF DOCUMENTS

Nearly all textbooks devoted to qualitative research methods discuss the use of documents as sources of data. There are numerous forms of documents that are useful to both consumer and organisational research. In particular, most organisations produce enormous volumes of text simply as part of their communication strategies and processes between different departments, functions and roles. Such written texts enable the co-ordination of interdependent tasks both within any organisation and between various organisations. So they are produced by people working together to facilitate interaction, and as a means of making requests, specifying requirements and outlining different responsibilities. Therefore, unlike interviews or focus groups, documents tend not to be generated directly by researchers themselves. They already exist! Of course, each researcher still has to make theoretically-informed decisions regarding the selection of appropriate documents. Documents are not 'objective' in the positivistic sense. Though they often exist independently of the specific researcher conducting the study, they are not independent of the people making and using the documents to facilitate their working lives. Because of this, documents must be understood in terms of their production and social purpose (Hammersley & Atkinson, 1995: 165–74). Documents also have specific effects; they do not simply describe some organisational social reality, they actively shape the practices and conduct of people. Indeed, certain documents are explicitly prescriptive; they are written *in order to* change or sustain the behaviour of workers and managers (think of work manuals, rosters, timetables, rulebooks).

But, we should be careful not to imagine such documents as floating free of specific social relations (bonds between people). Ultimately, documents are written, and they are written by people for other people to read. The extent to which people follow, ignore, adapt or change such written prescriptions is an aspect of the power ratio between writers and audiences (or between managers and subordinates in the context of organisations). There is a highly influential research tradition, following the work of Michel Foucault, within the humanities and social sciences, that stresses the power of discourses – a systematic order of statements pertaining to a given topic (Hall, cited in Tonkiss, 2004: 373) – to constitute the writer or speaker. In other words, even if we identify an author of a document, the conventional forms of speaking about the topic work through the particular author. He or she has read or been taught some managerial principle or procedure before and simply recycles it in a similar way. So the actual people who read and write documents become relatively marginalised (or decentred) compared to the discourse itself, e.g., the language of human resources or customer relations. For figurational researchers, the norms, disciplines and traditions of conceiving and communicating particular issues are important but, in order to understand why and how such norms change (and they do change), we need to locate such discursive changes within the dynamic context of broader social processes. The danger of emphasising 'discourse' as the prime mover in organisational and consumer research is that one can imagine language as autonomous from the generations of people that have used it. Elias (1983: 187) stresses the need to bring culture (which can be seen as a system of ideas and values, similar to discourse) 'back into contact with social development, within which alone cultural phenomena or, to use a different term, social traditions can be studied and explained'.

The list of documents that can be used for organisational and consumer research include manuals, advertisements, diaries, menus, shopping lists, websites, company reports, newspapers, magazines, memoirs, and letters (see Mason, 2002: 103). Researchers can also ask interviewees to generate their own documents by writing diaries containing details of consumption or work practices. This latter form of documents do not of course 'already exist', and tend to be used in conjunction with interviews and focus groups. However, because existing documents are in fact part of the functioning of organisations, they can reveal much about how organisations work. In the case of publicly-accessible documents, such as company reports or brochures, they also support the dependability of the findings as readers of the dissertation or research study can scrutinise such documents themselves. For the novice researcher, there is little danger of expecting the data to provide the answer to the research question directly. Many dissertation supervisors and examiners have seen (in writing) the practice of students asking the interviewee to answer the overarching research question directly! This of course relegates the student researcher to the position of reporter, and there is little need to conduct any analysis of the data (the answer is already there, fully formed in the interview transcript).

From a figurational perspective, the main advantage of documents is that they relate to a particular time in the history of an organisation or society (or, indeed, any social group that has produced written materials for various purposes).

PHILOSOPHY VERSUS SOCIOLOGY OF KNOWLEDGE

In the figurational consumption study briefly outlined below, there is an explicit use of historical documents. The recognition of the changing connotations of consumption and the consumer required the analysis (separating) and synthesis (connecting) of historical data. This can lead to questions often addressed by philosophers regarding the possibility of generating valid and reliable knowledge, or the difficulty of accessing reality, particularly historical reality. Elias maintains that philosophy provides a poor guide to the theoretical-empirical examination of societies. For Elias (1986: 20), 'the discovery, not the method, legitimizes research as scientific'. This is meant as a critique of standardised approaches to method, which imagine that faithful implementation will produce 'truth', irrespective of the object of investigation. Elias (1971a; 1971b; 1974; 1987) consistently argues for a sociology of knowledge perspective, rather than following particular philosophers who have not actually engaged in empirical research.

Any research method should be appropriate to the nature of the object of inquiry and cannot be posited prior to an understanding, theoretically informed, of the structure and dynamic processes immanent within such an object: 'The idea that people can discover a method or a tool of thought, independently of their conception of the subject matter about which knowledge is to be gained, is, however, a product of the philosophical imagination' (Elias, 1978: 57).

While contemporary philosophy of knowledge, or philosophical epistemology, might have developed interesting and relevant insights regarding the discovery of social scientific knowledge, it is not necessary to follow or adapt the methodological guidelines of such philosophies in order to produce such knowledge. Indeed, Kilminster (1998) argues for the displacement of philosophy as a guide to research in favour of a sociological epistemology. This, of course, could be depicted as a type of philosophical position, but such a view arguably would be untenable if philosophy as a discipline is to retain any coherent meaning or function.

Figurational research tends to prioritise the known nature of the object of investigation (for example, the practices, structures and values of the organisation or consuming social group), rather than elevate any particular method as 'superior'. What we know about such objects, of course, is inherited largely from one generation of researchers to the next. As Elias (1971a: 158-9) states:

> ... the knowledge which people have at any given time is derived from, and is a continuation of, a long process of knowledge acquisition of the past. It can be neither understood nor explained without reference to the structured sequence to which we refer when we speak of the 'growth of knowledge' or the 'development of knowledge' which, in turn, is part of the wider development of the societies where knowledge develops and, ultimately, of that of mankind.

The emphasis on the objects of inquiry in formulating appropriate methods may give the misleading impression that an inductive, empiricist position is being advocated. This has been a recurring criticism of Elias's work (Layder, 1986; see van Krieken, 1998). But Elias did not propose a separation of the subject and object of inquiry, nor did he follow an objectivist position familiar to positivists. According to Elias (1991: 3), 'anything that is not symbolically represented in the language of a language community is not known by its members: they cannot communicate about it with each other'. Similarly, he (1993: 125) states that '"knowledge", like "speech", presupposes a plurality of communicating people, not just an individual ... The "object" is a function of the fund of social knowledge existing at the time'. This is hardly the perspective of a naïve empiricist and Elias did not abide by the fiction of a 'neutral observation language'. Elias, and figurational researchers who follow him, use the word 'object' and 'fact' to distinguish the figurational or process approach from more speculative approaches that rely little on evidence of social events, processes, structures and experiences. The continued use of these words also distinguishes between a symbolic representation of an event, a fact, and an explanation for such an event by connecting it to other events or processes. This is how theories are developed but, as they are constructed from the theoretically-informed observation and interpretation of events and experiences, they cannot be considered as totally separate from those very events.

The purpose of research then, 'stripped of a good many philosophical encrustations … is to find out in what way perceived data are connected with each other' (Elias, 1987: 12). Researchers should seek a 'two-way traffic between two layers of knowledge: that of general ideas, theories or models and that of observations and perceptions of specific events' (Elias, 1987: 20). Elias's position on epistemology could be summarised as 'Forget Philosophy!', which may come as some relief to students working through Kant, Hegel and Popper. But some knowledge of 'philosophy of knowledge' questions probably remains valuable, at least while research methodology texts continue to cite them. Such knowledge also helps to recognise the distinctive nature of the figurational perspective. Before I demonstrate an application of this approach, it is necessary to briefly outline some key concepts.

FIGURATIONAL THEORY

There are many dimensions to Elias's concepts and theories, but for the purposes of this methodological discussion, I will focus on the key aspects. Perhaps the most important feature of figurational sociology is to see apparent social structures, attitudes, values, beliefs, traditions and practices as processes. In other words, every 'thing' in the social world is treated as 'in process', simply because these 'things' have histories. They are not natural or universal in the sense that they have always existed. Rather, they gradually developed over time. Obviously, particular organisations have not always existed. They were established by particular people at a particular point in time. Perhaps less obviously, once established, they continue to change. Through the competitive dynamic between other organisations, and through various shifting relations with other groups that the organisation depends upon (for example, customers, governments, suppliers, consultants, state bodies), the owners and managers of the organisation must adapt its structures, functions, corporate culture and conduct. The organisation is not static, and then suddenly is jolted into change until a new period of stability and equilibrium. Doubtless, most organisations have periods of accelerated change and relative calm, but change is normal. For figurational researchers, organisational change is not treated as dysfunctional or an aberration.

This brings us to the second critical factor in figurational research. Any organisation is an example of what Elias calls a figuration – a network of mutually dependent and oriented people. That means each person within this network is shaped, enabled and constrained by their relationships with everybody else, even if they are not fully aware of this. Consequently, we cannot understand and explain the beliefs and actions of any particular individual by examining them as individuals. Behaviour cannot be explained by traits or attributes that are somehow imagined to be innate properties of the individual. Even in consumption studies, we can use the concept of figuration to examine particular groups, like families, youth subcultures, spectators, social classes, ethnic groups, and gender. We can use figuration to correspond to various levels of social integration from a married couple, a housing estate, a suburb, a city, through to a nation-state and the globe itself. All of these levels are inter-related, such that changes in one level affect others. So, in order to be explained, organisational strategies, plans and actions, as well as consumer actions, beliefs, values and emotions, must be placed within a mobile network of social relations. This network consists of shifting interdependencies between numerous people, according to their roles, functions, or the kind of services, benefits and meanings they provide for each other. In more complex figurations, there are unstable power balances between people, usually organised in terms of group interests or identities, e.g., class, gender, ethnicity, generation, profession, trade.

In an organisational context, as business owners and managers become more dependent on their workers at various levels of authority within the organisation, within the context of centralising and expanding trade union formations, the power ratio between manager and worker becomes less uneven. This can lead to flatter organisational structures and more informal modes of interaction between employees at different levels (see de Swaan, 1981; Wouters, 1986; Wouters, 1990; Wouters, 1998). Elias & Dunning (1966) suggest that a football match can serve as a metaphor for relations and changes within organisations. Though the arrangement of players on a soccer pitch is far less complex than most organisations, and the rules are more agreed and codified, there are continually shifting movements on the field of play. Each player observes and reacts to the actions of every other player, such that no player is able to implement plans or intentions perfectly. In fact, the sequence of interactions on the pitch can only be explained in the context of the changing structure and order of the game itself (or the mobile network of the players themselves). Football games are not immune from wider social pressures, and so gradually the threshold of repugnance advances so that formerly acceptable displays of violence become disgusting to spectators. Governing bodies change the rules and players learn to adjust their conduct, and to monitor their own conduct in the face of more continuous monitoring by others (of course these days, footballers are observed not just by spectators in the stadium, but by many more through television broadcasts).

This leads us to another key figurational concept – habitus. This concept has been made famous by Pierre Bourdieu (1984), but it has a much older provenance. It refers to the second nature of a person, an embodied social learning, to the extent that one's actions, feelings and thoughts appear natural or habitual (see Mennell, 2004). It is closely related to the concepts of personality and identity, but people are less conscious of acting according to a specific habitus by virtue of its taken-for-granted nature. One of Elias's main arguments is that, gradually over time, people in many European societies increasingly saw themselves as detached or isolated from others. Their sense of themselves as individuals grew relative to their group affiliation (this is a relative balance, as social allegiances do not disappear). This occurs due to the lengthening chains of interdependence between more and more people. In other words, each person nowadays depends on many others for a wider variety of needs and desires compared to those in the Middle Ages. This growing interdependency is connected to increasing functional specialisation. As each person relies on so many more for their needs, actions and purposes to be fulfilled (think of a single member of a financial institution and all the other people she must deal with to complete her tasks and duties), they must exercise increasing self-constraint and self-awareness in the context of being appraised by others who have a vested interest in their conduct. As these interdependent links deepen and expand, societies develop new standards or codes of conduct, and indeed new words and other symbols to co-ordinate activities according to such standards. In other words, cultures change through changing social interdependencies.

Elias's most famous study, *The Civilizing Process* (2000), exclusively uses documents as sources of data. As a way of identifying cultural changes, and in particular the changes in habitus or how one conducted oneself in public settings, he examined multiple editions of etiquette texts. These prescriptive texts were written for young, minor noblemen who might aspire to enter some court society. They described the type of conduct, for example table manners, that was expected at court. By tracing the particular instructions that disappear in successive editions, Elias was able to show that these particular social standards no longer needed to be explicitly stated (though they often continue to be taught to small children). They had become 'internalised', or ingrained into the habitus. So the analysis of documents over time revealed changing expectations and conduct, changing culture, within a particular society – the court society.

The preceding discussion on the contrasts between a social and philosophical epistemology, as well as the theoretical orientation of figurational sociology, will frame the more specific procedures described below that relate to an account of the development of consumer subjectivity in Ireland. This account is summarised from broader studies (Dolan, 2005; 2009).

RESEARCH QUESTIONS

The central research problem of the study concerned the connection between changing beliefs and values regarding consumption, changing conceptions of the consumer and changing social figurations within Ireland. How are consumer subjectivities (or the consuming habitus) related to figurational characteristics? My understanding of subjectivity follows an Eliasian perspective, in that it refers to the individual's capacity and compulsion to act (including communication and emotional expression) within changing bonds of social interdependence. The study is not concerned exclusively with the explanation of consumption ideals and practices, but with using these as a way of understanding processes of individualisation and identity formation, in a similar way that Elias (2000), Mennell (1996), Dunning (1999), and Hughes (2004) have used aspects of consumer culture to examine developing modes of being and relating to others.

THE RESEARCH SITE

Ireland is a particularly interesting research site, due to its rapid industrialisation and urbanisation (concepts connoting denser social networks of more functionally differentiated people) during the 20th century. These changes include the restructuring of society from an agrarian to a post-industrial economy (Mennell, 1999), the rise and decline of the Roman Catholic Church (Inglis, 1998), the expansion of social welfare provision (Cousins, 2003), the formation of national democratic structures (Lee, 1989a), and the growing dependence on external markets and capital investment (Kennedy *et al.*, 1988). These are relative changes and do not imply complete discontinuity from earlier formations. Indeed, one of the challenges of process sociology is to illuminate both continuities and discontinuities in developing figurations.

DATA SELECTION

Several data sources were used for this study. In order to trace the development of the meanings of the relevant dimensions of consumption, parliamentary debates were analysed, both from the upper and lower houses of the Irish national parliament – Seanad Éireann and Dáil Éireann. The relevant debates were identified through the Irish government internet search engine of the parliamentary archives website (www.oireachtas-debates.gov.ie). The electronic form of the debates is a copy of the official public record of all parliamentary debates. The main advantage over the printed record is that debates can be searched by keywords through the electronic version. The identification of appropriate words proceeded somewhat on a trial and error basis, as it was through increasing familiarisation with the data that forms of expression relating to consumption became apparent. Words like 'consumerism' were rarely used by politicians, but the shifting contour of the debates can be discerned through the changing meaning and function of such phrases as 'standard of living', 'way of life', and 'identity' in conjunction with words related to ideals and practices of consumption such as 'luxury', 'need', 'shopping', 'spending' and new consumer objects such as 'television'. Individual debates were selected based on the nature of the debate and its relevance to the research questions. Debates that contained significant discussions of norms and ideals of consumption practices, as well as personal accounts or stories, were considered particularly relevant.

Parliamentary debates allow for the examination of multiple voices and perspectives within a social context of dialogue, argument, consensus building as well as rhetorical support and refutation. Parliament itself, as a social arena within a nation-state democratic system encompassing an adult franchise, provides a social space for the articulation of norms, beliefs and values pertinent to the concerns and worries not just of individual politicians but also of their constituents; 'In general, deliberative assemblies are a major social institution in every society, for conducting collective reflectivity, deliberation and decision-making' (Burns & Kamali, 2003: 262). Of course, parliamentary democracies are not necessarily transparent windows on the practices and norms of the entire electorate any more than etiquette texts, depth interviews or questionnaires are perfect imitations of social conduct and opinion. But politicians themselves are human beings who have been socialised within the multilevel figuration of Irish society and thus their statements and arguments represent broader social opinion. In fact, parliamentarians within democracies are expected to represent the views of their constituents. They depend on adults resident within a designated geographic area to vote for them in order to occupy the social role of parliamentarian within a competitive structure comprising other political candidates. They, along with such candidates and the electorate, comprise a social figuration with mutual interdependencies and shifting balances of power.

To provide a social structural or figurational context for changing meanings of consumption, I examined historiographic texts and census of population statistics as forms of data. There is no strict polarity between these texts, as political dialogue also provided evidence of changing figurations. Similarly, the historiographical texts contained evidence of norms and codes in particular periods. Evidence of practices and norms of consumption were also derived from government publications, such as household budget surveys and several biographical and autobiographical accounts. Thus, the various forms of data provided an interdependent support structure enabling greater verifiability. Sometimes, historians of Ireland make moral judgements on the actions of particular politicians, or assess their performance based on norms and ideals more appropriate to their own time and social position. These judgements have been disregarded, but not the events or practices to which they refer, provided contemporaneous evidence is presented, such as firsthand accounts or documents.

The Houses of the Oireachtas (Parliament) published a database of the full text of the *Official Report of the Parliamentary Debates of the Houses of the Oireachtas*, as published by the Stationery Office, on DVD in 2002 and this was used, as well as the website, to broaden the search for relevant debates between 1919 and 1980. While initially, debates were analysed in their entirety, gradually as the explanatory model developed, I was more selective in identifying key passages from debates. Thus, a dialectical process between data selection and analysis proceeded. While the selection of debates in the 1960s was relatively intensive, in that many debates were analysed, for other decades an approach more akin to postholing (see Sennett, 2002) was adopted, though selection was not done randomly or arbitrarily as debate headings often provided information indicating degree of relevance. Debates and statements were not avoided for fear of contradicting developing arguments, but rather used to refine such arguments.

DATA ANALYSIS & SYNTHESIS

As stated above, individual debates were analysed in full initially to develop tentative themes and connections. This ensures that the meaning of parliamentary speech is not decontextualised from the flow of the speech itself, but is rather understood in a more relational manner. These were subsequently written up and then reinterpreted to identify significant themes in relation to consumption, before undergoing reinterpretation again once the time frame was broadened. In other words, there was a 'constant two-way traffic' between data and developing themes. The main themes were based on the research questions of the study, intertwined with the prominent issues emergent in the initial data analysis. The theme of consumer subjectivity was based on a more explicit research objective which required the examination of changing meanings of 'the consumer', which was derived from the way politicians talked about consumption practices and ethics. Timeframes were constructed to examine these meaning changes. Thus, the process of analysis and synthesis involved the fluid coding of relevant extracts of parliamentary speeches. The approach diverges from conventional qualitative data analysis whereby codes are established to represent homogenous data extracts that are internally uniform and externally heterogeneous in relation to other codes (Mason, 2002: 150-65). Shifts, continuities and discontinuities in the meaning of themes and their fluid interconnections were identified.

Relevant biographies and autobiographies were integrated after the data interpretation of the debates, both as supplementary documentary evidence and as a further empirical test of the developing arguments and themes.

The analysis of the historiographical texts proceeded on the theoretically-informed basis that people are bonded together by various kinds of interdependencies. The historiographical texts generally did not offer models of such interdependencies, but rather a more empirically-oriented description of past events and individuals. Consequently, the figurations had to be constructed based on the identification of broader social relationships, the functions fulfilled and positions occupied by groups and individuals comprising such relationships, and the nature and extent of interdependencies. These interdependencies were also seen in processual form. Initially, the models of figurations were based on the analysis of the main relevant texts of one of the most cited modern Irish historians, Joseph Lee (1989a; 1989b), whose books *The Modernisation of Irish Society, 1848–1918* and *Ireland, 1912–1985: Politics & Society* are treated as standard texts by other historians. Subsequently, more specialist texts on narrower time periods and narrower social activities, such as economic histories, were analysed to refine the interpretation of figurational change. Further general 20th century histories, such as Dermot Keogh's (1994) *Twentieth Century Ireland* and Diarmaid Ferriter's (2004) *The Transformation of Ireland, 1900–2000* were read as empirical tests.

The above overview probably gives the impression of a clean, smooth process, eventually leading to a clear set of conclusions. However, data analysis and synthesis rarely proceeds smoothly. As I read and re-read the parliamentary debates, certain code words or phrases were noted in the margins to represent dimensions of the dialogue. These could be related to the social attitudes, ideals or expectations expressed, examples of specific consumption practices, and also the way such attitudes and experiences were expressed. The form of expression often indicated the norms of parliamentary conduct and, thus, the expected and experienced subjectivities of politicians themselves as public speakers.

This initial coding process produced hundreds of words and phrases, and is not unlike conventional coding practices (see Coffey and Atkinson, 1996; Spiggle, 1994). But the ultimate goal is to convert such minor codes into process-oriented codes. The latter codes are distinguished by their expression of changes along a particular dimension – very well-known ones include 'industrialisation', 'urbanisation' and 'individualisation'. But becoming industrialised entails many part processes. Process codes can also not normally be represented by a specific piece of data such as a statement in parliament or an extract from an interview transcript or memoir. In some instances, the 'author' of statements referring to past events or changes may imply specific processes, but these should not be taken at face value nor treated in isolation. To do so would elevate the 'author' to the position of expert and naively accept the data as unambiguously representing reality. Figurational research can treat such statements as supporting evidence, but ultimately data emanating from different phases (times) in the overall process is required.

The minor codes that the following example were based on include 'subjects of government intervention', 'protection', 'expertise', 'personality', 'Irish way of life', 'the economy', 'tradition', 'desire', 'emulation', 'habits', 'consumer knowledge', 'controlling consumption', 'self-reflection', 'self-image', 'materialism', 'patriotism', and 'freedom'. These codes can also be labelled in terms of valence; from the perspective of the speaker, they are seen as positive or negative. It is important that the researcher refrains from such moralising (at least for the duration of the analysis and synthesis; figurational researchers can and do adopt critical approaches to specific practices, institutions and people *based* on their analyses). The list of minor codes was then compared against the theories and research questions being examined in order to identify key codes (this is of course a spiral process, as data is selected with theory and questions in mind). I selected several master themes – standard of living / luxury, subjectivity and national identity. These comprised many of the minor codes, but inevitably the researcher has to make choices in terms of which themes warrant detailed analysis. It is important that the researcher keeps thinking of how all codes at various levels within a coding hierarchy are connected. Based on one key theme at a time, quotes from debates and other sources were mapped onto several A3 pages in order to visualise the changes in meaning and valence of certain codes, words, practices and identities. Quotes were also labelled in terms of the politician's name, political party, constituency, occupation, age and any other relevant and accessible information. This multiple coding allows for the identification of patterns and contradictions, which can often be explained by other differences. For example, older politicians were less willing to embrace the new subjectivity of the self-steering consumer that advanced in the 1960s. From a figurational perspective, the most important codes refer to changes in the network of interdependencies bonding Irish people together. This often, but not necessarily, changes in accordance with time, so specific quotes and extracts must be coded according to year. In so doing, we can also identify particular politicians who have 'changed their minds' over several years or even decades. Of course, the challenge is to interpret this change in the developing context of other changes.

In identifying long-term social processes, I then sought to represent 'oppositions' as well as less direct changes in the form of process codes. For example, the earlier parliamentary emphasis on one's duty to buy Irish or to limit one's needs recedes, while the licence to follow your own wishes in the market advances. These are not quite oppositional, as people at times still can be more collectively-oriented than self-oriented (for example, watching intercounty hurling matches or international soccer matches), but the code 'consumer individualisation' captures the process involved in the gradual, non-linear transformation in self and social expectations regarding consumption. Within such a process code, there will be 'moments' or specific years where the meaning of the consumer differs. Unlike conventional coding protocols, this does not signify a coding error, as the figurational researcher expects the meaning of identities and words to change. Any change can only be explained through other changes (normally there are many contributing processes and structural changes, so it is impossible and inadvisable to seek to locate some universal, eternal 'factor' or 'law'; as every 'thing' is moving, we must try to think processually rather than substantively).

The series of changes were then mapped again, including changes in the nature of the relationships (figurational changes) between various groups, e.g., employers and workers, Irish and foreign, men and women, clergy and lay people, young and old, landlords and tenants. Throughout the time period under study, some groups decline in power relative to others (according to Elias, power is always a relation rather than a property), and new groups may even be formed (such as the Free State). The shifting power ratios are associated with other processes like industrialisation, urbanisation, secularisation, commercialisation, mobilisation, specialisation, globalisation, monopolisation, privatisation, emigration and more specific ones like gaelicisation. The common suffix to all these words indicates their processual character; they do not refer to a practice, an event, a value, or an opinion, but to a long-term change that affects many people. Once these various processes and sets of relations are mapped visually, it becomes easier to imagine *how* they are connected.

THE RESEARCH EXAMPLE

This research example relies on data derived from parliamentary debates in Ireland, supplemented by diaries, reports, advertisements and memoirs, in order to see the changing moral and emotional connotations of the consumer, particularly in terms of the tension between the social duty to adhere to communal standards of consumption and the proclaimed sovereign right of each individual to follow their own dispositions and predilections. Compared to the broader study, only a tiny sample of quotes can be reproduced in this chapter. The goal is to show how quotes can be used as evidence, even though here their relative paucity is admittedly less than convincing. For dissertations of course, students have ample space to provide greater empirical support and to be attendant to the exceptions and contradictions in the data. Such 'irregularities' should not be treated as 'outliers', but as opportunities to refine and elaborate their explanations.

The Changing Consumer

Through the data, the identity and subjectivity of the 'consumer' was not always explicitly stated; meanings are often implicit and revealed by examining the norms and values concerning consumption. The movements in the meaning and function of the consumer do not follow a linear historical path; there are contradictory models of the ideal consumer. However, a shift in the direction from consumption as a collective and socially-regulated process towards a more self-determined process is clear. In Ireland, during the first half of the 20th century, a common social standard of consumption was emphasised. People were seen as having more or less common and constrained needs and desires. However, there is a class-specific aspect to this, in that different classes had different consumption practices, values and expectations. Politicians of a professional class habitus were also more likely to emphasise the individuality of the consumer earlier than other politicians. But generally, the individual became more centralised over that period as the subject of choice.

From the 1920s, politicians tried to impose constraints on consumption activities, justified in terms of patriotic duty. In the 1920 *Bill for the Protection of Irish Industries*,[1] the idea of state control was strongly endorsed: '… the protection of Irish Industries must take the form chiefly of discrimination by individual citizens in favour of Irish products'. Deputy Walsh, a trade unionist, argued that the 'Irish public were asleep

---

[1]   *Dáil Debates (DD)*, volume F column 229–31, 17 September 1920.

as regards their duty to support Irish manufacture'.[2] Ó Broin (1986: 7) recalls that as a child his father prohibited the purchase of foreign boots. If his mother sent him shopping to buy anything foreign, she would tell him 'not to tell [my father] where it came from' (Ó Broin, 1986: 8). So, although people were compelled to buy according to group norms, these could be evaded if one could avoid being observed. The lack of effective observation in many situations, coupled with very strict social observation and sanctions for norm transgression in others, meant that a stable, even, self-controlled habitus had less scope for development. From the perspective of analysing data, however, the theoretical meaning of these documented statements and experiences only becomes clear when compared against expectations of the consumer at a later stage of social development in Ireland. To produce a coherent narrative of change, it is often necessary for the writer to discuss these changed connotations at separated points in a research document, such as a dissertation, but the actual analytic procedure had juxtaposed these meanings (see discussion on mapping above).

Up to the 1940s, politicians emphasised self-reliance; people were expected to provide for their own needs. The pressure to meet certain needs was seen as vital in encouraging people to work. Politicians feared that some might not work at all and would thereby place extra demands on more productive citizens. According to Eamonn Coogan in 1947, 'Our attitude to these seekers of doles should be: "You will get nothing for nothing and damn little for a half penny."'[3] Though Coogan accepted that government should provide employment opportunities, where 'employment can be found, these people, provided they are fit, should be compelled to work'. So the ethic of self-reliance was inseparable from the felt need for strong social pressure. Coogan labelled 'work-shy gentlemen' as 'anti-social', meaning they had neglected their duty to take care of themselves and their families. In the same debate, Patrick Giles, a farmer, claimed that the nation had become 'a spoiled child', with people 'running to the shop and buying everything they need, instead of producing it'. This quote demonstrates not only a preference for more self-sufficient existence, but also an anxiety regarding the quickening pace of functional specialisation.

---

[2]   *DD*, volume F column 230, 17 September 1920
[3]   *DD*, volume 105 column 495, 28 March 1947; see also Vivian de Valera and Patrick Giles, column 502–8

By the 1960s, the emphasis on the social regulation of consumption practices had receded, while the scope and expectation of using consumption to express and distinguish the individual self had advanced. This, echoing Elias (1991), demonstrates a shift in the we–I balance towards the latter pole (but we-identities or we-images did not disappear). People did not rapidly shift their view of themselves in their relations with others, but there was a developing expectation among politicians that people either had, or should, become more self-steering in their conduct. In 1960, McGuire lamented the continuing mentality that expected others to prescribe appropriate courses of individual action: 'Many of our citizens are not only resigned to the State guiding and controlling their destinies and activities, but they acquiesce in that state of affairs; not only that, but many demand more and more State benevolence and control.'[4] Others, such as Patrick Donegan, doubted the ability of the State to control the television viewing habits of the Irish people: 'Our people – patriotic and nationally-minded as they may be – will sit down at night and look and listen to the programme they prefer.'[5] In 1962, politicians quoted reports of the government-established Committee on Industrial Organisation, which had expressed the view that patriotism would not protect business in Ireland from free-flowing imports following accession to the European Economic Community (EEC).[6] The decline in socially-expected patriotic consumption went hand-in-hand with a rising consciousness of a more differentiated, self-oriented consumer. One of the subsequent Committee (1964) reports on the furniture industry warned of inadequate product standards, lack of focus on design and the fact that 'no systematic investigation of the buying public's needs or *desires* has ever been made' (p. 73, my emphasis). Though specifying 'the buying public', they meant a more differentiated subject of consumption as they stressed the need for 'narrower specialisation' (p. 81) of production.

By the 1970s, expectation that the individual could, and should, find individual expression, distinction and fulfilment through consumption practices had taken hold in political dialogue. In 1974, Justin Keating welcomed proposed consumer protection legislation as it would help in 'satisfying the needs of a more sophisticated public'.[7] It would also benefit

---

[4] *Seanad Debates (SD)*, volume 52 column 123, 21 January 1960.

[5] Column 152.

[6] Norton, *DD*, volume 194 column 1818, 11 April 1962; McGilligan, *DD*, volume 195 column 408, 8 May 1962; Corish, *DD*, volume 195 column 98–9, 2 May 1962.

[7] *DD*, volume 272 column 94, 24 April 1974.

the retailing sector whose aim 'is to satisfy to the *highest* level the *wishes* and needs of the customers' (my emphasis). The escalating wishes of consumers and the corresponding growth in products and brands also meant the individual had no choice but to choose, and choices potentially became signs of the judgement, expertise and self-knowledge of each individual consumer. For many consumers, according to Paddy O'Toole, 'times have changed and ... consumers are now faced with a bewildering amount of products'.[8] The occupational or hereditary basis of social status was also assumed to be in decline as O'Toole thought many consumers were being persuaded that 'social status is measured by the frequency with which people can purchase and replace items'. Rising social pressure on each individual to find his or her own path as a consumer is also evident in O'Toole's comment that 'when a person makes what turns out to be a foolish purchase, we castigate him for being careless ... Sometimes these people are referred to as careless consumers'.

This increasing individualisation is also evident from the perspective of one person's life experiences. The memoirs of a retired schoolteacher demonstrate the unease of older people, brought up with different cultural values and social expectations, for modern conveniences; he recalls how girls used to wash their hair in rainwater without 'any medicated shampoos for greasy or dry hair or any of that nonsense' (O'Farrell, 1986: 25). Such 'nonsense' refers to the desire for product differentiation to meet greater subjective differentiation and variety.

Figurational Shifts

While it is difficult to summarise the data that led to the identification of changing connotations and expectations of the consumer, it is more daunting to demonstrate the figurational movements in Ireland in a brief section such as this. Essentially, I argue that, over the course of the 20th century, the network of mutual dependencies between people in Ireland became more extensive and intensive. Ireland became more enmeshed in wider figurations on a global level. People were increasingly subject to a greater variety of social pressures to adjust their actions to new social relations. Each individual is not necessarily fully aware of these new pressures, but the growing complexity between more and more people generates new models of conduct that develop and gradually diffuse throughout the population. Here, I can only briefly refer to the kinds of

---

[8]   *DD*, volume 309 column 1118–20, 16 November 1978.

documents that represent or provide evidence for this growing social complexity and functional specialisation. The indicators of this change are often quantitative indices such as population statistics, so the figurational approach adopts a 'mixed methods' strategy.

An example of greater interdependencies within Ireland occurred through increasing competition between Irish farmers and those from other states such as Denmark for consumers in Britain (Lee, 1989a; Lee, 1989b). As the pace and scope of industrialisation advanced during the 19th century in England, many people in Ireland specialised in the production of specific farming products or in specific phases of those production processes. The growing interdependencies between producers and consumers across national spaces (but within the same state formation at the time) encouraged further mechanisation of farming practices, which displaced much of the rural population. These people migrated to towns, to take up growing employment opportunities in administration and distribution, or emigrated, mainly to America. According to the *Census of Population* (1926 to 1981), 51 per cent of the labour force engaged in agricultural occupations in 1926, but this had declined to 16 per cent by 1981. This urbanisation process reflects increasing social interdependencies within Ireland but, even within the agricultural sector, the demand for consistent supplies of farm produce in the face of rising international competition stimulated the growth of agricultural co-operatives. Throughout the 20th century, these amalgamated and consolidated, embedding farmers and administrators in such organisations into tighter webs of interdependence.

The proportion of people living in towns comprising over 1,500 people rose from 32 per cent to 52 percent from 1900 to 1971 (Vaughan & Fitzpatrick, 1978). The growing urban population increased pressure for employment, and violent conflict between employing and working classes occasionally occurred. Power ratios between these interdependent groups became less unequal through the growth and consolidation of trade unions and, in a related process, the growth of employer organisations. This mutually constitutive process created multi-tiered social institutions with new social functions designed to mediate between opposing classes, which pacified relationships to some extent. People became subject to greater social constraints to exercise greater self-control.

However, the continuing lack of employment opportunities meant emigration became a growing source of shame for a new nation-state. As America restricted immigration, England became the main destination for Irish emigrants. Over 12,000 people emigrated to the USA in 1920 compared to only 469 to England (Vaughan & Fitzpatrick, 1978: 265–6). Of those born between 1936 and 1941, only 59 per cent remained in Ireland by 1961 (Rottman & O'Connell 1982: 69). This social and cultural crisis led politicians to abandon protectionist policies. Irish governments increasingly depended on foreign inward investment to provide employment, which intensified and multiplied social interdependencies between Irish people and other nationalities within a globalised system of production, exchange and consumption. While only 16 per cent of manufacturing output was exported in 1951, 64 per cent was exported in 1988 (O'Malley, 1992: 33–4). By then, foreign firms were responsible for 44 per cent of manufacturing employment and 75 per cent of manufacturing exports (O'Malley, 1992: 39).

In the course of these social changes, people had to attune their behaviour to unfamiliar social networks, depending on inadequate symbolic and emotional repertoires. The felt compulsion to watch oneself and others in these new social relationships produced tension and anxiety. Growing equalisation (without actually becoming equal) discouraged people from telling others how to behave, and so, lacking conduct models, people had to increasingly negotiate these networks as individuals. The development of the ideal of individuality was the unplanned, but ordered, outcome of figurational shifts. The increasingly individualised consumer is a version of this general individualisation trend.

CONCLUDING REMARKS

While 'historical social science' has been charged as untenable by both positivists and postmodernists alike, the principles derived from the sociology of knowledge and the adoption of a critical approach to sources offers the means to build explanations (Bryant, 2000). One criticism of Eliasian approaches, which could be applied to broadly conceived historical sociology, is that the meanings of words change over time and therefore the attribution of specific meanings by researchers is highly dubious, given their dependence on current meanings (for example, see van Krieken, 1989). However, this ignores the fact that it is precisely change that is the concern of process sociologists; fluid meanings are not ignored, but actively sought. The contemporary meaning of words can be deciphered by realising that words are simply a 'network of human sound-patterns' (Elias, 1991: 39), implying that words depend on each other for the establishment of meaning. By relating words to the interdependent context of surrounding words that comprise speeches and statements, interpretation becomes less arbitrary. An understanding of the shifting social figurational context also allows a more refined analysis and synthesis of political statements.

While Elias avoided the designation of 'historical sociology' to his approach, as he conceived it as axiomatic that sociologists should incorporate social change into their work, Calhoun's (2003: 383) endorsement of this subdiscipline captures the reasons for the sociological use of history:

> The most compelling reason for the existence of historical sociology is embarrassingly obvious (embarrassingly because so often ignored). This is the importance of studying social change. If it is remarkable that much sociology focuses on some combination of an illusory present and an even more illusory set of universal laws, it is still more remarkable that much history focuses not on crucial patterns, processes, trajectories and cases of social change but on aspects of the past divorced from their location in the course or context of social change.

In that respect, Calhoun (1998: 869) recommends a balance between explicit theory and narrative in the construction of explanations of change which approximates the position adopted here. The use and analysis of documents is indispensable in the comparison of cultures, whether consumer or organisational, over time.

REFERENCES

Bourdieu, P. (1984). *Distinction*. London: Routledge.

Bryant, J.M. (2000). 'On Sources and Narratives in Historical Social Science: A Realist Critique of Positivist and Posstmodern Epistemologies', *British Journal of Sociology* 51(3): 489–523.

Burns, T.R. & Kamali, M. (2003). 'The Evolution of Parliaments: A Comparative-Historical Perspective on Assemblies and Political Decision-Making', in Delanty, G. & Isin, E.F. (eds), *Handbook of Historical Sociology*, pp. 261–75. London: Sage.

Calhoun, C. (1998). 'Explanation in Historical Sociology: Narrative, General Theory and Historically Specific Theory', *American Journal of Sociology* 104(3): 846–71.

Calhoun, C. (2003). 'Afterword: Why Historical Sociology?' in Delanty, G. & Isin, E.F. (eds), *Handbook of Historical Sociology*, pp. 383–93. London: Sage.

Coffey, A. & Atkinson, P. (1996). *Making Sense of Qualitative Data*. London: Sage.

Cohen, L. (2003). *A Consumer's Republic: The Politics of Mass Consumption in Postwar America*. New York, NY: Knopf.

Committee on Industrial Organisation (1964). *Report on Survey of the Wood and Metal Furniture Industry (Pr. 7484)*. Dublin: The Stationery Office.

Cousins, M. (2003). *The Birth of Social Welfare in Ireland, 1922–1952*. Dublin: Four
    Courts Press.
De Grazia, V. (2005). *Irresistible Empire: America's Advance through Twentieth-Century
    Europe*. Cambridge, MA: Belknap Press of Harvard University Press.
De Swaan, A. (1981). 'The Politics of Agoraphobia: On Changes in Emotional and
    Relational Management', *Theory and Society* 10(3): 359–85.
Dolan, P. (2005). 'The Development of Consumer Culture, Subjectivity and
    National Identity in Ireland, 1900–1980', unpublished PhD, Goldsmiths College,
    University of London.
Dolan, P. (2009). 'Developing Consumer Subjectivity in Ireland: 1900–1980', *Journal
    of Consumer Culture* 9(1): 117–41.
Donohue, K.G. (2006). *Freedom from Want: American Liberalism and the Idea of the
    Consumer*. Baltimore, MD: Johns Hopkins University Press.
Dunning, E. (1999). *Sport Matters: Sociological Studies of Sport, Violence and Civilization*.
    London: Routledge.
Elias, N. (1971a). 'Sociology of Knowledge: New Perspectives, Part One', *Sociology*
    5(2): 149–68.
Elias, N. (1971b). 'Sociology of Knowledge: New Perspectives, Part Two', *Sociology*
    5(3): 355–70.
Elias, N. (1974). 'The Sciences: Towards a Theory', in Whitley, R. (ed), *Social
    Processes of Scientific Development*, pp. 21–42. London: Routledge & Kegan Paul.
Elias, N. (1978). *What is Sociology?* London: Hutchinson.
Elias, N. (1983). *The Court Society*. Oxford: Basil Blackwell.
Elias, N. (1986). 'Introduction', in Elias, N. & Dunning, E. (eds), *Quest For
    Excitement: Sport and Leisure in the Civilizing Process*, pp. 19–62. Oxford:
    Blackwell.
Elias, N. (1987). *Involvement and Detachment*. Oxford: Basil Blackwell.
Elias, N. (1991). *The Symbol Theory*. London: Sage.
Elias, N. (1993). *Time: An Essay*. Oxford: Blackwell Publishers.
Elias, N. (2000). *The Civilizing Process: Sociogenetic and Psychogenetic Investigations*,
    Revised Edition. Oxford: Blackwell Publishers.
Elias, N. & Dunning, E. (1966). 'Dynamics of Group Sports with Special Reference
    to Football', *British Journal of Sociology* 17(4): 388–402.
Ferriter, D. (2004). *The Transformation of Ireland, 1900–2000*. London: Profile Books.
Hammersley, M. & Atkinson, P. (1995). *Ethnography: Principles in Practice*, 2nd ed.
    London: Routledge.
Hughes, J. (2004). 'From Panacea to Pandemic: Tobacco-Use in the West', in
    Dunning, E. & Mennell, S. (eds), *Norbert Elias*. Vol.4, pp. 205–26. London: Sage.
Inglis, T. (1998). *Moral Monopoly: The Rise and Fall of the Catholic Church in Modern
    Ireland*, 2nd ed. Dublin: University College Dublin Press.
Kennedy, K.A., Giblin, T. & McHugh, D. (1988). *The Economic Development of Ireland
    in the Twentieth Century*. London: Routledge.
Keogh, D. (1994). *Twentieth-Century Ireland: Nation and State*. Dublin: Gill & Macmillan.

Kilminster, R. (1998). *The Sociological Revolution: From the Enlightenment to the Global Age.* London: Routledge.

Layder, D. (1986). 'Social Reality as Figuration: A Critique of Elias's Conception of Sociological Analysis', *Sociology* 20(3): 367–86.

Lee, J. (1989a). *Ireland 1912–1985: Politics and Society.* Cambridge: Cambridge University Press.

Lee, J. (1989b). *The Modernisation of Irish Society: 1848–1918.* Dublin: Gill & Macmillan.

Mason, J. (2002). *Qualitative Researching,* 2nd ed. London: Sage.

Mennell, S. (1996). *All Manners of Food: Eating and Taste in England and France from the Middle Ages to the Present,* 2nd ed. Urbana, IL: University of Illinois Press.

Mennell, S. (1998). *Norbert Elias: An Introduction.* Dublin: University College Dublin Press.

Mennell, S. (1999). 'From Agrarian to Post-Industrial Elites in One Generation? – Accelerated Social Change in Ireland', paper presented at Incontri Europei di Amalfi XI, 27–30 May.

Mennell, S. (2004). 'The Formation of We-Images: A Process Theory', in Dunning, E. & Mennell, S. (eds), *Norbert Elias.* Vol.2, pp. 367–86. London: Sage.

O'Malley, E. (1992). 'Problems of Industrialisation in Ireland', in Goldthorpe, J.H. & Whelan, C.T. (eds), *The Development of Industrial Society in Ireland,* pp. 31–52. Oxford: Oxford University Press.

Ó Broin, L. (1986). *Just Like Yesterday.* Dublin: Gill & Macmillan.

O'Farrell, P. (1986). *'Tell me, Sean O'Farrell': The Story of an Irish Schoolmaster.* Cork: Mercier Press.

Rottman, D.B. & O'Connell, P.J. (1982). 'The Changing Social Structure', in Litton, F. (ed), *Unequal Achievement: The Irish Experience, 1957–82,* pp. 63–88. Dublin: Institute of Public Administration.

Sennett, R. (2002). *The Fall of Public Man.* London: Penguin Books.

Spiggle, S. (1994). 'Analysis and Interpretation of Qualitative Data in Consumer Research', *Journal of Consumer Research* 21(3): 491–503.

Tonkiss, F. (2004). 'Analysing Text and Speech: Content and Discourse Analysis', in Seale, C. (ed), *Researching Society and Culture,* 2nd ed, pp. 367–82. London: Sage.

Van Krieken, R. (1989). 'Violence, Self-Discipline and Modernity: Beyond the "Civilizing Process"', *Sociological Review* 37(2): 193–218.

Van Krieken, R. (1998). *Norbert Elias.* London: Routledge.

Vaughan, W.E. & Fitzpatrick A.J. (eds) (1978). *Irish Historical Statistics: Population, 1821–1971.* Dublin: Royal Irish Academy.

Wouters, C. (1986). 'Formalization and Informalization: Changing Tension Balances in Civilizing Processes', *Theory, Culture & Society* 3(2): 1–18.

Wouters, C. (1990). 'Social Stratification and Informalization in Global Perspective', *Theory, Culture & Society* 7(4): 69–90.

Wouters, C. (1998). 'How Strange to Ourselves are our Feelings of Superiority and Inferiority? Notes on Fremde und Zivilisierung by Hans-Peter Waldhoff', *Theory, Culture & Society* 15(1): 131–50.

CHAPTER 9
AN OVERVIEW OF DISCOURSE ANALYTICAL APPROACHES TO RESEARCH

Brendan K. O'Rourke

INTRODUCTION

The field of discourse analysis (DA) is vast, varied and contested with traditions ranging from conversational analysis (Sacks, 1995, [1964-1972]), to more Foucauldian-inspired approaches (e.g., Kendall & Wickham, 1999), to critical discourse approaches (Van Dijk, 2001; Fairclough, 2003). This diversity means that this overview is necessarily selective. Nonetheless, this introduction should provide a platform from which readers then can investigate further those currents of DA that are of particular interest.

In order to locate DA within the range of methodology discussed in this volume, and to argue for the unity of various DA approaches, a short history is outlined. A survey of DA is then provided, organised by what various approaches mean by 'discourse' and by what theories and concepts they use for analysis. An illustrative exercise in the discourse analysis of some interview data then is given. Finally, a guide to further reading and resources is provided for the reader who wishes to study discourse analysis in greater depth.

THE UNITY & DISTINCTIVENESS OF DA

In this chapter, DA has a very broad meaning, incorporating such diverse approaches as the conversation analysis (CA) of Sacks (1995 [1964-1972]) and Schegloff (1999), the critical discourse analysis (CDA) of Van Dijk (2001) or Fairclough (1995), the discourse analysis for social psychology (DASP) of Potter & Wetherell (1987), the discourse theory of Laclau &

Mouffe (1985) and the discursive psychology of Harré & Gillet (1994). While these and other DA approaches differ on many issues, DA as a whole shares key differences from non-DA approaches. These differences will now be explored.

A central feature of DA is that language is understood as more than just a transparent descriptor of reality: rather, the use of language is seen as acting upon and creating what we take to be our reality. This is the case even where language is merely selecting, noticing and highlighting through description. Many non-DA approaches adopt or assume a reference theory of language, where a word or symbol is seen as a label for a separately knowable entity. For these approaches, the entity referred to could be an objective thing or concept. DA does not necessarily deny any referential aspects to language: contrast the critical realist approach of Fairclough (2005) with the more extensively-constructionist approach of Laclau & Mouffe (1985). Nonetheless, what all versions of DA share is the view that there is an active aspect to language, in which language functions to construct the world. While there are approaches that acknowledge this constructive view of language that would not label themselves as DA, DA focuses on this constructive work of language. For example, a non-DA approach to interview data is to treat the interview as a *resource* to, or way of, accessing – however imperfectly – some reality (be it the internal reality of an interviewee's mental state or the facts of the social world around the interviewee) beyond the interview. DA takes the interview as an example of the active nature of language to be studied for the sake of understanding that action itself. So, non-DA seeks information from an 'informant' using the interview as a *resource*, whereas DA studies the performance of talk of the interview itself as its *topic* (Potter & Wetherell, 1987). To understand the importance of this view of language and other distinctive features of DA, it is necessary to trace some of the history of what some have called the much broader 'linguistic turn' in Western thinking (Baghramian, 1998).

THE LINGUISTIC TURN

The linguistic turn was lead initially by philosophers like Gottlob Frege (1848-1925), Rudolf Carnap (1891-1970) and Bertrand Russell (1872-1970), all of whom felt that a lot of confusion in philosophy could be overcome by clarity in language (Russell, 1946:784-785). Such philosophical effort hoped for the application of logical analysis to all solvable philosophical problems and so tried to fashion ideal languages free from the errors of ordinary language. In opposition to many other approaches in science and philosophy, DA shares with these analytical philosophers their great focus on language and the concern that natural languages are not transparent mediators of thought. Analytical philosophy aimed to rid language of its rhetorical and grammatical flaws so that this purified language would be an ideal vehicle for the discovery of truth. However, DA rejects the analytical philosophers in their attempts to invent perfectly logical ideal languages, where the signs would correspond clearly to thoughts. In contrast, DA prefers to study the uses of natural languages in all their messiness.

Within philosophy, the view of language as active was advocated by Ludwig Wittgenstein (1889-1951). Wittgenstein, in the second half of his career, focused on the language games of ordinary language, rather than persisting in trying to find the ideal, perfectly referential language. Another philosopher, John Austin (1911-1960), also pursued speech act theory to understand the active nature of language. Grice (1998 [1957]) developed an understanding of how real languages aimed at co-operating to communicate meaning, rather than merely issuing logical descriptions. Though interested in the activity of ordinary language, Wittgenstein (1998 [1953]: 89-90) and Austin (1998 [1953]: 122) used hypothetical statements of their own construction to study language use. In contrast to these ordinary language philosophers, DA shuns hypothetical statements constructed by analysts and, instead, focuses on the 'naturally-occurring' language used in practice. In this sense, work like that of speech act theorists Labov & Fanshel (1977) moved towards DA in applying the ordinary language philosophy to real language in use. In this way, some of the pragmatics work inspired by Grice could be considered part of DA, but only where it is addressing real language in use.

While analytical philosophers were attempting to drive rhetorical and grammatical 'confusions' out of language, in order to make it ideal for the discovery of truth, linguists were pointing to a problem in trying to use language in such an attempt. De Saussure (1983 [1916]: 75) showed that the words and other signs in languages are related to corresponding ideas in only very loose, arbitrary ways. There is no stability in the sign or any firm way of fixing the meaning signified. Thus, it is impossible to create perfect correspondence between the sign and the signified. DA shares De Saussure's critique, in contrast with the analytical philosophers, of the reference theory of languages. However, De Saussure felt that actual instances of language use could not be studied systematically, so he stressed the structural elements of language. DA, in contrast, is committed to study language instances or practices in use.

De Saussure was a key influence on the predominately French intellectual movement known as structuralism. Developing from structuralism, an important range of thinkers, influential on DA, emerged. This range of thinkers is sometimes referred to as the post-structuralists. The word 'discourse' was in frequent and varied use in post-structural work (Diaz-Bone *et al.*, 2007). Famous phrases from these post-structuralists such as, 'There is nothing outside the text' (Derrida, 1976 [1967]: 158) and 'The death of the author' (Barthes, 1967), certainly seem to encourage DA's focus on the language used. Post-structuralism was particularly strong in the impact of literary criticism on DA. The most important of this highly varied group of thinkers for DA was Michel Foucault (1972; 1973; 1978; 1979). Foucault's major contribution to DA is at the level of discourse *theory*, rather than *analysis*, as he rarely engaged with a single text as topic for very long.

TREATING LANGUAGE IN USE AS TOPIC

Rhetoric, since the Greek philosophers and sophists, has studied the activity of language. The older view of rhetoric was that the activity of language was limited to its persuasive element. Nevertheless, there developed a vocabulary of language features and effects, which, as McCloskey (1998, [1985]) puts it, had some very useful thinking attached. There was a renaissance of rhetoric, both in literary (Booth, 1961) and in communication (McLuhan, 1951) studies. One of the outcomes of this resurgence is the recognition of rhetoric as not just persuasive but pervasive. Rhetoric is not mere style added to substance, but is inherent in substance and in science, as McCloskey's (1998, [1985]) *Rhetoric of Economics* shows. Billig (1991) brought a rhetorical perspective clearly into the mainstream of DA. He achieved this by extending rhetorical analysis from studies of academic and mass media discourse to the analysis of everyday talk. Billig (1991) showed that commonsense was rhetorical in nature.

Psychoanalysis, too, was undermining the reference theory of language. Freud showed, through studying the words of his patients, how language seemed to carry much more than the referential meaning that the purely rational mind might have intended. Lacan (1901-1981) argued for a return to Freud's work on slips of the tongue and felt that the unconscious was structured linguistically. Lacan's views on the importance of language, particularly in the formation of identity and through some specific Lacanian concepts (e.g., the role of 'suture' in Laclau & Mouffe, 1985) have been influential on some forms of DA. However, specific theories of the unconscious, like Lacan's, are not essential to DA.

Marxism, like psychoanalysis, shows that language as a pure reference system is corrupted but, in Marxism, this corruption is from power, rather than from the primordial drives of the unconscious. For Marxism, ideology, and so language, has always been part of the social reproduction of capitalism. Althusser (1971) developed two ideas from Marxism and psychoanalysis that have been important for at least some forms of DA. The first is *interpellation*, which points out the activity in calling a person into an identity. The famous example is how police shouting 'Hey, you!' has the active effect of getting the person hailed to respond and become a subject through that activity of language (Althusser, 1971: 174). Althusser's second concept of relevance to DA is the idea of the *ideological state apparatus*: institutions and practices, like the education system or the police, form the language that interpellates the subject in particular ways. These Althusserian concepts have been influential on DA through the medium of the post-structuralists (discussed above). They have also led to the stretching of the idea of discourse beyond language, to include the material practices and existence of the institutions that Althusser found so important in the interpellation process. In this Marxist view of ideology, there is a search for the processes behind language that shape it. This Althusserian form of Marxism treats the discourse as a resource (to get to a reality behind language), not a topic in and of itself. So while influential on DA, this approach is different from DA, for language use is always the topic focused upon by discourse analysts.

Within linguistics, the mainstream followed Chomsky (1998, [1972]) in keeping De Saussure's stress on the structure of language rather than particular performances of it. However, there was also another minority stream concerned more with language use than language structure. Hymes (1974), in studying language, stressed the social aspects of language, and developed, with John Gumperz, an ethnography of communication influential on many schools of DA.

While those studying language were becoming more aware of the social, sociologists were becoming more aware of language. Goffman (1959) added social interactional complications to the Ordinary Language philosophers' view of how language was used, giving rise to much discourse analytical work on politeness. The determination of ethnomethodology to study the accomplishment of society from the micro interactions amongst people up (rather than down from the *a priori* theories of grand social theorists) inspired Sacks' (1995, [1964-1972]) and Schlegoff's (1999) conversational analytical (CA) form of DA. CA and its ethnomethodological roots also inform many other schools of DA, for example, providing the resource *versus* topic distinction, discussed earlier and used throughout DA (Potter & Wetherell, 1987).

The above historical overview has sought to clarify the distinctiveness of DA compared to other approaches and shows how, despite its diverse influences, there is a certain unity to discourse analytical approaches. Having clarified this unity of DA, it is time to talk about its diversity.

DIFFERENT TYPES OF DA STUDIES

To illustrate the diversity of DA, a survey of studies, representative of the range of DA types, is presented here. As there are many forms of DA, the survey presented here is necessarily limited, both in its range and in the extent that it can give full explanations of all theories and concepts mentioned. It can, however, be used as a basis for further exploration. I have organised this survey according to two aspects: discourse and analysis. Organising DA studies according to these two principles does disguise that often what is considered discourse is intimately bound-up with how you might proceed to analyse it. Drawing attention to the 'discourse' aspect, as separate from the 'analysis' aspect, might also facilitate the erroneous view, warned against for example by Iedema (2007), that 'analysis' is somehow not discourse, but located outside and above it in some superior objective position. With these considerations in mind, this section proceeds to look at some discourse types. **Figure 9.1** below organises the various discourse studies that serve as examples of discourse types.

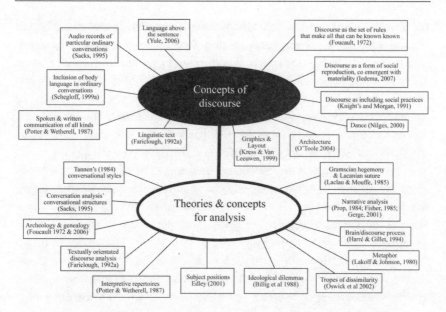

**Figure 9.1: Discourse Studies Organised by Type of Discourse &
Analysis Used (Source: Derived from the literature by the author)**

The top half of **Figure 9.1** illustrates the diversity of what is covered by the term 'discourse' in various DA studies. For Yule (2006:124), discourse refers to any amount of language larger than a sentence. For CA, discourse is spoken conversation in naturalistic settings, the study of which was made possible by the technology of audio recordings (Sacks, 1995, [1964-1972]), but extendable to the body language involved in natural conversations (Schegloff, 1999). Potter & Wetherell (1987:7) define discourse as including 'all forms of spoken interaction, formal and informal, and written texts of all kinds'. Fairclough (1992), too, prefers to focus on specific linguistic, usually printed, texts. Kress & Van Leeuwen (1999) focus on discourses of graphic communication, such as newspaper layout. The meaning of discourse can be expanded to include non-linguistic semiotic systems, such as architecture (O'Toole, 2004) or dance (Nilges, 2000). Knights & Morgan (1991:254) go beyond even this and view '... discourse as shorthand for a whole set of power / knowledge relations which are written, spoken, communicated and embedded in social practices'. Iedema (2007), too, shares such an encompassing view of discourse, as at times does Foucault (1972).

The other area of diversity in DA types illustrated in the lower half of **Figure 9.1** is the different concepts and theories from which the analysis can draw. Within the confines of this chapter, I can offer the reader merely a whistle-stop tour of the vast theoretical diversity involved. Interested readers can find more detail about particular approaches in the references cited. Tannen (1984) analyses similar kinds of discourse by looking for the different conversational styles of the participants. CA, following Sacks (1995, [1964-1972]), analyses conversational discourse with regard to '... the generic organisations for conversation ...' (Schegloff, 1999a: 412). Foucault approaches discourses in a much more historical way through his methods of archaeology – the examination of the conditions that make discourses possible (Foucault, 1966:31) – and genealogy – the tracing of the contingencies by which the particular discourse that has emerged (of all those that might have been possible) grew and intertwined itself in the world (Foucault, 2006 [1973]: 236). Fairclough (1992a) applies close textual analysis and concepts, such as, 'intertextuality' to examine critically how discourse constitutes representations, relations and identities in the context of non-discursive elements of society (which, for Fairclough, might be, for example, the power relations existing between employer and employee). Potter & Wetherell (1987) find it useful to identify interpretative repertoires – particular ways of speaking that, as they are creatively deployed, produce accounts. The idea of subject positions is used by Edley (2001) to look at how people use different, even contradictory, discourses to do the identity work of, say, constructing oneself as a heterosexual young man. Billig *et al.* (1988) draw on concepts of rhetoric and ideology to point to the usefulness of analysing discourse in terms of dilemmas. Analysing discourse using tropes of dissimilarity, rather than those based on similarity, such as metaphor, may be the way to open up new possibilities, argue Oswick *et al.* (2002). This contrasts with the emphasis of Lakoff & Johnson (1980) on the centrality of metaphor, which they see as central to the human way of thinking. Harré & Gillet (1994:79) attempt to relate rules of discursive activity to a model of brain activity and thus provide a realist grounding for DA. For others, narrative is the fundamental way that human thought is organised; the narrative approach to analysing discourse is promoted by many, including Propp (1984), Fisher (1985) and Gergen (2001). In contrast, Laclau & Mouffe (1985) stress the endless struggle for hegemony between discourses.

From the above survey, it is clear that there is a dizzying diversity of discourse analytical approaches. Novice researchers considering adopting a DA approach clearly need to be more specific about the particular approach they are adopting in their research. That choice will depend on many things, not least on the kind of guidance available to them in their particular circumstances. The survey provided in this section will help locate the particular approach they adopt in the wider literature that their library searches will present them with. Whatever DA approach a novice researcher might adopt, an engagement with data will be needed. It is to an illustration of such a discourse analytical exploration of data that the next section is devoted.

ILLUSTRATING A DISCOURSE ANALYTICAL APPROACH

The discourse analytical approach illustrated here is on researcher-generated dyadic interview data and uses an approach inspired by work such as Potter & Wetherell (1987) and McAuley *et al.* (2000).

Researcher-generated, one-to-one interview data is much used by social researchers, in general, and novice qualitative researchers, in particular. Despite its widespread use, there are often good reasons to avoid generating particularly researcher-involved dyadic interviews (Potter & Hepburn, 2005). For example, one disadvantage of interviews involving just the researcher and interviewee is that the researcher in her role as analyst of the interview transcript only has her own responses, as interviewer, to the single interviewee. In contrast, if there are multiple persons involved in the interaction, how they respond to each other can be a useful way of interpreting what is going on. In this regard, situations where there are multiple interviewees, such as focus groups, can be preferable to dyadic interviews, though as Freeman (2009) makes clear in this volume, focus groups, too, need to be handled with care. Novice researchers often feel obliged to expend resources on generating their own data, when imaginative use of already existing material can be used to produce first-class primary research as Dolan (2009) illustrates in an earlier chapter of this book. Dyadic researcher-involved interviews nevertheless can be the most suitable source of data for many kinds of research. For a further discussion of the research interview from a DA viewpoint, see O'Rourke & Pitt (2007). The interview data here provides rich material through which to illustrate how a discourse analytical approach can study the frequently-ignored interactional features of the interview.

The extracts presented here are from an interview I conducted as a part of a number of interviews with entrepreneurs. The interviews were primarily organised to talk with these entrepreneurs about the businesses they had started, but, frequently, we would talk about other businesses the entrepreneurs had been involved with. This is the case in the extracts presented here, as Eoin (a pseudonym) and I talked about a troubled company Eoin had been involved in managing.

In total, the entire interview involved 893 turns – a turn being counted each time another speaker begins to say something. The location of the extracts in the interview is indicated by the turn number displayed in the left-hand side column of the extracts. The meanings of the various symbols in the transcript are based on a system, known as Jeffersonian transcription, used in much DA work: the specific meanings attached to the symbols here are explained in **Appendix A** to this chapter. As can be seen from their turn numbers, the extracts shown here only involve a small proportion of that interview and are from early on in the interaction. The first extract is taken from near the beginning of the interview. Just before the extract shown below, Eoin had been describing his career before starting his own business and I begin the extract by inquiring about his involvement in the management of a business where there had been a crisis.

```
9    Brendan: Fair bit of crisis there, was there?
10   Eoin: (.) Emm, in what respect? (.) [Eh, towards the
     end?
11   Brendan: Did it ] nearly go bust [then wa
12   Eoin: To] Towards the end yes, em,.
```

Extract EB1 from an Interview between Eoin & Brendan
(Source: Transcript from a 66-minute Interview between 'Eoin' & Brendan)

In just these four turns of the interview, we can see some interesting interactional work being done. We see that the interview is a situation that puts interviewees in the position of having to account for themselves. In Turn 9, I rather undiplomatically ask (and clearly assume I am entitled to ask) if there had been – in a business Eoin had been running – a 'fair bit of crisis there, was there?' (Turn 9). After some hesitation, Eoin asks: '(.) Emm, in what respect? (.) [Eh, towards the end?' (Turn 10). Turn 10, therefore, as it is a question from the interviewee, seems awkward and occurs with other signs of awkwardness, such as over-lap and hesitation

(Fairclough, 1992). As an interviewer, despite the signalled awkwardness of asking about this, I clarify my question: 'Did it] nearly go bust [then wa' (Turn 11). Eoin's Turn 12 overlaps (another sign of the topic being an awkward one) with my clarification, but Eoin (as a good interviewee) accepts my topic by beginning to give an account of what happened in the firm. This account begins by Eoin mitigating my harsh summary of the firm given in Turn 11 ('go bust'). Eoin reduces this 'going bust' to being only a part of the story by confining the crisis of going bust to 'towards the end?' (Turn 12). In many conventional analyses of interviews, these awkward bits of interaction might be dismissed as merely poor communication of what 'is really going on' behind the interview. In contrast, DA stresses this kind of interactional work of talk as being key to what the interview itself is doing. My interpretation of what is being achieved in this bit of the interview is that the evaluation of what happened in the company, whether it was a success or failure, is being negotiated between me and Eoin.

After Turn 12 (in turns of the interview not shown here), the interaction between us becomes smoother, with Eoin providing an explanation of why the firm ran into difficulties, citing macro-economic factors and the decision of the majority shareholders as causes beyond his control. This concentration on reasons beyond Eoin's control necessarily portrays Eoin as rather powerless. At the beginning of **Extract EB2** below, Eoin begins to change this positioning of himself as powerless.

In **Extract EB2** below, Eoin manages to find at least some matters controlled by him and tells of making his 'own mind up anyway' amid this crisis: and points out how he 'wanted to do my own thing' (Turn 26). He uses the crisis as 'an exit mechanism' (Turn 28) that 'worked out quite well' (Turn 30) and was 'EDUCATIONAL' (Turn 34). Note how Eoin has turned what I described negatively as a 'fair bit of crisis … ' (Turn 9) into a much more positive 'exit mechanism' (Turn 28). Positivity, as Nelson's (2000) analysis shows, is a feature found much more frequently in business discourse. Eoin has shown himself as achieving such positivity, even in the evaluation of a situation I initially described as a crisis.

In turns after Turn 34, the interview interaction turns to other topics. In **Extract EB3** below we have returned to the discussion of the troubled company Eoin had managed.

26   **Eoin:** Everyone goes into a panic, yeah. I kind of, I
        made my own mind up anyway because I was with ((name
        of company)) for far too long, anyway and I wanted to
        do my own thing((detail excluded to avoid
        identification))
27   **Brendan:** Oh right. So this was change year.
28   **Eoin:** Yeah, yeah. This is the em, the year that I
        wanted to make that eh move, so and it kind of, well
        while I lost money, the money that I invested in the
        company eh, it was probably worth it in the end
        because it meant that em, that I had an exit
        mechanism
29   **Brendan:** Right, right, yeah.
30   **Eoin:** And eh, so it worked out quite well in that
        respect. And then I took what about six months off …
31   **Brendan:** Right, right.
32   **Eoin:** Em, so there are whole load of things there but
        it was (.)
33   **Brendan:** Had
34   **Eoin:** EDUCATIONAL

Extract EB2 from an Interview between Eoin & Brendan
(Source: Transcript of a 66-minute Interview between 'Eoin' & Brendan)

174   **Eoin:** but I had no idea because ((the name of the
        company)) for many years was run as a lifestyle
        business for one of the, the shareholders, ((detail
        excluded to avoid identification)) and I had really
        no idea what I was getting involved in
175   **Brendan:** Right
176   **Eoin:** I liked the idea of having a slice of the
        action em, but when I realised, em you know, how bad
        things were, em I got a bit nervy
177   Brendan: Right
178   **Eoin: But** em, having said that when we worked hard
        for the first year and a half and the first year, we
        actually made, the first time that we made a profit,
        the first time the company made a profit in a number
        of years
179   **Brendan:** Right, yeah
180   **Eoin:** Basically the company was being raped by one of
        the shareholders and he had an extraordinary
        lifestyle

Extract EB3 from an Interview between Eoin & Brendan
(Source: Transcript of a 66-minute Interview between 'Eoin' & Brendan)

In the above extract, Eoin describes that business as a 'lifestyle business', operated for the benefit of one of the shareholders (Turn 174). His comment that he 'had really no idea what I was getting involved in' (Turn 174) could be read as modesty or self-criticism, but it could also refer to the lack of transparency on the part of the board members. The talk that shows Eoin's competence and his achievements are much clearer. His achievement meant 'we made a profit, the first time the company made a profit in a number of years' (Turn 178); however, 'the company was being raped by one of the shareholders' (Turn 180). These are strong words and the word 'raped' makes a living person, a distinct corporate entity, of the organisation. The way in which the company was being drawn upon and run generally is discussed over the next five turns, which are excluded here for reasons of space, and because its presentation here adds nothing new to the analysis. **Extract EB4** below, however, allows us to see Eoin's summary of the internal difficulties inherent in the company he managed.

186   **Eoin:** It was yeah, it was, it was literally straight
      into the, into the frying pan and em, em but we tried
      to make it work and then, you know, we were dealing
      with, when we bought in, we were dealing with you
      know a company that had racked up significant losses.
187   **Brendan:** Mm.
188   **Eoin:** Em over you know a six, seven year period, to
      try and **eradicate** those losses in you know, a two or
      three-year period was very very difficult
189   **Brendan:** It was a tall order, to turn it around at
      all was an achievement
190   **Eoin:** And the money that we put in went nowhere near
      re-capitalising the company at all, em, eh, in fact,
      em the money that we put in went you know, a month or
      two later went out the backdoor again

Extract EB4 from an Interview between Eoin & Brendan
(Source: Transcript of a 66-minute Interview between 'Eoin' & Brendan)

In Turn 186 of the above extract, Eoin separates the actors like him who tried to improve the situation ('we tried to make it work') from the company 'that had racked up significant losses' before they had bought in. I co-operate in building this description of Eoin having to deal with a difficult situation, declaring that 'it was a tall order, to turn it around at all was an achievement' (Turn 189). Here non-DA approaches might seek to find out the truth of what really happened in the business, however DA not only shows that this might be very difficult to do, but more importantly illustrates how various versions of events, which may well be true, are built. In Turn 190, Eoin draws our attention to how the negative influence of some majority owners of the company persisted and made things more difficult: 'the money that we put in went you know, a month or two later went out the backdoor again'. In the next several turns (not shown here), Eoin stresses some of the achievements of his management of the company, including such successes as the recruitment of well-respected employees. In **Extract EB5**, Eoin closes discussion of the troubled company he managed in way that is worth explicating.

211   **Eoin:** You know, I think in publishing you can spend too much time dwelling on the successes of the past.
212   **Brendan:** Right, yeah, yeah, yeah.
213   **Eoin:** I mean it's a cut-throat world and you know, bloody hell, you know, em.

Extract EB5 from an Interview between Eoin & Brendan
(Source: Transcript of a 66-minute Interview between 'Eoin' & Brendan)

In **Extract EB5**, Eoin summarises his period in the troubled company as one involving 'successes of the past' (Turn 211). He cannot dwell on these successes because 'it's a cut-throat world' (Turn 213). This construction, accepted by us both at this stage, of Eoin's period in that troubled company contrasts greatly with my initial, more negative construction of it (Extract EB1's Turn 9): 'fair bit of crisis there, was there?'. Whatever else has been happening in the interview, much work has been achieved in changing the way we talk about Eoin's management of that company. By using business discourse in skilful ways, Eoin has constructed an account of himself as a successful businessman who is master of his own destiny. He has done all this, while also performing as a co-operative and competent interviewee. It is important to note that I do not mean to claim Eoin is not being authentic. For what it is worth, I found his story both genuine and admirable. However, the point of DA is not to adjudicate the truth of what might be behind the talk, but, rather, to illustrate what the talk itself does and how the constructions thus produced (e.g., Eoin's identity as a successful manager) are achieved.

CONCLUSION

So, DA does not necessarily doubt that people involved in creating an account are being authentic or sincere. Rather, discourse analysts regard language not as a transparent medium, but one whose very nature means it necessarily has a constructive action of its own. Important, too, to acknowledge is that DA does not necessarily deny that something real happened, which the words of an account may be referring to. However, DA's interest is primarily in focusing on the construction of the account as its topic, rather than using the account as a resource to find out what it was that 'really happened'. Taking the words of an account, such as that in the interview analysed in the last section as a transparent window into 'what really happened' in the firm concerned, would have been a very limited use of the interview material. By thinking of Eoin's account merely as giving an undistorted view of what happened, we would miss how he shapes his construction of 'what really happened' in ways that other accounts might not. DA reveals what kinds of positions are being established by those taking part in an interaction. In the analysis of the last section, we can see that I am positioned as the interviewer whose questions have to be answered. We can see, too, how Eoin builds his identity as both a competent interviewee who answers my questions and as a successful businessman, despite the crisis that occurred in that firm. We can see the details of how Eoin is able to show his success as manager and entrepreneur by carefully balancing the negative factors beyond his control (macroeconomic events, control by the board of directors) with the positive way he used the experience (how he had purchased an 'exit' mechanism and how the experience had been educational). The focus on what words or symbols do in terms of constructing a particular account is what unites all sorts of discourse analytical approaches.

Whereas DA might be united in certain respects, it can also be seen from this discussion that there is much diversity, even in the limited types of DA covered in this chapter. Elsewhere in this volume, Freeman (2009) shows how the insights of a more CA-influenced DA can be used in studying how young children act in talk. In addition to the related, but different, approaches taken by Freeman and I, there are many different discourse analytical approaches that might be of interest to the reader. However, for these different approaches, and for a deeper understanding than this short chapter can provide, interested readers will have to resort to further reading. I provide a brief guide to such resources below.

FURTHER READING & RESOURCES

The interested reader can draw on a variety of overviews of DA from different perspectives including De Beaugrande (1997); Van Dijk (1997); Potter (1998); Jaworski & Coupland (1999); Alvesson & Kärreman (2000); Mills (2004; 1997); and Iedema (2007). Indeed, there is an embarrassment of riches when it comes to further reading and resources concerning DA, so the challenge here is to put some limit on the recommendations so as not to overwhelm the reader. The selection highlighted here, therefore, is inevitably biased towards my own particular preferences and prejudices. For a more in-depth introduction to discourse analysis that illustrates a variety of approaches to a broad range of topics, Wetherell *et al.* (2001a; 2001b) have produced two volumes: one consisting of a collection of discourse studies (*Discourse as Data*) and the other, a volume more concerned with various theoretical standpoints within DA (*Discourse Theory & Practice*). Within the management field, Grant *et al.*'s (2004) *Sage Handbook of Organizational Discourse* is excellent, as is Bargiela-Chiappini *et al.*'s (2007) more linguistically-orientated and less organisationally-focused text. Discourse analytical papers appear in a vast range of prestigious peer-reviewed journals concerning particular topics and arising from a variety of disciplines. This makes it difficult to produce a comprehensive list of such journals that carry DA work. However, journals such as *Discourse & Society* and *Discourse Studies* give some sense of the variety of topics in association with which this increasingly popular methodology is used. There are also many web-based resources for discourse analysts, including http://www.dit.ie/research/centres/dag   and   Teun   van   Dijk's http://www.discourses.org. As well as having some interesting resources themselves, these two sites have up-to-date and extensive links to other DA resources on the web.

REFERENCES

Althusser, L. (1971). *Lenin & Philosophy and Other Essays* (B. Brewster, trans). New York, NY: Monthly Review Press.

Alvesson, M. & Kärreman, D. (2000). 'Taking the Linguistic Turn in Organisational Research: Challenges, Responses, Consequences', *The Journal of Applied Behavioural Science* 36(2), 136-58.

Atkinson, J.M. & Heritage, J. (1984). 'Transcription Notation', in Atkinson, J. & Heritage, J. (eds), *Structures of Social Interaction*, pp. ix-xvi. New York, NY: Cambridge University Press.

Austin, J.L. (1998, [1953]). 'Performatives and Constatives (trans)', in Baghramian, M. (ed), *Modern Philosophy of Language*, pp. 110-23. London: J.M. Dent.

Baghramian, M. (1998). 'Introduction and Commentaries', in Baghramian, M. (ed), *Modern Philosophy of Language*. London: J.M. Dent.

Barthes, R. (1967). 'The Death of the Author', *Aspen* 5/6.

Billig, M. (1991). *Ideology and Opinions: Studies in Rhetorical Psychology*. London: Sage.

Billig, M., Condor, S., Edwards, D., Gane, M., Middleton, D.J. & Radley, A.R. (1988). *Ideological Dilemmas: A Social Psychology of Everyday Thinking*. London: Sage.

Booth, W.C. (1961). *The Rhetoric of Fiction*. Chicago: University of Chicago Press.

Chomsky, N. (1998 [1972]). 'Form & Meaning in Natural Languages', in Baghramian, M. (ed), *Modern Philosophy of Language*, pp. 294-308. London: J.M. Dent.

De Beaugrande, R. (1997). 'The Story of Discourse Analysis', in Van Dijk, T.A. (ed), *Discourse as Structure & Process*, Vol.1, pp. 35-62. London: Sage.

De Saussure, F. (1983 [1916]). *Course in General Linguistics* (R. Harris, trans). London: Duckworth.

Derrida, J. (1976 [1967]). *Of Grammatology* (G.C. Spivak, trans). London: Baltimore.

Diaz-Bone, R., Bührmann, A.D., Gutiérrez Rodríguez, E., Schneider, W., Kendall, G. & Tirado, F. (2007). 'The Field of Foucaultian Discourse Analysis: Structures, Developments and Perspectives', *Forum Qualitative Sozialforschung / Forum: Qualitative Social Research* 8(2, Art.30): 52 paragraphs.

Dolan, P. (2009). 'Using Documents: A Figurational Approach', in Hogan, J., Dolan, P. & Donnelly, P. (eds), *Approaches to Qualitative Research: Theory & Its Practical Application*. Cork: Oak Tree Press.

Edley, N. & Wetherell, M. (1997). 'Jockeying for Position: The Construction of Masculine Identities', *Discourse & Society* 8(2): 203-17.

Fairclough, N. (1992). *Discourse & Social Change*. Cambridge: Polity Press.

Fairclough, N. (1995). *Critical Discourse Analysis: The Critical Study of Language*. London: Longman.

Fairclough, N. (2003). *Analysing Discourse: Textual Analysis for Social Research*. London: Routledge.

Fairclough, N. (2005). 'Peripheral Vision: Discourse Analysis in Organisation Studies: The Case for Critical Realism', *Organisation Studies* 26(6): 915-39.

Foucault, M. (1966). *The Order of Things*. London: Routledge.

Foucault, M. (1972). *The Archaeology of Knowledge* (A.M. Sheridan Smith, trans). London: Tavistock.

Foucault, M. (1973). *The Birth of the Clinic: An Archaeology of Medical Perception* (A.M. Sheridan Smith, trans). London: Routledge.

Foucault, M. (1978). *The History of Sexuality: Volume 1, an Introduction. The Will to Knowledge* (R. Hurley, trans). London: Penguin.

Foucault, M. (1979). *Discipline and Punish: The Birth of the Prison* (A. M. Sheridan Smith, trans). London: Penguin.

Foucault, M. (2006 [1973]). *Psychiatric Power: Lectures at the Collège de France 1973-1974* (with J. Lagrange & A.I. Davidson, eds; G. Burchell, trans). Basingstoke: Palgrave Macmillan.

Freeman, O. (2009). 'Analysing Focus Group Data', in Hogan, J., Dolan, P. & Donnelly, P. (eds), *Approaches to Qualitative Research: Theory and Its Practical Application*. Cork: Oak Tree Press.

Goffman, E. (1959). *The Presentation of Self in Everyday Life*. New York, NY: Doubleday.

Grant, D., Hardy, C., Oswick, C. & Putnam, L. (eds) (2004). *The Sage Handbook of Organizational Discourse*. Thousand Oaks, CA: Sage.

Grice, H.P. (1998 [1957]). 'Meaning', in Baghramian, M. (ed). *Modern Philosophy of Language*, pp. 127-36. London: J.M. Dent.

Harré, R. (2004). 'Staking Our Claim for Qualitative Psychology as Science', *Qualitative Research in Psychology* 1(1): 3-14.

Harré, R. & Gillet, G. (1994). *The Discursive Mind*. Thousand Oaks, CA: Sage.

Hymes, D. (1974). *Foundations of Sociolinguistics: An Ethnographic Approach*. Philadelphia, PA: University of Pennsylvania Press.

Iedema, R. (2007). 'On the Multi-modality, Materiality and Contingency of Organization Discourse', *Organization Studies* 28(6): 931-46.

Jaworski, A. & Coupland, N. (1999). 'Introduction: Perspectives on Discourse Analysis', in Jaworski, A. & Coupland, N. (eds), *The Discourse Reader*, pp. 1-44. London: Routledge.

Kendall, G. & Wickham, G. (1999). *Using Foucault's Methods*. London: Sage.

Knights, D. & Morgan, G. (1991). 'Corporate Strategy, Organizations & Subjectivity: A Critique', *Organization Studies* 12(2): 251-73.

Kress, G. & Van Leeuwen, T. (1999). 'Front Pages: Analysis of Newspaper Layout', in Bell, A. & Garret, P. (eds), *Approaches to Media Discourse*, pp. 186-218. Oxford: Blackwell.

Labov, W. & Fanshel, D. (1977). *Therapeutic Discourse: Psychotherapy as Conversation*. New York, NY: Academic Press.

Laclau, E. & Mouffe, C. (1985). *Hegemony and Socialist Strategy: Towards a Radical Democratic Politics* (W. Moore & P. Cammack, trans). London: Verso.

McAuley, J., Duberley, J. & Cohen, L. (2000). 'The Meaning Professionals Give to Management and Strategy', *Human Relations* 53(1): 87-116.

McCloskey, D.N. (1998). *The Rhetoric of Economics*, 2nd ed. Madison, WI: University of Wisconsin Press.

McLuhan, M. (1951). *The Mechanical Bride: Folklore of Industrial Man*. New York, NY: The Vanguard Press.

Mills, S. (2004 [1997]). *Discourse*, 2nd ed. London: Routledge.

Nilges, L.M. (2000). 'A Nonverbal Discourse Analysis of Gender in Undergraduate Educational Gymnastics Sequences Using Laban Effort Analysis', *Journal of Teaching in Physical Education* 19(3): 287-310.

O'Rourke, B.K. & Pitt, M. (2007). 'Using the Technology of the Confessional as an Analytical Resource: Four Analytical Stances Towards Research Interviews in

Discourse Analysis', *Forum Qualitative Sozialforschung / Forum: Qualitative Social Research* 8(2, Art. 3): 58 paragraphs.

O'Toole, M. (2004). 'Opera Ludentes: The Sydney Opera House at Work and Play', in O'Halloran, K. (ed), *Multimodal Discourse Analysis*, pp. 11-27. London: Continuum.

Potter, J. (1998). 'Discursive Social Psychology: From Attitudes to Evaluative Practices', in Stroebe, W. & Hewstone, M. (eds), *European Review of Social Psychology*, Vol.9, pp. 233-66. Chichester: Wiley.

Potter, J. & Wetherell, M. (1987). *Discourse and Social Psychology: Beyond Attitudes and Behaviour*. London: Sage.

Russell, B. (1946). *History of Western Philosophy*. London: Unwin.

Sacks, H. (1995 [1964-1972]). *Lectures on Conversation Volumes I & II*. Oxford: Basil Blackwell.

Schegloff, E.A. (1999). 'Discourse, Pragmatics, Conversation Analysis', *Discourse Studies* 1(4): 405-35.

Tannen, D. (1984). *Conversational Style: Analyzing Talk Among Friends*. Norwood, NJ: Ablex Publishing Corporation.

Van Dijk, T.A. (1997). 'The Study of Discourse', in Van Dijk, T.A. (ed), *Discourse as Structure and Process*, Vol.1, pp. 1-34. London: Sage.

Van Dijk, T.A. (2001). 'Critical Discourse Analysis', in Schiffrin, D., Tannen, D. & Hamilton, H.E. (eds), *The Handbook of Discourse Analysis*, pp. 352-71. Oxford: Blackwell Publishers.

Wetherell, M., Taylor, S. & Yates, S.J. (eds) (2001a). *Discourse as Data: A Guide for Analysis*. London: Sage.

Wetherell, M., Taylor, S. & Yates, S.J. (eds) (2001b). *Discourse Theory and Practice: A Reader*. London: Sage.

Wittgenstein, L. (1998 [1953]). 'Philosophical investigations' (G.E.M. Anscombe, trans), in Baghramian, M. (ed), *Modern Philosophy of Language*, pp. 89-106. London: J.M. Dent.

Yule, G. (2006) *The Study of Language,* 3rd ed. Cambridge: Cambridge University Press.

APPENDIX A: THE JEFFERSON–STYLE TRANSCRIPTION NOTATION USED

Symbol	Meaning
.	A stopping fall in tone firmly understood as a full stop
,	A brief pause understood as a comma
-	Indicates a sudden stop understood as breaking with previous sense
(.)	A brief but noticeable pause.
(#)	A timed paused where # is the number of seconds

Symbol	Meaning
.	A falling tone
?	A rising inflection understood as a question
-	A rising inflection not understood as a question
>text<	Enclosed speech was delivered more quickly than usual
<text>	Enclosed speech was delivered more slowly than usual
...	Deliberated excluded talk within a turn
[text]	Square brackets enclose overlapping speech
ALL CAPS	Shouted or increased-volume speech
°text°	Enclosed speech is noticeably softer than surrounding
Underlined text	Speaker is stressing the underlined speech.
(text)	Enclosed is transcriber's best guess of unclear speech.
((*text*))	Enclosed is a report of non-verbal activity, deliberate replacement of speech, or an inserted clarification.

Note: This transcription notation is based on the notation developed by Gail Jefferson, as described in Atkinson & Heritage (1984).

CHAPTER 10
ANALYSING FOCUS GROUP DATA

Olivia Freeman

INTRODUCTION

This chapter addresses the focus group method as a 'stand alone' element of the qualitative researcher's methodological toolkit. Focus groups generate primary research data that is discursive in nature and is best addressed through an analytical lens that is sensitive to the intricacies, complexities and subtleties of talk-in-interaction. There is an abundance of literature on the broad topic of focus groups including (i) *introductory texts* and *articles* aimed at a wide audience (Stewart *et al.*, 2007; Tonkiss, 2004) (ii) *critical texts and articles* aimed mainly at an academic audience (Barbour & Kitzinger, Bloor *et al.*, 2001; 1999; Catterall & Maclaran 1997; Kitzinger, 1994; Puchta & Potter, 2004) and (iii) *handbooks* aimed at both academic and commercial researchers (Edmunds, 1999; Fern, 2001; Greenbaum, 1998; Morgan, 1998). While some of the handbooks contain useful advice for the planning and moderation of focus group research, an immersion in these rather prescriptive texts might lead to the strait-jacketing of the intellectual and creative potential of the novice researcher.

Given the great quantity of material available on the focus group method, it is perhaps surprising that there is a dearth of discussion on the theoretical and practical aspects concerning the *analysis* of focus group data (Catterall & Maclaran, 1997; Kitzinger 1994; Litosseliti 2003). One of the reasons for this pertains to the fact that there is no 'best way' to analyse focus group data; indeed, a range of qualitative analytical procedures could be useful. Other reasons, however, relate to more deep-seated distinctions between the assumptions of the marketing research perspective on the use and value of focus groups *vis-à-vis* the assumptions of non-marketing research perspectives, which mainly derive from the social sciences (Catterall & Maclaran, 2006).

This chapter provides a discussion of the focus group method, with an emphasis on issues surrounding the analysis of focus group data. Disagreement in the wider literature base is highlighted in an effort to encourage the new researcher to engage critically with the various perspectives. Ultimately, it will signpost these perspectives and provide some guidance through what is a rather daunting and disharmonious volume of work on the focus group method. The first section briefly outlines the historical roots of the focus group method in an effort to shed light on the distinctive approaches that have developed over the last half-century. The second section addresses the interactive nature of focus groups and the relevance of this to decisions around research design and analysis. The third section points to some of the divergence in the literature with regard to managing and making sense of focus group data. The fourth section attempts to place some flesh on the bones of the preceding discussion, as two data extracts derived from focus groups exploring preschoolers' talk-in-interaction around commercial commodities are examined using a discursive analytical framework. Finally, some conclusions are drawn and suggestions for further reading made.

BRIEF HISTORICAL OUTLINE

The focus group method originated in the work of the Bureau of Applied Social Research at Columbia University in the 1940s. Bloor *et al.* (2001: 2) trace the founding of the method back to the work of sociologists, Paul Lazarsfeld and Robert Merton, who received 'a government contract from the "Office of Facts & Figures" to assess audience responses to the government's own wartime radio propaganda programmes'. They sought to add to the existing quantitative procedures for measuring audience response, which consisted of a button-response system that the subjects pressed depending on whether they were feeling positively or negatively towards what they were hearing. They set about using group-based interviews to obtain participant accounts of how they felt about the stimulus material.

Merton & Kendall (1946) documented these early developments. The main aim of the paper was to distinguish focused interviews from other types of research interviews, including in-depth interviews. The interviewer role was more active and, to an extent, more directive than that of the in-depth interviewer and the use of stimulus materials and verbal cues was encouraged. Merton & Kendall (1946: 541) set out four characteristics of 'focused interviews' and, given that Morgan (1998: 38) argues that there remains much similarity between current practices and the original description of group interviews, it is worth paraphrasing them:

♦ Persons interviewed are known to have been involved in a particular concrete situation.

♦ This situation has received previous analysis by the investigator.

♦ On the basis of this prior analysis, an interview guide has been formulated to aid in the obtaining of relevant information from the participants.

♦ The interview itself will focus on the subjective experiences of the participants to test the hypotheses under construction and perhaps to suggest inadvertently new hypotheses.

While Merton & Kendall (1946) did not actually coin the term 'focus group', the characteristics outlined above would shape the development of the 'focus group method' in marketing research. They concluded the article with an expression of hope that the focused interview would be 'substantially improved and its applications greatly extended' (1946: 557). The extent to which this development has occurred would appear limited. Indeed, Merton (1987:557) criticises the 'misuse' and 'abuse' of focus-group research. Bloor et al. (2001: 3) argue that, while the commercial potential of the focus group method has been exploited by the market research 'industry', it is only in the last three decades that social researchers have begun to engage with and develop the focus group method for academic research.

Stewart et al. (2007: 9) highlight some of the areas of commonality across a variety of approaches to focus groups, including: (i) an understanding that the purpose of focus groups is to gather individuals together who share some experience or set of characteristics that will aid them in focussing on a specific topic or set of topics for a set amount of time; (ii) an interest in group dynamics and how they affect individuals' contributions to the discussion; (iii) an in-depth approach to the task at hand; and (iv) a humanistic approach to interviewing, which encompasses openness, active listening and empathy. While they acknowledge that some of these elements are emphasised to a greater or lesser extent across disciplines, this attempt to gloss over fundamental differences in philosophy and approach can result in much confusion on the part of a researcher who is new to the method.

There are two major differences with regard to the use and value of focus groups across disciplines. The first concerns the **status** of focus groups in the methodological toolkit. For many marketing researchers, focus groups constitute an *auxiliary* method used to generate data to inform quantitative stages of a project or to aid interpretation of quantitative results, a kind of topping and tailing of the *main* research findings (Morgan, 1998; Stewart *et al.*, 2007). For academic researchers, however, focus groups are increasingly understood to constitute a *stand-alone* research method (Puchta & Potter, 2004). The second difference pertains to the **unit of analysis** as defined by the researcher. For marketing researchers, group interviews are synergetic; they produce more information than might be obtained through individual interviews of each of the members of the group. While the nature of group dynamics are observed to reveal the interactive work that results in unified answers to the pre-determined questions set forth by the group moderator, the *individual participants are the unit of analysis*. The report is a collection of insights derived directly from the mouths of the participants (Morgan, 1998: 1). For academic researchers, the group interaction itself is understood to hold the key to the generation of deeper insights into the phenomenon under study; the *unit of analysis is the group,* rather than the individuals taking part in the discussion (Tonkiss, 2004: 194).

The distinctions outlined above have significant implications for the design and analysis stages of focus group research and these will be discussed further in the sections that follow.

THE IMPORTANCE OF ANALYSING INTERACTION

Interaction as Resource

Litosseliti (2003: 2) emphasises two features of focus groups: (1) they are focused and thus involve some kind of collective activity around a small number of issues; and (2) they are interactive 'in that the group forces and dynamics are of the utmost importance'. This emphasis on interaction is shared by other social researchers (Barbour & Kitzinger, 1999; Kitzinger, 1994; Puchta & Potter 1999; Puchta & Potter 2004, Wilkinson, 2006) and indeed marketing academics (see Catterall & Maclaran, 1997).

However, some researchers feel that the cost of the synergy created by group dynamics, which leads to the generation of a greater quantity of information, must be weighed against the potential contamination of the views of individual members as a result of those very group dynamics (Edmunds, 1999; Fern, 2001). Thus, group effects are viewed as a constraint, rather than a resource for the researcher, or in Catterall & Maclaran's (2006: 257) terms the 'only distinctive feature of the focus group is presented as its primary strength as well as its main weakness'.

This concern has perhaps inadvertently led to the very effective concealment of group interaction in many research publications using focus groups to generate data. Kitzinger (1994:104) carried out an extensive review of focus group studies and concluded that from 'reading some such reports, it is hard to believe that there was ever more than one person in the room at the same time'. Social researchers are cognisant of the fact that talk generated in interaction in a group context will differ from that generated in a one-to-one interview, but this does not reduce its value as research data. Kitzinger (1994: 112) argues that, instead of attempting to generalise about group effects, we need to pay attention to group composition and how the characteristics of a group influence what is said and, thus, how social pressure impacts on the construction and communication of knowledge.

Munday (2006: 95) argues that the focus group interview has been treated primarily as a 'resource' with which to generate content (the expression of attitudes and opinions by participants). The focus group can also be treated as 'topic', with an emphasis being placed on analysing the process of talk-in-interaction as evidenced in the transcript. She (2006: 95) suggests that the content of the talk cannot be divorced from the circumstances in which it was produced and thus emphasis needs to be placed on both what is said and in what context it is said.

The concern with the ability to generalise findings on the part of marketing researchers, coupled with the view that group dynamics could prevent researchers accessing the authentic thoughts of individual participants, is evident in the prescriptive framework that has come to characterise some texts on focus groups. I will briefly address two contested areas:

- ◆ Selecting participants.
- ◆ Researching sensitive topics.

Selecting Participants

Many standard marketing research texts discourage the use of pre-existing groups, such as friendship groups, members of social clubs or work colleagues. Groups of strangers are seen to be more productive discussants, as they are viewed as more likely to express taken-for-granted opinions, views and experiences than are members of pre-existing groups who may already *know* each others' views on certain topics. In the same vein, groups of strangers may disclose more to each other than groups of friends, as a sense of security and privacy is established between group members for the duration of the focus group.

However, when research is concerned with the social context of public understanding (see Kitzinger, 1994: 104 for a study on participant's perceptions of AIDS) and in how people express opinions and ideas in the context of existing social relationships, then the employment of pre-existing groups is recommended (Munday, 2006:95). Friendship groups are also very useful when researching children, as familiar faces promote a relaxed atmosphere where the children can 'be themselves'.

Researching Sensitive Topics

As above, many standard marketing research texts advise researchers against using focus groups to explore sensitive topics, arguing that in-depth interviews are more appropriate. On the contrary, however, others argue that participants themselves might actually find the focus group setting an easier forum for the discussion of sensitive topics. Groups can facilitate discussion of otherwise 'taboo' topics, because the less inhibited members of the group 'break the ice' for shyer participants or one person's revelation of 'discrediting' information encourages others to disclose (Kitzinger, 1994: 111). Safety in numbers also increases the rate of participation and, in some cases, participants are grateful to be provided with an opportunity to gather with others who have shared knowledge of the sensitive topic under discussion.

MANAGING & MAKING SENSE OF DATA

The biggest advantage the focus group method has over other qualitative research techniques is that it provides for the generation of focused multi-party talk-in-interaction. A decision to use focus groups in academic research must be based on a commitment to keep intact the interactive integrity of the data throughout the research process. This section of the chapter will address some of the ways in which this might be achieved.

Use of the focus group method for academic purposes comprises three phases, which are depicted below in Figure **10.1**. A degree of overlap is evident across these three phases. In the majority of academic research projects at undergraduate or postgraduate level, the researcher moderates the group and transcribes the recorded data herself. Thus, analysis of the data begins with moderation, as the researcher cannot completely detach herself from her research aims as she engages with the participants. In the same vein, analysis takes place as the researcher enters the transcription phase of the process, identifying features of the data salient to the research aims as she engages in the act of transcribing. In practice, transcription of focus groups is an iterative process. After an initial transcription phase, interesting passages of talk are identified and isolated for closer transcription and this re-visiting of specific extracts can continue indefinitely.

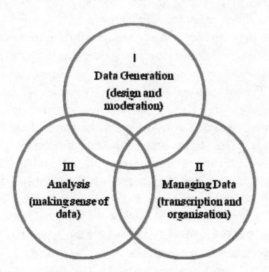

Figure 10.1: Focus Group Phases

While it is important to be aware of the overlap between phases, it is useful to address each in turn. The vast majority of the literature in the area addresses the focus group method as a data generation tool, and recommendations for further reading on the organisation and moderation of groups can be found at the end of this chapter. This section addresses the second two phases:

♦ Data management and transcription.

♦ Analysis.

Data Management & Transcription

One of the major benefits of successful focus groups is that they generate large quantities of talk among participants. While, traditionally, focus groups have been recorded using a dictaphone or digital recording device, increasingly, video recording equipment is used. The use of video has a number of advantages over audio alone, because it captures aspects of body language and facial expression and it greatly aids the transcription process as speakers can be easily identified. The video camera, or multiple cameras, can be placed in the background on tripods or alternatively, and more practically, an assistant can be employed to video the interaction taking place. The first step in managing the data involves transcribing the recorded interaction into an analysable format.

The burden of transcribing can be reduced through the employment of foot pedal systems, which allow the transcriber to control the playback in a hands-free manner, or through the use of open source software transcription packages, such as Transana (available from www.transana.org). This package provides a user-friendly transcription and management system for audio- or video-recorded data. Bloor *et al.* (2001: 59) estimate that a one-hour recording takes about eight hours to transcribe; however, while this provides a useful guideline for planning purposes, in certain circumstances, eight hours could be dedicated to the close transcription of one minute of recorded interaction. The length of time required will depend on the level of detail deemed necessary by the researcher and this, in turn, will depend on the type of analytical tools being employed following transcription.

Woofitt (2005: 10) explains that everyday speech, such as that generated in interviews or focus groups, does not resemble fictional depictions of talk; 'It is not grammatically neat and tidy, but appears on the surface to be disorganised and messy'. The following few rules of thumb, adapted from Bloor *et al.* (2001: 59), are useful with regard to transcribing recorded focus group data, while a short list of transcript notation conventions is included in the appendices to this chapter:

♦ All speech should be recorded, including unfinished sentences and brief utterances such as mm or eh.

♦ Overlapping speech (interruption) should be identified and, if
  indecipherable, this should be indicated.

♦ Speech should not be tidied up – hesitations, re-starts and pauses should
  be visible in the transcript.

♦ Marked body movements, gestures and laughter should be indicated.

♦ As far as possible, speakers should always be identified (pseudonyms
  are recommended).

♦ Volume of speech should be indicated where relevant (e.g., whispered
  speech, loud speech).

While adherence to these rules of thumb should result in transcripts that
are sufficiently detailed to reveal some of the subtleties and richness of the
generated data during the analytical phase, they are merely included in
this chapter to provide guidance to the researcher. In many cases, a very
close transcription is not necessary; for example, a researcher taking a
thematic approach to data analysis might be primarily concerned with the
content of the talk-in-interaction and, thus, not require the finer details of
speech delivery to be included in the transcripts.

Decisions around how best to analyse focus group data are perhaps
hampered by conflicting accounts in the literature, but are ultimately an
epistemological decision. For example, Stewart *et al.* (2007: 43) argue that
'the results of a focus group are extremely user-friendly and easy to
understand'. They advocate an analytical approach that sees the researcher
provide a 'descriptive' account of the transcribed data that is based on the
identification by the researcher of 'top-of-mind' responses, participants'
reasoning, time spent on issues, intensity of expression and internal
contradictions in participant responses (2007: 13). They view language as a
window through which the 'true' opinions, beliefs and attitudes of an
individual can be seen. They view interaction, not as a resource for
analytical discussion, but, as something that 'restricts the generalisability of
results' due to the interdependence of participant 'responses'.

While the promised ease and simplicity of their account of the focus
group method is appealing, this approach can result in a number of
problems for the academic researcher. Firstly, this approach can lead to the
positioning of the participants as experts by the researcher. Merton &
Kendall (1946: 541) warned against this approach in their early theorisation,
arguing that 'summary generalisations … inevitably mean that the
informant, not the investigator, in effect provides the interpretation'.

Litosseliti (2003: 92) warns that the researcher must be careful about taking participants' words and statements at face value and, instead, recommends considering them in their 'broader socio-cultural context', including factors, such as at what point in the discussion and in response to what comment or non-verbal cue was the talk uttered. Secondly, the concern with being able to generalise from the focus group to a larger population, along with the implication that interaction is something that should be glossed over, rather than addressed directly, is at odds with the philosophy behind interpretive research and leads to the richest and deepest insights to be garnered from focus group research being lost:

> Focus groups can provide a rich, complex and extensive data set for social researchers. However, many of the potential advantages of these data are lost in the absence of appropriate methods of analysis. There is a need to retain something of the richness of transcript data, while ensuring that the great mass of data thus generated are analysed systematically and not selectively. (Frankland & Bloor, 1999: 144-5)

Ultimately, the data generated through focus groups, once transcribed, can be analysed through a number of different lenses, including both quantitative (content analysis[1]) and qualitative (thematic analysis and discursive analysis) perspectives.[2] The next two sections of this chapter will address thematic and discursive approaches.

Thematic Analysis

The most common approach to the analysis of focus group data involves the identification of recurring themes across the transcribed talk. The search for thematic categories is guided by the specific research questions set during the research design phase and samples of talk, ranging from a couple of words to a multi-turned exchange between participants that fit the category, are coded using a colour-coding or alphabetic or numeric system. The coding process is iterative, with new categories emerging as the data is examined closely. The material is then 'cut' and 'pasted,' so that all data extracts sharing a common code can be placed together. This is commonly referred to as the scissor-and-sort technique (Stewart *et al.*, 2007: 116). The subsequent writing up of an interpretation is structured based on this coding process and can range from a fairly descriptive account of the

---

[1]   Content analysis is discussed in detail in Stewart *et al.* (2007).

[2]   See Silverman (2005) for a general introduction to qualitative analysis techniques that can be applied to focus group data.

major themes (common in market research reports) to a more in-depth analysis that addresses the relationships between themes. Both approaches quote from the selected extracts to support their interpretation of the data. However, it is not sufficient for the academic researcher to purely describe the content of the transcripts; she must also attempt to identify patterns in the data and, thus, relationships between themes across the data. Ultimately, the researcher must attempt to connect these findings to an existing body of theoretical argument.

Catterall & Maclaran (1997) view the interaction that takes place in focus groups as a resource to be analysed, from which 'important and potentially insightful communication and learning processes' can be viewed. They draw a photographic analogy to explain their position. A thematic analysis of the data is for them a 'snapshot approach' (1997: 6), which results in 'photographs (segments of text) [being] brought together as an album (report)'. As they are concerned with interaction they recommend the 'annotating-the-scripts' approach, '[which is] more likely to capture the whole moving picture of the unfolding script or story that is the focus group discussion' (1997: 6).

This latter approach involves reading the transcripts in a linear fashion and writing interpretations in the margins. The analyst can gain insight into the experience of the focus group, including the body language and tone that characterised the discussion. She can access the shared language on the topic, along with the taken-for-granted and challengeable aspects of the topic. She can identify specific arguments people use in topic-based discussions, along with individual trajectories of talk by one individual throughout the interview. Catterall & Maclaran (1997) emphasise that the only way to achieve this is to analyse the transcript off-screen in the first instance, as the researcher will be dealing with long passages of talk that cannot be viewed easily on-screen, but recommend a return to on-screen code and retrieve facilities to document recurrent themes.

Discursive Analysis

Tonkiss (2004: 204) argues that, given focus groups 'capture something of the situated communicative processes through which social meanings are made and produced', focus group data is well suited to discourse or conversation analysis techniques[3]. Puchta & Potter (2004) provide a comprehensive overview of analytical approaches to the study of talk-in-interaction, specifically talk generated through the use of the focus group method. These approaches entail an interest in the 'business of talking', including an interest in what people say, the way they say it and why they say it (2004: 25).

A key difference between discourse analyses and more general thematic analyses is that variability, ambiguity and contradiction, rather than consensus, both between and within accounts, is predicted and explored. These differences between analytical techniques and foci are not merely superficial; they are symptomatic of deeper views on interpretive research. Gilbert & Mulkay (1984), who were amongst the founders of Discourse Analysis (DA), argue that a basic four step procedure informs much qualitative research:

♦ Obtain statements by interview or by observation in a natural setting.

♦ Look for broad similarities between the statements.

♦ If there are similarities that occur frequently, take these statements at face value, that is, as accurate accounts of what is really going on.

♦ Construct a generalised version of participants' accounts of what is going on and present this as one's own analytic conclusions.

This type of procedure allows many analysts to overcome problems posed by variability, but, according to Gilbert & Mulkay (1984), it also rests on a 'naïve' view of language in which it is assumed that any social event has one 'true' meaning. For the majority of qualitative researchers, language is conceived of as a medium through which we pass thoughts (ideas, intentions, information) between each other. However, discursive approaches focus on utterances as performing actions and displaying action orientations respectively (Woofitt, 2005).

Conversation Analysis (CA) (Hutchby & Wooffitt, 1998; Sacks, 1995) aims to provide an elaborate account of the way in which talk-in-interaction is constructed and understood by the speakers (Kitzinger & Frith 1999). CA tells a story in which (i) turns and, hence, (ii) individual speakers are the heroes (and villains) of the drama of the talk. CA is concerned with the intricacies of talk and, therefore, employs an elaborate transcription system designed to preserve these tiny details of speech, including the singular utterances, the pauses, the sighs, the inhalations and exhalations, the overlap

---

[3]   I make a distinction between conversation analysis and discourse analysis in the discussion that follows, however, in many cases, conversation analysis is placed under the broad umbrella of discourse analytic approaches.

and the whisper; and it is through this activity that a detailed interpretation is constructed. Talk is understood as a process that occurs *turn by turn* and as something that is characterised by *delays*, both within and between turns, by *overlap* between speakers and by *repair*, including re-starts and hesitations. These features are time-consuming to transcribe and result in 'messy' transcripts, but they are central to understanding the 'how' of interaction. Other features of conversation include the doing of *accountability*, whereby speakers provide an account for why they have made a particular statement, remark, or decision, *evaluations* and *assessments*, which are often carefully crafted depending on the audience, and *agreement* and *disagreement* between speakers as they compete to hold the floor. The identification of these conversational features in a passage of talk provides the researcher with a way of describing the interaction taking place.

Discourse Analysis (DA) looks at language in a broader context.[4] As people engage in conversation, they set up various accounts and versions of events, and these accounts and versions often alter during the course of the social interaction. DA offers a number of analytic concepts.[5] The term *discourse* is used interchangeably with talk or talk-in-interaction to describe the words spoken or the content of the talk, i.e., management discourse centres on management topics. *Repertoires* serve to position speakers within a specific social context and this action is referred to as *positioning* or *subject positioning*, i.e., employing a gender-based repertoire in talk serves to construct oneself or others in a gender-specific light, as defined by the speaker; an expertise-based repertoire serves to construct oneself or others as knowledgeable or lacking in knowledge. 'As we speak, we are positioned and position ourselves in particular ways which serve certain functions' (Aldred & Burman, 2005: 179). The emphasis here is on how the language functions to construct social identities and positions.

> It's not just the mental furniture that gets moved around and reshaped in interaction; the whole house gets changed. The identity of the speaker is managed and reworked as people converse. People's talk is put together to present themselves as clever or naïve, mysterious or ordinary. Again the fundamental issue is what people are doing with their talk. Identities get varied according to the business being done. For example, we might imagine that mostly we would like to appear

---

[4] For a more detailed discussion of DA, see O'Rourke in this volume. For an introduction to the distinctions between CA and DA, see Woofitt (2005).

[5] Potter & Wetherell's (1987) brand of DA is drawn upon for discussion in this chapter.

extraordinary or clever or imaginative. But there are situations where you really want to appear ordinary. (Puchta & Potter, 2004:27)

The next section of the chapter will attempt to contextualise some of the above discussion. This should not be read as a formula or a 'how- to' with regard to carrying out data analysis of focus groups; it is intended, rather, as an illustration of one style of data analysis in practice.

ANALYSING GROUP DATA

Background

The data extracts addressed below are taken from focus groups conducted with preschoolers[6] (mostly aged between three and four years). The broad aim of the research project for which these focus groups were conducted was to investigate children's construction of social identities and social structures through talk-in-interaction around brands. The focus group method was employed to generate talk-in-interaction among small pre-existing friendship groups. The method was employed as a stand-alone method and the talk generated was transcribed using a close transcription style. The interaction has been analysed in depth using a combination of conversation analysis and discourse analysis. The analytical discussion that follows illustrates an emphasis on understanding the focus group method as both resource and topic. In other words, both the content and the interaction are integrated in the analytical discussion.

Sociological theory on childhood suggests that, while studies of childhood consumer culture tell us a lot about children's preferences and roles in terms of consumer decision-making, they rarely explore children's use and transformation of symbolic and material goods within peer cultures (Corsaro, 2005). This formed part of the rationale behind an investigation into what we can learn about what children 'do' with consumer culture by

---

[6]   It is essential that researchers familiarise themselves with ethical codes of practice prior to conducting research with children. Most third level institutions provide guidelines for child-related research and, in many cases, the proposed research project may not proceed until it is approved by an ethics committee. Obvious prerequisites include the need to obtain written parental consent and written or verbal child consent and it is essential that the child is reminded that s/he may withdraw from the research activity at any time. For an interesting discussion of this topic, see Hill, M. (2005).

studying talk-in-interaction around topics such as children's branded toys and TV programmes.[7] How are these resources employed in children's talk-in-interaction to construct social worlds and identities?

Data Generation

The focus groups were activity-based (Eder & Fingerson, 2003) and took place in preschool settings, including Montessori schools and community-based preschools. The groups comprised me, as moderator, and three to four children, who were classmates and, in some cases, friends outside of the preschool environment. A classroom assistant or teacher sat in the background to ensure the children were comfortable throughout the process. Two activities were employed: (i) a 'bingo' game, which used brand logos, some of which were specific to children's cultures and some of which were non-specific; and (ii) a creativity exercise, which involved the children choosing laminated Velcro-backed cards taken from a toy catalogue with which to decorate a felt Christmas tree. The groups lasted between 15 and 45 minutes, depending on the children's levels of concentration and involvement in the tasks. This is considerably shorter than a focus group with adults, which would normally last between one and two hours. The focus groups were recorded using a digital handycam. The raw data consisted of video footage recorded on digital video cassettes. These were then converted to MPEG video files and transcribed with the aid of the software package Transana.[8] The Jeffersonian transcription system was employed (Jefferson, 1984).

Data Analysis

While data generation techniques, such as, interviews or focus groups, are adapted to suit children's physical, social and cognitive needs, the analytical techniques of CA and DA can be applied to children's talk in the same way that they might be applied to adult talk. The analytical approach taken here is a CA-informed discourse analysis and draws on a number of

---

[7]   Space does not permit a detailed discussion of researching children. For an
      excellent introduction, see Greene, S. & Hogan, D. (eds) (2005).

[8]   Transana is designed to facilitate the transcription and qualitative analysis of
      video and audio data. It provides a way to view video, create a transcript, and
      link places in the transcript to frames in the video. This software was designed
      by Chris Fassnacht and David Woods at the Wisconsin Centre for Educational
      Research and is available free from www.transana.org.

influences, including Gilbert & Mulkay (1985), Potter & Wetherell (1987), Edley & Wetherell (1997), Kyratzis (2000) and Goodwin (2006). It should be noted that this approach is not the 'best' or 'only' way to analyse focus group data; rather, it is the method I have used in recent research and, thus, have decided to employ for demonstrative purposes here. Traditionally, CA does not concern itself with issues or categories outside those demonstrated explicitly by the speakers themselves and, thus, it represents a bottom-up approach.[9] Some forms of discourse analysis take a top-down orientation, for example, Critical Discourse Analysis is concerned with how conventional ways of talking and writing within a culture serve political or ideological functions and, thus, mould how people think and act as social beings. The CA-informed discourse analytic approach proposed here, however, retains a bottom-up orientation to research by drawing on Potter & Wetherell's (1987) brand of DA.

This approach uses a combination of both methods. CA is used to describe the finer detail of interaction, specifically the ways in which children use linguistic devices to negotiate meanings and to build identities and relations turn by turn. CA identifies a myriad of specific conversational features, for example, children's use of assessment or evaluative statements, narrative, agreement or disagreement, as well as the use of intonation, volubility and silence. These features can be understood as social actions that build social relations, such as alliances, hierarchies, friendships and conflicts. The main concern here is 'the doing of the talk'. DA is concerned with how talk-in-interaction functions in the here-and-now to construct various and fluid accounts and versions of events, which often alter during the course of the social interaction (Edley & Wetherell, 1999; Potter & Wetherell, 1987). DA identifies the cultural themes of the linguistic repertoires being constructed through talk and the subsequent meanings, social identities and social relations built through collaboration and / or conflict in terms of repertoire usage. The main concern here is 'what the talk is doing' or the functionality of language-in-use. The presence of me, an adult researcher, is of course central to the interaction taking place. Analysis of my own talk-in-interaction must, therefore, be integrated into the overall analysis. Specific attention is given to the role I play in reinforcing or challenging a sense of solidarity or discord between the children throughout the analytical discussion. It is important to note that this does not imply an assessment of the impact my presence is having on the children, in fact that is completely outside the

---

[9]   See Goodwin (2006:14)

remit of a DA perspective, but, rather, I must address how my own talk is functioning within the context of the group.

In practice, the analytic approach employed here comprised of four phases, some of which occurred simultaneously. The aim is to provide a textured description and a rich interpretation of the multi-party interaction that took place:

◆ Data corpus is transcribed using Jeffersonian transcription style in an attempt to capture accurately the turn-by-turn interaction of all participants.

◆ Data is sampled or broken down for further analysis, mainly in terms of topic-based sequences of interaction.

◆ Data is analysed using CA and DA to *identify* specific conversational features (linguistic devices[10] and linguistic repertoires[11]) and the positioning and social action being achieved through employment of these features – this is a descriptive process.

◆ Interpretation of 'talk as action' reveals the negotiated sense-making that leads to the construction of selves, relations and things in social context – this is an explanatory process.

The two extracts below have been selected from two separate focus groups. Both sequences of topic-based interaction were stimulated by the presentation of a 'bingo' card as part of a match-and-win activity. The children temporarily switched focus from the object of the game (filling up their card and winning) to the engagement in brand-related interaction around 'Bob the Builder' (extract one) and 'Dora the Explorer' (extract two). The analysis that follows aims to (i) demonstrate the value of detailed transcription conventions in capturing the subtleties of talk-in-

---

[10] Linguistic devices refers to features of conversation that produce social action, including use of assessment, narrative, agreement / disagreement, repetition, making affiliative references, teasing, use of reported dialogue (see Kyratzis (2004) for specific comment on linguistic devices and children's peer cultures.)

[11] DA's main conceptual tool is the linguistic repertoire, defined as related or themed terms such as metaphors or figures of speech, used in particular kinds of ways (Woofitt, 2005: 80). Potter & Wetherell (1987) define an interpretative repertoire as a culturally familiar and habitual line of argument comprised of recognisable themes, common places and tropes. Repertoires position people socially; hence to speak a repertoire is to speak from a subject position or to build a social identity.

interaction for analytical purposes; (ii) make plain the importance of analysing interaction (including that of the moderator) in the context of the broader conversation taking place; and (iii) provide an illustration of how the techniques of conversation analysis (CA) and discourse analysis (DA) can be employed to *read* the data generated in focus groups.

In summary, the analysis below is concerned with the ways in which preschoolers explore and build relationships through talk-in-interaction around brands. Does the interaction result in a show of solidarity or discord or both? Conversational features, including agreement / disagreement, echoing, silencing and volubility, are revealing in this regard. The construction and negotiation of social identities are also demonstrated in these extracts. They are revealed through the identification of discursive repertoires that serve to colour the discourse produced. A guide to transcription conventions is included in **Appendix 1**. Arrows in the margins guide the reader to specific areas for discussion. It is recommended that each extract be read through in full prior to reading the analysis that follows.

EXTRACT ONE – 'BOB THE BUILDER'

In the commercially-based discourse surrounding 'Bob the Builder',[12] talk-in-interaction is sustained for two-and-a-half minutes (see **Extract 1** below). This focus group comprised two girls, Anna and Cathy, and two boys, Ewen and Luke.

```
312   Olivia: Okay and the ↑ last one. (1.3) °what is
              it ((Bob the Builder card is presented))
313   Cathy:  (.hhh) Mih (.) I CAN HAVE IT
314   Olivia: ↑ >You have it!<
315   Luke:   You've to put that blue ( ) down ( )
              ((leans body inwards and points to token
              demonstrating that Cathy needs to put a
              token on her bingo card))
316   Olivia: Well done ↓ and Hh ↑ Who is this guy ↓
317   Anna:   [Bob the builder]
```

---

12 Bob the Builder is a children's television clay character. Bob appears as a construction contractor in a stop motion animated programme with his colleague Wendy, various neighbours and friends, and their gang of anthropomorphised work-vehicles and equipment (all made of clay). In each episode, Bob and his gang help with renovations, construction, and repairs and with other projects as needed. The show emphasises conflict resolution, co-operation, socialisation and various learning skills. Bob's catchphrase is "Can we fix it?". It's shown in 30 countries and is owned by HIT Productions.

```
      318   Ewen:    [Bob the builder]
      319   Cathy:   Bob the builder
  →   320   Olivia:  Do you like him ↑
      321   Anna:    [Yeah       ]
      322   Cathy:   [I HAVE IT !]
      323   Olivia:  Do you like it Ewen ↑
  →   324   Anna:    Eh He sings (1.0)Bo:::b the buil:↓der
                     [can you fix it] ((sung))
      325   Cathy:                  [ ... oo fix it]
      326   Anna:    [BO::::B THE BUIL↓DER] ((sung))
      327   Cathy:   [°Bob the builder    ] ((sung))
      328   Anna:    YES YOU [CAN] ((sung))
      329   Cathy:           [can]
      330   Anna:    >Scoop ( ) and [Diz:↓zy and Ro↑ly too↓]
                     Lof:↑ty and Wen:↓dy=<
      331   Cathy:                  [Dizzy   (2.0)   too ]
                     ((sung))
      332   Anna:    and join ↑ the [queue↓] ((sung))
      333   Cathy:                  [queue ] ((sung))
      334   Anna:    [Bob and his g:ang↓] and so much (.)fun
                     working toge:↓ther=
      335   Cathy:   [mmm mmm     ang ]
      336   Anna:    to get the job ↓done [BO:::B THE
                     BUIL↓DER  can he fix it ]=
      337   Cathy:                        [°Bo:::b the
                     buil↓der can he fix it ]=
      338   Anna:      =[BO:::B THE BUIL:↓DER YES HE CAN]
                     ((hammering actions))
  →   339   Cathy:   =[Bo::b the buil↓der yes he can]
  →   340   Olivia:  We:ll↓ done(.) do you not know that song
                     Luke do you know it?
  →   341   Luke:    N::o
      342   Olivia:  Ewen
      343   Cathy:   I did ((hands in the air))
  →   344   Ewen:    ((shakes head))
      345   Olivia:  No↑ well give yourselves a big clap for
                     an excellent game
                     ((all clap hands))
  →   346   Anna:    They're on:ly new children ((points in
                     the direction of Luke and Ewen)
      347   Olivia:  They're new children are they ↓I see
      348   Anna:    And I'm not a new ( )
      349   Olivia:  You were here last year were you Anna↓
  →   350   Anna:    Yeah No I was only a little baby when I
                     used to go to the creche
      351   Olivia:  And what are you now
      352   Anna:    A big girl ((smiles))
      353   Ewen:    But when I was staying at my home and I
                     was goin' very fast down the and then I
                     went very fast running
      354   Olivia:  Really ↑ok would you ↓like to play
                     another quick game?
```

```
355   Anna:    yeah
356   Ewen:    ((nods))
```

Description of Events

This passage of talk-in-interaction occurred in the middle segment of this focus group. A game of brand-related bingo is about to be completed and the last card features 'Bob the Builder', an icon in terms of children's consumer culture. Talk based around the commodities of consumer culture tends to be characterised by evaluations and assessments. I invite Ewen to evaluate Bob the Builder following his correct identification of the character (line 320). However, he does not respond as Anna takes the floor and begins to sing the theme tune from this popular children's programme (lines 324 to 338). She is joined by Cathy, who plays a supporting role in singing the song, coming in with certain phrases (lines 325, 327, 329, 331, 333, 335) and eventually joining in. The two boys remain completely silent throughout this rendition and a hierarchical structure emerges, comprising Anna at the top of the hierarchy (she gains and maintains the floor throughout this passage of talk), Cathy and myself, who support Anna's position (Cathy through following her lead throughout the performance of the song, and me through support and praise, see line 340) and, finally, Ewen and Luke, who through remaining silent, neither seek to challenge the emergent structure nor construct an alternative one where either one of them might attempt to take the floor.

Explanation of Events

Following completion of the song by Anna and Cathy, I highlight the non-participation of the boys by asking them if they are familiar with the theme tune to which they each respond that they are not (lines 341 and 344). I thus make salient their silence as a feature of the group interaction and to an extent provide Anna with the opportunity to reinforce the emergent hierarchy. She provides an account for their lack of participation and draws a distinction between new members and old members of the wider social group (i.e., the child-care facility) in the process. Her use of the intensifier 'only' preceding her description of the boys as 'new' (line 346) emphasises their lower status among the group and it also provides an excuse for their lack of participation.

From a discourse analytic perspective, Anna *positions* the boys as outsiders (line 346) and contrasts this with her own position as an experienced insider (line 350); she has been attending this childcare centre since she was a 'little baby' being cared for in the crèche.

Anna uses the 'Bob the Builder' themed discourse to construct herself as an expert within the group. She demonstrates expert knowledge on 'Bob the Builder' through a full rendition of the theme tune and also provides accounts for non-participation of other members of the group. Her status is supported by Cathy, who follows her lead, but remains the less dominant of the two girls, and me, through support and praise and the making salient of the fact that the boys have remained silent. The hierarchical community emergent in this group is reinforced further by Anna's distinguishing between 'new' and 'old' members of the group. She displays a high level of social competence in positioning herself as a well-established member of the childcare facility, more broadly, and as an expert and leader in the context of the focus group setting.

EXTRACT TWO – 'DORA THE EXPLORER'

In the commercially-based discourse surrounding 'Dora the Explorer',[13] talk is sustained for two minutes (see **Extract Two** below). This group comprised two boys, Josh and Keane, and two girls, Claire and Millie.

```
374   Olivia:  [Okay are we >ready for the next↑ one<]
375   Claire:  [°the two of us have it               ]
376   Josh:    YEAH:::
377   Millie:  ((claps in response to Claire))
378   Claire:  ((claps in response to Millie))
379   Olivia:  OKAY everybody read:::::y ((I hold up
               'Dora the Explorer' card))(1.0) ((Josh
               raises his hand followed by Millie and
               Claire))
380   Josh:    [Do::ra
381   Claire:  [Dora
382   Millie:  [Me::: (.) I have it
383   Olivia:  You have it great
384   Claire:  I [I have it too]
385   Josh:    [Do::ra (.) that's Dora ]
386   Olivia:  Okay
387   Keane:   ( .. )
```

---

13 Dora the Explorer is an American animated television series for preschool children, broadcast on Nickelodeon in the United States. It first aired in 2000. In every episode, seven-year-old Dora goes on a quest, usually to help someone in trouble or otherwise do a good deed for someone. Dora also enjoys sports, as she is on a baseball team with her best friend, Boots, and her other friends and coached by her father. She loves soccer and is very good at it.

→ 388 Olivia: Keane tell me about Dora (.)
  389 Claire: <Me Too>
  390 Keane: What?
→ 391 Olivia: [Tell me about Dora]
→ 392 Josh: [↑DO YOU KNOW ALL] ABOUT Dora↑ (1.5)
               ((to Olivia))
  393 Olivia: I don't ↓((shakes head))
  394 Josh: Well (.) she's [she's an]
               explo:::wa↓(.hhh)sh and the =
  395 Millie: [I like it]
  396 Josh: = >she has a little monkey< and his name
               is Boots but the
[they call him Boots because]=
→ 397 Claire: [<u>NO</u>   <u>NO</u>   <u>NO</u>   ]=

  398 Josh: = [he wears boots on his feet]
→ 399 Claire: = [NO (.)   Her   ] monkey's
               name is Fro:gee
→ 400 Olivia: Her monkey's name is Frogee↓
  401 Claire: Yeah
→ 402 Josh: No no <it's not <u>Fro</u>gee(.)it's <u>Boots</u> cos
               he's> called Boots because he wears
               boots on his <u>feet</u> ((Millie and Claire
               are focussed on Josh, Keane has risen
               from his place in the circle and is
               walking behind Josh))
→ 403 Olivia: He wears boots and Millie y' you said
               you like Dora do you↓
→ 404 Millie: Yeah
→ 405 Claire: I   [I like Dora]
→ 406 Josh: [Muh me too I] LOVE HIM too I love
               her too ((pointing to himself))
→ 407 Olivia: Mmm hmm and Keane↑ do you like Dora the
               Explorer?
→ 408 Keane: No (.)
→ 409 Olivia: You don't ↓
→ 410 Keane: (Spiderman)
→ 411 Josh: YES her name is Dora the Explorer
               (.hh)'cos (.hh) her name is Dora the
               explorer 'cos she explores and his name
               is =
  412 Keane: [I love Spiderman]
→ 413 Josh: = [<u>Boots</u> 'cos he] wears <u>boots</u> on his
               feet
→ 414 Olivia: And can you get a doll of her
  415 Millie: [Yeah!]
→ 416 Josh: [YES] YOU CAN (.) I've the doll of her
  417 Olivia: >You ↑have the doll↓ of her< do you↓
  418 Josh: Yes
→ 419 Claire: But she's only for girls ↓(.)
→ 420 Josh: Sh She's for boys too↑
  421 Olivia: Is she↑ ((to Claire))

```
     422   Josh:    I've got a doll (.) of her((points to
                    himself))
     423   Claire:  [I (.) I]
→    424   Josh:    [sh she ] has no clothes on her [she's
                    in her  ] swimmin' suit
→    425   Claire:                                      [I I
                    have (hhh)]
     426   Olivia:  Is she
→    427   Claire:  Yeah I have two dolls of her too
                    ((points to herself))
     428   Olivia:  Really
     429   Millie:  ° I don't
     430   Olivia:  You don't Millie
→    431   Josh:    Well I I I HAVEN'T got[two dolls( I    I
                    I        )       ].
     432   Olivia:                          [Do you want a bit
                    of help with your] shoe there ((to
                    Keane))
→    433   Josh:    I no .hh I haven't got two dolls I have
                    only got one and she's at- in the beach
                    (.) she's at the beach
     434   Olivia:  She's at the beach is she
     435   Josh:    But she has no clothes on her
     436   Olivia:  Right ((I am putting Keane's shoe back
                    on him))
     437   Josh:    Only her swimmin suit (.) only her
                    bathin' suit
     438   Olivia:  And would you like to ge- get a Dora
                    Millie
     439   Millie:  Yeah
     440   Olivia:  You would
→    441   Claire:  <And (.)but I already have two>
     442   Olivia:  Well ↑lucky you↓ Are we ready for the
                    next one↓
     443   Josh:    Yeah
     444   Claire:  Yeah
```

Description of Events

This lengthy passage of talk-in-interaction was also generated while playing a game of bingo using brand-related stimulus materials. The card displayed featured the character 'Dora the Explorer', another TV-based character popular among preschool children. I twice invite Keane, the only member of the group who has not responded to the presentation of the card, to tell me about this character (lines 388 and 391). Following the second attempt, Josh takes the floor and responds by turning the conventional question-answer (interviewer-respondent) sequence around and asking me if I know anything about Dora (line 392). I respond in the negative and Josh then takes the floor and begins to describe the character. Josh displays social competence here in negotiating control of the floor; his question successfully wins him an invitation to tell me about this character. He continues to dominate talk throughout this passage, however, the talk-in-interaction is characterised by disagreement and general discord and Josh's expertise and dominance is challenged on a number of occasions. Claire challenges Josh on his description of Dora's monkey as being named 'Boots' (lines 397 and 399). I support her to an extent by tying my next turn to her statement that the monkey's name is 'Frogee' and repeating the statement; however, I do so using a questioning tone (line 400). Josh then substantiates his claimed accuracy on the name of the monkey when he explains for the second time that the monkey is named Boots because he 'wears boots on his feet' (line 402). I acknowledge his description by reiterating the statement he wears boots, but immediately attempt to bring Millie into the discussion (line 403). Millie and Claire demonstrate positive affiliation for the character (lines 404 and 405) and Josh takes the floor again declaring his own positive affiliation for 'Dora' (line 406). Again, Josh receives little support or acknowledgement from me, as I am not directing questions at him in spite of his demonstrated expertise. I invite Keane to share his evaluation and, for the first time in the passage, I use Dora's full title 'Dora the Explorer' (line 407). Keane responds negatively and, instead, favouring 'Spiderman' (lines 408 and 410). Josh immediately interrupts Keane tying with my use of the full term 'Dora the Explorer' and again provides the logical explanation that the monkey's name is Boots because he wears boots, in the same way that she is called Dora the *Explorer* because she explores (lines 411 and 413). I again invoke a topic change and fail to provide ratification of Josh's account, this time inquiring as to whether Dora exists in the form of a doll (line 414). Josh affirms that a Dora doll exists and substantiates this by claiming he possesses one (line 416) and providing a description of her (line 424). Claire challenges the appropriateness of Josh's ownership of this doll on the basis of gender (line 419), when she states that the doll is 'only for girls', to which Josh responds that she is for boys too (line 420). Claire attempts to gain the floor (line 425) and finally wins it attempting one-upmanship on Josh by twice stating she owns two of these dolls (lines 427 and 441). Josh does not challenge this, reiterating that he only has one (lines 431 and 433), and ultimately Claire wins the final word on the topic the second time she claims that she possesses two 'Dora' dolls (line 441) along with positive affirmation from me (line 442).

Explanation of Events

This passage of talk-in-interaction is complex in terms of social organisation. Josh clearly dominates the floor both in terms of gaining and maintaining strategies and in terms of voluminous interruption / overlap patterns. Josh attempts to position himself as an expert on 'Dora the Explorer'. He provides qualified descriptions, for example, in his repeated attempts to prove that Dora's monkey is called 'Boots' because they are a feature of his appearance. However, his construction of himself as an expert and his search for ramification receives no support from the other children and very limited support from me. Analysis of my talk in this passage demonstrates a concern or quest for the inclusion of Keane and Millie, the two children who are saying the least (lines 388, 391, 403, 407, 438). I don't address Claire or Josh directly at any point, despite Josh providing all the answers to my general questions about 'Dora'. Interaction between the children themselves is confined mainly to disagreement, the first between Josh and Claire, in relation to the name of Dora's monkey, and the second which is again between Josh and Claire, in relation to the gender-based nature of ownership of the Dora doll. Neither Claire nor Josh receives support for their arguments from the other members of the group, including me. An overarching concern with inclusion of *all* children by me sees a hierarchical structure emerge, which I appear to control and which serves to exclude Josh as a valued participant, instead placing him at the peripheries of the group. So, while he is successful in gaining and holding the floor, he is unsuccessful in gaining the support of the other group members and his frustration with this is demonstrated by his repetition of the same description and account concerning the monkey three times between lines 396 and 413. The community which emerges here is a hierarchical one led by me, an adult, followed by Claire and Josh, who compete for my approval of their claims, Millie, who remains interested and is positively oriented towards the topic, i.e., 'Dora', and, finally, Keane, who disassociates himself from the topic and affiliates himself firmly with 'Spiderman' instead.

Two types of repertoires (expertise and gender) emerge from the 'Dora the Explorer' discourse. The use of expertise to gain and hold the floor has been discussed above. In addition, Claire colours the discourse with a gender-based repertoire with her 'only for girls' remark to Josh (line 419). It might be extrapolated that perhaps Keane indirectly supports this characterisation of Dora, given that he does not engage in the conversation, instead, claiming sole affiliation for 'Spiderman'. Josh negotiates gender in a complex manner. He disagrees with Claire and argues the universal appeal of 'Dora' when he states that she's for 'boys too' (line 420) and he supports this argument stating personal possession of the doll. He proceeds with a detailed description of the doll, placing her in a seaside context dressed in a swimsuit (line 433). Dora is a seven-year-old character in the TV programme, so it is possible that Josh is making a strong distinction here between the 'Dora' doll he owns and a baby doll, the possession of which might be more gendered. He also remains steadfast in his claim as to only possessing one Dora doll (lines 431 and 433), thus allowing Claire to win one-upmanship through her declared ownership of two dolls.

DATA ANALYSIS SUMMARY

The analysis applied to the first extract emphasises the social actions being achieved by the features and content of the talk-in-interaction taking place. While the rendition of 'Bob the Builder' provides an indication of the salience of this TV character in children's lives, knowledge around the character is used to build hierarchy within the group. The overt lack of participation on the part of two children in this sing-song routine tells us less about their *actual* knowledge of 'Bob the Builder' and more about the relationship between the children themselves. Indeed, their lack of participation is used by Cathy to reinforce her 'insider' status and their 'outsider' status as crèche members. I, as researcher and moderator, appear to support her in this quest by my highlighting of their silence. It is important, however, to point out that this is just one extract plucked from a focus group that lasted 24 minutes. Silence on the part of the boys did not prevail throughout this time period. Social identities and relations appear to be fluid and temporary among preschoolers and this temporality is evidenced in the context of the focus group. Thus, one extract provides a snapshot of interaction, but a detailed snapshot and one that provides evidence of the ways in which the resources of consumer culture can be used in social interaction.

The second extract is also analysed in terms of both topic and resource. Here numerous linguistic features, including, agreement / disagreement, evaluative statements, affiliative references, repetition, volubility and silence, are revelatory of the social organisation being accomplished in the course of talk-in-interaction. In addition, we see repertoires around gender and expertise being employed to do the work of positioning selves and others. What is perhaps most interesting in this extract is the manner in which a shared cultural object, i.e., 'Dora the Explorer', is negotiated, discussed and used as a resource for the co-construction of social identities and relations.

CONCLUSION

The main aim of this chapter is to address theoretically, and illustrate via empirical examples, the issue of analysing focus group data. A brief historical overview of the focus group method is provided as a basis from which to discuss some of the most prominent areas of disagreement within the literature. These include: the conceptualisation of focus groups as either auxiliary *or* stand-alone method; the unit of analysis as individual *or* group; and, perhaps most saliently, the issue of focus group data as topic *or* resource, where topic implies an analytical emphasis on the interaction taking place within the context of the group setting and resource suggests an analytical emphasis on the content of the talk generated through the group. The importance of analysing interaction is highlighted and a three-phased model depicting how to use the focus group method for academic purposes is suggested. Issues of data management and transcription are also discussed in some detail.

The second half of the chapter discusses possible approaches to the analysis of focus group generated talk-in-interaction, including thematic and discursive approaches. A discussion of discourse analytical approaches precedes a detailed illustration of one type of analysis in practice, i.e., a CA-informed discourse analysis. I have attempted to detail the 'how' of managing, transcribing and analysing focus group data and have included some rules of thumb and step-by-step outlines, which, while not prescriptive, are intended to provide guidance to the novice researcher. While many researchers reading this chapter may not intend to use a discourse analytical approach, it is hoped that this illustration might serve to demonstrate the value of the focus group method for researching the co-construction of meaning between participants in the context of group interaction and that it might help to demystify the process of *reading* focus group data.

RECOMMENDATIONS FOR FURTHER READING

For a comprehensive and easily accessible introduction to the focus group method:

Litosseliti, L. (2003). *Using Focus Groups in Research*. London: Continuum.
Tonkiss, F. (2004). 'Using Focus Groups', in Seale, C. (ed), *Researching Society & Culture*. London: Sage.

For more advanced engagement:

Barbour, R. S. & Kitzinger, J. (eds) (1999). *Developing Focus Group Research: Politics, Theory and Practice*. London: Sage.
Puchta, C. & Potter, J. (2004). *Focus Group Practice*. London: Sage.

For organisation and moderation of focus groups:

Stewart, D.W., Shamdasani, P.N. & Rook, D.W. (2007). *Focus Groups: Theory and Practice*. London: Sage.

REFERENCES

Alldred, P. & Burman, E. (2005). 'Analysing Children's Accounts Using Discourse Analysis', in Greene, S. & Hogan, D. (eds), *Researching Children's Experience Approaches & Methods*, pp. 175-98. London: Sage.

Barbour, R.S. & Kitzinger, J. (eds) (1999). *Developing Focus Group Research: Politics, Theory & Practice*. London: Sage.

Bloor, M., Frankland, J. & Thomas, M. (2001). *Focus Groups in Social Research*. London: Sage.

Catterall, M. & Maclaran, P. (1997). *Focus Group Data and Qualitative Analysis Programs: Coding the Moving Picture as Well as the Snapshots* [Online]. Available: http://www.socresonline.org.uk/2/1/6.html (last accessed 14 March 2009).

Catterall, M. & Maclaran, P. (2006). 'Focus Groups in Marketing Research', in Belk, R.W. (ed), *Handbook of Qualitative Research Methods in Marketing*, pp. 255-67. Cheltenham: Edward Elgar.

Corsaro, W.A. (2005). *The Sociology of Childhood*. Thousand Oaks, CA: Pine Forge Press.

Eder, D. & Fingerson, L. (2003). 'Interviewing Children and Adolescents', in Holstein, J.A. & Gubrium, J.F. (eds), *Inside Interviewing New Lenses, New Concerns*, pp. 181-201. London: Sage.

Edley, N. & Wetherell, M. (1997). 'Jockeying for Position: The Construction of Masculine Identities', *Discourse & Society* 8(2): 203-17.

Edley, N. & Wetherell, M. (1999). 'Imagined Futures: Young Men's Talk About Fatherhood and Domestic Life', *British Journal of Social Psychology* 38(2): 181-94.

Edmunds, H. (1999). *The Focus Group Research Handbook*. Chicago, IL: American Marketing Association & NTC Business Books.

Fern, E.F. (2001). *Advanced Focus Group Research.* London: Sage.

Frankland, J. & Bloor, M. (1999). 'Some Issues Arising in the Systematic Analysis of Focus Group Materials', in Barbour, R. & Kitzinger, J. (eds), *Developing Focus Group Research: Politics, Theory & Practice,* pp. 144-55. London, Sage.

Gilbert, G.N. & Mulkay, M. (1984). *Opening Pandora's Box: A Sociological Analysis of Scientists' Discourse.* Cambridge: Cambridge University Press.

Goodwin, M.H. (2006). *The Hidden Life of Girls.* Malden: Blackwell Publishing.

Greenbaum, T.L. (1998). *The Handbook for Focus Group Research.* London: Sage.

Greene, S. & Hogan, D. (eds) (2005). *Researching Children's Experience: Approaches and Methods.* London: Sage.

Hill, M. (2005). 'Ethical Considerations in Researching Children's Experiences', in Greene, S. & Hogan, D. (eds), *Researching Children's Experience: Approaches and Methods,* pp. 61-87. London: Sage.

Hutchby, I. & Wooffitt, R. (1998). *Conversation Analysis: Principles, Practices and Applications.* Cambridge: Polity.

Jefferson, G. (1984). 'Transcription Notation' in Atkinson, J. & Heritage, J. (eds), *Structures of Social Interaction,* pp. ix-xvi. New York, NY: Cambridge University Press.

Kitzinger, C. & Frith, H. (1999). 'Just Say No? The Use of Conversation Analysis in Developing a Feminist Perspective on Sexual Refusal', *Discourse & Society* 10(3): 293-316.

Kitzinger, J. (1994). 'The Methodology of Focus Groups: The Importance of Interaction Between Research Participants', *Sociology of Health and Illness,* 16(1): 103-21.

Kyratzis, A. (2000). 'Tactical Uses of Narratives in Nursery School Same-Sex Groups', *Discourse Processes,* 29(3): 269-99.

Kyratzis, A. (2004). 'Talk & Interaction among Children and the Co-construction of Peer Groups and Peer Culture', *Annual Review of Anthropology,* 33: 625-49.

Litosseliti, L. (2003). *Using Focus Groups in Research.* London: Continuum.

Merton, R.K. (1987). 'The Focussed Interview and Focus Groups – Continuities and Discontinuities', *Public Opinion Quarterly,* 51: 550-66.

Merton, R.K. & Kendall, P.L. (1946). 'The Focused Interview', *The American Journal of Sociology* 51(6): 541-57.

Morgan, D.L. (1998). *The Focus Group Guidebook: Focus Group Kit 1.* London: Sage.

Munday, J. (2006). 'Identity in Focus: The Use of Focus Groups to Study the Construction of Collective Identity', *Sociology* 40(1): 89-105.

Potter, J. & Wetherell, M. (1987). *Discourse and Social Psychology: Beyond Attitudes and Behaviour.* London: Sage.

Puchta, C. & Potter, J. (1999). 'Asking Elaborate Questions: Focus Groups and the Management of Spontaneity', *Journal of Sociolinguistics* 3(3): 314-45.

Puchta, C. & Potter, J. (2004). *Focus Group Practice.* London: Sage.

Sacks, H. (1995). *Lectures on Conversation Volume I.* Cambridge, MA: Blackwell.

Sacks, H. (1995). *Lectures on Conversation Volume II.* Cambridge, MA: Blackwell.

Silverman, D. (2005). *Doing Conversational Analysis.* London: Sage.

Stewart, D.W., Shamdasani, P.N. & Rook, D.W. (2007). *Focus Groups: Theory and Practice.* London: Sage.

Tonkiss, F. (2004). 'Using Focus Groups', in Seale, C. (ed), *Researching Society and Culture*, pp. 193-206. London: Sage.

Wilkinosn, S. (2006). 'Analysing Interaction in Focus Groups', in Drew, P., Raymond, G. & Weinberg, D. (eds). *Talk and Interaction in Social Methods*, pp. 50-63. London: Sage.

Woofitt, R. (2005). *Conversation Analysis & Discourse Analysis: A Comparative and Critical Introduction.* London: Sage.

APPENDIX ONE – LIST OF TRANSCRIPTION CONVENTIONS

Symbol	Name	Use
Turn – Taking Transcription Conventions		
[text]	Brackets	Indicates the start and end points of overlapping speech
[[	Double Brackets	Indicates the speakers start a turn simultaneously
=	Latching	Indicates the break and subsequent continuation of a single interrupted utterance
-	Hyphen	Indicates an abrupt halt or interruption in utterance
Speech Delivery Transcription Conventions		
(# of seconds)	Timed Pause	A number in parentheses indicates the time, in seconds, of a pause in speech
(.)	Micro pause	A brief pause, usually less than 0.2 seconds
. or ⊚	Period or Down Arrow	Indicates falling pitch
>text<	Greater than/ Less than	Indicates that the enclosed speech was delivered more rapidly than usual for the speaker
<text>	Less than/Greater than	Indicates that the enclosed speech was delivered more slowly than usual for the speaker
°	Degree symbol	Indicates whisper or reduced volume speech
ALL CAPS	Capitalised text	Indicates shouted or increased volume speech
underline	Underlined text	Indicates the speaker is emphasising or stressing the speech
:::	Colon(s)	Indicates prolongation of an utterance

Symbol	Name	Use
(hhh)		Audible exhalation
? or (.hhh)	High Dot	Audible inhalation
Extra-Conversation Conventions		
(guess)		Indicates transcriber's best guess
((*italic text*))	Double Parentheses	Annotation of non-verbal activity
◎	Left margin arrows	Specific parts of an extract discussed in the text

Jeffersonian Transcription Notation is described in Jefferson, G. (1984).
'Transcription Notation', in Atkinson, J. & Heritage, J. (eds), *Structures of Social Interaction*, pp. ix-xvi. New York, NY: Cambridge University Press.

CHAPTER 11
QUALITATIVE METHODOLOGY DISCUSSION

**Discussants: Marian Crowley-Henry, Paddy Dolan,
Paul Donnelly, Olivia Freeman, Conor Horan
& Brendan O'Rourke**

Transcribed & Edited: John Hogan & Brendan K. O'Rourke

INTRODUCTION

During the writing of this book, we, the contributors, found ourselves discussing and debating the best way for students to conduct qualitative research-based dissertations, especially if it was their first time conducting such research. In these debates, we learned a lot from each other, as we each came at methodology from a different disciplinary perspective, with different training and bodies of literature behind us. Such conversations made us aware of how we differed on many issues. However, we also came to agree upon a great many points, recognising the common ground that exists between our various disciplines. Many of the lessons resulting from these conversations are sprinkled throughout the various chapters of this volume. However, we felt that readers might gain a more immediate and fresher perspective by having access to some of our conversations on qualitative research. This chapter tries to provide such an insight, by reproducing a conversation among seven of the contributors.

THE CONVERSATION

John Hogan (Moderator): How should a student begin to do research?

Brendan O'Rourke: I think, for academic research, the student should begin with a passionate interest in one of their courses, or one of their lecture series. Where they get a sense that there is something interesting happening in the literature and that they want to contribute to that. Or, they are excited by a particular debate in the literature. I think students should have a feeling of entering a conversation.

Paul Donnelly: Looking at this slightly differently, students could look to faculty and see what their research interests are. This could overlap with courses they've taken and with what interests them. If a student is to link up with a faculty member who has an interest in her research, she is potentially going to benefit more from the experience. This kind of contact could lead on to postgraduate, and potentially PhD, research.

Paddy Dolan: I think one of the problems is that students often change their thesis topics quite late in the process. I think that this is because they just lose interest. They need to be excited by the substantive area, not just the theory. They have to pick something they love, whether it is football, or music, or ... whatever, it doesn't really matter. So they can combine their interest in the object, with some of the theory they have come across through their various lectures.

Paul Donnelly: Perhaps, by linking up with a faculty member, students' loss of interest in their chosen research topic could be prevented. Whereas, if left to their own devices, interest can diminish. If students think that they are under pressure – they've got nine months – and a more interesting topic comes to their attention, they can think 'I've seen more literature on that'. Whereas, if they are working with a faculty member, they can be shown that there is a lot of literature out there on their initial choice.

Conor Horan: I find that, when taught masters students, who've come through from undergrad, are looking for a dissertation topic, they tend to rely upon academic sources. Whereas, MBA students tend to rely upon a managerial source that interests them. My advice to the MBA student, or the practitioner-type student, coming into a masters course – is that, in order to get a balance, they have to go back to the academic literature and understand how academics discuss managerial problems. Whereas, with the undergrads, I recommend that they go in the other direction. They have to discover why this is an important issue in practice, because most of their background is academic. The advice varies then for the different types of students. For me, it's trying to get to the conversation, because it highlights understanding the language that's used in both fields. So, whatever angle you're coming at it from, getting the right balance is what the students have to do in the first stages of the process.

Marian Crowley-Henry: I think that being interested in a subject area is where the research starts from. If that interest wanes, maybe the faculty can help re-invigorate it by feeding in their own research interest(s). But, an interest in the subject is important.

Conor Horan: Academic guidance is critical.

Brendan O'Rourke: I'm a little nervous of the kind of interest / excitement thing, which admittedly I do talk a lot about myself. This is because students sometimes experience a feeling that they have to bring incredible originality when undertaking research. Yes, sure they need to be excited about it, but, they need to get it done as well, as it's usually a course requirement.

Paddy Dolan: I think if they're excited about their research, they look forward to doing it in their free time.

Brendan O'Rourke: Yes.

Paddy Dolan: We should make a distinction between being excited and being original.

Brendan O'Rourke: Absolutely, maybe that's a better distinction.

Paul Donnelly: It's all to do with doability then?

Conor Horan: Often, in the methodology books, it says that the researcher has to add fresh insight and, when students read that, they get really afraid. Well, fresh insight can be a tweaking of a theory, or an application of a theory in a new context, and that can be enough. I think some of the textbooks with these requirements can be really scary for students. Students end up feeling that they have to come up with a completely new theory, and this scares them off.

Paul Donnelly: Something to go along with the issue of interest is that of ownership. Research is something that students should own as a process.

Brendan O'Rourke: Absolutely.

Paul Donnelly: As opposed to going along to a supervisor and it's the supervisor who owns the idea.

Paddy Dolan: Yes.

Paul Donnelly: Having ownership brings with it a sense of responsibility. This can help the student in general.

Paddy Dolan: I think that it is a balance between the student claiming ownership and following the research interests of potential supervisors. There is a balancing act there because, if the student looks to the supervisor as the source of all ideas, this can lead to uncertainty as to how to proceed.

Conor Horan: The student has to come up with the research objectives. The danger is where the supervisor puts in place a set of objectives. But, if the student is not writing their own objectives, following their own path in the general area, then that can be very dangerous.

Brendan O'Rourke: It's a delicate balance for the students, between saying: 'I have to do something for the course requirements, I need to do this; and I want to follow my passion'. But, there is also a limited amount of resources available. They should be coming to the supervisor in terms of what can they get out of this limited resource – like most supervisors are – rather than coming in a very abstract way with a vague interest. It has to be something that they're building themselves, and that they're using the supervisor as a resource.

John Hogan (Moderator): How should the student balance interest in the topic and its doability?

Paul Donnelly: That's where working with a supervisor provides the understanding that it's a nine-month process for the final year undergrads or taught postgrads; whereas, if it's an MPhil student, then there is more time involved and more room for manoeuvre. Some students come along with brilliant ideas; others with a whole kitchen sink of things. Then, through discussion with their supervisor, they funnel that down to something that can be done in the time available.

Marian Crowley-Henry: I'd say for undergrads more emphasis should be placed on the thesis being done in the nine months that are provided. Whereas, if it's a research masters, or a PhD, and you have to keep it going for a period of years, then there is more room to manoeuvre in terms of balancing this longer timeframe with the project's doability. However, even in this case, doability is still the essential factor.

Olivia Freeman: I think one of the things that undergrads need to do, at the beginning of the process, is read complete articles that have empirical components. Because many of them won't have done that.

Paul Donnelly: Even though, of course, they should have.

Brendan O'Rourke: They might go to the library and have a look at some finished dissertations, and scan through them. But, I think that if they have an area of interest, they need to go and find five or six peer-reviewed articles, coming from different methodological approaches to that area of research. This will allow them say that they are interested in this area, and 'out of all of the approaches, this particular one by John Smith, or whoever, is probably the one that's most doable for me, and that I'm most interested in'. Most of my students do qualitative research. But I don't think there is anything wrong with what quantitative researchers would call a replication study. This would involve the student taking a fairly interesting article that they would have liked to do themselves, and essentially retrying it in a different context. Citing it fully, and following it, and learning from it. If they are interested in an area, and they come across an empirical-based article, like Olivia was saying, I think that's a brilliant way to balance doability and interest.

Paddy Dolan: This is because it has been done already, and they can see it in the article. I think one of the problems we have with a lot of undergraduates is that they have confused ideas about the nature of theory. This is particularly prevalent in business subjects, which can be quite managerialist, and understandably so. Business subjects can be quite prescriptive: 'this is what you should do to run a proper business - this is what you should do in order to design advertising'. Some students see that as theory. But, very often those kinds of prescriptive theories, or even moral theories, can't really be examined through empirical data. They are just models of what we should be doing. There can be ways of translating them into questions that require empirical data, but that requires a lot of work. So, what I always try and say to the students, particularly the undergraduates, is that they should avoid prescriptive and normative theories about telling people what they should be doing because you cannot answer these by getting data.

Brendan O'Rourke: I think it is useful sometimes to use the distinction between pure and applied research. I think that if you steer students with experience towards the pure academic research, it can be easier research. Whereas, for those students without experience, particularly undergraduate students, as opposed to MBA students, they are so anxious to get their career going that, if they're working in a business and they come across a practical problem, they're almost dying to solve that practical problem.

Conor Horan: I think that when a student comes in trying to solve an actual problem in industry, solving that problem can be enormous within the given timeframe. I tell them that they have only nine months, and I'm going to assume that they have no time and no resources. So, within those constraints, a relevance issue kicks in. They have to make practical shortcuts along the way to some degree. I find what's useful for me is to revert back to a cause and effect-type argument, as they tend to have a complex and muddled view of the world. It's not that they will go and measure cause and effect between two variables, but they might want to try and understand it. Or they might want to look at how these variables are related in some shape or form. Even though we tend to talk about qualitative research, for me that's a great grounding for them to start from. To get them thinking that way is useful at the beginning. I know that, when I get students to write the thesis proposal, I nearly have to force them. It's a deductive structure and, if you look at the chapter that's in the typical methodology textbook, it's very much 'here's a research topic, now how do you refine it?'. But, once that proposal is in, then let them mould it, and go back into more qualitative issues. I find from teaching it that structure is helpful. Now, I'm sure there are philosophical positions as to biasing of a student in their research process, if you want to get into that type of discussion. But, for me, that's how I would break it down for them, and get them to narrow and focus in on something that they can do within a nine month timeframe.

Brendan O'Rourke: I think that can be useful, but the trouble is it's not the only way.

Conor Horan: There are a variety of ways.

Brendan O'Rourke: There isn't one right way. There are many different traditions of research, and that is what I think is very useful about Olivia's suggestion that the students go away and they read journal articles, and see what they are attracted to. Because there are so many different ways of looking at an issue, and you are joining in a particular conversation.

Conor Horan: Yes.

Brendan O'Rourke: Any particular academic conversation will have norms and traditions and priorities within it, and I think that it is important to engage with the research conversation.

Conor Horan: If they don't engage in the conversation, they're not building up their research skills. And that's something we tend not to talk about – that the process over the nine months is a skill-building exercise. How to do research is an analytical skill that you have to build. You don't get that unless you engage with the seminal articles, and look at different things, and different approaches.

John Hogan (Moderator): What skills are needed in order for a student to undertake a dissertation?

Olivia Freeman: I think the most important skill is time management. A lot of undergraduate theses are very structured, and I think that there's a tendency, especially with such a short timeframe, to say I'll have a lit review done by this date, and a methodology by that date, and the analysis by the final date. I guide my students through it that way, but I emphasise the importance of thinking about the methodology as one progresses with the literature review. So, I think there needs to be a huge amount of time put in at the beginning. Then the students can probably take a step back timewise, before dedicating another large chunk of time towards the end. But, it's getting across the importance of spending the first six weeks of the timeframe reading a huge amount of material, that you're not necessarily going to use. That is difficult.

Conor Horan: I think what happens is that students are told 'go read literature'. But, they translate this as meaning they have to go and do their literature reviews. But that's not the correct way of doing it from my point of view, in that you have to go and examine the seminal articles. What I tell my students is to find out what these research articles say. Why have they asked the particular questions that they have. From that, you'll have a conversation with the literature where you pull out the objectives. But I see students spending two or three months writing. They're told 'write 7,000 words on this topic', and they come back with a piece of work that looks like a textbook, and students often expect that this translates into a dissertation. You'll see them in the library writing, and they've no research objectives! As far as I'm concerned, that's a wasted two months. Yes, they've informed themselves, but not in a way that is contributing to what research questions should be asked.

Paddy Dolan: But, I think the need to think critically, and to be able to evaluate different explanations, really can't be separated from the other skills that are needed. From the beginning I think students need to think of the literature review as an explanation. They need to judge different theories in that context, and come up with explanations that either support, refute, modify, extend, or whatever, existing explanations.

Conor Horan: Whereas, if you're just reading for two months …

Paddy Dolan: Well, that's the thing, that task is just filling in space.

Conor Horan: Yes.

Olivia Freeman: What's needed is immersion really, the student deciding that they are going to completely immerse themselves in the literature.

Paul Donnelly: It is equally a skill of identifying what are the seminal articles, then reading past the whole Wikipedia thing, and getting into what is there at the heart of the matter. Judicious selection requires critical skills in terms of thinking things through. It means reading recent articles that seem to be very strong, looking at the bibliography, the reference section, and getting a sense of patterns – which articles seem to be coming up all the time. Then going and getting those articles and immersing yourself in them. It's a matter of developing skills in terms of searching and selectivity. What are the key words that seem to be important so they can be searched on library databases, Google™ Scholar, etc. It's also a matter of being able to avoid stuff that's out there masquerading as research of merit. So, it's about developing a range of skills.

Olivia Freeman: I think one of the things you said there is probably the most important of all, that is, getting students to read the references at the end of an academic article. An article does not finish with that last full stop in the conclusion section.

Paul Donnelly: In terms of their relationship with their supervisors, students can ask questions and build up a sense of owning the process. Students should prepare in advance for meetings with supervisors, so that they've got questions ready, to get as much out of the limited time that's available to them. So, there's a skill in managing the relationship with the supervisor, to get the best out of it.

Brendan O'Rourke: It's true that it's often the case that you pick up a literature review that the students have spent a lot of time on, and it reads like a textbook, or a general survey of the area, when what we want to see is a thesis that is making an argument from a critical point of view, and that will contribute to the academic conversation by making that argument. We often get the same thing in the students' methodology chapters. These chapters read like somebody giving us a course in methodology.

Conor Horan: Yes, rather than employing what they are learning.

Brendan O'Rourke: Rather than employing their learning and using it in the process of making their own contribution to the conversation. It's interesting that we're asking what skills students need to do research, and what skills they'll get, and the answers seem to be the same.

Paddy Dolan: Yes.

Brendan O'Rourke: This sounds very tough for a novice researcher. I think that there is an iterative process going on: finding an article, being impressed by it, then realising that it isn't peer-reviewed. Going away and looking up a reference, and realising, actually, that most of the ideas in the article you've just read come from that original source, and there's little new in the article you'd been reading. I think that somebody listening to our conversation, who hasn't done research before, could be scared by the idea that they need to know how to do research before they ever start to do research.

Paul Donnelly: But, that equally points back to whatever preparation they may have gotten in previous years: doing research for projects and learning through faculty members to differentiate between a trade journal-type article and a more academic piece. So, it involves building on, and going back to, what they will have done in previous years, and taking from that.

Paddy Dolan: I don't think we can ever expect that the dissertation will teach them everything they need in order to do a dissertation.

Paul Donnelly: Because there is reflection as well.

Paddy Dolan: Yes, this occurs in the final year of programmes.

Paul Donnelly: Paddy's absolutely right. One of the main objectives of most courses would be to develop critical thinking skills. So students should have moved a fair distance by their dissertation year.

Marian Crowley-Henry: I'd agree. I think the critical thinking is vital. I've had students hand up article reviews, as opposed to what they were asked for – a critique of the key elements within the article.

Paddy Dolan: And sometimes only a series of summaries of articles.

Marian Crowley-Henry: It takes a while for students to actually realise that, instead of giving summaries, they have to pick out critical elements.

John Hogan (Moderator): What do students learn from dissertation work?

Paddy Dolan: There is a need for the student to think about the skills they have in order to undertake qualitative research, particularly important are interviewing techniques and focus group skills. I think that some students, for whatever reason, are better suited to having structured questionnaires compared to the kind of flexibility and reflexive interviewing that's required of open-ended questioning.

Brendan O'Rourke: One of the things I try to say to my students is that they might be good at qualitative research, if they are getting good marks in discursive subjects.

Paddy Dolan: Very often students don't get much training in qualitative methods. There is a huge emphasis on statistics, quantitative methods. Marketing research is mostly sampling theory, etc.

Paul Donnelly: Yes.

Paddy Dolan: Students learn qualitative methods by trial and error.

Conor Horan: But, I find that when students get into the realm of doing a dissertation, it's as if the knowledge they've accumulated over the previous years in college, including statistical methods, is packaged away, and pushed into a corner somewhere. They can't translate what they've previously learned into the process of doing research. I've seen that in many cases, because a lot of the statistical analysis I've examined tends to be poor. They've done factor analysis, regression, etc. and I can't understand why they didn't apply this.

Paddy Dolan: They learn a style of questioning from doing quantitative methods. You really have to think hard to get out of that. Very often, when I ask my students to write a topic guide, they'll come back with 20-odd questions, mostly closed-ended, because it's what they're used to. And if you're an interviewee faced with that, I think that you're going to help the student out. Because, it appears to the interviewee as if the student just wants to get through the interview quickly with their closed-ended questions. Students need to learn how to think on their feet, to rephrase or delete questions instantly during an interview, and make those decisions on the spot. It's a difficult skill to master.

Brendan O'Rourke: Students also need to be critically reflective of having done that, or not having done that, afterwards.

Paddy Dolan: But, I think an interview has to feel like a conversation from the interviewee's perspective. Whereas, very often, novice qualitative researchers impose a certain style of, you could hardly call it conversation, a style of interaction that is not ideal.

Conor Horan: Or students expect an interviewee to fill in all the pregnant pauses they've created.

Marian Crowley-Henry: Conducting pilot interviews is useful for students to transcribe and see what material they end up with. Then they should discuss with their supervisor the issues they may have encountered in trying to get the respondents to open up. I find that, unless they go out and see for themselves how the interview worked (or didn't), any interview preparation discussion they may have with a supervisor just seems too remote to them.

Olivia Freeman: Yes, I agree with Marian and to get back to John's question as to what do students learn from dissertation work, I think the answer very much depends on the student's level of engagement with the task. I believe it is possible to learn very little from the dissertation process, particularly if the student compartmentalises it into three or four discrete tasks – lit review, methodology, industry review, analysis – and essentially works on these in isolation before pasting them together. If, however, the student immerses themselves in a field of literature, comes up with an interesting angle of exploration into that field and an appropriate way of gaining access to the data required and, if they then place that data under an analytical lens and actually see patterns emerge that they can write up as insights, I think this can be a very satisfying experience. I think the student who experiences this learns about long-term project planning, how to deal with the challenges and frustrations that come with long deadlines and, perhaps, most importantly, how perseverance and attention to detail pays off as the finished product demonstrates a rigorous commitment to the task.

John Hogan (Moderator): How can the supervisor and student ensure that a good working relationship is maintained throughout the research process?

Paddy Dolan: Listening to your supervisor is the most important thing.

Paul Donnelly: Come to meetings prepared.

Marian Crowley-Henry: Yes, the responsibility is on the student.

Paddy Dolan: One of the things that annoys supervisors is when they email dissertation students feedback, and advice, adding comments to Word files, and provide the most up-to-date style guide. I also write supervisory notes, for all my students, of what I expect from them, and then they obviously don't read any of these. You get new material back that's not referenced properly, and doesn't even have a list of references at the end. This is so easy to do – just to read the feedback. There's no excuse for not doing it.

Conor Horan: This is true, because it unfortunately has an influence on the relationship. You look at this person who's coming in completely unprepared, or doesn't have any work done, and they sit there and go 'Ok, tell me what to do?'.

Paddy Dolan: We know far more than the students about how to write successful dissertations. So they should listen to us!

Olivia Freeman: Another colleague came up with this diary, weekly reports, that a few of us are using. The students fill in the number of hours they've worked, what they've read, what they've achieved, and what they felt was difficult. It actually gives an agenda to every supervision meeting. It enables students to face the fact that they may not be managing their time well. It makes us face the fact that they've read loads and we need to be on top of it.

Paul Donnelly: They send that at the start of the meeting?

Olivia Freeman: They send it the day before, ideally.

Paul Donnelly: That goes back to the whole thing of ownership …

Conor Horan: But, this also comes back to the style of supervision …

Paul Donnelly: Owning the process.

Conor Horan: … that you want to engage in. I know we all have very different styles.

Olivia Freeman: I think supervisors should be prepared to commit to a Word document feedback on draft material. Not every single week, because you can't … it's …

Paddy Dolan: Dissertation students won't write every week.

Olivia Freeman: You don't want drafts coming back with an extra three lines that you're supposed to magically figure out are the new bit. For a dissertation project, say beginning in September and submitting in June, I would have a deadline in November by which they have to send me 3,000 words, and another in January. I have an agreement with them in September that, on receiving the 3,000 words, I will do detailed comments on it, and email it back to them. The whole thing is electronically recorded. So it's not just them coming in and getting a bit of a chat from me saying 'I think you're getting on grand'. It's more detailed than that. It's all set out at the beginning. It's communication really, so that the two of you – supervisor and novice researcher – have an agreement on what will work.

Paul Donnelly: For a project with that timing, I suggest a completed literature review by December. What Marian, John and I do is a slight variation on what you are doing, Olivia. At the end of every meeting, the students write up a summary of what they did up to the previous week, what was discussed in the meeting, and what are the deliverables for the next meeting. Then, of course, a supervisor can read over that and see, well, did the student understand what we covered in the meeting and you can correct any misunderstandings. Plus, it's a record, no different to what you have, of what's happening at every meeting. It's something that the student can look over and see, 'Well, gosh, I haven't really been doing an awful lot', it's there on paper, or 'I have been doing a lot'. The summary of the meeting is about ownership, the students owning the process.

Marian Crowley-Henry: What's important is having these milestones. It gives the students some guidance on their progress.

Paul Donnelly: They can build on what they've already done.

Brendan O'Rourke: I generally have an idea of what I expect them to do across the period of the dissertation – a rule of thumb – if you will. But, it does vary with the methodology, and it does vary with the particular student.

Paul Donnelly: Absolutely.

Brendan O'Rourke: I was going take up a theme that Paul's been talking about – ownership – because it's so important. In some ways, I'm not sure that the relationship between supervisor and supervisee is that important. I think sometimes students overestimate the importance of the relationship. Sure, you'd be an idiot to be a supervisee who doesn't take account of the fact that you're facing your judge and examiner, to some extent, and you have to be appropriately cognisant of that. Sure, you'd be an idiot of a supervisee not to listen to someone who's been through this process and guided others through the process before. But, I think, sometimes, you see very good students engage in a kind of game of pleasing their supervisor from week to week, instead of really owning the document, and realising that they have to produce this. I'm a good supervisor, but my two minutes of thought about a problem they've been working on for a week doesn't always exceed their effort, and I think they should have a sense of ownership about that. Sure, it's nice to have a working relationship, and I think I've certainly become friends with some of my supervisees, and I'm sure lots of us have over the years. And that's nice, that's lovely. But I think it should be product-focused – 'friend or not, produce the dissertation!'.

Paul Donnelly: But, I feel, in order to have that product focus, there has to be a good working relationship. Fostering such a relationship is incumbent upon both parties.

Brendan O'Rourke: I've had troubled, argumentative, relationships with some brilliant supervisees. I felt they were grossly mismanaging their time, and, as it turned out, they delivered at the end of the day. They used me in a way that, I think, was most useful for themselves, and that is fair enough if they produce the document. I do feel, particularly with some better students, that they are often trying to please you too much.

Paul Donnelly: That's something we must look out for as well, and tell the students that they are not in the business of pleasing us. We have respect for the relationship, but, get out there and do the work, and if there's something we disagree on, well, let's have a discussion.

Conor Horan: Could I come back to the issue of milestones? I know we tend to be focusing a lot on undergraduates. With most of the master's courses, with a 12-month dissertation period, what I do as the methodology lecturer, is to have a definite milestone in week 8. It's like Olivia was saying, they are required to answer how have other researchers researched my topic. They have to submit two pieces, a literature review and a methodology. Then, in January, they submit their dissertation proposals. That really starts the conversation off with their supervisors, as my role as methodology lecturer is completed. I'm intrigued by that structure, because you have a methodology lecturer for the first part of the course, and then the supervisor system in the second part. It's a much bigger process, and we rarely talk about it. We just talk about the student and the supervisor. I think discussion of that bigger process would be something I'd like to see more of. Such as, see how the relationship of staff to students is managed. If you want to get good research out of final year undergrads and masters students setting milestones, and good student / staff relationships, are important.

John Hogan (Moderator): This volume addresses qualitative research, what is the relationship between qualitative and quantitative research?

Conor Horan: You can use quantitative and qualitative approaches in all paradigms, and I think this divide between qualitative and quantitative approaches is talked about too much. I see it in the methodology sections of the dissertations in the library, and to me those bits of methodology sections shouldn't be there.

Paddy Dolan: I agree with you, I don't think philosophy is the answer.

Conor Horan: But, there's an overemphasis on this division!

Paddy Dolan: Yes and no. I agree that there is an overemphasis on the idea that these approaches are thought of philosophically as distinct and separate. But, I think they are, in themselves, quite distinct methods, and are useful for different purposes.

Conor Horan: Right, yes.

Paddy Dolan: The problem is where people start to think there's no difference, and you can use them any way you want. I think that's quite dangerous. There are very clear reasons why you might follow an ethnographic approach, for example. That does make a real difference. I mean, you can't then start counting things. You have to observe how people behave.

Conor Horan: Like doing six interviews and saying, 'Oh well, four people said this, thus it must be two thirds of the respondents-type thing'.

Paddy Dolan: If you're doing organisational research, it's quite possible you could distribute a survey to all the employees. If it's a large organisation, you might have hundreds of respondents. But, if you have the same research questions, and adopt a qualitative approach, whether it be ethnographic, an interviewing approach, or even get them to do focus groups, you'll have very different answers.

Brendan O'Rourke: I totally agree with Conor and Paddy that the distinction between the approaches is not at all philosophical. For me, there are three components to research. There's the literature, the methodology, and the context you work in. One of the questions I ask students who are particularly clueless about what they're going to do is – what were their results in quantitative subjects and what were their results in discursive subjects? So, I think the qualitative *versus* quantitative distinction is very handy for a beginning researcher, trying to see what general approach they might begin to take, provided you don't take it too seriously.

Conor Horan: It's true!

Brendan O'Rourke: I think there's a kind of natural division. When you are arguing qualitatively, you do quite different things from when you are using quantitative techniques; consequently, I think, for novice researchers, it's really silly to try and mix methods in anything but a very small case study. Therefore, I think this qual / quant divide is useful, but, a very rough distinction.

Paddy Dolan: If you're doing quantitative research, it's usually on the basis that you're going to empirically generalise to some population. That's not the purpose of qualitative research. I think there are very clear differences. I think it's important that researchers understand that the approach we pick is not simply down to a matter of opinion. Certain problems require quantitative data, and certain other problems require qualitative data.

Olivia Freeman: I'm at a point now in my own research where, having used only qualitative methods for so long, I am now using some very basic quant research. For me, the whole thing about analysing this quantitative data is about patterns, about exploring the patterns and clusters in the data that I'm finding.

Conor Horan: I think there is the danger if you're doing qualitative research that you completely ignore any kind of numbers coming in. Sometimes, people get locked into a qualitative or quantitative mindset to the detriment of their research.

Paddy Dolan: I'd agree with that. It really all just depends on what you're tying to find out.

Conor Horan: Absolutely.

Paul Donnelly: It's the same thing for those who are very quantitatively-minded. Sometimes, they will engage with some qualitative work to try and build up a sense of what they might need to inform a questionnaire.

Conor Horan: Yes, but I think in a complex world you have to know that the positivist is looking for statistics, for very structured patterns.

Marian Crowley-Henry: It's all about what it is that you want to find out.

Paul Donnelly: It's understanding in different ways.

Paddy Dolan: The qualitative approach is also quite suited to looking for structure, within organisations, within other social groups, and looking for relations. I think that, if you have a multiple regression equation, for example, it's like adding up the components of particular variables to a particular outcome, but it doesn't really get to grips with the structure of the relationships of the people involved.

Conor Horan: I was looking at a paper at a conference a number of years ago, where this lady had measured 56 different variables within business-to-business relationships. But, when you asked her anything about the relationships, she couldn't describe them, because all she was looking at were cause and effects, regression. She couldn't tell you anything about the meaning, or the meat in the relationships in terms of the day-to-day process of it. It sounded bizarre to me.

Olivia Freeman: That's made me think of something else that's really important in terms of undergrads doing research. A lot of the time, whether they do adopt a qualitative, or quantitative approach, all they end up doing is describing. They never even attempt an explanation. It's important that novice researchers think from the outset that they have to try to explain something.

Brendan O'Rourke: It's the critical thinking and insight again that one is looking for. I think, ultimately, qual and quant are not different philosophies. I think that skilled researchers can meld them quite well. However, novice researchers need to understand that there are different questions that are answered by numbers than are answered by words.

Paddy Dolan: Yes, but some things are fine to measure by numbers.

Brendan O'Rourke: Absolutely. But, I think that for a novice researcher, who is beginning to undertake primary research, it is very hard to do both at the same time, and so I do think that the distinction is useful.

Paddy Dolan: But, I think that the way Potter & Wetherell (1987) deal with attitudes, compared to Fishbein & Ajzen (1975), is great, as it brilliantly summarises the advantages of qualitative research compared to quantitative. In Fishbein & Ajzen (1975), there was a particular way of measuring attitudes that became popular. They decided that ordinal data could be called metric by labelling it near interval. How near, who knows, near enough? They treated attitude as if it's a property of each individual, so every individual has a certain amount of attitude towards a particular object, or activity, or whatever. So we all have attitudes within us.

Olivia Freeman: Positive or negative, isn't it?

Paddy Dolan: Exactly, attitudes have a certain valence. But, that's not tested by any theory, or any data generation, it's just assumed. Then, you see, depending on how much of this property you have, whether you are more likely to perform a certain act. Like, in consumer behaviour, will you buy something or not. It's a methodologically individualistic approach to social phenomena.

Olivia Freeman: Whereas Potter & Wetherell (1987) would say that attitude is not a fixed entity. It's something that is constructed, through interactions, and functions for somebody in a particular context, at a particular moment.

Paddy Dolan: Attitude is context-specific.

Olivia Freeman: Yes, it can entirely change from one situation to another.

Brendan O'Rourke: So, we have two ways of thinking about attitudes. In one, the Fishbein & Ajzen (1975) way, there is this thing inside individuals that can be measured through surveys. It's seen as fixed for individuals across situations, it's measurable, and all of the same type. That may not be a bad assumption in some work, when you're asking some type of questions, but it's an awful assumption if you're trying to understand how things like attitudes are constructed where the Potter & Wetherell (1987) way of looking at things is much more insightful.

Paddy Dolan: Norbert Elias talked about attitudes, decades ago, and said the important thing about attitudes is not that you have them, but that they have history, they have been formed through social interaction and interdependence. So, if you want to understand this thing that you understand to be an entity and object, you have to translate it into a process, because that's actually what it is. So, again it's quite a fundamental difference.

John Hogan (Moderator): There is much talk about methodological and philosophical issues, is this important in research?

Paddy Dolan: Well, I think methodological issues are! I think it's somewhere in the purpose of this book!

GENERAL LAUGHTER

Paddy Dolan: I don't think philosophy is. Traditionally speaking, philosophers don't generate and analyse empirical data.

Conor Horan: I think a student getting into philosophy can fall into a pit of philosophical discussion, and never get on with doing the empirical research work. I direct students to get on with their research, and reflect on their position using philosophy. With undergrads, I wouldn't get into it too deeply, but with some of the masters students I get into it a little bit more, in terms of just understanding how other researchers might actually look at their research, particularly if that other researcher is coming from a different philosophical stance. In this way, it gives students a grounding as to grouping bodies of literature, and an understanding of what philosophical approach that body of literature is coming from. I do think it's a good way of opening your mind. But, to start off a piece of research by saying I'm a positivist, a postpositivist, a critical realist, etc. is damaging. That's because, by declaring your philosophical position, you immediately close the doors on all other paradigms. You have immediately boxed yourself in to one way of thinking. I think that the whole process of doing a dissertation, a PhD, research, or whatever, is a journey.

Paul Donnelly: There's a journey that can be taken through philosophy, in terms of getting a sense of where do I feel comfortable, and how do I see the world.

Conor Horan: I'm not saying that you should leave philosophy reading until the end. I think you should open your mind philosophically as you go through your process. I don't think you should just read philosophy at the end of your research, and reflect back in that structured way. I think it's always good that you expose yourself to the basics of philosophy. Use it to open your mind, look at other things, but don't fall into the hole of philosophy.

Paul Donnelly: Little did I realise that, during my own PhD research, I was coming to it from a very managerialist perspective. Having worked in an organisation, that's how I was thinking. But, when I was exposed to various philosophies, suddenly, so many different ways of thinking about the world opened up to me. Then, it was a matter of trying to figure out 'where do I feel comfortable philosophically?'. I certainly moved away from a managerialist position. I grew to understand that all reality is constructed; we construct it through interaction. You start thinking about it and realise that you've got an affinity with that.

Conor Horan: Let me rephrase what I'm saying in terms of an ongoing reflection. I think it's an ongoing reflection on where you are and your extant position.

Paul Donnelly: Absolutely.

Conor Horan: Not reflection at the end of the process.

Paul Donnelly: To be opened up to philosophical reflection is a great help, because that can help in terms of how you want to do research, what sort of questions do you have, and what sort of questions can you now explore that you didn't before.

Conor Horan: So, do you think this makes sense in the context of undergraduate students, who've a short time to come to grips with the basics of research?

Paul Donnelly: Absolutely, as it starts the process of opening their minds, and can continue long after the dissertation is completed. I'd see it as part of the whole experience of being.

Olivia Freeman: I don't think that an undergraduate student will necessarily come to that point that you talk about. But, I think that they need to engage with, or be aware of, the fact that there are all these 'isms', and that they have consequences.

Paul Donnelly: I'll just give you a quick example. One of our research students was very stuck in a quantitative approach. She was resisting getting into any area that could be described as philosophy, thinking about ontology, and so on. However, when she was exposed to it, her mind opened up immensely. She first redefined herself as an interpretivist and then a critical realist. She may find feminism, for example. Who knows? But, she's on a learning journey, and she really appreciates that journey.

Conor Horan: I was observing some PhD students, one of whom had a completely managerial approach to research, just as you were mentioning. However, after a couple of days attending a course on philosophy, he'd completely opened up. He said, 'Wow, I'm seeing this whole new spectrum of life'. I think it's lovely to see that in someone.

Brendan O'Rourke: I think philosophy is very useful for opening up your mind. But, I also think there is a danger that it can close minds. If you take Burrell & Morgan (1979), for instance, they lay out four basic philosophic positions. You've essentially got to assume an isolationist strategy where you adopt one of these. I think this approach was probably useful in the late 1970s when there was so little toleration for different philosophical or methodological points of view. But, I think it's dangerous now, and can be an excuse for not answering an argument.

Paul Donnelly: That book came out at a particular moment in time, but the thinking has moved on since then.

Conor Horan: I've used Burrell & Morgan (1979) in the past and found it helpful.

Paul Donnelly: It's an entrée.

Brendan O'Rourke: Mike Reed (1985) has some really good criticisms of the isolationist strategy of Burrell & Morgan (1979)

Conor Horan: I found it good in presenting a body of literature that was coherent. It can be a good introduction.

Brendan O'Rourke: An advantage of understanding the basics of philosophy is it stops you making what we'd call 'schoolboy errors'. That is, taking bits from various approaches that are mutually contradictory and ending up making a fool of yourself. I think the way to overcome that is through engaging with the literature into which your contribution, your research, fits. If you engage in the literature, and listen to that conversation, you won't make those mistakes, because you'll be within that conversation.

Paddy Dolan: People can learn how to do methodology from the kind of articles that Olivia was talking about. Rather than reading say the German philosopher Martin Heidegger on the nature of being and time, and seeing how Heidegger might solve some empirical problem, better to engage with the work of those who are empirically engaging with some research problem and see how they are doing it.

Conor Horan: I think that a lot of the knowledge on methodology and philosophy should be employed, not just described. Students should use it as a way to inform their thinking, to inform a decision-making process regarding whatever problem, or whatever extraneous affair, has to be handled.

John Hogan (Moderator): On that note, we will draw our conversation to a conclusion. Thank you all very much.

CONCLUSION

From the above conversation, we can see some commonalities in the advice that the various participants would give to novice researchers. Novice researchers should combine their personal passions with research work they find in the literature. They should try to join in the conversation of researchers looking at a particular area. They should study some research philosophy to open themselves to broader vistas, but they should immerse themselves in studies of the matter they are interested in. They should take ownership of their dissertations and, all agreed, they should draw on, and listen to, their supervisors wisely! Evident, too, in the conversation were the differences in viewpoints among these researchers who have worked so closely together. This is the world that the novice researcher is entering into when taking on research and, while a challenge, we hope that this conversation conveys the sense of excitement and fun most feel when engaged in research.

REFERENCES

Burell, G. & Morgan, G. (1979). *Sociological Paradigms and Organizational Analysis*. Aldershot: Ashgate.

Fishbein, M. & Ajzen, I. (1975). *Belief, Attitude, Intention and Behavior: An Introduction to Theory and Research*. Reading, MA: Addison-Wesley.

Potter, J. & Wetherell, M. (1987). *Discourse and Social Psychology: Beyond Attitudes and Behaviour*. London: Sage.

Reed, M. (1985). *Redirections in Organizational Analysis*. London: Tavistock.

INDEX

academic knowledge 75
analysis 3, 14, 16, 28, 34, 38, 43, 47,
    58, 71, 91, 100, 113, 118,
    134, 156, 188, 196, 197,
    198, 206, 209, 210, 214,
    216, 230, 232, 235, 237,
    239, 242, 244, 245, 246,
    253, 254, 255, 267, 271
  causal, *see* causal analysis
  content, *see* content analysis
  critical juncture(s), *see* critical
  juncture(s) analysis
  discursive, *see* discursive
  analysis
  event structure, *see* event
  structure analysis
  factor, *see* factor analysis
  institutionalist, *see*
  institutionalist analysis
  narrative, *see* narrative analysis
  of focus group generated talk-
  in-interaction 255
  path dependence, *see* path
  dependence analysis
  rhetorical, *see* rhetorical analysis
  statistical, *see* statistical analysis
  textual, *see* textual analysis
  thematic, *see* thematic analysis
  unit of 232, 255
anthropology 38, 39, 65, 77
  cultural 39, 53
  fieldwork 41

fieldwork and classic
  ethnography 41
  social 39
applied research 21, 25, 265
artefact(s) 15, 43, 77, 80, 81, 99
Atlasti 119
attitude
  consumer, *see* consumer
  attitude
attitude(s) 28, 66, 190, 197,
    201, 233, 237, 278
Austin, John 211
auto-ethnographic research 58
auto-ethnography 12, 58, 77
  combined with ethnography 77

Bank of England 160
Bhabha, Homi 12, 71
  framework(s) 71, 74
bias 11, 28, 31, 54, 60
  interviewer(s) 54, 60
  investigator(s) 139
  researcher(s) 54
bibliography 268
*Bill for the Protection of Irish
  Industries, 1920* 200
Bob the Builder 245, 246-249, 254
body language 215, 236, 239
Boots 252, 253
Bourdieu, Pierre 192
brand knowledge 15

Bridging Silicon Valley and Turkey
conference 78
Britain 13
1979 160, 165-166,
171-172, 174
Bureau of Applied Social Research,
Columbia University (USA) 230
business school knowledge 75

CA *see* conversation analysis
Callaghan, James 165, 171
career(s) 42, 45, 47, 211,
218, 265
construction 40, 54, 58
element(s) 58
framework(s) 58
influence(s) 47
reason(s) 54
trajectory 106, 114
Carnap, Rudolf 210
causal analysis 137
causal logic 19, 133
causal narrative(s) 137
CDA *see* critical discourse analysis
Census of Population 204
Central Bank 159
Chamber of Commerce 115
change agent(s) 162-163,
173, 174, 175
children 15, 105, 106, 108,
109, 110, 112, 115, 119,
120, 121, 193, 223, 234,
243, 244, 245, 253, 254
birthday parties 120
branded toys 243
construction of social identities
242, 253
consumer culture 248
conversation 15

preferences 242
preschool 251
researching 234
roles 242
scrapbook(s) 116
talk-in-interaction 15, 243
TV programme(s) 243
Cisco Systems 79
civil society organisation(s) 163
coding 5, 14, 118, 196,
197-199, 238
colour, *see* colour-coding
focused 118, 119
open 118
collectivism 66
colour-coding 238
Committee on Industrial
Organisation 202
conceptual framework 20
consumer attitude 31, 186
consumer behaviour 21
consumer culture 10, 14, 15, 185,
193, 248, 254
childhood / children's 242, 248
consumer individualisation 199
consumer knowledge 198
consumer research 3, 14, 185,
186, 187
consumer researcher(s) 15
content analysis 238
context 11, 26, 38, 46, 48-51,
58, 59, 60, 72, 73, 87, 89,
99, 122, 126, 127, 138, 263
group 233, 245
institutional 131
organisational 191
research, *see* research context
social 48-51, 55, 135,
195, 234, 241, 245
social figurational 195, 206

social structural   195
socio-cultural   238
temporal   48-51, 55, 186
conventional economics   129, 130
conversation analysis   10, 214,
                        215, 216, 240-241,
                        242, 244, 245, 246
    accountability   241
    agreement   241
    application to children's
    talk   243
    assessment(s)   241
    delay(s)   241
    disagreement   241
    evaluation(s)   241
    overlap   241, 253
    repair   241
    turn by turn   241
Coogan, Eamonn   201
corporate culture   190
corporate social responsibility
    strategy   23
counting   6, 275
critical discourse analysis   209, 244
critical juncture(s)   10, 13, 134,
                    135, 137, 141, 142, 143,
                    144, 152, 153, 154, 162,
                    169, 173, 174, 175, 176
    analysis   153, 155
    characteristics of approach
                                           155-156
    criteria for examining   154, 174
    framework(s)   152, 153,
                                        154, 175
    in macroeconomic policy,
    elements of   153
    postdictive   153
    potentially predictive   153
    use of approach   155-156

CSR see corporate social
    responsibility
culture   3, 28, 37, 38, 39, 40,
                    41, 42, 43, 44, 45, 47,
                    48, 52, 53, 55, 58, 59,
                    60, 66, 67, 68, 69, 71,
                    74, 77, 89, 128, 185, 187,
                    191, 192, 193, 206, 244
    consumer, see consumer culture
    corporate, see corporate culture
    organisational, see
    organisational culture
    peer, see peer culture

DA see discourse analysis
Dáil Éireann   194
Data
    collection   16, 23, 25, 33, 35, 38,
                    43, 52, 55, 57, 59, 76,
                    78, 80-81, 108, 113-117
    management   100, 113, 117-119,
                                236-238, 255
    primary, see primary data
de Valera, Eamonn   165
demographics   28, 109
Department of Finance   170
Department of Industry &
    Commerce   138
Department of Labor (USA)   160
Desmond, Daniel   165
discourse   15, 71, 75, 79, 80, 187,
                    209, 212, 213, 214, 215,
                    216, 241, 246, 249, 253
    business   219, 222
    gendered   75
    international management   73
    management   241
    meaning of   215

orientalising   88
studies   224
theory   212
Discourse & Society journal   220
discourse analysis   8, 10, 14-15,
                240, 241, 242,
                244, 245, 246
and conversational analysis   14,
                209, 214
and language   210, 241
application to children's
talk   243
CA-influenced   219
CA-informed   15, 243-244, 255
central feature   210
critical analysis   209
critical analysis, *see also* critical
discourse analysis
critical discourse
approach(es)   14
critical discourse approach(es),
see also critical discourse
analysis
critical, *see* critical discourse
analysis
critical, *see* critical discourse
analysis
discourse   241
discursive psychology   210
distinctiveness   209-210
diversity   214-217
exemplars of empirical work   15
for social psychology   209
Foucauldian-inspired
approach(es)   14, 209
history of   14, 209-214
interview data   217
Jeffersonian transcription   218,
                227-228
language   219

positioning   241, 248, 253, 254
psychological perspective   14
repertoire(s)   241, 253, 254
research approach(es)   209-228
subject positioning   241
survey   15
talk   241
talk-in-interaction   241
turn   218
unity   209-210
Discourse Studies journal   220
discursive analysis   238
discursive analytical
framework(s)   230
dissertation   1, 2, 3, 4, 7, 8,
                9, 11, 12, 15, 22, 23, 25,
                33, 34, 57, 200, 201, 265,
                267, 269, 270, 271, 272,
                273, 274, 275, 279, 280
examiner(s)   188
fieldwork   41
functional focus of   32-33
minor   29, 52
MPhil   1
ownership of   280
PhD   1
postgraduate   1, 2
proposal   30
reader(s) of   188
research-based   261
supervisor(s)   188
topic   262
topic selection   20
undergraduate   1, 2, 28, 47
word-count   1
document(s)   3, 14, 115, 117,
                118, 195, 206
analysis of   185, 193
figurational approach   185-208
historical   188

primary, *see* primary
document(s)
research   38, 201
source(s)   59, 186
types of   187
use of   186-188
documentary
  evidence   197
  evidence, use of   185
  source(s)   30
documentation   4
Donegan, Patrick   202
Dora the Explorer   245,
                                          249-254, 255

Economic Development   165
economics   10, 28, 65, 131
  qualitative approaches to   10
  transaction cost   127
  use of path dependence in
                                            130-131
efficiency   127
Elias, Norbert   14, 185,
                                      188, 199, 278
  approach   185
  distinction between history
  and sociology   185
  position on philosophy   190
emigration   170, 199, 204-205
employer organisation(s)   170, 204
Employer-Labour Conference   170
Enlightenment   69
Enterprise Ireland   138
entrepreneur(s)   73, 78, 79, 81, 82,
                                    90, 99, 218, 223
  high-tech, *see* high-tech
  entrepreneur
  identity formation   89

international, *see* international
entrepreneur
research   105
Turkish   75, 78, 79, 82,
                                      83, 87, 88, 89
US   78
women   13, 99, 105
entrepreneurial
  activities   74, 102
  community   79
  identity-formation   89
  leadership   170
entrepreneurship   74, 99, 100,
                                  104, 107, 119
  'doing' of   99-124
  gendering of   99
  international, *see* international
  entrepreneurship
epistemology   61, 72, 75,
                                  189, 190, 237
  constructivist critical   76
  Elias's position on   190
  feminist   100
  philosophical   189, 193
  social   193
  sociological   189
ESA *see* event structure analysis
ETHNO   139, 141
ethnographic
  fieldwork   44, 83
  observation   83
ethnography   12, 13, 37-63, 76, 77
  as a research approach   38, 39
  auto-ethnographic approach   58
  bias   60
  boundaries with qualitative
  research   48
  Chicago School   41
  classic approach   12, 39, 40-41

classic approach and
anthropological fieldwork   41
combined with auto-
ethnography   77
context   48
critical and reflexive
approach   42-45
cultural and social
approach   39-40
data collection   38
epistemological justification   38
epistemological position of
researcher   44
features of approach   46-47
immersion   52-53, 54, 55
insider-outsider   53
interpretive   44
limitations   59-69
Margaret Mead   37
method(s)   38
methodological justification   38
objectivity   42
of language   213
ontological justification   38
ontological position of
researcher   44
overview of literature   37-63
range of approaches   58
reflexive approach 39, 53, 58, 60
sociological school of   58
urban approach   41-42, 58
urban approach and 'deviant
subculture'   41
urban approach and
sociological fieldwork   41
ethnomethodology 13, 99, 101, 102,
                103-104, 118, 121, 214
ethnonarrative(s)   77
European Economic
Community   202

event structure analysis   137, 139,
                           140-141
    ETHNO   139
    use of, in industrial and
    interracial unionism   140
    use of, in organisational
    change   140
    use of, in organisational
    decline / life histories   140
Export Profits Relief Tax   164

facial expression   236
factor analysis   270
family   2, 13, 45, 90, 99, 100, 102,
           104, 105, 106, 107, 112,
           117, 119, 120, 121, 122
familying   102
FDI   90
Feldt, K-O   172
feminism   13, 102, 280
    socialist   13, 104, 121, 122
feminist
    epistemology   100
    socialist analysis   101, 102
    socialist theory   13, 99, 102
    Western   71
Ferriter, Diarmuid   197
    Transformation of Ireland,
    1900-2000, The   197
Fianna Fáil   165
field observation   114, 115
fieldnote(s)   12, 37, 38, 40, 41, 44,
               45, 48, 49, 50, 52, 54,
               55, 56, 57, 58, 59, 85
fieldwork   12, 41, 45, 48, 51-52,
               57, 60, 66, 69, 77,
               78, 79, 80, 81, 82,
               83, 86, 91, 113-117

anthropological, *see*
anthropological fieldwork
ethnographic, *see* ethnographic
fieldwork
international management, *see*
international management,
fieldwork
international, *see* international
fieldwork
postcolonial, *see* postcolonial,
fieldwork
sociological, *see* sociological
fieldwork
figuration(s)   186, 191, 194,
                             195, 197, 203
   social   193, 195
figurational
   approach   204
   approach, *and* Norbert Elias   14
   assumption study   188
   characteristics   193
   context   195, 206
   movement(s)   203
   perspective   188, 190, 198
   research   189, 191, 198
   researcher(s)   187, 189, 191,
                               198, 199
   shift(s)   203-205
   sociology   185, 190, 193
   theory   190-193
Financial Times, The   165, 167
Financing Our High-Tech Future:
   Investments in Turkey
   conference   80
First Programme for Economic
   Expansion   165, 170
First Thursday(s)   80, 81
focus group method   229-259

focus group(s)   4, 5, 185,
                             186, 187, 217
   analysing data   229-259,
                               242-246
   and conversation
   analysis   239-240
   and discourse analysis   239-240
   areas of commonality across
   approaches   231
   characteristics of   231
   coding   238-239
   content analysis   238
   discursive analysis 238, 239-242
   group dynamics   233
   interaction as a resource 232-233
   marketing research
   perspective   229, 231, 232,
                               233, 234
   non-marketing research
   perspective   229, 232, 234
   selecting participants   234
   status of   232
   thematic analysis   238, 238-239
   Transana   236
   transcription   235, 236-238
   unit of analysis of   232
   use of video   236
Forbairt   138
Forfás   138
Foucault, Michel   187
framework(s) 13, 19, 47, 58, 72, 104,
                153, 154, 155, 156, 233
   Bhabha, *see* Bhabha,
   framework(s)
   career, *see* career framework(s)
   conceptual, *see* conceptual
   framework(s)
   critical juncture(s), *see* critical
   juncture(s) framework(s)

discursive analytical, *see*
discursive analytical
framework(s)
Hofstede, *see* Hofstede,
framework(s)
ontological, *see* ontological
framework(s)
postcolonial, Said, *see* Said,
postcolonial framework(s)
postcolonial, *see* postcolonial
framework(s)
postmodern, *see* postmodern
framework(s)
post-structuralist, *see* post-
structuralist framework(s)
Spivak, *see* Spivak,
framework(s)
systems, *see* systems
framework(s)
theoretical, *see* theoretical
framework(s)
Frege, Gottlob   210
Freud, Sigmund   212
Friedman, Milton   166
Frogee   252

gender   12, 76, 89, 100-101,
                     104, 105, 107, 122,
                     191, 252, 253-254
    and postcolonial   76
    and Spivak   89
    as a 'display'   104
    as a performance   104
    as an accomplishment   104
    difference(s)   66. 67
    discrimination   55, 56
    'doing' of   99-124
    relations   75
gender-based   241, 253

gendered   76, 254
    assumption(s)   90
    complexities   91
    discourse   75
    discourse(s)   75
    division of global labour   75
    divisions   101
    high-technology
    entrepreneurial self   90
    high-technology
    entrepreneurial self   90
    implications   104
    member   101
    place   75
    postcolonial subject   71, 75
    power relations   72
    practices   90, 101
    processes   100, 101, 105, 117
    self   86
    social structures   101
    structure   121
    substructure   101
    work as   101
gendering   89
    of entrepreneurship   99
    of organisational analysis
    literature   100
    processes and practices   101
gender-specific   241
Giles, Patrick   201
glass ceiling   55
global / local dichotomy   67-68
globalisation   12, 13, 58, 65, 67, 68,
                     73-74, 75, 76, 77, 87,
                     89, 90, 91, 92, 199
    and people   66-70
    dynamic conceptualisations
    of   66
    processes   74, 86, 90, 91

processes related to identity-
   formation   74
GLOBE project   67
Google™ Scholar   268
Grande École   56
Gumperz, John   213

habitus   192, 193, 200, 201
Hayek, Friedrich   166
Hegel, Georg   190
Heidegger, Martin   281
hermeneutics   37, 40, 61
high-tech entrepreneur(s) 78, 89, 90
high-technology business
   knowledge   89
historical
   institutionalism   10, 151-153
   institutionalist(s)   153, 164
   knowledge   126
   narrative(s)   127, 140
   sociology   205, 206
historiography   138
history   13, 60, 65, 73,
                           126, 127, 128, 129, 131,
                           134, 135, 139, 143, 151,
                           152, 185, 188, 210, 278
   modernist, see modernist
   history
   narrative, see narrative history
   of discourse analysis   14, 209
   of organisational
   populations   128
   scientific, see scientific history
   sociological use of   206
Hofstede, Geert   67
   framework(s)   67
Humanism   69
humanities   187

hybridity   74, 76, 80, 87
hypothesis(es)   13
   generation   126

IDA see Industrial Development
   Authority
ideational change 153, 154, 162, 168,
                           169, 174, 175, 176
   change agents   162-163
   identification of   162-164
   two-stage conceptualisation
   of   163
identity   12, 40, 56, 67, 72, 74,
                           75, 76, 101, 192, 194,
                           200, 213, 216, 222, 223
   constitution of   67
   construction   47, 50, 54
   formation   68, 72, 73, 74,
                           77, 78, 80, 82,
                           83, 86, 193, 213
   formation of researcher's
   own   77
   formation of, under
   globalisation   76, 86-87
   formation, entrepreneurial   89
   globalisation processes
   related to   74
   Mexican   88
   national   198
   reconstruction   45
   research, see research identity
   Turkish   88
identity-formation
   as discursive process   83
   cultural differences approach 89
   entrepreneurial, see
   entrepreneurial identity-
   formation

from postcolonial
perspectives   78
narrative(s)   73, 76, 80
processes   85, 87, 89
IM *see* international management
imagery71
IMF *see* International Monetary
Fund
in-depth interview(s)   8, 55,
                         195, 230, 234
individualisation 193, 197, 203, 205
consumer, *see* consumer
individualisation
individualism   66
industrial and interracial unionism,
use of event structure analysis
in   140
Industrial Development Agency
Ireland   138
Industrial Development
Authority   138, 141,
                       142, 143, 164
inefficiency   131
institutional
arrangement(s)   130, 132,
                       155, 157, 162
change   152, 155, 157, 175
character   170
choice(s)   152
context   131
development   132
emergence   132
evolution   131
factor(s)   137, 143
innovation   135
matrix   132
path dependence   131-133
pattern(s)   137, 144
perspective   136
scholar(s)   132

sociology, use of path
dependence in   130
stability   155
theory   125, 126, 127
void   130
institutionalisation   142, 163
institutionalism
historical, *see* historical
institutionalism
institutionalist analysis   152
institutionalist(s)   152
historical, *see* historical
institutionalist(s)
Internal Revenue Service   112
international entrepreneur   13,
                        73-76, 87
international entrepreneurship   74
international fieldwork   13
international management   12-13,
                            65-98
approach(es)   70
audience   86
discourse   73
field(s)   69, 74, 92
fieldwork   65-98
fieldwork   65-98
nation-specific theories and
methodology   69
postcolonial contributions to 91
relevance of postcolonial
theory   72-73
research   12, 65-98
scholar(s)   68, 69
scholarship   68
state of field   66
theory   12, 66. 68, 69, 71, 75, 91
International Monetary
Fund   160, 163
international organisation(s)   159,
                              163

international trade
  development of, use of path
  dependence in   130
inter-organisational
  relationship(s)   28
interpretive methodology   37, 61
interpretivism   3
intertextuality   216
interview(s)   4, 5, 8, 12, 30,
                                 37, 38, 39, 40, 41, 42,
                                 47, 50, 52, 54, 55, 56,
                                 57, 61, 77, 79, 80, 81,
                                 82, 83, 85, 87, 90, 108,
                                 114, 115, 185, 186, 187,
                                 210, 217, 218, 219, 222,
                                 223, 230, 231, 233, 236,
                                 239, 240, 243, 270, 271
  data 40, 58, 59, 139, 209, 210, 217
  dyadic   217
  focus group(s)   233
  focused   230, 231
  focused, see also focus group(s)
  group(s)   231, 232
  guide   114, 231
  in-depth, see in-depth
  interview(s)
  informal   113, 114
  material   138, 223
  process   40, 49
  researcher-involved   217
  semi-structured   113, 114, 138
  structured   54
  transcript(s)   12, 44, 47, 55,
                                   56, 58, 117, 118,
                                   188, 198, 217
  transcript(s), see also
  transcript(s)
  see also interviewing

interviewee(s)   12, 80, 83, 187,
                         188, 210, 217, 218, 219,
                         222, 223, 231, 270, 271
  account(s)   139
  mental state   210
  narrative(s)   40,50
interviewer(s)   57, 217, 219, 223
  bias   54, 60
  in-depth   230
  role of   230
interviewing   14, 45, 55, 57,
                                 113, 231, 275
  reflexive   270
  technique(s)   270
  see also interview(s)
introspection   4
investigator(s)
  bias   139
Ireland   13
  1959   159, 164-165,
                                   169-170, 174
  as a research site   194
Ireland, 1912-1985: Politics &
  Society   197

Jeffersonian transcription
  system   218, 227-228,
                                   243, 245
Joseph, Sir Keith   166

Kant, Immanuel   190
Kennedy, John F   160
Keogh, Dermot   197
  Twentieth Century Ireland   197
Kiwanis   115
knowledge   2, 6, 8, 11, 25, 27,
                        40, 59, 61, 70, 72, 76,

77, 82, 92, 101, 106,
135, 138, 141, 189, 190,
241, 249, 254, 270, 281
academic, *see* academic
knowledge
body of   25, 27, 33
brand, *see* brand knowledge
business school, *see* business
school knowledge
canonical   70
claim(s)   12, 82
communication of   233
consumer, *see* consumer
knowledge
contextual   58
high-technology business, *see*
high-technology business
knowledge
historical, *see* historical
knowledge
management, see management
knowledge
media, see media knowledge
philosophical   3, 189, 190
philosophy *v* sociology 188-190
production of   75
self, see self-knowledge
social scientific, see social
scientific knowledge
social, see social knowledge
sociology of, see sociology of
knowledge
Western academic   71
Western forms of   72
knowledge creation
process   6
knowledge-intensive   130

Labour party   165

Labour party (UK)   160
Landsorganisationen i Sverige
(Sweden)   173
language   7, 19, 34, 61, 76, 77, 80,
83, 85, 187, 189, 210,
211, 212, 214, 215, 223,
237, 239, 240, 241, 262
activity of   212, 213
and discourse analysis   210
body, *see* body language
community   189
constructive view of   210
of representation   72
reference theory of   210,
211, 212
representative view of   15
shared   239
language-in-use   244
Lazarsfeld, Paul   230
Le Pen, Jean-Marie   45
leadership   28, 67
entrepreneurial, *see*
entrepreneurial leadership
Lee, Joseph   197
*Ireland, 1912-1985: Politics &
Society*   197
*Modernisation of Irish Society,
1848-1918, The*   197
Lemass, Sean
Minister for Industry &
Commerce   165, 170
Taoiseach   159, 165, 170
linguistic
device(s)   244, 245
features   254
practice(s), Western   73
repertoire(s)   244, 245
text(s)   215, 224
turn   210-212
linguistics   213

literature   28, 29, 31, 32, 34,
                      54, 66, 217, 230, 262,
                      268, 271, 276, 282
    academic   21, 25, 262
    anthropological   43
    body of   23, 29, 31, 32,
                      261, 262, 279, 281
    business academic   11
    career   47
    contemporary   12, 37
    critical juncture(s) 154, 155-156,
                                   157
    entrepreneurship   106
    ethnography   12
    focus group(s)   229, 230,
                          235, 237, 255
    gendering of organisational
    analysis   100
    immersion in   268, 271
    international
    entrepreneurship   87
    international human resource
    management   47
    international management   66,
                          69, 73, 74, 75
    management   67
    organisational   13, 14, 125
    organisational analysis   100
    organisational analysis,
    gendering of   100
    peer-reviewed   27
    qualitative inquiry   99
    review(s)   2, 3, 9, 13, 267,
                          268, 273, 274
    traditional   37
    work-family   106
logic
    causal, see causal logic

longitudinal studies / research   12,
                               46, 127

macroeconomic crisis(es)   153, 154,
                      157, 158, 159, 162,
                      168, 169, 174, 175
    as starting point for change 152
    definition of   157
    identification of   157-159
macroeconomic event(s)   223
macroeconomic policy   10, 13,
                           151-184
    change in   153, 154, 157
    change in, identification
    of   169-174
    elements of critical
    juncture(s)   153, 174
    Ireland   151-184
    third order changes in   174
    UK   151-184
management   218, 222
    discourse   241
    field   224
    international, see international
    management
    knowledge   73
    time, see time management
    topic(s)   241
    values   66
market dynamics   28-29
Marxism   213
McGuire, Edward   202
Mead, Margaret   37
media knowledge   75
memoir   198
Merton, Robert   230
methodology   8, 9, 11, 13, 14, 61,
                  104-105, 106, 209, 224

books / texts   9, 190
choice of   11
development, sequence of 13-14
formulation   8
interpretive, *see* interpretive
  methodology
nation-specific   69
qualitative, *see* qualitative
  methodology
research, *see* research
  methodology
section / chapter   3, 9, 27
selection of   11
study design   76-80
testing of   13
mimicry   71, 76, 78, 80
moderation   235
of focus group research 229, 256
moderator(s)   15, 243, 246, 254
group   232
Modernisation of Irish Society, 1848-
  1918, The   197
modernist
  historian(s)   126
  history   126
  philosophy   69

narrative(s)   38, 40, 45, 47, 49,
                   50, 55, 76, 80, 138,
                   139, 140, 141, 152,
                   206, 216, 244
  analysis   83, 137, 140-141
  causal, *see* causal narrative(s)
  chronology of   141
  description   140
  event(s)   141
  explanation   140
  historical, *see* historical
    narrative(s)

history   128
identity formation   73, 76, 80
of change   185, 201
path dependence, see path
  dependence narrative(s)
text(s)   55
Western   71
native self   86
naturalism   61
new positive feedback
  economics   130
New York Times, The   161
Newsweek   171
Nixon, Richard   160

O'Toole, Paddy   203
observation   4, 12, 37, 38, 44,
                   46, 50, 51, 60, 61,
                   113, 114, 201, 240
  categories of   117
  direct   3, 12
  ethnographic, *see* ethnographic
    observation
  field, *see* field observation
  language   189
  method   105
  self, *see* self-observation
  theoretically-informed   190
observation(s)   28, 40, 41, 42, 46, 49,
                   50, 51, 54, 57, 58, 77,
                   83, 113, 114, 115, 190
OECD *see* Organisation for
  Economic Co-operation &
  Development
Official Report of the Parliamentary
  Debates of the Houses of the
  Oireachtas   196
ontological
  framework(s)   61

pustification   38
position   44
underpinning   102
ontology   60-61, 280
Ordinary Language
    philosophers   213
    philosophy   211
Organisation for Economic Co-
    operation & Development   156,
                        159, 160, 163, 170
organisation studies   122, 126,
                                    128, 130
    use of history in   126
    use of history in, integrationist
    position   126, 128-129
    use of history in,
    reorientationist position   126
    use of history in,
    supplementarist
    position   126-128
    use of path dependence in   130
organisation theory   13
organisation(s)   4, 6, 14, 30, 32,
                            34, 52, 54, 55,
                        56, 78, 101, 107, 127,
                        132, 135, 136, 152, 186,
                        187, 189, 190, 191, 204,
                        216, 221, 275, 277, 280
    civil society, see civil society
    organisation(s)
    employer, see employer
    organisation(s)
    gendered substructure of   101
    international, see international
    organisation(s)
    women business owner, see
    women business owner
    organisation(s)

women business, see women
    business organisation(s)
organisational
    actions   191
    activities   136
    behaviour   21
    change   140
    change, use of event structure
    analysis in   140
    context   191
    culture   6, 206
    decision-making procedures 28
    decline   140
    decline / life histories, use of
    event structure analysis in   140
    ecologist(s)   128
    ecology   126, 127
    field(s)   127
    form   143
    form(s)   125, 127, 132
    forming   138, 141
    intervention(s)   128
    justice   67
    level(s)   28, 101, 125
    multinational   74
    perspective   136
    plans   191
    population(s)   127
    processes   30
    research   3, 14, 186, 187, 275
    research   14, 186
    role(s)   2
    scholar(s)   101, 132
    social   253, 254
    social reality   186, 191
    strategies   191
    structure(s)   6, 10, 186, 191
    theorising   10, 13, 125, 133
    theory   10, 126, 127, 128,129

theory, as a process 125
theory, assimilation of history
into 126-127
theory, historically-
informed 126
variability 128
outsourcing 90

Parliamentary debate(s) 14,
194-196, 200
Parsons, Talcott 103
participant observation 12, 37,
39, 41, 43, 45,
46, 50, 51-52, 55,
56, 59, 77, 80, 81, 85
overview of literature 37-63
path dependence 10, 13
analysis 138, 143
and government policies 151
and technology 130-131,
135-136
antecedent conditions 134
as an integrationist
position 129-133
chronology 138
critical juncture(s) 134, 135, 154
data analyses 139-140
defining characteristics of
analyses 133
doing 133-143
event structure analysis 140-141
explanation 141-143
institutional, *see* institutional
path dependence
interpretation 141-143
narrative analysis 140-141
narrative(s) 142
outcomes 136-139
reactive sequences 136-139

structural persistence 135-136
theory 125-150
path dependency 13
peer culture 242
peer review system 26-27
petro-states 156
phenomenon(a)
social, *see* social
phenomenon(a)
philosophy 12, 60, 61, 188,
189, 210, 211, 232,
238, 275, 279-282
analytical 211
discussion of 3
economic 159
Irish economic 170
market-oriented 171
of knowledge 3, 189, 190
Ordinary Language, *see*
Ordinary Language philosophy
Western 70
Western modernist 69
policy, entrepreneur(s) 162, 165
policy studies, use of path
dependence in 130
politeness 214
political, entrepreneur(s) 174
political science, use of path
dependence in 10, 65, 130
polity 151
Popper, Karl 190
population ecology 125, 127
positivism 3, 61
postcolonial 12, 13, 65-98
and gender 76
fieldwork 82, 91
framework(s) 12, 13, 70-73, 76,
80, 85, 86, 90, 91, 92
framework(s), Said, *see* Said,
postcolonial frameworks

studies 70
theory, relevance to international management 72-73
postmodern framework(s) 70
postmodernist(s) 205
post-structural work 212
post-structuralism 212
post-structuralist framework(s) 70, 76
post-structuralist(s) 212, 213
Powell, Enoch 166
power 12, 27, 100, 165, 166, 195, 213
  balance(s) 191
  of discourse 187
  ratio 187, 191, 199, 204
  relations 72, 73, 74, 75, 76, 80, 88, 100, 101, 122, 215, 216
  trade union 166
preschool(s) 243
preschooler(s) 10, 15, 230, 242, 246, 251
  social identity among 254
  talk-in-interaction 230
primary
  data 30, 35
  document(s) 30
process sociology 185, 194
protean career concept 58
psychoanalysis 212, 213
public / private divide 13
Public Sector Borrowing Requirement (UK) 171
pure research 25, 265

qualitative methodology 8, 9, 16, 17

books 10
discussion 261-282
roundtable discussion 261-282
qualitative methods 2, 3, 5, 6, 7, 14, 270, 276
  for consumer research 185
qualitative research 1, 2, 3, 4, 7, 11, 16, 19, 30, 38, 48, 57, 59, 60, 106, 234, 240, 261, 265, 266, 270
  all ethnographic 38
  and media 4
  approaches to 4, 6, 7, 9, 17, 46
  as a tool 15
  boundaries with ethnography 48
  complexity 6
  concepts underlying 7, 17
  conduct of 3, 11, 17
  discourse analytical 8
  dissertation(s) 261
  distinguished from quantitative research 5-7, 16
  diverse approaches 6
  ethnographic approaches 45
  involvement of researcher(s) 5, 6
  iterative process 17
  methodologies 9
  nature of 15
  not subjective 4
  not value-free 17
  popular representation of 6
  reflexive nature of 44
  relationship with quantitative research 275-278
  researchers' reflections 6, 7
  role of researcher in 44

sampling in   5
textbook / guide   3, 35, 186
use of software   119
qualitative researcher(s)   4, 5, 59,
         60, 217, 229, 240, 271
qualitative software, pitfalls of 119
qualitative-quantitative
   distinction   5, 275-278
quantitative methods   2, 6, 270
quantitative research   7, 16, 19,
                            275-278
   distinguished from qualitative
   research   5-7, 16
   relationship with qualitative
   research   275-278
   sample size   5
quantitative researcher(s)   3, 265

Reciprocal Trade Agreements Act
   1934   156
reflexivity   44, 54, 70
   by researcher 46, 52, 56, 77, 86
regional studies, use of path
   dependence in   130
regression(s)   2, 270, 277
religion   28
repertoire
   expertise   253, 254
   gender   253, 254
   gender-based   241, 253
replication study   265
representation   6, 12, 15, 69,
                     70, 71, 72, 73,
                     74, 77, 92, 216
   language of   72
   symbolic   190
representational
   strategies   72, 75
   view of language   15

research
   agenda   38
   applied, *see* applied research
   auto-ethnographic, *see* auto-
   ethnographic research
   boundary   21
   children   234
   choice of perspective(s)   23
   consumer, *see* consumer
   research
   context   91
   conversation analysis-
   informed discourse analytic
   approach   15
   directionally-focused   28-30
   discourse analytical
   approach(es)   209-228
   dissertation, functional focus
   of   32-33
   doability   264
   entrepreneur   105
   evaluation   26-28
   figurational   189
   findings   3, 24-25, 47
   focus group(s)   229-259
   front   22
   goal(s)   70
   idea   19, 22-24, 31
   identifiable group(s) for
   research   30-32
   identity   69
   international management, *see*
   international management
   research
   interpretive   240
   methodology   1, 2, 7
   methodology 1, 2, 7, 10, 43, 58
   methodology, application in
   practice   8, 9

methodology, importance of
chapter in dissertation   27
methodology, selection of   2
objectives   2, 264, 267
organisational   3, 186
participant(s)   83
process   1, 19-20
process, guidelines   11-12
pure, *see* pure research
purpose statement   19, 33-35
qualitative, *see* qualitative
research
quantitative, *see* quantitative
research
question(s)   1, 2, 821, 25,
                   29, 33-35, 47
question(s), *and* mental schema30
rationale   21
rationale, developing   24-26, 28
replication study   265
rigour   26
social   3
strategy   3
subject   69
topic   1, 31
topic, finding   21-22
topic, refining
topic, relevance   21
topic, selection and
development   19-36
transparency in   21-22, 27
value judgement(s)   26-28
researcher(s)
bias   54
researcher-as-storyteller   140
rhetoric   71, 195, 211,
                   212, 216
rhetorical analysis   212
Riksdag (Sweden)   166

role(s)
family   2
organisational   2
personal   2
social   2
Roman Catholic Church   194
roundtable discussion   16
Russell, Bertrand   210

Sabanci University, Istanbul   86
    School of Management   80
Said, Edward   12, 71
    postcolonial framework(s)   71
sampling   5, 43, 106
    criterion-based   106
    in qualitative research   5
    purposive   106
    theory   270
scholar(s)
    institutional, *see* institutional
    scholar(s)
    organisational, *see*
    organisational scholar(s)
scientific
    choice   21
    history   6
scientistic approach   43
Seanad Éireann   194
Secretary of the Treasury
    (USA)   160
self   67, 69, 74, 75, 86,
            91, 92, 101, 199, 202
    conceptualisation of   73
    constitution of   67
    construction of   67
    cultural identification of   88
    entrepreneurial   90
    gendered   86

gendered high-technology
entrepreneurial 90
hybrid 86, 87
political identification of 88
self-analysis 56
self-awareness 192
self-constraint 192
self-construct 74
self-control 204
self-criticism 221
self-image 198
self-knowledge 203
self-observation 80
self-reflection 198
self-regulation 66
self-reinforcement 131
self-reliance 201
semiotic systems 215
semiotics 61
shadowing 105, 113-117
Sinerjiturk 80, 81, 86
Small Business Development
Center (USA) 107
social class 28, 191
social constructionist
argument(s) 104
Social Democrat party
(Sweden) 167, 172
social feminism 121
social identity 245
among preschoolers 254
construction of 241
construction of by children 242
social knowledge 189
social phenomenon(a) 2, 4, 278
social reality 101, 102, 103, 186
social resource(s) 15
social science
historical 205
research 60

researcher(s) 43
social science(s) 7, 29, 30, 34,
65, 151, 155,
185, 187, 229
social scientific knowledge 189
social symbol(s) 7
socialist feminist
analysis 102
analytical approach 101
argument(s) 104
perspective 102, 122
theorising 13, 102
theory 99, 102, 121-122
sociological
epistemology 189
fieldwork 41
perspective 23, 185
studies 52
theory, on childhood 242
use of history 206
sociology 8, 10, 65, 185
fieldwork and urban
ethnography 41
figurational, *see* figurational
sociology
historical, *see* historical
sociology
of knowledge 205
process, *see* process sociology
Sophia Professional Women's
Network (France) 49
spatial location of production, use
of path dependence in 130
Spiderman 252, 253
Spivak, Gayatri 12, 71, 72
and gender 89
framework(s) 72
SPWN *see* Sophia Professional
Women's Network

Stanford Graduate School of
  Business High Tech Club
  (USA)   78
Stanford Turkish Student
  Association (USA)   78
Stationery Office   196
statistical
  analysis   270
  correlation(s)   2
  regression(s)   2, 270, 277
storytelling   140
strategy   6, 74, 130, 164,
                            165, 170, 172, 204
  corporate social
    responsibility   23
  economic   170
  isolationist   281
  text(s)   32
  use of path dependence in   130
structural contingency
  theory   125, 127
structuralism   212
student-supervisor
  relationship   271-275
subaltern   75, 89
  agency   86
subalternity   76, 89, 90
subject
  research, see research subject
Sweden   13
  1982   160-161, 166-168,
                                172-173, 174
Swedish Employers'
  Federation   167
symbolic interactionism   13, 99,
                            102-103, 104, 121
synthesis   14, 188, 196,
                                197, 198, 206
systems framework(s)   50

TABC see Turkish American
  Business Connection
talk as action   245
talk-in-interaction   15, 229, 240, 242,
                            243, 245-246, 248,
                            251-252, 253, 254
  focus group generated,
    analysis of   255
    study of   240
text
  data   81, 83
  message(s)   4
text(s)   4, 14, 32, 37, 40, 41, 42, 44,
                        48, 52, 55, 58, 59, 61,
                        71, 72, 75, 76, 80, 81,
                        85, 119, 186, 190, 212,
                        215, 224, 229, 233, 239
  etiquette   193, 195
  historiographic   195, 197
  marketing research   234
textbook(s)   3, 6, 11, 19, 21, 22, 28,
                            186, 263, 266, 267, 268
textual
  analysis   216
  mapping   119
  material   118
Thatcher, Margaret   160, 165, 166,
                                    171, 172
The Economist   166
The Third Road (Sweden)   172
The Times   160, 165
thematic analysis   238
theoretical framework(s)   5, 6, 14,
                                100, 121, 134
theory
  development   126
  nature of   265
theory-practice debate   21
Third World   76

Time International   159
time management   267
transaction cost theory   125, 127
Transana   236, 243
transcription   235, 236, 240, 242
   convention(s)   245, 246, 258-259
   issues   255
   Jeffersonian   218, 243, 245
   notation   227-228
   of focus group(s)   235
   process   236
   software   236
Transformation of Ireland, 1900-2000,
   The   197
Turkey's Role in the Global High
   Technology Market
   conference   80
Turkish American Business
   Connection (USA)   78, 79,
               80, 81, 86
Twentieth Century Ireland   197
Twitter   4

USA   13
   1960   159-160, 174

value   5, 7, 8, 9, 24, 52, 67,
           73, 75, 126, 127, 136,
      153, 199, 203, 232, 233
   judgement(s)   26, 27
   measurement   27

values   11, 30, 66, 67, 103,
         185, 187, 189, 190,
      191, 193, 195, 200, 203
   management, *see* management
   values
   work-related, *see* work-related
   values
van Dijk, Teun   220
variables   2
Vetterberg, Hans   167
vocabulary   71, 212

Walsh, Deputy   200-201
Whitaker, T.K.   165
   Economic Development   165
Wikipedia   268
Wittgenstein, Ludwig   211
women business
   organisation(s)   115
women business owner
   organisation(s)   107
work   99, 102
   as gendered   101
work-family   13, 99, 100,
             104, 122
   'doing' of   99-124
   balance   99, 122
   gendered study of, in
   entrepreneurship   100-102
   research   105
work-related values   67
World Bank   163

OAK TREE PRESS
is Ireland's leading business book publisher.

It develops and delivers
information, advice and resources
to entrepreneurs and managers –
and those who educate and support them.

Its print, software and web materials are in use in
Ireland, the UK, Finland, Greece, Norway, Slovenia,
India, Pakistan and Sri Lanka.

OAK TREE PRESS
19 Rutland Street
Cork, Ireland
T: + 353 21 4313855
F: + 353 21 4313496
E: info@oaktreepress.com
W: www.oaktreepress.com